BY RICH COHEN

WHEN THE GAME WAS WAR

WHEN THE GAME WAS WAR

The NBA's Greatest Season

RICH COHEN

RANDOM HOUSE

NEW YORK

Published in the United States by Random House,
an imprint and division of Penguin Random House LLC, New York.

RANDOM HOUSE and the HOUSE colophon are registered trademarks
of Penguin Random House LLC.

LIBRARY OF CONGRESS CATALOGING-IN-PUBLICATION DATA
Names: Cohen, Rich, author.
Title: When the game was war: the NBA's greatest season / Rich Cohen.
Description: First edition. | New York, N.Y. : Random House, [2023] |
Includes bibliographical references and index.
Identifiers: LCCN 2022042514 (print) | LCCN 2022042515 (ebook) |
ISBN 9780593229545 (hardcover) | ISBN 9780593229569 (ebook)
Subjects: LCSH: National Basketball Association—History. | Basketball—
United States—History. | Boston Celtics (Basketball team)—History. |
Los Angeles Lakers (Basketball team)—History. | Detroit Pistons
(Basketball team)—History. | Chicago Bulls (Basketball team)—History. |
Bird, Larry, 1956- | Johnson, Earvin, 1959- | Thomas, Isiah, 1961- |
Jordan, Michael, 1963-
Classification: LCC GV885.515.N37 C65 2023 (print) |
LCC GV885.515.N37 (ebook) | DDC 796.323/64—dc23/eng/20220930
LC record available at https://lccn.loc.gov/2022042514
LC ebook record available at https://lccn.loc.gov/2022042515

Printed in the United States of America on acid-free paper

randomhousebooks.com

3rd Printing

Book design by Alexis Capitini

To Aaron, Nate, Micah, and Elia

All matadors are gored dangerously, painfully and very close to fatally, sooner or later, in their careers, and until a matador has undergone this first severe wound you cannot tell what his permanent value will be.

—Ernest Hemingway, *Death in the Afternoon*

CONTENTS

WHEN
THE GAME
WAS
WAR

PRE-GAME

You wouldn't think a single basketball game could turn a person into a fanatic, but that's what happened. Of course, it wasn't just any game. It was Game 6 of the 1988 NBA Finals. I was nineteen years old, and the Los Angeles Lakers, the great and godly Showtime Lakers of Kareem and Magic and Worthy, were trying to deliver on their coach Pat Riley's promise, made twelve months earlier in a champagne-filled locker room, to repeat as NBA champions. But it was looking like Riley was about to make a fool of himself: By Game 6, the Detroit Pistons, the so-called Bad Boys made up of Isiah, Laimbeer, and Rodman, were threatening to spoil the Lakers' dreams of a repeat.

It was clear the oddsmakers had underestimated Detroit, a team that had thwarted two dynasties, one of the past (the Celtics) and one of the future (the Bulls) on their way to the finals. The Pistons, up three games to two in the best-of-seven series, were looking to finish off the Lakers in their own arena, the "Fabulous Forum," in front of their own celebrity fans, which in this world is akin to getting stomped in front of your parents.

I spent the afternoon preparing for the game by playing one-on-one, twenty-one, and HORSE in the driveway with my father, a Brooklyn-born basketball coach and the man who taught me to admire the Pistons. "L.A. is class and flash," he explained, "but Detroit knows how to win."

Having spent his childhood on outdoor courts in Benson-hurst and Coney Island, he recognized in the Pistons what he called the "playground" or "Brooklyn" style. He demonstrated this style during our driveway contests by moving me around with his butt, hitting from the same spot again and again, and getting into my head by spewing a series of not-very-nice comments about my mother and my manhood. "Hey, Mama's boy. I think you've got a little drool on your collar. Want me to get Mama to wipe it up?"

He recognized the same ethos in the Pistons, and that's what he admired. There were no easy layups against Detroit. That team made certain that, when morning came, you'd remember you'd been in a fight. They lived by the Avenue X maxim: "If we ain't gonna beat you, we're at least gonna beat you up."

It did not hurt that the Pistons were led by 27-year-old Isiah (Zeke) Thomas, who was not only great-looking and charismatic but was also, in the relative terms of the NBA, small. Five-ten in shoes, Isiah was a short man in a tall man's game, which meant, my father explained, he did not have to be merely as good as the others; he had to be better. Most fans today don't remember Isiah as he was in the late 1980s, when he was the best player on the best team. Say what you want about Michael and LeBron, but, pound for pound, inch for inch, grading on a curve, Isiah was the GOAT.

And he was local, a Chicago-area product just like me, and so, though my home team wasn't in the finals that year, Isiah—a short, underestimated, baby-faced Chicagoan—became my avatar. The Pistons were looking to close out the defending champions in six games, eager to inaugurate their own dynasty (they would go on to win in 1989 and 1990). Pat Riley trademarked the term "three-peat" for the Lakers, but the Pistons would have used it first had they also won in 1988, putting them among the all-time greats instead of the not-quites. Today, the Bad Boys are remembered mostly as a foil—what, in the world of pro wrestling, they call a "heel."

That night, Isiah and the Pistons were hanging in midway through the second half, when, on what looked like an otherwise routine play, Isiah ran over the foot of L.A. guard Michael Cooper, turning his ankle ninety degrees. Isiah fell to the floor, reached for his foot, and screamed.

The Forum got quiet—it was the kind of uncanny silence only a crowd can make. Jack Nicholson was on his feet. Barbra Streisand looked concerned.

A trainer helped Isiah to the bench, where he sat, leg extended, as trainers and doctors worked all around him. The injury capped off what had been a punishing postseason for Zeke, who had been cut, tripped, banged, and knocked out over the course of the last seven weeks. The game continued. The announcer said Zeke was probably done for the night; my father—we were watching on the Magnavox in the family room—agreed. "You roll an ankle like that," he said, "it blows up, then you can't put any weight on it."

Isiah, who seemingly had the same thought—*I've got to do what I can while I can still walk!*—somehow got his busted self back onto the floor. It was as if, knowing his ankle would soon triple in size, he decided that this was his best chance to push his team across the finish line.

He took an inbound pass, then went to work. Though hobbled—he moved like a supermarket cart with a punk wheel—he set up plays, delivered pinpoint passes, hit shots from all over the floor, and now and then, in that third quarter that seemed to stretch into a lifetime, even drove the basket, going one-on-one with players who were a foot taller and a hundred pounds heavier, including Magic Johnson, who had been (but would soon no longer be) one of Isiah's best friends.

The *Detroit Free Press* later ran a list of all the shots Isiah hit in the third quarter.

11:01	2 free throws	LAKERS 56—50
10:31	Follow up 5 footer	LAKERS 56—52
10:06	18 foot jumper from the key	LAKERS 58—54
9:37	12 footer from the right side off drive	LAKERS 62—56
8:14	14 foot bank shot from left side	LAKERS 64—58
7:38	12 foot jumper on left side, from Dumars	LAKERS 64—60
6:22	Breakaway lay-up, from Dumars	LAKERS 66—62
3:29	12 foot jumper on left baseline from Dantley	LAKERS 74—68
2:59	14 foot bank shot from [Vinnie Johnson], Cooper fouled on play—Zeke missed free throw	LAKERS 76—70
1:13	26 foot 3 pointer, from Vinnie Johnson	TIES SCORE AT 77
0:46	Breakaway lay-up from Rodman	TIED 79—79
0:02	20 footer from left corner, from Johnson	PISTONS 81—79

Isiah's 25-point third quarter remains a postseason record. But it wasn't just the numbers that dazzled. It was the grit, the determination, the way this small man at play in a world of giants put his team on his back and nearly delivered them: The Pistons came up just short, and many believed they were hosed by the refs with a bad call at the end.

Isiah became a symbol in those twelve minutes, an embodiment of everything that a person who wants to live ecstatically should be. He played with fury and joy. He loved his teammates and his opponents—you could see it in every move. He never gave up, never stopped trying. He did this not in spite of his injury but because of it. As a professional athlete, he knew it would only get worse, that it was now or never, that the pain did not matter if he did not notice it, that, in this league, there is only today, this quarter, right now. He was like a protagonist out of a Camus novel—I'd taken existentialism in college that year—who is free because he knows he will die.

That's the night I fell in love with the NBA.

For a Chicago sports fan in the early 1980s, life was pain. The Cubs had not won a World Series since 1908. The White Sox had not won since 1917, and, what's worse, the last time they should've won, in 1919, they took money to throw the games instead, shrouding the entire city in shame. The Blackhawks had not won the Stanley Cup since 1961—seven years before I was born. True, the Bears won the Super Bowl in 1986, which was incredible— but only for a moment, as, over the next few years, we had to sit on our hands and watch as the McCaskeys, the family that owns the Bears, dismantled the team, possibly because they'd realized losing can be more profitable than winning.

And so, for much of my childhood, I focused my attention on amateur basketball. DePaul had a great team in the 1980s, a team stacked with future NBA stars. The Loyola Ramblers were good. Even the Northwestern Wildcats were interesting. But the best games were played at the high school level—not my high school, New Trier, which was constantly being outjumped and outmuscled, but the great downtown public and Catholic school teams of the era.

There were dozens of basketball powerhouses in the city: Westinghouse, where Mark Aguirre and Hersey Hawkins played; Simeon, the alma mater of Derrick Rose and Ben Wilson; Carver, which had been put on the map by Cazzie Russell. There were also far-flung Catholic schools, such as St. Joseph's in Westchester, Illinois, where coach Gene Pingatore built a state champion around the teenage Isiah Thomas in 1978.

My father would drive us to gyms across the state to watch the best teams compete. Dull fluorescent light, linoleum, flickering numbers on rickety scoreboards, cheerleaders and uniforms and freaked-out parents, my father instructing, whispering in my ear—"See how he boxes the man out? Notice how he always goes to his right? The kid can't play with his left hand"—top prospects showing off for the scouts, who, even if you couldn't see them, were always there. That's what I remember.

I saw Isiah play against Westinghouse in December 1978. It was dark at 5:00 P.M. and bitterly cold. Even then, amid high school teammates and opponents, most of whom would go on to lead ordinary adult lives, Isiah looked small, fragile. On many plays, he was shadowed by two or three defenders who hung over him like oak trees, which did not matter when Isiah decided he was going to the basket. His height, or lack of, made him a lodestar for every undersized would-be in Chicagoland. He was electric that evening, scoring from inside and out, securing the win on the last shot. The smooth efficiency of his style made you want to find something, anything, you could do half as well.

Though everyone in Northern Illinois knew about Isiah, he did not yet exist to the rest of the world. He was a secret we knew we'd have only for a little while, and it made us proud. A memory of the adolescent Isiah is also a memory of childhood, which is what made it so painful when Michael Jordan turned Zeke into a foil, and when Zeke, who'd been Daniel in the lions' den, went from hero to antihero.

You could watch Isiah and a dozen other local standouts mix it up on the city playgrounds most weekend afternoons. The courts were gritty, the neighborhoods run-down, but the games, the quality of talent, were unreal. In 1970s and 1980s Chicago, the playground standouts pushed each other toward greatness, until, in the way of a local music scene—Liverpool in the 1960s, say; Seattle in the 1990s—they all seemed to emerge on the national map at once. You recognized them by their style. It was a Chicago style, created by the realities of the city. It was, according to Isiah, characterized by hard, physical play—not because Chicago is tough, but because the weather is so nasty. They played all winter on the West Side, which meant wind and snow. Even the prettiest shot won't fall when the gale-force wind is blowing off the plains. Even the most eagle-eyed playmaker won't deliver when the flurries swirl. To be effective in February, you learned to keep opponents off-balance and take the ball to the hoop; the wind can't spoil a dunk. It was a stingy style that could be seen across the NBA. The 1987 All-Star Game featured a half dozen players who'd grown up on the West Side courts, including Mark Aguirre, Mo Cheeks, Doc Rivers, and Isiah Thomas.

Of course, Chicagoans, though happy to serve as a talent pool, wanted a great NBA team of their own. The city had had a star-crossed relationship with the pro game. Several teams had come and gone since the first professional league was founded in 1898. There'd been the Chicago Bruins of the American Basketball League, the American Gears of the National Basketball League, and the Chicago Zephyrs of the National Association. The Bulls, a 1966 expansion club, were meant to fill a hole left by the Zephyrs, who moved first to Baltimore, then to Washington, where they still play as the Wizards.

The Bulls posted a few decent seasons in the 1970s, then collapsed. They were a joke by the early 1980s, known mostly for blown draft picks and head-case flameouts. Quintin Dailey, drafted in the first round in 1982, is remembered less for how he played than for something he did on the road in 1985. Pulled from a game early, he sent a ball boy for a slice of pizza, nachos, popcorn, and a soda, which he ate on the bench.

This finally began to change in 1984, with the coming of Michael Jordan. Watching Jordan, especially when he was young and seemingly made of springs, was amazing, but just as amazing was watching Jerry Krause, the dumpy general manager—Jordan called him "Crumbs"—rebuild the team around its star. 1985. 1986. 1987. 1988. Krause experimented with players and coaches, searching for just the right combination, the mix that would best support Michael Jordan. Once the ingredients were in place, you watched the players develop, alone and together, season after season. You followed them as you might follow a talented group of freshmen as they make their way through college. You got to see them learn how to work together, cooperate, sacrifice, share. You got to see them learn how to lose and learn how to win. It was not mere happiness you felt when they finally figured out how to overcome an obstacle like the Detroit Pistons. It was pride, a satisfaction unknown in a time of nearly unlimited free agency. These days, when buying a Bulls jersey, I ask the guy to put the name of the owner on the back; everyone else will soon be gone.

As the years went by, as I moved away from Chicago and into the world, as I watched the rise and fall of political leaders, political parties, and even ideologies, I found myself thinking not less but more about the Bulls and the great NBA teams of the late 1980s. In them, I recognized the same historical process I was seeing in the news. In the 1980s, NBA teams took time to build, to adapt— draft by draft and trade by trade—in order to defeat their most dangerous rivals. The Pistons were built to overcome the Celtics just as America was built to overcome Russia. Get bigger, faster, and better or end up on the ash heap of history.

In an attempt to relive and understand that era, which for me began the night Isiah scored 25 points in one quarter on one leg, I've read every book and every memoir about every team and by every player from that decade. I have watched all the old games, read all the old articles and stories. I have tracked down and interviewed all the old players, coaches, executives, writers, and broadcasters, or as many as I could find. I've had hundreds of conversations about everything from the nature of Bill Laimbeer

("Pussy! Guy'd jump on you just like you were a piece of bubble wrap!") to the trouble a tall man faces when flying coach ("They folded me up like an accordion!").

I spoke to Bill Laimbeer, Danny Ainge, Red Auerbach, Bill Cartwright, Johnny Dawkins, Sam Perkins, and Dominique Wilkins, who, in May 1988, matched Larry Bird shot for shot in what many consider the greatest postseason showdown. I spoke to stars, journeymen, role players. I spoke to Jerry Sichting, who was brought to Boston to give the Celtics an outside shooting threat. He'd been a high school and college star in Indiana, but spent his first NBA seasons searching for a role. One day, he pitched himself in a handwritten letter to Celtics president Red Auerbach. *Watch the film,* Sichting wrote Auerbach. *When your big men are in the lane, the two guard is always open at fifteen. Put me in that spot and I will hit that shot every time. I am the missing piece.*

I spoke to Mychal Thompson, who was brought to L.A. for the sole purpose of stopping Boston forward Kevin McHale. (The two had faced each other every day in practice in college.) I spoke to Wes Matthews, a generational talent whose career was cut short by drugs, and I spoke to the Bulls' Craig Hodges, who won the 3-point shooting contest in 1990, 1991, and 1992. I spoke to some of the greatest coaches in history: K. C. Jones, Larry Brown, Bill Fitch, Rudy Tomjanovich, Johnny Bach. I spoke to Sam Vincent, who played against Jordan in high school, then was traded before the start of the 1987–88 season from Boston to Seattle, then, mid-season, from Seattle to Chicago, which gave him unique insight into contrasting locker rooms. I spoke to commentators and reporters who covered the games night after night.

In the course of all these conversations, I came up with a notion that hardened into a thesis: The 1987–88 season was the greatest season in NBA history.

Why?

The superstars, the incredible pool of talent. Because of that once-in-a-lifetime collection of players, rookies and veterans, the level of competition in 1987–88 was greater than it had ever been and—arguably—has been since. There were more future Hall of Famers in action that season than in any other single season; among them were young stars who would continue on in the league for years, and old stars who'd debuted in the distant past. At twenty-two, Scottie Pippen and Reggie Miller were the youngest. At forty, Kareem Abdul-Jabbar was the oldest. Between them, youngest to oldest, were twenty-nine other future Hall of Famers: Michael Jordan (24), Chris Mullin (24), Karl Malone (24), Joe Dumars (24), Charles Barkley (24), Hakeem Olajuwon (24); Patrick Ewing (25), Clyde Drexler (25), John Stockton (25); Dennis Rodman (26), Isiah Thomas (26), James Worthy (26); Ralph Sampson (27), Dominique Wilkins (27); Magic Johnson (28); Sidney Moncrief (30), Kevin McHale (30); Larry Bird (31), Bernard King (31), Mo Cheeks (31); Adrian Dantley (32), Jack Sikma (32), Moses Malone (32); Dennis Johnson (33), Alex English (33); Robert Parish (34); Bill Walton (35); Bob McAdoo (36); Artis Gilmore (38). Taken together, these players encompass nearly the entire history of the league. Kareem played his first game in 1969, when Bob Cousy, who'd played his first game in 1950—just four years after the NBA was founded—was still active. He played his last seasons in the league with Reggie Miller, who continued until 2005, when he (Miller) played with Dwight Howard, who was still going in 2022.

Four of the NBA's dynasties, each at a different stage of development, competed in 1987–88. The Celtics, who won three titles in the 1980s, were beginning to slip but were still the Celtics. The Lakers, who'd won five titles that decade, though slightly past their peak—call it five after midnight—were still among the best ever. The Pistons were just reaching cruising altitude and might well have been the best team in the game that year, even if few realized it. And the Bulls, in whom, though nascent and very much in the act of becoming, the contours of the great dynasty—six titles in eight seasons—could already be seen.

When I ran this notion by basketball experts—Was the 1987–88 season really that good, or was it that I was nineteen and, when you're nineteen, everything looks that good?—none really disagreed.

"It's difficult to compare seasons," NBA commissioner Adam Silver told me. "But you're right that the 1987–88 season had an incredible mix of established superstars and emerging young players who would go on to have Hall of Fame careers."

"I wouldn't argue with that thesis," said Jack McCallum, who covered the NBA for *Sports Illustrated* in the 1980s. "The old greats were still great in 1987–88, and the young greats were great already. Kareem was still relevant," he explained. "MJ was just coming into his own. That era, in general, I think, we can safely call the golden age of the NBA. It was as good as it ever got in basketball.

"Here's how you know it was the best era," he added. "Think of all the teams that did not win but would have won at any other time: the Cavaliers, the Knicks, the Sonics, the Trail Blazers. They just happened to be great at the toughest basketball moment."

When I told Danny Ainge about all the future Hall of Famers who were active in 1987–88, he laughed and said, "I hadn't done the math, but it doesn't surprise me. You could feel it. There was so much talent and depth, so many great teams. In what other time are Dominique Wilkins and the Hawks not NBA champions? And then, when you battled all the way through the playoffs, who was waiting for you but the Pistons, or the Lakers, or, later, the Bulls. Come on!

"That year was the peak of a kind of basketball you don't see in the league anymore," added Ainge, who spoke to me as he drove to the Jazz practice facility in Salt Lake. "The physicality, the toughness. We knew it would be a fight whenever we went against Detroit. And we wanted the fight. We don't have much tolerance for that anymore. The league doesn't and society doesn't. It's not just basketball. All the major sports have become less physical. You get something when you do that. Guys play longer, and score more. But you give up something, too. You lose the game as an example and model for how to deal with the adversity and hardness of life. Like Kevin McHale playing an entire post-season on a broken foot. When will you ever see that again?"

The game was still violent in 1987–88; teams still adhered to playground rules. But it had also become as fast and elegant as it would ever be. The fashion that dominated out West—that pass-drunk, run-crazy fast-break basketball—was the game as dreamed of by Bob Cousy, and Walt Frazier, and Dr. J, and all the other airborne legends. If chronicled with care, I believed, that season could stand for the glory of the game at its best.

I decided to tell it as a story not of eighty-two contests but of just four games, plus the postseason—four games to stand for all the others, four games to tell a story that, at its core, is the story of four teams, which, at its core, is the story of four players—Bird, Magic, Isiah, Michael—and the revolution they brought to the league.

THE PLAYERS

THE FLIGHTLESS BIRD

Bird was the oldest. He was born in 1956, three years before Magic, five ahead of Isiah. He was half a generation older than Michael, who was in high school when Larry broke in to the NBA in 1979.

Bird began as a kind of rumor: There were whispers of a hoop-shooting hick in the Indiana scrub, the southern part of the state, down where the Klan was still strong. It was said he was beating college teams single-handed, playing in a way no white player had played since Cousy had a decade before.

In 1977, Red Auerbach, president of the Celtics, sent K. C. Jones, an assistant coach who'd anchored the 1960s Boston dynasty, west to investigate. He was skeptical when he left, but aglow when he returned.

"I told Red that Bird was the most confident athlete I had ever seen in my life, in any sport, anywhere," Jones said. "Picture this: The Indiana State team is playing I think it was Southern Methodist. Larry is being double- and triple-teamed every time he touches the ball. He gets away on a fast break but there are two guys hanging on him as he goes downcourt. Larry fires the ball off the backboard at an angle, simultaneously zigging away from the two defenders. They think he's just thrown up a crazy shot. Larry goes right to where he knows the ball will come off the board, and in the air, he takes the pass he's just made to himself! And dunks. I had never seen anybody have the presence of mind and self-confidence and ability to put something like that together."

Bird was an Indiana dream personified, a character out of the movie *Hoosiers,* the raw talent hitting jump shot after jump shot on a dirt court behind his mother's house in French Lick, metal pole shaking, ragged net sighing, hayfields rolling away. French Lick was a faded resort, a blink-and-miss-it hot spring beside Highway 56. There was a small high school, a dilapidated hotel, a piano factory. There were no elite summer camps for Larry Bird, no personal trainers, no showcases. Like politics, sports in such a town is local. Kids do not play in mesh uniforms. They play in jeans, shirts or skins. Larry's father did not help. He could neither hold a job nor pay the rent. If not employed at the piano factory, he was looking for work or drinking. Joe Bird fought in the Korean War, an experience that unhinged him. He was restless when he returned, prone to mood swings and bad decisions. When Larry's mother filed for divorce, Joe became an untethered balloon, drifting in a blue sky. He told his kids they'd be better off without him. One afternoon, he called the house and told his wife what he planned to do. He shot himself that day.

Larry Bird got into a lot of fights growing up. You could see it later, in the way he went after opposing players in the NBA. The look in his eyes was for real. If not fighting for himself, he fought for his brothers. It was the code he'd learned from his father: Protect your family. "My father taught us all to watch out for one another, no matter what the circumstances," Bird said later. "He told us that if he ever heard we didn't stick up for one another, we shouldn't bother coming home."

Larry grew a foot between his junior and senior years of high school. He did not stop growing until he really did look like a bird, a crane—the long spindly legs, the tangle of dirty-blond hair, the beak of a nose.

Asked if Larry was strong, locals would say, "Not weight-room strong."

Then what?

"Cock strong"—a term of high praise in Southern Indiana, meaning naturally powerful, Herculean without resorting to the weight room.

Larry said he was better at softball than at basketball—slow-pitch beneath the arc lights. He played in a beer league with his brothers, a rangy center fielder with hitting power. He could drive the ball three hundred feet into the gloaming. He mumbled to himself as he rounded the bases: *Fuckers shouldn't play me so shallow.* He said he was even better at badminton than at softball, but it was the basketball court he loved; that's where the world made sense to him, where the variables became manageable.

Never an especially athletic player, Bird relied on his uncanny sense of the game, his instinct. You don't have to be a superhuman athlete if you know what will happen next. "He was such a quiet rebounder," Celtics general manager Jan Volk told me. "He prepared for rebounds in ways that didn't draw any attention. He'd just drift over to his spot without being noticed and was usually there waiting when the game delivered the ball into his hands."

"I can visualize possible situations on the court before they happen," Bird explained. "That's how I come up with steals in the closing moments. Some golfers say they visualize everything about a shot before they take it. That's how I feel about playing defense."

He'd never seen a pro game before he played in one. He learned about the NBA and its history the way he learned about everything else: from the older kids in French Lick. "When we weren't playing ball, we hung out at a pool hall owned by a midget named Shorty Reader," Bird wrote in his memoir, *Drive: The Story of My Life.* "Shorty had a Volkswagen and we used to drive over to Northwood, Indiana, where we could pick up Chicago Cubs games on the car radio."

Bird found the best competition on the court behind the French Lick Springs Hotel, where a group of employees, all Black, had a regular game. He bluffed his way in, then studied the action like a student. This was different than the game played at the high school. It was quicker, open and free, built around unexpected passes, slashing moves to the hoop. He knew he was finally seeing the game as it was meant to be played. "I've always thought of basketball as a Black man's game," he said. "I just tried to do everything I could to fit in." It was attitude as well as talent. The players behind the hotel were not polite like the other kids he knew. They cursed and razzed each other constantly. It was in those games that Bird learned to trash-talk.

Larry dominated in high school. It was a classic case of man against boys. It seemed like he broke a town or district record every other week. "There was one night when I had a helluva game going," Bird said. "I had thirty-something points in the first half, and people were thinking I was going to break the Orange County record. My dad was at home. He didn't go to many games. Well, my uncle called him at halftime and said, 'You'd better get down here. Your boy is going to do it tonight.' We didn't have no car, but he walked over. I ended up with fifty-four points and thirty-eight rebounds."

The fact that Bird played at a tiny school in a rural area in the barren wilds of Indiana kept most of the big-time college scouts away. They dismissed him at a distance, calling his competition weak, his fundamentals awful. His movements looked awkward on film. "All I ever heard as I'd been playing was about everything I wasn't or everything I couldn't do," Bird said. "It was always: He's from a small town; he can't run and can't jump. He can't play against bigger guys. He's a step slow. He can't play defense."

Bird was also said to be sensitive and stubborn, a bit of a head case.

"He went to a real small school and wasn't Mr. Basketball or anything," Jerry Sichting told me. "But he was good enough to get invited to the high school all-star series they had every year. Indiana versus Kentucky. The coach didn't start him, and didn't use him. When he finally tried to put him in at the end, Bird refused to play. That's when he got the bad rap."

Indiana University coach Bobby Knight offered Bird a scholarship just in case he turned out to be a player. He'd rather Bird sit on the bench in Bloomington than become a starter somewhere else. Larry left French Lick with fanfare—for an Indiana kid, there was nothing bigger than playing for Bobby Knight. But Bird floundered at Indiana. The sprawling campus, all those classrooms, all those teachers, and all those kids—it was too big for him. He did not play varsity, so he wallowed, one of a dozen scholarship nobodies. He was hazed, as was every newbie, by the squad's upperclassmen, particularly Kent Benson, on whom Bird would revenge himself in the pros. (Benson spent a dozen years in the NBA, mostly as a Piston.) According to Seth Davis, author of *When March Went Mad,* the last straw for Larry was a first-semester bowling class he was required to take but could not afford.

He left Bloomington a month after he arrived, returning—quietly, anonymously—to French Lick, where he took jobs cutting down trees, painting signs, hauling trash. He was living with his mother and brothers in a wood house by the railroad, paint peeling. If you'd seen Larry walking the streets of French Lick on one of those afternoons, you'd have thought you could see his future, too. Loveless marriage, backbreaking work, early death. But he was saved by his talent and ambition. He began playing pickup in local games. And dominated. He was tapped for bigger games against stiffer competition, money games where middle-aged men stood along the fence, cash in hand. He was asked to suit up for Amateur Athletic Union (AAU) showcase tournaments. He'd improved since high school. He already had that otherworldly vision. There was nothing he did not anticipate. A recruiter from Indiana State—a small school in Terre Haute—began to turn up at Bird's games. Scouts live for such moments, catching sight of a feral genius at play in the wild. This was Bill Hodges, an assistant coach at the university. He'd seen Bird in high school and never forgot him. Hodges spoke to Indiana State head coach Bob King. He asked King to include Bird in a game featuring Indiana's top high school talent. King reluctantly agreed.

I mean, who is this garbage-hauling townie?

Bird went straight to the arena from work—he'd been stacking wheat on a farm. Noticing the scratches on Bird's arms, Coach King asked if he'd been "putting up hay."

"Yes, sir," said Bird.

"I bet your arms are pretty tired," said the coach.

"I can barely lift them."

Bird dominated the game even so, collecting 43 points, 15 assists, and 25 rebounds. By the fall, he was bound for Terre Haute.

In his first year at Indiana State, Bird could practice but not play—that was the rule for D-1 transfers. The Sycamores went 13–12 as Bird watched. The next year, with Bird in the lineup, the same team went 25–3. Magazines sent reporters. Fans lined up for tickets. Bird averaged 32.8 points a game. But it wasn't just the points that made him famous. It was his style, how he played. The icy calm, the passes to teammates who didn't even know they were open. By his second season in Terre Haute, he'd become a top NBA prospect. *If he plays like that as a Sycamore, imagine what he'll do if we put real talent around him.*

Most NBA executives stopped scouting Bird when he said he'd return to college for his senior year. Common wisdom: Drafting a kid who isn't ready to go pro is like giving up on a season before it starts. But that's not how Red Auerbach saw it. To

Auerbach, a Larry Bird you had to wait for looked like an under-valued commodity. Boston had the sixth overall pick in the 1978 draft, but Auerbach saw no one with the sort of generational talent he could rebuild around. In a notorious bit of draft-day brilliance, Auerbach used his first round pick on Bird—the player who said he would not go pro for another year. (In May 1979, seemingly in response to Auerbach's unprecedented move, the NBA passed the so-called Bird Collegiate Rule: A player must renounce college eligibility before he can enter the draft.) "I knew Bird would go one or two in the draft next season," Auerbach explained. "I also knew I wasn't planning to have the worst record in the league, so this was my only shot at him, and I was thinking long-term. We weren't going to win anything next season anyway. But here was someone I thought could help us win in the future." It was an executive's equivalent of a no-look pass.

"I wasn't paying attention to the 1978 draft," Bird said. "I was out playing golf in Santa Claus, Indiana, when a man came up to me on one of the fairways and told me the Celtics had taken me sixth in the draft. I said, 'What's that mean?' He said, 'I don't know. Watch the evening news.'"

Bird returned for his senior year at Indiana State, determined to make a run at the national title. The Sycamores, a collection of big country kids who'd soon return to their family farms—not a single player from that team, other than Bird, made a career in the NBA—defeated several college powerhouses (Purdue, Creighton, New Mexico) en route to a perfect record.

Meanwhile, a brilliant, charismatic, generational talent—a point guard trapped in the body of a power forward—was watching closely from a distance. Magic Johnson, who had turned the Michigan State Spartans into a powerhouse, checked the newspaper each morning to see how Bird had done. Against NC State. Against Bradley. Against Wichita. Magic had in fact played with Bird in a college all-star game. They'd clicked on the floor, and Magic had followed Bird ever since. "He was like no white player

I'd ever seen," Magic explained. "It wasn't only his talent; it was his attitude. When you were on the court with him he gave off that you-can't-touch-me aura. The fact that he talked trash, and Larry really did talk trash, was even more surprising. That's playground stuff, and Blacks weren't used to hearing it from a white guy. It used to bother some Black players. They wondered, 'Is he talking that stuff to me?' But Larry backed it up night after night."

The Sycamores blazed through the early rounds of the 1979 NCAA tournament as Magic led his team through the opposite bracket, working his way toward his first showdown with Bird. Michigan State beat Penn to reach the final. The entire Michigan State team, including several future NBA players, gathered in the stands to watch Indiana State play DePaul in the semifinal. The Blue Demons had several standouts, including Mark Aguirre, who was in the process of rewriting the NCAA record book. The Sycamores had Bird. Arguing with teammates—a dozen men in Michigan State jackets, most of whom believed DePaul would win easily—Magic said, "You don't know my boy Larry. Don't underestimate Larry."

Bird took control in the first half. Hit jumpers, battled for rebounds, dunked. He scored 35 points. Indiana State won by 2.

The 1979 NCAA Final was played in Salt Lake City, Utah. Historians say it was this game, in which Bird and Magic went head-to-head before a national audience, that marked the birth of the modern NBA. The league had been struggling. There were few transcendent stars, few great teams. The pro game had become plodding, violent, slow. There was too much off-court news—players arrested for gun possession, drug possession, assault. Attendance was down, as were revenues. Many games were not even carried on live TV. Then here came Bird and Johnson, sharp and sober and wildly talented, prodigies who seemed to be playing for the love of the game.

Purity.

There was also the perfect contrast of the matchup. The city

(Lansing, Michigan) vs. the farm (Terre Haute, Indiana). Black vs. white. Flash vs. . . . well, not substance, because Magic Johnson had plenty of substance, but the old hustling, sweaty American way of getting a dirty job done epitomized by Bird vs. what looked like effortless Magic. Bird had already been drafted by the Celtics. Johnson would be drafted first overall in 1979, meaning that the NCAA Final marked the beginning, not the end, of the rivalry.

Magic and Larry crossed paths in the tunnel before the game. Reaching a hand out to Larry, Magic said, "Yo, Bird!" Larry left Magic hanging, turned and walked away. Magic could be friends with an opponent. Not Bird. "Earvin is an outgoing guy," Bird said later. "He's got the big smile. He loves everybody, loves to high-five. For me, when you compete, you're really not friends. You need to keep that edge. I never let myself forget: My goal is to take three of them teeth home with me."

The final was not especially close. The Spartans came with a simple strategy and executed it perfectly. As soon as Bird had the ball in his hands, two or three Spartans swarmed, bumped, swatted, fouled. In a normal case, a player breaks such a trap by getting the ball to teammates—they were open all over the floor—and letting them score easy baskets while occupying the defense. But Bird did not have the kind of teammates at Indiana State who could beat any of the Spartans one-on-one. Magic Johnson scored 24 points that night. But two of his teammates—Sam Vincent and Greg Kesler, both headed for the NBA—also scored double digits. Bird got 19 points, but had to do it with crazy, off-balance shots. Michigan won 75–64. It was a lesson for Bird and Magic: No matter how good, any single player can be stopped. To go all the way, a team needs many sources of offense.

The Spartans raced to center court when the buzzer sounded. They celebrated, then cut down the nets. Magic looked at the Indiana State bench. "I'll never forget what I saw," he later said. "While half the arena was screaming with joy, Larry Bird was sitting with his face buried in a towel. He was obviously crying, and my heart went out to him. As happy as I was, I knew that if things had gone a little differently, I would have been the one with his face in a towel. I take losses the same way."

Red Auerbach asked Bird to fly to Boston and finish the 1978 NBA season with the Celtics. He would've been the first man to play in college and the NBA in the same season. Bird demurred. He wanted to return to Terre Haute with his teammates, mourn the loss, finish school, graduate. When he did turn up at the Celtics facility for rookie camp at the end of the summer, half the veterans—for them, these early practices were optional—were waiting. According to the newspapers, Auerbach had agreed to pay Bird over $600,000, the most ever paid a rookie, which irritated Celtic veterans like Cedric Maxwell, who'd come to camp to school Bird.

Bird played forward with a handful of different partners that week. He was gangly, tall and stooped, hands on hips, blond fuzz springing from ruddy cheeks. He had the face of a pioneer or a frontiersman. The Hick from French Lick—he gave *himself* that name at a press conference.

Cedric Maxwell, twenty-four and going into his third NBA season, joined with Tiny Archibald and M. L. Carr in an effort to embarrass Bird. The resulting scrimmages were fast and physical; everyone took a run at the rookie, who blossomed under the pressure. Maxwell pushed him farther and farther outside, but no matter how distant, no matter how hard he'd been jostled, Bird made the shot. "After a week of camp my opinion completely changed," Maxwell said. "There was no denying it: The white kid could really play."

It was Bird's passing that impressed veterans the most. Here was a big forward who moved the ball like a guard. He seemed to know where you were going before you knew yourself. Even as a rookie, Bird did that thing an athlete must do to be considered great: made his teammates look better than they really were.

Most college stars struggle when they enter the NBA. For the first time, many are facing opponents who can run just as fast, jump just as high, and shoot just as accurately as them. And maybe, for the first time, they are not the best player on the floor.

Whenever I asked a veteran about the adjustment, I was given a variation of the following: "I was still a kid when I arrived, and now I was playing against men." Bird was an exception. He was actually better as a pro than he'd been in college. The better the opposition, the better he performed. He was big and physical under the hoop, a style that suited the franchise perfectly. John Havlicek, a legendary Celtic, told *The Boston Globe* "[I] never would have retired if I had known there was a chance to play with someone like [Bird]."

The Celtics were predicted to finish at the bottom of their division in 1979–80, Bird's first year. They'd gone 29–53 the previous season and failed to make the playoffs. Their best player, center Dave Cowens, was a broken-down old man of thirty-one in 1979. This would also be the last Celtic season for the once great Bob McAdoo, who was overweight and not mentally present in 1979. Celtic fans called him "McAdon't." The team had hired a new coach, a disciplinarian named Bill Fitch. A few weeks before the opener, Fitch handed Bird a piece of paper and asked him to write down how many games he thought the Celtics would win.

Bird thought a moment, then scribbled a number.

Fitch looked at it and snickered. "Forty-seven?" he said incredulously. "That's awfully high. From twenty-nine to forty-seven? You must really think something is going to happen around here."

The Celtics would finish the season at 61–21, first place in the Eastern Conference.

"I'm still waiting for Coach Fitch to come back on that one," Bird said later.

For many rookies, the schedule is a bigger adjustment than the game. All that traveling, all those arenas, all those heckling fans, many of them drunk, all the reporters and hotels. NBA teams traveled commercial back then. Night games usually ended after the last flight out. Per league rules, teams had to take the first flight to the next city in the morning, which meant a 5:00 A.M. jump to D.C., Philly, Detroit. While the GMs and coaches were drinking Bloody Marys in first class, the players were trying to get comfortable in coach, tall men crammed into small seats, sweat suits, and neck pillows, the flight attendant navigating the drink cart around the long limbs like a sea dog rounding Cape Horn.

Bird loved it. Playing on the road in the NBA meant having to think about only one thing: basketball. The rest of it, the confusion and hassle of everyday life, vanished. "The first three months or so of that season were neat," he said. "I was just traveling and playing and I didn't have to worry about anything else."

The Celtics made it to the semifinals in Bird's rookie year, then lost in five games to Philadelphia. The 76ers were the class of the NBA, a powerful team flush with talent. Dr. J, Doug Collins, Darryl Dawkins, Mo Cheeks. To understand why Boston played the way they did in the 1980s, you have to look at those 76ers. You'd need a steamroller to get by Philly, so that's what Red Auerbach built: a steamroller. Bird had merely been the first piece.

Bird won Rookie of the Year in 1979–80 and finished high in the MVP voting, astonishingly so for a first-year player. He averaged 21.3 points a game and was outstanding in the playoffs. In one year, he'd returned the Celtics to the center of the basketball conversation. And yet, he was not happy. Until he'd avenged his NCAA loss to Magic Johnson, he'd never really feel like he'd accomplished anything.

MAGIC

Magic was everything Bird was not: athletic, extroverted, affectionate, press-friendly. He always seemed to be having a blast. While Larry was a white kid in a Black man's game who, before anything else, wanted to prove he belonged, Magic was transcendent—

a revolutionary talent. Don't get me wrong, Bird wanted to dominate. But always within the existing structure of the game, at one of the known positions on the floor.

Magic, a Black kid playing a Black game, wanted more than that. It was not enough to simply excel. He wanted to change the game as he played it, rewrite the code from within the Matrix. Before him, point guards tended to be small slick operators like Bob Cousy. Magic was different because he'd been relatively short in grade school, when positions were first assigned. His early coaches put him at point guard because he was small, and it was as a small guard that he mastered the tricks little men use to outwit giants. Dribbling and ball handling, feinting and fooling. Then he grew. Six-two. Six-three. Six-four. When he reached 6'8", coaches began asking him to play forward, but he refused. He had his position, loved it, and would not change. He liked carrying the ball and setting the tempo. The result was a phenomenon new to the game: the skills and mindset of a point guard in the body of a power forward. He was often half a foot or more taller than the player tasked with defending him. This helped explain his court vision: He could usually see over the defender's head. He could take in every player and every open lane at a glance.

"It was that vision that made Magic into Mozart," Jeff Lamp, who played with Magic on the Lakers, told me. Lamp, who was a superstar at the University of Virginia, spoke to me from his office at the National Basketball Players Association in L.A. during the COVID-19 quarantine. "There was his leadership, of course; he was the greatest leader I've ever been around," Lamp continued. "And he could run like the wind and shoot the lights out. But it was his vision that set him apart. I've never seen anybody else with that kind of vision; he used it to control the game. Here was a guy who could dominate without scoring a single point."

Magic's Michigan childhood consisted of playgrounds. He lived across the street from one, down the street from another, two blocks from a third. He spent every free minute on the basketball courts at those playgrounds. Earvin Jr.—not yet Magic—was the sixth of nine children. His mother was a school cafeteria supervisor, and his father, Earvin Sr., worked long hours at Fisher Body Plant. He volunteered for the graveyard shift—4:48 P.M. to 3:18 A.M.—because it paid overtime. Though he did not see much of his son—Earvin Sr. was asleep when Earvin Jr. left for school—he taught by example. The lesson was simple: Work hard, provide, never give in to despair.

Though Earvin Jr. admired his father, he did not want to live like that. Earvin Jr. wanted money, freedom, fame. When he was five, his father gave him a basketball. He grasped it like a magician grasps a wand. He carried it everywhere, dribbled it up and down the block, among potholes and parked cars. His left hand dribbled while his right hand waved hello. He hung out of the car window, dribbling it on the street while his mother drove. He bounced the ball off the walls at home, off the lockers at school. It was confiscated, returned, confiscated again. He spent hours watching the older kids in the park, turning the ball in his hands, waiting for his chance. *You need a ball? Let me play.* He was the grade-schooler competing with teenagers, finding the open man, making the pass, hitting the shot.

His junior high coach took the team to see the Pistons. It was the first pro game Earvin Jr. had been to. He was dazzled by the size of the players, their skill and speed, the TV cameras, the glass backboards, the glossy floor, the wild crowd. Bob Lanier was playing for Detroit, along with Dave Bing and Jimmy Walker. The visiting Milwaukee Bucks, one of the best teams in the NBA, were a mix of youth and age. The Big O, Oscar Robertson, was the point guard. Kareem Abdul-Jabbar, who'd recently changed his name from Lew Alcindor, was the center. Earvin Jr.'s team visited the Bucks locker room after the game. Little Earvin, program and pen in hand, stood beside 7'2" Kareem's locker, watching him towel off. He wanted an autograph, but was afraid to ask. He opened his mouth; nothing came out. Kareem, notoriously prickly with fans, especially kids, stared into Earvin's eyes, then turned to the kid next to Earvin Jr. and said, "What does this young blood want from me?"

"Your autograph, sir."

Abdul-Jabbar pulled the program from Earvin's hand, scribbled his name, gave it back, got up, and went to the showers. They would meet again a decade later.

Earvin Jr. planned to play for his neighborhood high school, a top athletic power. He knew the colors, the words of the fight song, the names and proclivities of the varsity basketball team's starting five. But shortly before he was to matriculate, the state enacted its plan to desegregate the public schools. Instead of going to the school down the block, Earvin was bused to Everett, a mostly white school in South Lansing. There was tension in the hallways those first weeks. To the principal, who was monitoring the situation closely—this was a great experiment, with much in the balance—the basketball team was a beacon of hope. Unlike when they were in the classroom or on the playground, the kids on the team would be forced to work together if they wanted to win. If things worked out, they could serve as an example for the rest of the students. Earvin Johnson, Jr., who already had the big smile and could seemingly get along with anyone, became the linchpin. He was a bridge builder by nature; bringing people together had always been his thing. Love for everything and everyone—it shined from him like a light.

Everett, a longtime also-ran in the state's Class A division, became a contender as soon as Earvin Jr. arrived. He only got bigger and better. He was 6'8" by his senior year, when he averaged 28 points a game and led Everett to the state title. He got his nickname then, too. He'd spoken to a local reporter after a game and did not think of it again until he saw the headline that identified him as EVERETT'S EARVIN "MAGIC" JOHNSON. He was embarrassed at first. It sounded like bragging. But once people picked up the name, and it showed signs of permanence, he embraced it.

Wilt the Stilt, Pistol Pete, "the Iceman" Gervin—every star needs a nickname.

The scouts were fixated on the question: Where will Earvin Johnson play college ball? He'd considered UCLA and North Carolina before narrowing the field to the classic Motor City dilemma: University of Michigan or Michigan State? Michigan had the better team and was a more established sporting power, but he went with State. Mainly because the Wolverines coach wanted Magic to play forward while the Spartans coach said something like, "Hey, you come here, you can play any position you want."

Magic did for Michigan State exactly what he'd done for Everett. While averaging 17 points a game as a freshman, he led the Spartans to the Elite 8 of the NCAA tournament, where they lost to Kentucky. He worked on his left hand and outside shooting over the summer, then returned for his sophomore year an even better version of himself. The Spartans entered the 1979 tournament as a favorite. They beat LSU, Notre Dame, Penn, and Indiana State to win the first NCAA championship in Michigan State history.

Magic announced his eligibility for the draft as soon as he was back in Lansing. He'd won two titles in three seasons: a Michigan state high school championship and an NCAA championship. He was ready for the big time. He seemed likely to go number one in the draft, which meant either the Bulls or the Lakers—the Bulls because they were awful, the Lakers because they'd traded up. A coin toss would decide who picked first. It was the Bulls' general manager, Rod Thorn, picking against the Lakers' general manager, Jerry West. Thorn called heads. It was tails, so instead of heading across Lake Michigan to Chicago, Magic went across the country to Los Angeles, where he'd play for the team Jerry West had built around Kareem Abdul-Jabbar. It seemed like another piece of bad luck for the Bulls, but, by losing that toss and remaining awful, they'd get a shot at an even better player a few years later.

On advice from Jerry West, Lakers owner Jack Kent Cooke planned to draft Sidney Moncrief—Sid the Squid, a shooting guard who'd broken collegiate records at the University of Arkansas. But Kent Cooke was in the process of selling the Lakers to Jerry Buss, a cowboy-boot-wearing entrepreneur from Wyoming, and he yielded when Buss made it clear he wanted Magic.

As with Bird in Boston, every Laker veteran turned out for the optional summer camp to meet the rookie. Magic soon found himself on the floor with players who were not only better than any he'd ever played with—Norm Nixon, Michael Cooper, Kareem Abdul-Jabbar—but entirely unfamiliar with his style. Those first no-look passes caught the veterans by surprise. They'd be racing down the floor, covered like a glove, then turn, and suddenly, there was the ball. Magic's passes hit them in the face, hit them in the back of the head. Guys fell down, and got up bitching.

What the fuck?

"If you can see me, I can see you," said Magic. "If I can see you, you're getting the ball."

Magic was promptly tested by his new teammates; some were jealous of his celebrity, some of his contract. (He signed for nearly $500,000, slightly less than Bird, but still the second-highest rookie contract in the league's history.) Some hated the big toothy grin, and the passes that came from nowhere and hit you mid-thought. But Magic rose to the occasion, redoubling his effort when challenged. He came to blows—actual fisticuffs—with Norm Nixon, who'd been the Lakers' top guard before Magic arrived. In the end, Nixon would be traded for the sake of team cohesion. He'd been a fan favorite, and it took some of the L.A. faithful years to forgive Magic, but that early struggle was something else to Magic's teammates. It was the kid making his bones.

This was when the veterans began to regard Earvin Johnson as something more than just another rookie. He was a leader with the will to take his place atop the hierarchy. (Some of these events were revisited in HBO's *Winning Time,* in which Magic is played by Quincy Isaiah and Nixon is played by his own son DeVaughn.)

Magic was given another nickname that summer. Earvin at home, Magic in public, he became "Buck" to teammates. This either denoted his manner—with those long legs and wide eyes, he looked like a gamboling young deer—or his other personality, the nighttime Earvin who haunted the clubs, went everywhere and loved everything, sometimes two or three at a time. This was 1979, the beginning of the Showtime Lakers, which meant speed on the floor and shenanigans at the disco. Play all day, dance all night, behavior not merely tolerated but encouraged by Jerry Buss, who turned the staid old Forum Club, where season ticket holders once enjoyed buffet dinners, into the hottest nightspot in town.

Each rookie was assigned a mentor, a veteran to shadow, learn from, and, in many cases, be hazed by. Some veterans humiliated their charges, made them sing in the locker room, wash their cars, go to the store for condoms and wine. Kareem, who'd been given charge of Earvin Jr., required only two things from his rookie: Every morning on the road, Magic was to bring Kareem a copy of *The New York Times* and the *Herald Examiner;* at every practice, he was to fetch his Gatorade.

Assigning Magic to Kareem was the coach's way of getting the team's best players to bond. Magic tried to befriend Kareem, but the older man remained standoffish. It was only on the court that he seemed present, and not always even then. "When I first came to the Lakers, Kareem was so aloof, so distant, and so completely different from the other players that some of the guys referred to him as the 'brother from another planet,'" Magic wrote in his memoir.

Magic searched for a connection, a key to open the door into

Kareem's life. He found it by showing an interest in Kareem's art. One day, after practice, Johnson asked if Abdul-Jabbar would teach him how to shoot the skyhook, Kareem's signature weapon. As of 1979, the skyhook was the most beautiful shot in the game, satisfyingly elegant and all but unstoppable. It evolved from the straight hook, a shot that had been around forever. Kareem's variation, stumbled across while he was playing in high school, was to combine the classic hook with the jumper. Hence: skyhook. Turning his back to the basket, Kareem, with the ball in his palm and the hoop in his periphery, would extend his arm to its limit, leap from one foot, raise his shooting hand up and away, then roll the ball off his fingers at the top of his jump. It seemed less like he was shooting the ball than setting it free. Relying on the skyhook, Kareem made .574 percent of his shots in 1971–72, his third season in the NBA, and averaged 34.8 points a game. A .559 lifetime shooter, he'd go on to score 38,387 points in his twenty-year career, putting him atop the all-time list, a record he held for thirty-eight years. LeBron finally broke it on February 7, 2023.

Kareem is 7'2". At its point of release, the skyhooked ball was twelve feet off the ground, two feet *above* the rim. "Even if you dropped from the ceiling," Oscar Robertson said, "you couldn't block that thing." And yet, maybe because it was so uniquely Kareem's, no one ever asked how the trick was done. Magic was the first. The mere act of being asked pleased Kareem and created a bond. Magic's interest meant that Kareem's signature move might live on after he retired. That's culture: invent, perfect, bequeath.

Magic played his first pro game in Seattle on October 12, 1979. Everything fans and teammates would come to love about Johnson was on display that night. He led the offense, made gorgeous passes, rebounded like a big man, dribbled like a small man, scored from the inside and the outside, high-fived, fist-pumped, and looked like he was having the time of his life; 26 points, 8 rebounds, 4 assists. The game was decided on the last possession. The Lakers were down 102–101. Kareem got the ball at the top of the key with two seconds on the clock. He looked like he might drive, then stepped away, turned, jumped, and hit the skyhook.

Magic, who'd been under the basket waiting for a rebound, raised his arms in victory and ran up-court, where he grabbed and held stoical Kareem like a lost brother, leaned back, and laughed. The game was being broadcast on national TV. The same audience that had seen Magic win the NCAA Final a few months before was now seeing him hug Kareem Abdul-Jabbar.

"I was still in college, but I remember watching that game on TV and it was nuts," Jeff Lamp told me. "It was like Magic was still in school, and brought all those tough old pros back there with him. Back to Lansing. Back to a time when every game mattered. Kareem, having just hit that skyhook, was walking off the court, like, you know, another day at the office, and here comes Magic, jumping all over him. Kareem pushed Magic away and said, 'What the hell are you doing? We've got another eighty-one games. Pace yourself.'"

The Lakers built their attack around their star rookie. It was a speed offense, characterized by the fast break. Magic's height, dribbling, passing skills, and quickness were what made it possible. No guard in the NBA could screen him. "We could play blindingly fast when Magic was handling the ball," Lamp continued. "That kind of speed opens everything. Each time down the floor, Magic would see three or four scoring options—things no one else would see. Once we got cooking, we could push the tempo, the intensity. Just keep pushing it. Then, if he didn't see anything he liked, he'd just take it to the hoop himself."

"Every missed shot by you was a fast break for them," Michael Holton, a Phoenix Suns guard who battled the Showtime Lakers in the 1980s, told me. "My first year in Phoenix, they swept us in the playoffs by an average of thirty points a game. Every time we blew a shot, they made a basket. It was ridiculous."

1980. 1981. 1982. This was when so-called playground basketball, distinguished by its athleticism and its speed, fully triumphed in the NBA. It was different than the game played in the earth-bound 1950s and '60s. It was razzle-dazzle, rock and roll. It was "Every time they miss, we score." It was the game as it was played on public courts in predominantly Black neighborhoods like Har-lem and Watts, the South Side of Chicago and East Lansing, Michigan. It had been dismissed by many white coaches as un-sound, not good team basketball, vulnerable to a smart, carefully devised defense.

To the historian Harry Edwards, such views were merely evi-dence of racism. "In 1928, for example, the all-black Renaissance Five defeated the famed all-white Celtics—the leading white bas-ketball team of the time—and several other all-white aggrega-tions," he writes in *The Revolt of the Black Athlete*. "And these victories were not atypical, although they seemingly went unno-ticed by the white sports-reporting establishment of the day."

According to Edwards, the bias against playground ball was less about fundamentals than about resentment: Historically, basketball had been a white game, invented by James Naismith in 1891 to keep kids occupied during the long New England winters. Black athletes took it, reinvented it, then returned it as something better and new—and, increasingly, more profitable.

Magic Johnson's gift for comradeship could be seen in his unself-ish passing, the way he got every other player involved. His arrival in L.A. elicited a late-career flowering from Kareem. Revived by Magic's passing, Kareem won his sixth NBA MVP and helped lead the Lakers to the 1980 finals, where they faced the Philadel-phia 76ers. But when Kareem rolled his ankle in Game 5, Magic stepped forward to play center in Game 6, a position he'd never played before. Magic lost the opening tip but dominated the rest of the game, winning Finals MVP. Larry Bird was watching on a 22-inch TV in French Lick, Indiana. Here's what Bird was thinking: *Son of a bitch! Two years in a row!*

That marked the dawn of the Magic Johnson era. *Showtime.* The Lakers had signed Kareem Abdul-Jabbar in 1975, but did not win it all until they added Magic. It was his skill and energy, his personality. Kareem was cranky and distant. He seemed old even when he was young. Magic, on the other hand, would always be a kid. That's what he gave the team. At the Forum Club, it was high fives and confabs. On the court, it was speed and creativity. His gift for friendship bonded him with players across the league, especially rookies. He sought out those who approached the game with the same intensity, had the same spark. With these people he formed a kind of brotherhood. There were phone calls, dinners, off-season pickup games. Why? Because the game is bigger and more important than any single rivalry or team. And not just rookies, but high school and college standouts too, anyone he recognized as a kindred spirit. The greatest example, the friendship that defined the era, was the bond Magic Johnson formed with the young Isiah Thomas. Magic loved Isiah because Isiah understood.

ISIAH

Born in 1959, Magic grew up watching guards like the Lakers' Jerry West and the Pistons' Dave Bing, future Hall of Famers both listed at 6'3". Born in 1961, Isiah grew up watching Magic, listed at 6'9". Still in high school when Johnson led Michigan State over Bird in the NCAA Final, Isiah, just 5'10", was swept up in the way Magic redefined the point guard position. Despite his height, Isiah actually tried to play like Magic. This was one of Isiah's most admirable qualities: He did not let size define him. He determined, from his first appearance on Chicago's West Side courts, to play the game exactly the way he wanted.

There were a dozen playgrounds within three miles of Isiah's childhood home, but Gladys was his favorite. Its real name was Gunderson Park, in honor of Gladys Gunderson, a member of a prominent Chicago family, but everyone called it Gladys. It was a small square of concrete at the corner of South Spaulding and West Gladys, three blocks from the I-290 overpass amid a stretch of bleak low-slung tenements.

"Gladys was a ghetto playground with all the standard ghetto amenities," Thomas said later. "Broken glass. Dry drinking fountains. Steel bars across the restroom doors. Hot and cold running gang fights. Its basketball courts had more pits, cracks, and craters than the old parquet floor at Boston Garden. Weed and gravel claimed equal shares of what was not worn down to bare dirt. And then there was the Hole, the man-eating abyss that gaped directly beneath one of the baskets. The Hole swallowed up balls, players, entire teams. You had to watch out for the Hole when you went to the bucket at Gladys Park."

The 1970s were a golden age of neighborhood basketball in Chicago, a world with many levels. Up top were the Bulls, an expansion franchise that debuted in 1966. The Bulls were licensed to replace Chicago's earlier pro teams, the Stags, the Majors, the Zephyrs, and the American Gears. Old-timey white men in short-shorts, delivering crisp bounce passes. The Stags and Majors played at Chicago Stadium, a barn on West Madison Street on the city's Near West Side, five miles from the Loop. The rodeo played the stadium, as did Led Zeppelin, the Blackhawks, and the Ice Capades.

The interstate separated the Near West Side from the rest of the city, isolating it and starving it of services until it became a vast ghetto, Chicago's most dangerous neighborhood. Blocks were controlled by rival gangs in the 1970s and '80s. The Black Disciples. The Vice Lords. The Blackstone Rangers. Trains ran express from the Loop on game days. "Whatever you do," people would say, "don't get off before your stop."

Though Isiah grew up less than a mile from the stadium, he'd never seen a Bulls game live because he couldn't afford a ticket. He'd wait by the players' entrance after the parking lot emptied. These were the Bob Love, Jerry Sloan, Norm Van Lier days in Chicago. "We'd beg for merchandise, anything they could give us," Thomas said. "We'd take an autograph, but we really wanted a jersey, shoes, shorts, and, oh my God, maybe a ball. Anything we could sell."

Then there was the college basketball scene. The Chicago State Cougars were solid in the 1970s. The DePaul Blue Demons were dominant. The Loyola Ramblers, the first NCAA team to break the color line, went on storied postseason runs. Northwestern had the best coach, Tex Winter, who would introduce the triangle offense to Phil Jackson and the Bulls in the 1980s. And there was the competitive high school scene, with powerhouses like Thornridge, where Quinn Buckner played; Westinghouse (some consider the 1977 Westinghouse Warriors the greatest high school team ever); Simeon Career Academy, where Derrick Rose played; and St. Joseph's, a Catholic school in the western suburbs where Coach Gene Pingatore built a basketball factory.

But the playgrounds were where you'd see the most uninhibited form of basketball. Great playground players are often stymied by an organized system; if you want to see them at their best, working to impress only each other, you have to go to the park, where the game is played without coaches. When you remove the authorities, the kids establish their own hierarchy. It doesn't matter what the scouts think or who shoots the best percentage. At Gladys, there was only one question: Can he play?

Mark Aguirre, Doc Rivers, Mo Cheeks, and Isiah Thomas all faced each other at Gladys before they met again in the NBA. There was also Lord Henry, Zeke's older brother—Isiah was the youngest of nine—whom Zeke ranked with the best. Lord Henry, who was ten years older, taught Zeke how to dribble, shoot, carry himself. "He had elusive speed, was deceptive, and could move from the top of the key to the basket faster than anyone I have ever seen," Thomas said. "He could use his eyes to move people off the mark, to make space. If he got an inch of daylight, he was gone."

Lord Henry served Zeke as example and counterexample. "He could've been a great college player," Thomas said. "He would have been an even better pro. They would have put his name on a shoe and sent him to Europe with Magic and Michael, dressed in red, white, and blue. He became an addict instead, an intravenous drug user. He abused himself right out of the game."

Isiah's mother, Mary Thomas, learned from Lord Henry too. *Never again.* She stood on her porch with a shotgun when members of the Vice Lords or Blackstone Rangers came for her children. "My boys are not here for you," she'd say. "They are *my* boys. Now get going or you won't go anywhere again."

Mary Thomas became a neighborhood legend in Chicago. Disney even made a movie about her: *A Mother's Courage: The Mary Thomas Story.* It starts with Mary as a child in Vicksburg, Mississippi, and ends with her holding that shotgun. Isiah's father came and went, so it all depended on Mary. She posted house rules on the front door: *No insulting anyone else, ever; be home before sundown; don't take things that don't belong to you.* "And they usually followed those rules and did what I said, so I didn't have to whup them much," she told the *Chicago Tribune.* "But I did hit my kids. I don't believe you can't spank your children. Still, it was easy for them to talk to me. If they would tell me someone came up to them and asked them to do something not right, I'd tell them, 'Don't follow no one nowhere.'"

This is what made basketball so important to Isiah. Gladys was the only place he could get out from under his mother, the only place he felt free. He was already a great player at thirteen. He held out his hands and the ball came—like a yo-yo or a dog. He loved to pass because he knew the ball would come back. He was even more deceptive on the court than Lord Henry. It was not just his game that deceived, but his looks. How could a person that adorable—his eyes twinkled, his smile flashed, his cheeks were smooth—play so viciously? There were no easy baskets when you played Isiah. If you went up and over, he'd drive you into the pole. If you went around, he'd check you to the concrete. That's how everyone played at Gladys.

Gene Pingatore recruited Isiah to play at St. Joseph's in Westchester, Illinois, a dozen miles west of the city. It was a three-hour commute for Zeke. He left in the dark and returned in the dark: the bleakness of the gray Chicago winter. He took the 5:30 A.M. bus to the end of the line, then walked the last mile and a half. During that walk, white friends would drive by in cars with their parents but wouldn't stop. "It's cold in Chicago," Isiah said, "and by the time I got to school, I'd say, 'Hey, man, didn't you see me?' And they'd say, 'Well, I'm not like that but Mom and Dad are from a different generation.'"

Gene Pingatore was a great coach, and Isiah loved him. He'd been born in Cicero, played high school ball at St. Mel's, attended Loyola in Los Angeles, then returned to Chicago to pursue his vocation, which was not just winning games but "raising men." It was Pingatore who taught Isiah how to play in a system, as part of a machine. Isiah continued to call Pingatore even as an NBA star. When the Pistons were being stymied by the Knicks' full-court trap in the 1983 playoffs, it was not Detroit coach Chuck Daly who came up with the solution. It was Gene Pingatore, who told Isiah to "run the press breaker," a defensive scheme drilled at St. Joseph's high school.

Isiah, whose team finished second in the Illinois High School Basketball Championship his junior year, spent much of his senior year meeting with college recruiters. The most determined presented themselves at the Thomas home to be questioned by Mary Thomas and Lord Henry. Some came with offers of cars and money. Some with guarantees of a starring role, a national championship, a path to the NBA. Isiah wanted to play at DePaul with his friend Mark Aguirre. Mary wanted him out of the city and off at a "real college," like those she'd seen in the movies.

Bobby Knight had been coaching at Indiana University for a decade when he met Mary. He was tougher than most college coaches. At Indiana, it was Knight, not the players, who ran the offense. His kids followed his system; if you did not buy in to it, you did not play. Most coaches flattered Isiah during their visits, but Knight focused his attention on Mary. At times, he spoke only to her, which infuriated Lord Henry, who had heard all the terrible Bobby Knight stories. The yelling, the tantrums, the abuse. He argued with Knight, who ignored Lord Henry until Lord Henry became impossible to ignore.

"Do you have something you want to say to me, son?" Knight asked Lord Henry.

"When Junior is down there in Bloomington, if something goes down with the Klan, who's going to take care of him?" Lord Henry asked.

"Well, if we're winning, the Klan will," said Knight.

This was a joke that did not land.

Lord Henry started screaming. Knight, who was thirty-nine years old, asked Lord Henry if he wanted to step outside. He stood up, took off his coat. Mary Thomas told Lord Henry to shut up, then asked Knight to continue. Turning back to her, he said, "I'm going to offer your son three things. One: He's gonna graduate [he did, but only much later]. Two: He's gonna be a gentleman [he isn't]. Three: Everything I know about basketball, I'll teach him [he did]."

Mary Thomas convened a press conference the next day. With Isiah sitting glumly at her side, she told the world that her son would be playing for Bobby Knight at Indiana University.

Isiah got off to a rocky start in Bloomington. Bobby Knight coached like a marine sergeant, constantly shouting, insulting, grabbing, shoving. His aim was to break down and rebuild freshmen to fit his scheme. Zeke resisted; fireworks ensued. Knight threatened to send Isiah home. When that didn't work, he threatened to keep him on scholarship but off the floor. Win or lose, it did not matter to Knight. He'd sit Zeke until Zeke gave in. This meant most of that first preseason. But it was the coach who finally bent. It happened in December 1979, when, looking for a spark against Miami of Ohio, Knight sent Isiah out onto the floor, where he took over the game. By January, Isiah was a leader. He called plays, made passes, managed the clock. The team began to hum, and, by the spring of 1980, Isiah had emerged as a star. He carried Indiana to the NCAA tournament and took them all the way to the Sweet Sixteen, where they lost to Purdue.

He was named captain before his sophomore year. Coach Knight had come to trust the boyish twenty-year-old he called "Pee Wee." Listed at six feet, Zeke was shorter. In interviews, he sometimes gave his own height—teams tend to puff up in press materials and on roster sheets—as 5'10". He was beloved by fans, who chanted his name and hung a biblically inspired banner from the bleachers: "AND A LITTLE CHILD SHALL LEAD THEM," ISAIAH 11:6.

I'd followed Isiah since he was in high school. He was the first star I'd been able to watch develop, to grow from fledgling to hawk. I'd hoped he'd go to DePaul so I could see him live; the Blue Demons played at the Rosemont Horizon, which was just thirty minutes from my house. But I understood his choice of Indiana. There was no greater name in college sports than Bobby Knight, who'd turned a dozen raw kids into NBA players. My father took me to see Isiah and the Hoosiers blow out Northwestern in Evanston in February 1980. Zeke had filled out and settled into a rhythm at Indiana—he became a great team player in college—but he was still electric and still small, even smaller when compared to his teammates, many of whom were 6'7" or above.

The Hoosiers went into the 1981 NCAA tournament ranked third in the Midwest—Isiah was a sophomore—then upset everyone en route to the final, where they beat a North Carolina team that included Sam Perkins and James Worthy to win the championship. Isiah appeared on the cover of *Sports Illustrated* on April 6, 1981. Hoisted by fans, he cuts down the basketball net, handling the scissors as carefully as a five-year-old working on an art project. *And a little child shall lead them.* He announced his eligibility for the NBA draft a month later. Two years and out was the fashion of the moment. He wanted to play for the Bulls and tried to make it happen. The Dallas Mavericks had the top pick that year. On a visit to Texas to meet the top brass, Zeke made himself unwanted, trashing the coach and the owner, then refusing to wear a Stetson at the press conference.

"No way," he said publicly at the time, "I'm not into that cowboy [shit]."

The Mavericks took Mark Aguirre first overall instead.

Isiah tried to repeat the performance in Detroit, which had the number two pick. But the Pistons had a new general manager, Jack McCloskey, who knew what he wanted and could not be manipulated. Zeke's size did not bother McCloskey, nor did his behavior. "I saw him play at Indiana and it was a perfect game," McCloskey said. "Isiah didn't do anything wrong. And the extraordinary thing about it is he was absolutely demanding everything from everybody. You could tell that he was a great leader. To me, this was a no-brainer."

When Zeke started acting like a jerk in Detroit, McCloskey cut him off, saying, "I saw what you did in Dallas. It won't work here."

"I don't want to play here. I want to play in Chicago," said Isiah.

"That doesn't matter because we're going to draft you and you're going to play here," said McCloskey.

(The Bulls, with the sixth pick that year, drafted Notre Dame's Orlando Woolridge.)

The Pistons were awful when Isiah arrived. They'd gone

21–61 the previous season. For most of Detroit's veterans, there was no ambition greater than survival. *Don't get cut.* Zeke changed that. "He was the leader from the start," Pistons forward Earl Cureton told me. "He had the championship on his mind from the moment he arrived. I remember him saying it, and I looked around the locker room, and I'm like, 'Nah, not this bunch,' but he started changing the mood fast."

Thomas played in seventy-two games in 1981–82, averaged 17 points a game, made the All-Star Team, and was named Rookie of the Year. He worked hard on and off the court. He studied Bird and Magic, the most successful players of the time, searching for the secret to winning. He decided it was sublimation. For a team to be successful, its best players have to sublimate their own talent, sacrifice playing time and point totals in pursuit of a balanced attack. Which means less glory, less fame, less money, for the individual. It can be a tough sell. "I didn't just watch films of role model players, I tried to think like them," Isiah said. "I came to see that a star player stands out from his teammates. A leader doesn't stand out at all. I adjusted my game by focusing more on creating opportunities for my teammates. From that point on, my scoring and assists dropped. Instead of standing out, I'd fit in."

Isiah's breakout game came on Halloween 1981 in Chicago. He'd left over a dozen tickets at Will Call: All his friends and family were there. He scored 28 against the Bulls that night, and smiled as he left the floor, fist raised. It had always been his dream to be the all-time-best player in Chicago. And it was a dream that might have come true if not for an eighteen-year-old UNC freshman who, at that point, seemed like just another long-shot prospect.

MICHAEL

For basketball players, the first dunk is a baptism of sorts, an essential milestone. Michael Jordan, who spent much of his childhood as a short kid, had been working his way toward that feat for years. He'd hang from a pole in his bedroom to stretch his frame, squirt lemon juice on his toes at bedtime, which his mother said would help him grow. He worked at it till he could touch the net, then the rim. When he was fourteen, he was able to get his hand above the basket. But his first real, in-game dunk did not come until later. He was a sophomore at Laney High School in Wilmington, North Carolina. A player on the other team threw a lazy pass. Jordan, then still known as Mike, picked it off and ran upcourt. At fifteen, he was barely six feet, seemingly not tall enough to dunk. He took off just inside the free throw line, hung above the rim, finished with authority. The backboard rattled. The kids in the foldout bleachers, including members of the varsity team who'd come to watch, went wild.

Michael learned to play hoops in the driveway of his family's suburban ranch house. His father, James, after a career in the U.S. Air Force, had taken a job at G.E. as a mechanic. He'd eventually become a manager, a white-collar executive who spent weekends fiddling with cars in the garage, tearing down and rebuilding engines. If he stuck out his tongue as he worked, it meant he was concentrating—a gesture picked up by his son. Michael Jordan hanging above the rim with his tongue out is iconic. When a kid goes for a reverse layup in the driveway with their tongue sticking out, they might think they are imitating the GOAT, but are in fact copying a G.E. mechanic fiddling under the hood of a '56 Plymouth Belvedere.

James and his wife, Deloris, raised five children: James, Larry, Deloris, Michael, and Roslyn. The brother who was closest to Michael in age, Larry, was his primary rival. Larry was one year Michael's senior, and domineering. For MJ, afternoons meant basketball humiliation. The brothers would play on as the sun went down, pressing and challenging each other. He started with a modest goal: Beat Larry. That was the engine that drove him. He had the little brother fire and practiced the little brother religion.

No matter who he was facing later, Michael was always battling his brother. "Michael got so good because Larry beat him all the time," said their father, James Jordan. "He took it hard."

"What's he doing out there?" a Bulls team psychologist later asked rhetorically. "He's having a dialogue with [his brother] Larry. He's telling Larry that he's had enough and now it's his turn."

Larry was as good as Michael, but did not grow. Before Michael, no one in the Jordan family had been taller than 5'8". How did Michael defy genetics? Maybe it was luck, or a solar flare, or the lemon juice, or the power of human will. Michael was 5'5" in seventh grade and 5'9" his freshman year. He was a midsize kid who excelled at every sport, especially baseball. He pitched multiple 12U no-hitters. But it was basketball that interested him, and, as a Laney sophomore, he expected to make varsity, where Larry, wearing number *45,* had starred a few years before. Jordan asked for number *23,* as that was a bit more than half of *45,* which is how Michael saw himself at the time: a bit more than half as good as Larry, but improving fast.

Michael prepared for the tryout with his friend Leroy Smith. Jordan was better than Smith, and everyone knew it, but it was Smith, not Jordan, who made varsity. Why? Possibly because Leroy Smith was 6'7". Not making the top team as a sophomore is part of the legend. Every kid who does not make *the* team is consoled with the story of Michael Jordan. *Do you know who else didn't make* the *team?* The slight drove Jordan the same way he'd been driven by Larry. He broke every JV record as a sophomore, then left for the summer. That's when the miracle happened. He grew four inches in three months and returned with a new body. "He came back a different guy," said Todd Parker, who played with Michael at Laney. "No longer skinny little Mike. He was jumping out of the gym. I'm like, 'What?'"

Jordan was the star of the varsity team his junior and senior years. Playing against Laney meant having to contain Jordan, who spent half the game above the rim. He attracted recruiters from nearly every Division I school in America. In the spring of his senior year, he drove a sports car—how did he afford it?—with vanity plates that said MAGIC, though Magic Johnson was not his role model; that was David Thompson, who played at North Carolina State. Thompson was the proto–Air Jordan, a 6'6" guard who could do just about everything that would make Jordan famous. He should've been a star, but his career, like Lord Henry Thomas's, was cut short by drugs.

Jordan was not the most polished high school recruit, but he had a surfeit of that quality coaches and scouts call "upside." There were better high school players in 1981, but none had Mike Jordan's potential—those intangibles that have to do with the sort of physical and mental skills that cannot be taught. Court vision, Jordan's uncanny sense of the game, of how the action will unfold. His ambition, that nearly physical need to win. The other things, the weaknesses—his outside shooting, his defense—could be fixed. No telling what he'd be in two or three years. A good scout sees the player on the floor; a great scout sees what that player can become.

Jordan participated in the McDonald's All-American Boys Game that spring. It was the weekend that marked his arrival on the national scene. "I played with Michael in that game," Sam Vincent, who was taken in the first round of the 1985 draft, told me. "It was in Wichita, Kansas. I knew how good he was from the moment he first carried the ball. He was probably six-foot at that time, but played above everybody. He could score whenever he felt like it. Of course, I did not know what kind of player he'd turn out to be, but you could see, by the end of high school, that he was turning into something unique."

Jordan wanted to attend college close to home, which meant the Atlantic Coast Conference. Duke. Virginia. Wake Forest. In the end, it was University of North Carolina coach Dean Smith who won him over. UNC basketball was storied, with alumni scattered around the NBA. The team was led by James Worthy and Sam Perkins when Jordan arrived. Coach Smith had a general policy—freshmen don't start—but ignored it for Jordan. (Michael was, in fact, just the fourth freshman to start his first game in UNC history.) He'd been electric in the early practices, 6'4" and still growing. He had close-cropped hair and a sweet face. And he was cocky, constantly challenging the upperclassmen, talking trash and dunking over them.

"When Mike arrived on campus, I thought, *Oh, no, here comes another country boy*," Sam Perkins, who would play sixteen NBA seasons, told me. "I'm from Brooklyn," Perkins went on, "you know, big-time, so of course I didn't know much about Wilmington, North Carolina. Then, when we had that first scrimmage, and Mike was doing all kinds of crazy things, wagging his tongue, hanging in the air. And we thought, man, Little Brother is fixing to bite his tongue off! But we didn't know how good he was or how great he'd become. We really didn't. We just thought he was another fancy finesse kid who lacked mental toughness."

"After he started to get better, he would pick on Sam Perkins and me," said James Worthy. "He'd say, 'Let's play one-on-one. Let's play one-on-one.' Finally I did. We played three games and I won one or two that I know of."

No one not on that team knew how good Jordan was, because Jordan played in Dean Smith's system, which raised up the weak and sublimated the strong. Jordan was not allowed to freelance or roam at UNC. No individual moments. No showboating. "It was hard for pro scouts to tell how good Carolina players were because the program made certain players look better than they really were," David Halberstam writes in *Playing for Keeps*. "They became the beneficiary of the system, their strengths magnified, their flaws hidden, or at least partially hidden—and at the same time it often suppressed the talents of great individual stars who might average ten or fifteen points a game in another system."

"I don't think Coach Smith ever bragged on Michael, but I

remember playing golf with [UNC assistant] Roy Williams and he said they had a hell of a player named Jordan," UNC alum and NBA player and coach George Karl told me. "But Coach Smith never said it. Because that's not Christian. He was a humble man. And I don't even think they really understood how good Jordan was going to be. I mean, they knew he was good. But they couldn't know what he'd become."

Teammates began to name Jordan's more outlandish dunks. He debuted the "rock the cradle" against Maryland at the end of his freshman year. Freed by a long pass from Worthy, Jordan loped downcourt, leapt with the ball held in the crook of his arm, then: SLAM! He did it in violation of Dean Smith's rule against showboating, to send a message to Maryland's coach, who Jordan believed had once disrespected him.

In Jordan's freshman year, UNC played the Georgetown Hoyas, coached by John Thompson and led by center Patrick Ewing, for the NCAA championship. The Hoyas won the first half 32–31. The Tar Heels won the second 32–30. Eric "Sleepy" Floyd hit a shot with 57 seconds left to give the Hoyas the lead. Dean Smith called time. Jordan took a seat at the end of the bench, his face buried in a towel. The seniors stood in a circle. Coach Smith laid out a plan: Jimmy Black inbounds to Michael, who passes to Matt Doherty, who carries the ball up-court, then passes to one of the big men inside, Worthy or Perkins, for the last shot. But if they're covered, said Smith, look for Jordan.

"You get me the ball," Jordan told Doherty as they went back onto the floor. "I'll make the shot."

Georgetown led 62–61. Thirty-two seconds left. Black in-bounded to Jordan, who passed to Doherty, who looked inside and, seeing no free teammates, passed to Black, who faked inside, then went crosscourt to Jordan, who stood all alone seventeen feet from the basket. Michael stepped left, then, with fourteen seconds on the clock, went up and hit the shot. His composure was what amazed people. Eight months before, he'd been in high school. "Once you get in the moment, things move slowly," he explained. "You start to see the court very well."

The shot is famous not because of the physical accomplishment—it was an everyday jumper—but because of the context. At nineteen, Michael hit the winning basket of the NCAA Final with fourteen seconds left. That's the stuff of dreams—a fantasy you concoct when you're shooting around in your driveway. Michael later said he'd seen himself making the shot in a dream the night before. If he looked composed, he explained, it was because he was not just taking the shot but taking it *again*. He called the outcome predestined. *It had to happen because it was meant to happen.* That shot changed Jordan's life. He returned to campus a star. The crowd that greeted the team chanted for "Mike," who stood before them in sunglasses. "Yeah, I wanted it," he said. "And, when I got it, I knew. I always knew. I've always known."

Jordan wanted to turn pro after his sophomore year, but Coach Smith dissuaded him. It was not Michael's diploma the coach worried about. It was his basketball education. As good as Jordan had become, his training was still incomplete.

"Come back," said Smith, "and I will teach you how to play defense."

A year later, after Jordan had indeed learned to play at both ends, it was Smith who said, "And now, Mike, I've taught you everything. It's time for you to leave."

The Rockets had among the worst records in the NBA in 1983–84, which put them in a coin flip for the top pick. If Houston lost the flip, they'd take Jordan with the second overall pick. If Houston won the flip, they'd take Hakeem Olajuwon, a seven-foot center predicted to be the NBA's next great big man, at number one, leaving the Portland Trail Blazers to pick second. Since Portland already had a "Jordan-like" guard in Clyde Drexler, they would use the number two pick to take Sam Bowie, a seven-foot center from Kentucky.

The Bulls would pick third.

Bobby Knight put in an emergency call to his friend Stu Inman, the Portland GM, a few days before the draft. "You've got to take [Jordan]," said Knight. "He's going to be the best."

"But we need a center," said Inman.

"Well, play him at center then," said Knight.

Houston won the coin toss and took Olajuwon. Portland took Bowie, a pick now considered the worst in league history. Not only did they pass on Jordan, they ended up with a weak-kneed center who spent most of his career on the injured list.

The Bulls' front office had a long history of wasting first round picks. They'd taken David Greenwood first in 1979—didn't pan out. They'd taken Kelvin Ransey first in 1980—didn't pan out. They'd taken Orlando Woolridge, a brilliant dunker who disappeared on defense, first in 1981—didn't pan out. They'd taken Quintin Dailey, an electric talent who'd been convicted of sexual assault and had a drug problem, first in 1982—didn't pan out. They'd taken Sidney Green first in 1983—didn't pan out.

Then, in 1984, they took Jordan. The front office believed he'd be good, but only sensed how good that summer when he played in the Olympics. The 1984 men's Olympic basketball team was one of the last made entirely of amateurs. Bobby Knight, who'd been hired to coach, held fiercely competitive tryouts. Joe Dumars, Charles Barkley, John Stockton—the players who didn't make the cut now fill the Hall of Fame. According to Knight, Jordan had a single weakness. "If this kid develops a consistent jump shot," said Knight, "he's going to be the best to ever play this game."

The 1984 Olympic team was stacked with future stars, including Patrick Ewing, Sam Perkins, Chris Mullin, and Michael Jordan. Most telling were the tune-up games that pitted the Olympians against pickup teams of NBA veterans. It was off-season for the pros, many of whom were not in game shape, and the lineups consisted of players who didn't normally play together; even so, the results were surprising. Not only did the amateurs compete, they dominated, winning all eight contests. Embarrassed by the poor showing in game one, NBA commissioner David Stern called in ringers. Isiah Thomas, Robert Parish, Kevin McHale, Magic Johnson, Alex English—it was the first time many of the league's standouts would face Jordan.

Michael missed a pass during the pre-game warm-up one night. The ball rolled to the far end of the court, where Larry Bird stopped it with his foot. When Jordan went over smiling, Bird kicked the ball high over Jordan's head. Bobby Knight had encouraged the pros to be mean, play tough, and "give the kids a challenge," but probably got more than he wanted.

Oscar Robertson, who was coaching the NBA side, tasked Mike Dunleavy with shutting down Jordan. The game was played at the Bucks, arena in Milwaukee. Dunleavy, who'd been taking a break from the NBA—he spent eight months in the middle of his career selling bonds for Merrill Lynch—flew in from New York for the game. "I'd heard so much about Michael that I wanted to see if I could stop him," Dunleavy, who went on to coach in the NBA and college, told me. "Turns out I couldn't and neither could any of the other players. It was a nasty game. No whistles, nothing. Patrick Ewing's elbow was a windmill. *Wham! Wham! Wham!* I saw Michael driving the hoop. I ran over to intercept. He'd just dunked the ball so hard it hit one of our guys on top of the head. Michael loved to rock it back then, do the double pump, do the double clutch. And I'm like, no way, not again. I grew up in Brooklyn, so in a game like this, it's Brooklyn rules. Whatever you have to do. He jumps and is holding the ball right in front of his face. Rookie mistake. I punch the ball and it hits him in the mouth. That put him on the ground. He pops up, cursing and bloody. He wants to fight! I'm like, 'Dude, I get it, but it was an accident.' Then he goes off. He scored and scored that night.

"I faced him again that season when I was playing for the Bucks," Dunleavy went on. "He looks over, sees me, and stiffens. He comes right at me on the next play. I move to take the charge, but he basically walks through the air and up my body, then slams the ball in the basket."

Jordan, who would soon be surrounded by an entourage—trainers, handlers, college teammates who'd flunked out of the pros, city aldermen, downtown preachers, Nike executives—was alone when he first arrived in Chicago, tall and handsome and impossibly young in sneakers and sweats, headphones pressed to his ears. Most of his teammates listened to rap. Run-DMC. LL Cool J. It was hip-hop's first golden age. Jordan, who'd grown up in suburbia, preferred Chaka Khan and Billy Ocean, the softer side of the radio dial. He was probably listening to Whitney Houston as he stepped out of O'Hare. It was August, when the airport smells of diesel. Cars whip through the drop-off as cops blow their whistles.

There'd obviously been a screwup at the front office; no one came to meet the Bulls' top pick. He had the name of a hotel north of the city, but was otherwise at sea. The highways coiled away. The Chicago skyline lurked to the east. A cab slowed; the window opened. The driver offered to help. Jordan explained his situation and showed the address. Five minutes later, Jordan was seated in the back of the car, staring out as I-90 merged into I-294. They exited at Willow, then zoomed past the regional landing strip, the landfill, the cornfields, the housing developments. The driver was named George. He joked, told stories, explained the city—Chicago is filled with explainers. George would become the first member of Michael's entourage, and, as of 2022, works for Jordan still.

Jordan's first house was on Essex Drive in Northbrook, a suburb twenty miles north of the city. Northbrook, like the affluent towns surrounding it, was almost entirely white. Because it was also close to the Bulls' practice facility and gym—the team worked out in a public health club, the Equinox, in Deerfield—it was where many Bulls lived. Professional athletes—several Chicago Bears lived in Northbrook, too—formed a sort of colony. On Chicago's North Shore in the 1980s, there was nothing more thrilling than an MJ sighting.

Jordan was twenty-one when he first suited up. On the floor, he found himself in the company of the overpaid and addicted. The 1984 Bulls were coached by Kevin Loughery, who, unlike Dean Smith, let Jordan indulge his driveway style of play. The Bulls, in the process of being sold, were just beginning to rebuild, and Jordan, who lit up Chicago Stadium night after night, became the cornerstone.

His professional breakthrough came on November 15, 1984. Chicago lost to Boston at the stadium, but Jordan scored 27. Asked after the game where Jordan ranked, Larry Bird said, "Best. Never seen anyone like him. Unlike anyone I've ever seen. Phenomenal. One of a kind. At this stage in his career, he's doing more than I ever did. I couldn't do what he did as a rookie. Heck, there was one drive where Michael had the ball up in his right hand, then he took it down, then he brought it back up. I got a hand on it, fouled him, and he *still* scored. And all the while, he's in the air! I'd seen a little of him before, and wasn't that impressed. I mean, I thought he'd be good, but not *this* good. Ain't nothing he can't do."

Jordan excelled whenever the Bulls played the Celtics. He had a way of rising to the occasion, of playing his best against the best, the most famous instance being Game 2 in the first round of the 1986 playoffs. Chicago lost to Boston in overtime, but Jordan scored 63 points. It was not just the total that impressed Bird but the way MJ scored—not by playing his own game, but within the flow. "That wasn't Michael Jordan out there," Bird said. "It was God disguised as Michael Jordan."

"Jordan is always in what I call a ready position," said Celtics legend Bob Cousy. "Like a jungle animal, who is always alert, stalking, searching . . . Jordan has that awareness, and that costs you physically. If you do it, you are so exhausted you have trouble getting out of bed in the morning. Not many athletes do it."

Jordan played every game as if it mattered, as if he were still battling his brother Larry as the sun went down. He did not just turn the Bulls around; he revived the franchise. Their record improved, attendance skyrocketed. A team that had routinely drawn fewer than 7,000 fans a game began selling out the stadium. The Bulls had been considered B-list in Chicago, below the Bears, the Cubs, the White Sox, and even the Blackhawks. Michael changed that. This was the era of sporting stars in Chicago. Bears quarterback Jim McMahon was in his prime, as was running back Walter Payton. Cubs second baseman Ryne Sandberg won the National League MVP in 1984. Carlton Fisk was behind the plate at Comiskey Park. But Jordan was bigger than all of them. Not just because he was a great athlete, but because he was beautiful.

There was one knock on Jordan in the 1980s: He was great, but the Bulls did not win a title. Not a team player, that's what the skeptics insisted. Bird laughed at this, saying, "That's because he doesn't have a team."

That would begin to change in the summer of 1987.

THE SEASON

THE CELTICS

The 1987–88 NBA campaign promised to be special from the first. The previous season had ended with a dramatic showdown between the era's great rivals, the Celtics and the Lakers. Magic, now an eight-year veteran, had driven in the final spike in the most dramatic way—by hitting a hook shot from about eight feet, which seemed both unprecedented and familiar, an homage to the shot made famous by Kareem. By the next morning, it was already being referred to as if part of American history, up there with George Washington's cherry tree and Charles Lindbergh's Atlantic crossing.

They called it "the baby skyhook."

For the Boston Celtics, who were aging but still excellent, the mission was clear: Get back to the finals and defeat the Lakers, whose vainglorious coach had not merely predicted a repeat title—no team had repeated in a generation—but had guaranteed it. And yet, as the Celtics chased the Lakers, they were being chased by their own mad pursuer, the Detroit Pistons, soon to be tagged the Bad Boys, a team built big and mean with the express purpose of defeating Boston. The Pistons had lost to the Celtics in the seven-game Eastern Conference Finals in 1987, but most of the players on Detroit, and even some on Boston, considered it a fluke.

Detroit had Game 5 in the bag in Boston. All they had to do was inbound the ball, kill a few seconds, and they'd be heading home, where Detroit almost never lost, to close out the series. But Isiah, given the ball to inbound, fell for Bird's fake—Larry leaned this way, went that way—and floated a pass to Laimbeer that Bird intercepted and then, while falling out of bounds, delivered to Dennis Johnson, who hit the game-winning layup with less than a second on the clock. The play was like a spinning propeller—so fast it was a blur.

Isiah spent hours on the phone with Magic after the game. Johnson later said Isiah cried and cried. For Detroit, who went on to lose in Game 7 in Boston Garden, the object of the 1987–88 season was so simple it glowed: Get back to the Eastern Conference Finals and do to Boston what Boston had done to them.

Meanwhile, the Pistons had a mad pursuer, too: the Chicago Bulls, a team that, for years, had been a one-man show—they were derided as "Michael and the Jordanaires" (if you're an Elvis fan, you get the reference)—but had recently beefed up with two rookies, Scottie Pippen and Horace Grant, who would eventually become stars.

For Jordan and the Bulls, the goal was more basic still: Respect. Michael was already considered the best athlete and maybe the best player in the league, but here was the rub: They said he could not play team ball, and, as only a team can beat a team, he could not win in the postseason. Entering his fourth pro campaign, he'd yet to advance the Bulls beyond the first round of the playoffs.

The NBA was filled with other contenders in 1987–88, half a dozen of them probably good enough to go all the way in a typical season. The Washington Bullets had Bernard King and Moses

Malone, Manute Bol, the league's tallest player (7'7"), and Muggsy Bogues, the league's shortest (5'3"). The New York Knicks had Patrick Ewing, Mark Jackson, Gerald Wilkins, and Bill Cartwright. The Atlanta Hawks had Dominique Wilkins, the greatest dunker in history, Antoine Carr, Tree Rollins, Kevin Willis, and 5'6" Spud Webb.

There were even better teams out West. The Denver Nuggets were coached by Doug Moe and led by future Hall of Famer Alex English. The Portland Trail Blazers had Jerome Kersey, Kevin Duckworth, Terry Porter, and the transcendent Clyde Drexler. The Dallas Mavericks had playground legend Mark Aguirre, Jordan's UNC teammate Sam Perkins, Derek Harper, Roy Tarpley, and one of the league's first European stars, Detlef Schrempf. The Utah Jazz had John Stockton and Karl Malone, who were just starting to gel; the Houston Rockets were coached by former Celtic Bill Fitch, who was experimenting with a scheme he called the Twin Towers Offense, which featured two of the game's dominant young centers, 7'4" Ralph Sampson and 7' Hakeem Olajuwon. There was tremendous parity in the league, which is partly what made the games so exciting.

Boston, which began the season with a nearly 20-point win over the Milwaukee Bucks at Boston Garden on Friday, November 6, got off to a jackrabbit start. Six straight victories. What's more, Bird, who'd been banged up the previous year, looked like his old self, trash-talking and scoring. The NBA named him Player of the Week for its first seven days. He'd appear in seventy-six of eighty-two regular season games in 1987–88, averaging 22 points a night. He'd end the season among the league leaders in points and rebounds, possibly because he felt he had something to prove. At thirty-one years old and recovering from a bad back, he wanted to show that he could still compete at the highest level, could still lead his team to the finals, could still dethrone Magic.

Of course, when you talk about Bird and the Celtics, you are also talking about Boston Garden; no team in history was more closely associated with its arena. A concrete fortress built above North Station in one of the city's toughest neighborhoods, the Garden was a sacred place in American sports, a cathedral and a madhouse, paradise and the pit of hell. Train tracks emerged from it like tentacles, each car bringing another batch of besotted crazies. On winter afternoons, it seemed to glower beneath dark clouds like a haunted castle.

It was designed by Tex Rickard, who also designed the original Madison Square Garden in New York. It was neither hockey nor basketball Rickard had in mind. It was boxing, the top-drawing sport in the 1920s, when Rickard worked. His stated goal was to seat every fan close enough to "see the sweat on the fighter's brow." Boston Garden was surprisingly intimate when retrofitted for hoops. In no other venue were fans so close and players so exposed.

The seats were steeply banked and climbed nearly to the roof. You might feel dizzy in the top rows, but never lonely. Cigarette smoke pooled; the cheap seats drifted in a blue haze. Some were obstructed, others precariously perched. Players complained about the locker rooms, which were small and dank. You froze in the winter, broiled in the summer. Reporters had mixed feelings about Boston Garden, as did visiting executives and owners. But basketball fans loved the place. It wasn't just the proximity, the fact that you could hear the trash talk; it was the sense of community. You felt like you were part of a nation at Celtic home games.

Walter Brown, who'd managed the Garden before there was an NBA, was always on the lookout for new tenants, fresh spectacles to fill his arena—pro wrestling, monster trucks, political conventions, the circus. He helped create the Ice Capades for this purpose in 1940. In 1946, in partnership with several other arena owners, he created what became the NBA. In other words, the Garden was not created for the team; the team was created for the Garden.

The league began with eleven clubs, including the Boston

Celtics, the New York Knickerbockers, the Philadelphia Warriors, and the Providence Steamrollers. The Celtics were woeful in those first few seasons. Their fortunes began to change in 1950, when Walter Brown hired Red Auerbach, a 33-year-old coach who'd had basketball success in Washington, D.C. Auerbach, a thickset red-haired street kid from Williamsburg, Brooklyn, arrived in Boston with no great fanfare, but would remain with the team until 2001, becoming the most successful coach and executive in NBA history.

He was old-school. He wore sweats to practice, a whistle around his neck. He was less like the celebrity coaches of today than like a middle school gym teacher. He always had a ball under his arm and was never far from a blackboard. A hardcourt innovator, he traded and drafted not for pedigree but for smarts, speed, size. He said the most important thing in a game is the most obvious: possession. *If we have the ball, they can't score.* To control possession, you need rebounds. A team that collects twice as many rebounds only needs to make half as many shots to achieve the same point total. With that in mind, Red went after big players who could battle for position under the rim.

Red could be fiery—he slugged a fan who spit on him in Cincinnati in 1962. When certain of a win, he'd light a cigar and smoke it on the bench. This became known as Red's victory cigar. Opposing players and coaches and NBA officials loathed the gesture. "When the league was picking on me, I tried to think of something that would aggravate the higher-ups," Auerbach told *The Boston Globe*'s Dan Shaughnessy. "I wasn't having much luck until one day I lighted up a cigar during a game. Afterward, I got a little note, saying, 'It doesn't look good for you to be smoking cigars on the bench.' I haven't been without one since."

Auerbach's greatest skill was talent-spotting. "He could watch a game and see what all ten players were doing at the same time," Jan Volk, general manager of the Celtics in the 1980s, told me. "He had this magical ability to see and digest. And he understood people. He understood what drove them. And he worked very hard, even when he was older. He went to see everyone, all the players. He felt that the most important part of scouting a college player was seeing how he practiced. How does the kid prepare? How does he interact with his teammates? He'd see things in a player that were invisible to everyone else."

Red built his greatest Boston teams around a key piece, a cornerstone, the first of these being Bill Russell, a 6'10" center from the University of San Francisco whom he heard about via his network of unofficial scouts—old teammates and army buddies scattered across the Lower 48. A phone ringing in the middle of the night: "There's a kid out here, Red. You gotta see him. He's your kind of kid." Red's "kind of kid" meant speed and size. "I can teach a lot of things," Auerbach explained, "but I can't teach a kid how to be tall."

Auerbach saw and wanted Russell, but there was a problem. Boston would not pick until late in the first round in 1956, by which time the big center would be gone. Red went into his office at the Garden, shut the door, worked the problem. The Rochester Royals had the first draft pick in 1956. *Maybe the Royals can use a player like Russell,* Red told himself, *but that's not what they need. What they need is money.* The team, owned and coached by Les Harrison, was behind in the rent payments on its stadium. Instead of trading the Royals a package of players for the top pick, Auerbach convinced Walter Brown to offer the owner of the Rochester War Memorial Arena, where the Royals played, several weeks of performances by the Ice Capades in lieu of the Royals' back rent.

Bill Russell arrived in Boston in September 1956. The Celtics won their first championship the following spring. The good times continued. Auerbach's team appeared in every NBA Finals between 1956 and 1966, winning nine out of ten. They won again in 1968 and 1969. Eleven championships in thirteen years. Visiting teams came to hate Boston Garden as a result. To make matters worse, the arena had been allowed to dilapidate. It was a wreck by the 1960s. Worst was the parquet floor. Like the ivy at Wrigley Field or the Green Monster at Fenway Park, Boston Garden's parquet was a lovable eccentricity unless you had to play on it.

Consisting of 274 panels of Tennessee red oak and arranged in a parquet pattern known to anyone who's ever rented an apartment in Manhattan, the Garden floor had been designed to be quickly removable for hockey games. It was beat to hell by the time Bird, McHale, and Parish arrived, resulting in dead spots that visiting teams discovered by losing possession. "The Celtics would force you onto those dead places," Bulls forward Charles Davis told me. "You'd dribble and the ball would stay down and they'd get possession and score and that would be the difference, the reason you lost."

"None of that is true," said Bird, who claims the dead spots changed every time the floor was taken up and put back, that in the 1980s, the Celtics were playing atop a kaleidoscope.

Red Auerbach actively looked for ways to make opponents uncomfortable. "He'd put us in locker rooms where the keys didn't work, the towels went missing, and the heat was set over a hundred degrees, and you couldn't open the windows," Bulls coach Phil Jackson said. "For [one] series, he put us in a different locker room for every game, and the last one, for Game Seven, was a cramped janitor's locker with no lockers and a ceiling so low many of us had to stoop to get dressed."

"That arena was old and creepy," Earl Cureton, who played for the 76ers and the Bulls in the 1980s, told me. "You always felt like some supernatural force was working against you when you played there."

Cureton is referring to the Garden Mystique, the fact that the place could seem possessed. In the Garden, weird bounces turned wins into losses, which equaled a serious home court advantage. In 1985–86, the Celtics went 40–1 at home. They hardly ever lost there in the postseason. Some credited "the Leprechaun," the fighting Irishman painted at center court.

"The Boston Mystique isn't leprechauns hiding in the floorboards," Pat Riley protested. "It isn't blood and guts. It's a willingness to use any tactic to upset an opponent. Turn up the heat when it's already hot. Shut off the visitors' water heaters. Instigate hard fouls on the court. It's [Auerbach] chasing officials all the way to the dressing room to try to intimidate them. To hell with dignity. To hell with fair play. The Boston Mystique encourages the lowest common denominator of fan behavior. It grows directly out of the low-rent attitudes of the Boston management. They're the Klingons of the NBA."

The fact that spectators sat so close at the Garden could make games nightmarish for visiting players, especially for Black players. "The fans in Boston were ruthless," Charles Davis told me. "They'd say the nastiest things, throw stuff and spit at you."

Even some of the greatest Celtics experienced racism in their home city, from their own fans. Bill Russell was abused when he arrived in 1956. It was nearly impossible for him to buy a house, and once he finally did, it was broken into and vandalized. Racial slurs were painted on the walls. In his memoir *Second Wind,* Russell describes Boston as "a flea market of racism." "If Paul Revere were riding today," he wrote, "it would be for racism. 'The [n-words] are coming! The [n-words] are coming!'"

When Russell went to Auerbach with the problem, Auerbach commiserated. Auerbach said he, as a Jew, also had trouble finding a house, which is why he lived in the Lenox Hotel. His family stayed in D.C.; he slept in Boston only when necessary. The result was an unbreakable bond between Auerbach and Russell. These men loved each other because they understood each other, and what it felt like to be outsiders. Here, in essence, is what Auerbach told Russell: *We don't play for Boston, or the fans; we play for each other.*

In others words, the franchise was better than its fans. In

1964, and it's a fascinating irony, the Celtics put the NBA's first all-Black team on the floor. Bill Russell, Sam Jones, Satch Sanders, K. C. Jones, Willie Naulls. Most remarkable is the fact that Auerbach didn't even know he'd done it. When asked to comment, he said he was entirely unaware he'd broken a line, or done something historic, or even sent out an all-Black team. "I just put the best guys we had on the floor," he explained.

Bill Russell became the NBA's first Black head coach in 1966, when Auerbach kicked himself upstairs. Russell continued to lead from the floor as well as the bench, as the team's player/coach. At thirty-four, he was slowing down, but still among the NBA's top centers. He coached Boston to two more championships. He left the Celtics after the 1969 season.

Boston declined in the post-Russell years. They stumbled to championships in 1974 and 1976—these clubs were led by Dave Cowens—then completely fell apart. Gloom set in, a basketball fallow, the hangover that follows the spree. Eighteen titles in twenty-five years. Worse than being bad was being mediocre, no better than the Bullets or the Pacers. Boston suffered through two losing seasons, then Auerbach started to rebuild. It was not one more championship he wanted, but a perennial contender, which is why, in 1978, he forfeited short-term success by drafting Bird, who would not be a Celtic for another fifteen months.

I met Red Auerbach in New Orleans in 1986. This was the peak of the Bird/McHale/Parish years. Red's Celtics were as good as any team had ever been. We had dinner a few hours before Larry King, who'd invited me along, was to interview Auerbach on his late-night radio show. We ate peeled shrimp and gumbo at Pascal's Manale on Napoleon Avenue. Auerbach was big and round, stuffed into a blue blazer at least two sizes too small. He was a *dese,*

dems, and *dose* type of New Yorker, a native of that part of Brooklyn where "toilet" is pronounced *turlet.* He waved his cigar as he spoke, stuck it between his teeth, grinned. That cigar, which remained unlit, had come to mean something more than just victory in a game. It meant victory in life. Auerbach, who'd played college ball when the pro game was a sideshow, had helped, with his years of excellence in Boston, the NBA reach the stratosphere; it's become bigger than baseball and more exciting than football.

Larry King and Red Auerbach talked about the standouts of their youth, the action on the Coney Island courts, where even the stars accepted the playground rules: You could hit that layup, but you'd pay for it. Larry told Red that Sandy Koufax injured his left elbow—the injury that would send him into retirement at thirty-one—not on the pitcher's mound but at a public court in Bensonhurst, where, after hitting a 2, he was driven into a metal stanchion.

Auerbach talked about Bird and McHale and how the 1986 Celtics would deal with injuries and age. He talked about the astronomical salaries of the game's top players, an onslaught he said began with Magic and Bird. "I'd already agreed to pay Bird three and a quarter million for a five-year contract, which would make him the highest-paid rookie in NBA history, topping the contract Jerry Buss had given Magic," said Auerbach. "Then Bird's agent, Bob Woolf, he says, 'OK, we also want a 100K bonus if Bird makes the All-Rookie team.' And I'm like, are you kidding? I'm already paying him more than any first-year ever. How about you give me *back* 100K if he *doesn't* make the All-Rookie team?"

Auerbach believed Bird was worth paying, because Bird was the sort of player you could build around, a cornerstone. But for Auerbach, the crucial moment in franchise building came not with Bird's acquisition but a year later, during the summer before Bird's second pro season.

Behind nearly every NBA dynasty is a trade that looks like a crime. The 1968 deal that sent three Lakers—Darrall Imhoff, Jerry Chambers, and Archie Clark—to the Philadelphia 76ers for Wilt Chamberlain looks like a crime; as does the 1977 deal that sent Dr. J from the Nets to the 76ers for three million dollars; as does the 1998 deal that sent Robert "Tractor" Traylor from the Bucks to the Mavericks for Pat Garrity and Dirk Nowitzki.

Auerbach's dynasty-building crime came with a geometrical insight: Looking over the draft boards and rosters before the 1980–81 season, he saw a way to land two undervalued players with a single move. Detroit had the first pick in 1980, but there was no one in the draft class they wanted as much as Bob McAdoo, the Celtics' underperforming forward. Auerbach traded McAdoo for the Pistons' first round pick, waited a moment, then swapped that number-one pick to the Golden State Warriors, who were angling to draft Joe Barry Carroll, a center from Purdue whom Auerbach considered overrated. Auerbach got Golden State's first round pick in return—they were picking third overall—then, in the way of a man who might ask a clothing salesman to throw in a free tie with a new suit, Auerbach said, in essence, "And since we're giving you a number one for a number three, how about you throw in that center you never play—what's his name?—Parish."

To the Warriors, Robert Parish, a 7'1" center who'd played at a small college in Louisiana, was a washout, a wasted pick. He was overweight and unmotivated and his game suffered as a result. Auerbach knew he'd perform when he felt there was a reason to perform.

Auerbach then used the number three pick to draft another seven-footer, Kevin McHale, from the University of Minnesota, who Auerbach said he would have taken ahead of Joe Barry Carroll in any case. In sum: Auerbach swapped McAdoo and Carroll for Parish and McHale. Together with Bird, these men would make up the most formidable front line in the NBA.

Auerbach was after size, physicality. To return to the finals, the Celtics would have to beat the 76ers, the best team in the East. So here, through a rent in the fabric, you can see NBA history in motion. The Celtics evolved to beat the 76ers, who had evolved to beat the Lakers, who had evolved to beat an earlier iteration of the Celtics. History is not a line. It's a pattern.

Once he had his core players, Auerbach merely needed to fill holes, put out fires, and ride the train as long as the train would go.

Danny Ainge arrived in a roundabout way. Born in Eugene, Oregon, Ainge was the only athlete in Oregon history to be first-team All-American in three sports. He led his high school basketball team to three championships. Football scouts ranked him among the top wide receivers in the country. He was drafted to play infield for the Toronto Blue Jays before he turned eighteen. He actually intended to focus on baseball, not basketball. Having decided to go to college, he worked out with the Blue Jays in the spring and summer, which left him time to play basketball for BYU in the fall and winter. He led the Cougars to the 1981 NCAA tournament his sophomore year. He hit the layup that eliminated Notre Dame in the Sweet Sixteen. He probably played well because he played loose. For him, it was all gravy—basketball wasn't even his sport. On June 2, 1979, he became the youngest player in Blue Jays history to hit a home run. He appeared in part of three major league baseball seasons, collecting 146 hits but batting just .220. Auerbach, who'd taken Ainge in the second round of the 1981 draft—he did it the way you buy a lottery ticket, because you never know—approached Ainge in the gray hour that followed another disappointing MLB season. He asked Danny a simple question: "Would you rather be known as a weak-hitting Toronto Blue Jay, or as a member of the greatest basketball team of all time?"

According to Ainge, it was less the Celtics' mystique that enticed him than the prospect of playing with Bird. "Larry was a magician, and I wanted to get a chance to be on the other side of the curtain," Ainge told me. "That just seemed so exciting."

The Blue Jays, who had counted Ainge among their future stars, sued for breach of contract. The Celtics settled for $800,000, a decision they possibly questioned following Ainge's performance at rookie camp, which many consider the worst debut in franchise history. He shot oh for nineteen in his first scrimmage, then continued to brick, clank, and bumble. Bad practices followed bad scrimmages. Boston coach Bill Fitch tried to motivate with mockery. He called Ainge a disappointment, and shouted as he ran laps: "Hey, Ainge! Your shooting percentage is worse than your batting average!"

For most players, hitting shots isn't about hustle. It's about finding the stroke, that heavenly groove. It's less work than grace, and the harder Fitch pushed, the further Ainge fell from grace. He found it only when Fitch was replaced by K. C. Jones in 1983.

Ainge became a good 3-point shooter who got even better in the clutch. He was also a dramatic flopper. If bumped, he went down grimacing, holding his knee. Long-haired and apple-cheeked, he was said to have "the most punchable" face in the NBA. He came across as small and whiny on TV, which was a distortion. "Danny is actually six-five but, for some reason, he looks more like five-six out on the court," K. C. Jones said. "But he is six-five and does it all. He hustles and scraps on the defensive end, and runs like the wind on the fast break."

Dennis Johnson, who would play guard beside Ainge for nearly ten years, was another key acquisition. When he arrived in Boston in 1983, Johnson was already a star, the most interesting sort of star, the sort trailed by nasty rumors and a bad reputation. He won a championship with the 1979 Seattle SuperSonics, who'd taken the point guard in the second round in 1976. He was named Finals MVP. But the fact that he was an All-Star, and one of the league's top defenders, did not prevent the Sonics from trading him to the Phoenix Suns. In explaining himself, Sonics coach Lenny Wilkens hung the worst label on DJ: *locker room cancer.* His attitude sucked. His work ethic sucked. If he didn't like a drill, he'd leave the court and watch from the bleachers. It was not just his manner but the way he looked, the architecture of his body. Johnson had dark circles under his eyes, his shoulders sagged, and he seemed to be jogging even when he was running, which could disguise the fact that he was one of the game's great team players.

Dennis knew how to get along with people because Dennis had fifteen siblings. He also knew what it meant to be overlooked, underappreciated. He grew up in Compton and was only twelve years old when riots swept Los Angeles. One of his first memories was burning buildings and police truncheons.

He loved basketball but was handicapped by size. Small in stature, big in ambition—that's what they said. He was 5'9" his senior year at Dominguez High School. He was lucky if he saw two minutes of action in a game. It was only after graduation that he started to grow. He perfected his craft on the playground as he waited for his body to catch up with his dream. He was 6'4" when a coach from Los Angeles Harbor College "discovered" him.

Lenny Wilkens said Dennis Johnson walked instead of ran, and dribbled as the shot clock ran down, but it only seemed that way if you didn't really look. A creative ball handler, Johnson was usually doing much more than you noticed. He set the tempo and always knew when to kick it into a higher gear. In the famous play at the end of Game 5 of the 1987 Eastern Conference Finals described above—Larry stole Isiah's inbound pass, turned, and dished to Dennis Johnson for the winner—much is made of Bird's heady interception. But it would have been pointless without Dennis, who read the moment same as Larry, broke for the hoop, and hit the layup with such speed it's recalled mostly as a blur. "People say, 'How did it happen?'" Johnson said. "Well, I don't know how the hell it happened; it just happened."

Dennis played one season at Pepperdine, a peripheral basketball school he turned into a contender. He led the Waves to a top 20 ranking in 1976, averaging over 15 points a game. It was his performance in the 1976 NCAA tournament that put him on the draft board. He was a strange prospect—much better than the stats said he should be. That's what led to the trouble in Seattle and Phoenix: Surrounded by first round picks who did not perform, Johnson found himself in battle with teammates. They did not want to change their game—their style—to make space for the kind of game Johnson played—pass-drunk, cerebral, defensive. When Phoenix general manager Jerry Colangelo finally decided to trade Johnson—Colangelo claimed Johnson demanded a trade—he could hardly find any takers.

Who wants locker room cancer?

For Auerbach, the result was yet another perfect crime. In return for Dennis Johnson, who would play seven seasons in Boston, quarterback the offense, lead the defense, and have his number retired, Auerbach sent two future second round picks to Phoenix, along with Rick Robey, a broken-down center who appeared in just fifty games with the Suns before retiring.

Johnson arrived in Boston as a project, a risk. He'd alienated two coaches and two teams. He seemed to be the kind of player who, instead of making everyone better, might make everyone angry or worse. Danny Ainge nicknamed him "Chemo" because "that's what we'd been told we'd need after spending a few weeks around Dennis."

Johnson insisted that he'd merely been waiting for a team with good teammates and the right coach, where he could settle into his role instead of fighting players not willing to do what had to be done. Years later, when his jersey was hung from the rafters, Magic Johnson sent a telegram to be read aloud at the ceremony. It called DJ "the best backcourt defender of all time."

Bird has identified the arrival of Dennis Johnson as the moment the Celtics ascended. "DJ is simply the best player I've ever played with on the Celtics," Bird explained. "Kevin is great. Robert is great. I've played with other great players. But when I look at the teams, there's always a player on that team who seems to symbolize the whole team. When I think of our own team, the guy I think of is DJ. When I look at him, I think, 'The guy will do anything to win.'"

"Bird and me, we never talked about what we were going to do on the floor, never made a signal for it," Johnson said. "We just knew. I'd be coming down the court and I'd hear the other team's coach saying, 'Watch it, watch Bird off the pick, watch . . .' And it'd be too late."

And then, in addition to all this, Bird kept getting better. After the final loss that ended all but a championship season, he'd go home, climb into bed, stare at the ceiling, and ask himself, *What can I do to get better?*

"Every summer, Bird went back home to Indiana and worked diligently, trying not only to stay in the best of shape with a strict regimen, but to improve his game by adding shots," David Halberstam writes. "One year it was an up-and-under shot coming off a fake. Another year it was a shot designed to add a degree of separation for a player who was not getting any younger, a faked drive forward followed by a quick backward step as he released the ball. One year it was improvement on his left hand; he had come into the league with a good left-handed shot, but as his career progressed, he sensed the need for that additional option and refined it. On the first days of Celtics' preseason camps, the other players liked to see what Bird had added to his game over the summer."

On February 14, 1986, during a game against the Trail Blazers, in an effort to both work on craft and fight tedium, Bird played forty-eight minutes and scored 47 points using only his left hand. Explaining himself to the press, he said, "I'm saving my right hand for the Lakers."

Bill Russell's Celtics, the team that dominated in the 1960s, had been mostly Black. Larry Bird's Celtics, the team that dominated in the 1980s, were mostly white—a fact that did not go unnoticed. To some, the Celtics, in their pale homogeneity, embodied Boston as it was in the 1980s, with its haunted arena and bile-spewing fans. But it was hard to argue with performance. Boston reached the finals in 1981, 1984, and 1985, attaining an otherworldly brilliance in 1985–86 with a team some consider the best of all time. Auerbach had added the aging, injury-prone future Hall of Fame center Bill Walton to the roster. Despite bad feet, bad ankles, and bad knees, Walton managed to appear in eighty games. His style was the style Bird loved most: complicated, elegant, deft; full of behind-the-back, through-the-legs, over-the-shoulder passes. It was like Cirque du Soleil when it worked. This one would throw to that one, who'd underhand to this one, who'd flip to that one, and now it's over . . . no, wait . . . now it's over . . . no, wait . . . now it's over there. They progressed via touch pass. Walton tapped the ball to Bird, who tapped it to McHale, who laid it gently off the glass. This team was not tempted by rim-rattling jam. Their game was quiet. Each play unfolded like a maze; each maze ended at the basket.

I asked NBA veterans which of the four teams—Lakers, Pistons, Celtics, Bulls—had been the best at their best. Each team had its loyalists, but the 1985–86 Celtics won by a plurality.

"The 1986 Celtics were the best ever," Bulls guard Craig Hodges told me. "It wasn't just all the stars, but how much fun they had tricking your ass. You never knew where the ball was gonna turn up. You'd have to slap your own face, or be mesmerized."

"It was Boston," said Sam Perkins. "They had more real players than the Bulls, Pistons, or Lakers, and were more fluid and loose on the floor together. The Lakers could seem like a bunch of great stars playing a two-man or a three-man game, but the Celtics were all five guys firing, meshing."

The Celtics swept the Bulls in the 1986 playoffs, beat the Hawks in five, swept the Bucks to reach the finals—their third straight appearance—then beat the Rockets in six to win Boston's sixteenth NBA championship.

At the start of the 1986 off-season, the Celtics' continued dominance seemed assured. Not only had Boston won the title, Auerbach had somehow acquired the number two pick in the draft. And he knew exactly who he was going to take: Len Bias, a once-in-a-generation talent from Maryland. Auerbach had been scouting Bias since he was in high school. "When Red saw Bias, he was convinced he was looking at one of the greatest players he had ever seen," John Feinstein writes in *Let Me Tell You a Story: A Lifetime in the Game*. "Bias was six-foot-eight, with guard quickness and a feathery jump shot. He could shoot off the dribble and jump so high it was almost impossible to block his shot."

Bias, whom one Celtics scout called "the closest thing to Michael Jordan," was the sort of player who, in a fallow time, Auerbach would have made the cornerstone of a dynasty. Because of that famous luck, he'd instead be adding him to what was already the best team in the league. Not only could a player like Bias contribute points and defense, he'd lighten the workload for Bird and McHale, allowing them to extend their careers.

And then: Len Bias was gone. He'd visited Boston on draft day, worn a Celtics jersey for the press, flown back to Maryland to celebrate with friends, inhaled a mountain of cocaine, and died.

Auerbach got the call at 4:00 A.M. The old coach, wild-haired, bolted upright in bed, hearing but not registering. *What do you mean, dead?* "It was one of those deals where you understand what has happened but can't believe it," Auerbach said. "I mean, I'd been with the kid a few hours earlier, and he couldn't have been healthier or happier."

"I was in Indiana when I got the news," Boston guard Jerry Sichting told me. "I was staying at my in-laws'. My wife came in and woke me. What a nightmare. I thought I was dreaming."

Bird said the news hit him like a physical blow; he called it the cruelest thing he had ever heard.

At that moment, every needle on the Celtics, dashboard quivered and fell. The team, which, with Bias, could have continued to compete for another decade, suddenly looked old. "He would have been a perfect fit," said Sichting. "That became apparent the very next year when Walton got hurt. Bird and McHale had to play so many hard minutes, their bodies started to break. Bias would have given those guys a rest. It would have made a world of difference."

"It's difficult not to speculate how much Bias would have helped," said Bird. "I can say that I felt that he was the player who would be able to take my place. He wasn't Michael Jordan, but was in that mold. He was a runner and jumper unlike anyone on our team, and he was as tough as nails. I think he would have been a lot better in the pros than he was in college. I think he could do more things than, say, James Worthy. I was so excited when we drafted him. I thought, 'Oh, boy, here we go, we're on a roll now.'"

It was the kind of tragedy that hangs over a franchise. The Celtics, who'd always been blessed, suddenly seemed cursed. "It's hard for people to understand what losing Bias did," Auerbach said. "We were riding high. We'd just won another title. And [Bias] was going to be the next generation, the way we'd always done it, bring in great young players to take the place of other great players as they got older. You aren't talking about an injury, you're talking about losing a guy who would have been an all-star for ten years—at least—and losing him in the worst possible way. But it wasn't just that. There was a pall cast. It was almost like a foreboding of doom."

The Celtics repeated as Atlantic Division champs in 1987, but without the same verve. It was only guts and luck that got them by the Pistons in the Eastern Conference Finals. They'd as much as lost Game 5 in the Garden when Bird picked off Zeke's stupid inbound pass and DJ laid it in with 1.7 seconds to go. (In real time, it looked like this: pass, steal, pass, shoot, game.)

It was in the locker room after Game 7 that Detroit rookie Dennis Rodman brought the issue of race, which was always there but usually sublimated, to the surface. He scowled when asked about the loss, called Bird overrated, then said Bird had only been named MVP because "he's white."

"I think Larry is a very, very good basketball player, an exceptional talent," Isiah said when asked to comment on Rodman's comment. "But I'd have to agree with Rodman. If he was Black, he'd be just another good guy."

In his anger and disappointment, Isiah had inadvertently ripped off the lid, bringing all the questions that must never be asked about race and the game into the open. Why does it seem like Black players are better than white players? Why is it that great white players are described as *hardworking* and *heady* while great Black players are described as *gifted* and *athletic*? Why are almost all the coaches and owners white, while almost all the players are Black? Why are almost all the fans white? Is it true that every Black player believes, in his heart, that he can defeat any white player one-on-one, even an MVP like Larry Bird?

To Bird, Isiah's comment was nothing more than dumb talk from a player who'd just been defeated. To reporters and fans, it was something else. It was Isiah telling the public what Black players really think about their white opponents. Isiah has called the hours that followed the worst of his NBA career, a period that cast him in a new light, that changed his reputation from sunshine and charm to sour-grape discontent, from smiling good guy to smiling bad guy, which is how most people still view him thirty-five years later. Isiah had been a little too honest.

LAKERS AT CELTICS

When the Lakers faced the Celtics in Boston Garden on December 11, 1987, it was the first time the teams had played each other since the Lakers beat Boston in Game 6 of the 1987 NBA Finals.

The Celtics' season had seemed promising that fall. Bird was healthy for the first time in years—it would be the most productive offensive season of his career. McHale had recovered from foot and ankle surgery. Ainge and Johnson, though not perfect, felt good enough to play. And yet, when stone-faced Robert Parish met Kareem for the opening tip, you got a shiver of anxiety. Parish was thirty-four. Bird was thirty-two. McHale was thirty. DJ was thirty-four. Ainge was the only starter still in his twenties. There was no way around it—the Celtics were getting old. If this was a dynasty, it was a dynasty in decline.

Bird scored the first points of the game, going under Worthy and off the glass for 2. For long stretches, Bird did nothing but score that night. From inside and outside. Off the backboard or with a *swish*. He did not have to look to find his teammates. He knew. When double-teamed, he stared at DJ but passed to McHale, who, though he resembled Frankenstein's monster, was surprisingly graceful. Bird described McHale as "the ultimate bailout." "No matter how much trouble I'll be in," he explained, "I know I can always throw the ball to Kevin, and he'll get to the basket and take the pressure off." And yet you had the sense that Bird was often a little disappointed in McHale; that, as good as he was, Larry wanted him to be better. According to Bird, McHale "*could be* the top defender" in the league. According to Bird, Kevin "is so awesome on *some* nights."

"Kevin reminds me of my little brother, Eddie," Bird explained. "He makes everything look so easy, and when you say something about him working harder, he just kind of mopes around."

Even when McHale played his best, Bird seemed determined to top him, to show him that more was still possible, that a perfect game could at least be imagined. On March 3, 1985, McHale scored 56 points, a Celtics record that was broken a week later when Bird scored 60.

"The most important thing in life to Larry is basketball," Celtics radio broadcaster Glenn Ordway said. "The most important thing to Kevin is, at various times, family, fun, recreation, friends, and basketball. Basketball is somewhere in the top five, but, frankly, might be closer to five than to one. I think Larry resented that night after night he's out bustin' his butt for basketball, basketball, basketball, and there is Kevin with a totally different set of priorities. On the court, Kevin is as fierce a competitor as anyone, but, at other moments, he's always talking about his family or his golf game or his fishing. That got to Larry."

McHale grew up in Hibbing, Minnesota. His father was a mill worker, and never let Kevin forget that basketball is just a game. "I think what I got from my father was that a man got up and went to work every day, whether it was thirty below or thirty above," said McHale, who spent summers working beside his father. Returning to school in September, he'd tell friends he'd spent vacation as "a blast furnace guy."

He attended the University of Minnesota on a basketball scholarship, where he played with the Bahamian center Mychal Thompson, whom he'd face again in the NBA. The Lakers acquired Thompson in 1986 specifically to stop McHale, whose game Thompson had decoded in the Minnesota gymnasium.

McHale had not watched pro basketball when he was in college, nor followed the NBA draft. First he ever heard about it was from one of the football players, who congratulated him for being taken in the top five.

"Top five of what?" asked McHale.

He figured it was a fraternity thing.

By the end of his rookie year in Boston, McHale had become one of the game's premier post-up players, meaning he'd get close to the basket, turn his back on the defender, hold up his hands, and wait for the ball. His most effective move was tagged the "up-and-under." He'd fake like he was going to jump, get the defender in the air, then go under him en route to the hoop, often drawing a foul. When it worked, the up-and-under was good for 3 points.

And there were a dozen other ways he could score inside. The secret was his footwork. It might look like improvisation, but he in fact spent hours perfecting each stutter step, change of direction, fadeaway. He was so tricky, so deft and unpredictable, that he fooled not just opponents but officials, who now and then, having been fooled, blew the whistle. In other words, he was so good it looked like cheating.

"McHale's drop-step, twisting, up-and-under move sometimes drew a traveling violation," Dan Shaughnessy writes in *Wish It Lasted Forever*. "Referees assumed he must be dragging his pivot foot to beat defenders. It turned out to be an optical illusion. The zebras studied video of McHale in slow motion and discovered that he was not traveling—he was simply a physical freak with the quickness and agility to get underhand layups without taking a third step."

"I didn't know they studied up on it," McHale said, "but I remember in games I would sometimes tell the refs, 'Please go in at halftime and watch the tape and just watch my feet. As long as my left foot is my pivot foot, I can move my right foot seventeen times. It doesn't matter.' They'd sometimes come out and say, 'You know, you're right.'"

McHale was a physical wonder: 6'10", 210 pounds, with an eight-foot wingspan and an almost biological need to shoot. They called him "the Black Hole" because once you tossed the ball into that maw, it was never coming back out. He was usually assigned to guard the other team's power forward. Against the Lakers, he often covered James Worthy. Not being able to stop Worthy—no one could—he'd play him opportunistically. The best way to stymie Worthy? Put him on the bench. McHale was aggressive on offense, driving on Worthy, trying to get him into foul trouble.

Once a player picks up the third or fourth foul, he'll back off. Six fouls, he's out. McHale let Worthy get his points while waiting for a mistake, a moment he could exploit.

McHale anticipated Worthy's jump shot late in the first quarter at the Garden that December. He swatted the ball out of Worthy's hand and across the floor to Bird, who passed it to Parish, who passed it back to McHale—that indomitable Boston front line, racing up-court, zipping the ball back and forth as the crowd howled. McHale finished the play with a soft layup. No need to elaborate when you're being successful.

Magic Johnson slowed the tempo when he got the ball. Basketball rides on surges, swings. It's the job of the point guard to direct those surges, staunch and feed, snuff and ignite. Never let yourself be carried away by the other team's momentum. *It's our movie, not theirs.* Magic passed the ball to Kareem in the post. This was Abdul-Jabbar's second-to-last season. He couldn't run like he used to, and didn't seem to care as much as he once did, but used the right way, he could still be effective. Kareem, being tightly guarded by Parish, dribbled twice, stepped away, and launched the skyhook.

Bird is a forward. Magic is a guard. They do not cover each other, nor play man-on-man. Dennis Johnson guards Magic. Michael Cooper covers Bird. If you see Bird posting up Magic, something has gone wrong. And yet, whenever they were on the same floor, it felt like they were connected by a hidden wire. They answered each other shot for shot in the first quarter. There was a "take that" vibe to the game. After all, these men were linked by history. It was their rivalry that had brought the NBA back from the dead and set it on the path to becoming America's grandest spectacle. Theirs was a fast, elegant game that perfectly suited modern fans. By the late 1980s, the NBA had become what America wanted to be—fast, athletic, diverse.

The Lakers vs. the Celtics had long been the league's great rivalry. Magic and Larry merely breathed life back into a fire that had been blazing since the 1960s, when it was Bill Russell driving on Elgin Baylor. But by the 1987–88 season, while the Celtics were starting to fade, the Showtime Lakers were still going strong.

Bird scored 15 points in the first twelve minutes of that game, putting Boston ahead 29–27 early. Then Worthy picked up his third foul. Thinking the call ticky-tack, he stood before the referee, palms raised in appeal, beard bristling, eyes wide behind enormous goggles, shouting, "Come on, now! Come on! Come on! Come on! Come on, now!"

When foul trouble sent Worthy to the bench, he was replaced by Lakers fan favorite Kurt Rambis. He'd been a starter, but the team had upgraded via the draft, leaving Rambis with no obvious role. TBS announcer Bob Neal said, "Here comes Rambis! The fans in L.A. call him Clark Kent."

"Unfortunately," said color commentator and Hall of Famer Rick Barry, "he also *plays* like Clark Kent."

Rambis dribbled off his foot soon after he checked in. Robert Parish dove for the loose ball, got it, then hit Dennis Johnson with a long pass from a sitting position. In this moment, you saw how badly the Celtics wanted to win. Early season game or not, beating L.A. always meant something.

There are two units of NBA time. There is the season, and there is the moment. The season is important, but it's made up of moments. When you are in the moment, there is no important or unimportant. There is no season. There is only the moment.

Bird scored his 22nd point to start the second half, then missed six shots in a row. With Bird off target, the Celtics seemed overwhelmed. That was the thing about the Showtime Lakers: If you got them down, you had to step on their neck. As long as they could see a path, they could come back and win. They had so many weapons.

Magic took over in the fourth. Always tall for his position, he had been slight in college, but had grown thick and strong as a pro. He wore a Fu Manchu mustache in 1987–88. He always seemed to be smiling. When the Celtics responded to his run with a double-team, he turned into a bandleader, finding open men—Byron Scott for a 3; James Worthy for a runner in the lane; A. C. Green for a jam; Kareem for a skyhook—all over the court.

Bird answered Kareem's skyhook by taking the ball end to end and hitting a layup that put Boston ahead by 2, with 1:44 left to play. The lead changed hands three more times in the last minute. Cooper tied the game with a jumper, with twenty-six seconds left. Boston scored, then got the ball back with a chance to score again. Ainge missed from fifteen feet, but drew a foul. Then missed both free throws.

Pat Riley called time-out. The players gathered round as he diagrammed the last play. Magic was smiling down at Riley. Kareem was sitting at the end of the bench, a towel over his head.

Michael Cooper waved the ball over his head on the sideline, searching for an inbound pass. He found Magic across the floor with just enough time for Johnson to put up a one-handed off-balance 3, less shot than throw, the way you throw a crumpled piece of paper into the trash. Magic later said he'd perfected this shot in the games of HORSE he played with Byron Scott before and after practice. It fell in at the buzzer. Magic ran across the floor shouting, high-fiving, jumping up and down. Bird slouched as he went into the tunnel. Magic had done it to him again.

THE BULLS

By mid-January, the landscape of the season begins to come into focus. The shooting stars have burned out, the contenders emerged. The regular season is eighty-two games. It's an endurance test, and it tends to favor experience and depth.

The NBA's Eastern and Western Conferences were each divided into two divisions: the Midwest and Pacific in the West, the Central and Atlantic in the East. The Lakers, who led the Pacific Division first to last in 1987–88, had the best record in the NBA on January 16, 1988. At 26–7, they were six games ahead of Seattle and Portland. Byron Scott, the third or even the fourth best player on L.A., had been named NBA Player of the Week on January 10, which shows the depth of that team.

The Dallas Mavericks led in the Midwest Division, closely trailed by the Denver Nuggets and Houston Rockets. At 24–10, the Celtics led in the Atlantic, six games ahead of the Philadelphia 76ers, a once great team recovering from the retirement of their star, Dr. J. The 76ers were led by Charles Barkley, who, at twenty-four years old, was already an All-Star.

To general surprise, the Atlanta Hawks (25–9) seemed to be running away with the Central Division, leaving both the Pistons (20–11) and Bulls (20–14) behind. When Atlanta star Dominique Wilkins began to be identified simply as "Nique," the established powers knew it was time to take Atlanta seriously. That team, built by general manager Stan Kasten, the only executive to field winning clubs in three sports—baseball (Dodgers); hockey (Thrashers); basketball (Hawks)—was nearly as deep as the Lakers. Even so, the Celtics knew their real challenger would be the Pistons, not the Hawks. And the Pistons knew that while the Celtics blocked the path ahead, it was the Bulls closing in from behind.

The Pistons dominated the Bulls in those years. They beat them on the floor and in their heads. The Pistons had the Bulls' number, but the gap kept narrowing. "It was like, no matter what we did, every time we looked in the rearview mirror, there was Jordan and the Bulls, a little bit closer," Bill Laimbeer told me. "It was like a horror movie: We just couldn't shake them."

For Detroit coach Chuck Daly and his players, the long-term strategy was simple: Stomp on the Bulls, bruise and bloody and pound them until they break. "It was like, every time we played them, they were laughing at us and saying, 'Who's your daddy?'" Bulls veteran Charles Davis told me. "They were so far inside our heads, they could have moved in furniture." That's why every game between the teams became so heated, why each fight for possession either threatened to turn into a brawl or *did* turn into a brawl.

The fans who paid to see the Bulls play the Pistons at Chicago Stadium on January 16, 1988, expected a good performance from their team. Scottie Pippen and Horace Grant, who had arrived in the 1987 draft, added skill, size, speed, and youth to the roster. Michael Jordan, at twenty-five and in his fourth season, was at his athletic peak. Like the wizard in a children's story, he'd finally mastered his powers. He'd lead the league in scoring that season, averaging 35 points a game, and win the first of his five NBA MVPs. (According to experts, he should have won at least nine.) Charles Oakley was still on the club. It was his job, as the team's power forward and heavy, to win possession—he led the league in rebounds that season—and protect Jordan, especially when the Bulls played Detroit. Chicago, a franchise that had never made it beyond the second round of the playoffs, got off to their best start in years in 1987–88.

Informed fans credited Jordan with the turnaround, but they knew it wasn't only Jordan. There was also general manager Jerry Krause, who began making moves soon after he was hired by Bulls owner Jerry Reinsdorf in 1985. Jordan was already on the roster when Krause took over, so Krause set his task as assembling the pieces that would complement Jordan and turning the Bulls into a team.

Krause was a local, having grown up in Norwood Park on the city's Northwest Side. He was a backup catcher on the Taft High School baseball team and served as a kind of gopher for the football and basketball teams. To many, Krause, short and stocky with a weird squinty eye, seemed like a wannabe jock, the sort of hanger-on who invites ridicule. He made a mess of himself when he ate, which is why Jordan, whose "good guy" image was just that, called him "Crumbs." But Reinsdorf recognized Krause for what he was—a workaholic with a genius for spotting talent. He'd scouted baseball as well as basketball. His most famous find to that point had been Earl Monroe, a future NBA Hall of Famer who Krause had seen playing at a small college in 1966. Recognizing hidden value, raw talent—that was the art. Krause could spot upside where others saw only a hopeless project. It was Krause who made the trades and picks that turned the Bulls into a dynasty. If he's not been given proper credit—he *is* a member of the NBA Hall of Fame—it's only because he didn't look the part. "I'm ugly and fat, and that's why people hate me," he told the *Chicago Tribune*. "But I have a lot of friends who are fat and ugly, and I don't hate them."

There were good and bad things about Jerry Krause.

First the bad: He was aggressive and stubborn and spoke too honestly. If you heard him say, "Do you want to hear what I really think?" you'd be well advised to say, "No." He spoke harshly and without filter. It earned him enemies, and having enemies made him resentful and suspicious. He thought he was being given the high hat. He blabbed to reporters. He was what Chicagoans call a pop-off artist. His belief that he was not given proper credit made him mistrust his own players, some of whom he came to think of as interchangeable. He wanted love and appreciation from reporters and fans, but fans don't love executives, and short, fat businessmen don't sell newspapers.

Now the good: He understood what it takes to win. Success in the NBA is not merely the cumulative effect of smart trades and sound draft picks. It's the product of a design. Great teams are painstakingly built with a specific plan, style, and goal in mind. Whereas most GMs operate from draft to draft, taking whoever seems best among the current crop, Krause focused on the middle distance. He saw what the kid was doing now, but imagined what he would be doing in three to five years.

When you praise Krause for his role in building the Bulls, someone will always say, "But Jerry Krause didn't draft Michael Jordan! The GOAT was on the roster when Krause arrived. Any GM could have won with Michael."

But Jordan played six seasons without winning, or even getting very far in the playoffs. And yes, Jordan was the key, and no, Krause did not pick him, but that's the point: You don't need to be Jerry Krause to draft Michael Jordan. Any college basketball fan could have done that. Building an effective organization around Jordan—that was Krause's historical role.

He started with the staff. Jordan needed direction, and the team needed leadership. By 1987–88, Krause had assembled the most interesting front office in the NBA. Tex Winter, a basketball old-timer who'd been born in Wellington, Texas, in 1922, served as guiding spirit and guru, a basketball preacher whose gospel was the "triangle offense," the scheme the Bulls would introduce in the 1990s. Johnny Bach, another old-timer, this one from the East—he was born in Brooklyn in 1924 and played in New York's Catholic league—served as scout and assistant. Phil Jackson, who'd won as a player with the Knicks and as a coach in the Continental Basketball Association with the Albany Patroons, was an assistant coach and advance man, traveling ahead of the Bulls in 1987–88 to scout the next team on the schedule. "Phil's reports were filled with tons of details, large and small," Scottie Pippen said. "Which side of the floor players preferred to operate from. Which hand they liked to dribble with. Where any of them might be a little soft on the defensive end. Which plays the opposing coach would usually run at different stages in the game." But more than that, Phil Jackson was the prince-in-waiting, positioned to take over if and when head coach Doug Collins stumbled.

Jackson had already developed his oddball philosophy when he reached Chicago. He said he'd based it on Zen Buddhism, Native American philosophy, the game as he learned it from Knicks coach Red Holzman, and his love of music. A 6'8" preacher's son from Deer Lodge, Montana, Jackson was a tie-dye-wearing hippie in 1987, a jazz nut, and a serious Deadhead.

He advised players to heed the wisdom of the great Thelonious Monk:

1. Just because you're not a drummer, doesn't mean you don't have to keep time.
2. Stop playing all those weird notes (that's bullshit), play the melody!
3. Make the drummer sound good.
4. Don't play the piano part, I'm playing that.
5. Don't play everything (or every time); let some things go by . . . What you don't play can be more important than what you do.
6. When you're swinging, swing more.
7. Whatever you think can't be done, somebody will come along and do it. A genius is the one most like himself.
8. You've got to dig it to dig it, you dig?

Jackson wanted his teams to function like a jazz ensemble in 4/4 time. "The basic rule was, the player with the ball had to do something with it before the third beat," he said. "Either pass, shoot, or start to dribble. When everyone is keeping time, it makes it easier to harmonize."

There is footage of Jackson quoting Kipling in the locker room before a big game:

Now this is the Law of the Jungle—
As old and as true as the sky;
And the Wolf that shall keep it may prosper,
But the Wolf that shall break it must die.
As the creeper that girdles the tree-trunk,
The Law runneth forward and back—
For the strength of the Pack is the Wolf,
And the strength of the Wolf is the Pack.

Jackson did not mind working as an assistant. He wanted to spend a year or two in the background, watching and learning from Doug Collins, a onetime standout whose playing career had been cut short by injury. Collins was just thirty-five when he took over the Bulls. Having been an NBA star, he was expected to understand the pressure on Michael Jordan, the challenge of growing up in the spotlight.

Doug and Phil—there could be no greater contrast. Collins still behaved like a star; as if he were essential. He threw up his hands, mugged, screamed. "He was way too animated," said Pippen. "A coach in the NBA shouldn't be running up and down the sidelines. In the locker room after the game, his shirt and jacket were drenched with sweat as if he, too, had been playing." Collins ended every night in a lather, his curly hair unkinked and damp. In short, Doug ran hot. Phil ran cool. He was about detachment, knowing his role, letting the players play. When someone screwed up on the court, Collins yanked him. Phil liked it when there was a screwup, and let the player carry on. How else do you improve? How else do you become resilient?

"I learned early that one of the most important qualities of a leader is listening without judgment, or with what the Buddhists call bare attention," Jackson explained.

"What made Phil a good player is what made Phil a good coach," Celtics coach Jimmy Rodgers, who scouted Jackson when he was in college, told me. "It takes a certain mindset: You have to be able to put ego aside and understand your role and what you can and can't do for the team. It could seem like Doug was doing everything, while Phil was doing nothing at all."

"Doug was a very excitable, high-strung personality," Pete Babcock, the Nuggets vice president in 1987–88, told me. "Phil was the opposite. They had completely different approaches. At a certain point in their development, the Bulls needed Doug. Then, at a later point, they'd need Phil."

"Jerry Reinsdorf told me he thought people are motivated by one of two forces: fear or greed," Phil Jackson wrote in his book *Eleven Rings: The Soul of Success*. "That may be true, but I also think that people are motivated by love. Whether they're willing to acknowledge it or not, what drives most basketball players is not

money or adulation, but their love of the game. They love the moments when they can lose themselves completely in the action,
and experience the pure joy of competition. One of the main jobs
of a coach is to reawaken the spirits so players can blend together
effortlessly."

When Jerry Krause took over in 1985, he saw a team in need of
gut renovation.

Tear it down, then build it up.

First, demolition. The list of once valued players—including
high draft picks—that Krause cut includes David Greenwood,
Ennis Whatley, Quintin Dailey, and Orlando Woolridge. "I had
nine players I didn't want and three I did," Krause said. "I wanted
Dave Corzine. I wanted Rod Higgins, and I wanted Michael. The
rest of them I couldn't have cared less about. And they were talented. All of them were very talented. But it wasn't a question of
talent."

Then, construction. Jordan was helpful with this, and not only
on the court. On most teams, when a new talent arrives, there is
an immediate jockeying for position. This gets worse as the team
gets better. Everyone wants to be top dog—the best paid, the
most interviewed. But that was never an issue in Chicago because,
in Chicago, everyone knew that Jordan was king. Most of Krause's
acquisitions were scouted and acquired in reference to Michael:
How can they help Michael? How will they mesh?

Charles Oakley was a perfect example. A playground legend
from Cleveland, Ohio, who attended a small university (Virginia
Union), Oakley was brought to the Bulls to fight for position and
protect Jordan. He averaged 12 points and 13 rebounds a game in
1987–88. But the stats only tell part of the story. They can never
explain a person's personality, their drive. Looking at Oakley's

numbers, you might have a hard time understanding his choice of schools. Virginia Union is a small Black university that plays in the NCAA's second division. Why would a premier athlete like Oakley—he was big and fast, a standout in football and basketball who could've easily played Division I—bury himself in the sticks?

Well, that's a story.

The youngest of six children, Oakley grew up on the corner of East 123rd Street and Superior Avenue in a working-class neighborhood of Cleveland. He spent summers and a few of his middle school years with his grandmother in Alabama, an experience he claims enabled him to bond with Jordan. "We're both Southerners," he said. "We were both the youngest in our family, which meant we both had that same chip, the same feeling of being looked down on. And we were both raised right, the Southern way, good manners and taught to follow the law, which is whatever your parents say it is."

But the most important things to happen to the young Charles Oakley—the misadventures and dustups, the playground battles and Friday night football games with their bell-ringing hits—happened in Cleveland. He loved the city—it gave him his code and his edge—yet was terrified by what might happen if he stayed. It was in fact a single event—his presence seemed accidental—that made him want to get as far away as possible, even if that meant giving up a big-time college career.

"I was seventeen and saw a man get shot four times," Oakley wrote in his book, *The Last Enforcer.*

> It took place in the basement of a house in Cleveland, where a guy was running a game of craps on a pool table. I had won some money gambling the week before, so I decided to take $1,500 and test my luck, seeing if I could make some more before I headed off to college. It seemed like most of the people in the basement knew each other and like they were all having

a good time as they were shooting dice. I was standing off to the side near the staircase, watching and waiting for my turn. I had been there about fifteen minutes when one guy pulled out a gun and said: "This is a stickup. Give me all the money." I was thinking this must be a joke. How was he going to rob everyone and get away when most of the people there knew who he was? But he wasn't playing around. He took some of the money off the table and started making his way to the staircase. All of a sudden, there was a series of loud "bap, bap, bap, bap" sounds.

A man next to Oakley was hit twice in the chest and spun like a target in a shooting gallery, then was hit twice more in the back. Oakley ran and, in a sense, did not stop running until he reached Virginia Union. It turned out to be a good thing, a blessing. Oakley excelled in the small pond, learned the game and his place in it—he would always be a bruiser, crashing the boards, tearing down rebounds. He was mature, prepared for the NBA, by his senior season. He averaged 24 points and 17.3 rebounds a game, and led his team to the NCAA Division II tournament.

A handful of scouts had noticed Oakley, including Bulls GM Jerry Krause. Dismissing the doubters, Krause chased his vision. It was less college senior Oakley that interested Krause than the player he believed Oakley would become: a tough inside presence who could get the ball to Jordan. When Krause selected Oakley ninth overall in the 1985 draft, the Bulls fans who'd gathered outside the Hyatt Regency on Michigan Avenue booed.

Asked for a response, Oakley, then just twenty years old, said, "Talk is cheap and actions speak louder than words. I'm the real deal."

"Krause was nicknamed 'the Sleuth' because of his uncanny ability to find extraordinary prospects at small, out-of-the-way colleges where nobody else bothered to look," said Phil Jackson.

Michael Jordan came to loathe Jerry Krause, but Oakley never forgot what the GM did for him, how he'd seen what no one else could see and gave him a shot. Jordan skipped the memorial that followed Krause's death in 2017, but Oakley, whom Krause traded after three seasons in Chicago, flew in to pay his respects. "Krause was one of the greatest general managers in NBA history," Oakley said. "He was inducted into the 2017 Basketball Hall of Fame class posthumously. I think that honor should have come years earlier. I always appreciated everything Jerry did for me. He brought me to Chicago. He respected me, and I had a lot of respect for him."

The Oakley pick was remarkable, especially considering some of the washouts—Benoit Benjamin, Jon Koncak—who were taken before him. Oakley played in seventy-seven games his rookie season, and soon became one of the league's best rebounders. "Oakley was huge for us," Bulls center Dave Corzine—who spoke from his office at DePaul, where he works as an assistant to the athletic director—told me. "He would have been huge for anybody—he became a star in New York—but he was exactly who we needed to back up Michael. Jerry's strong suit was talent. He never lost his willingness to be surprised."

No matter how many seasons he played, and he played forever, you could always recognize joy in Oakley's game. It was the joy of a kid who'd seen a man gunned down beside him, who'd missed those bullets by inches, and appreciated every moment that followed. "This close," he'd say, marking the distance with his fingers.

In what felt like a gift to longtime Bulls fans, Krause signed veteran Artis Gilmore in 1987. Gilmore was a sad case, a great player whose trajectory did not align with his times. The Bulls took Gilmore, a 7'2" monster in college, first in the 1971 draft, but, having gone early in the ABA draft as well, Artis opted for the free-spending, slam-dunk-crazed upstart league with the red-white-and-blue ball instead. There were great players in the ABA—Dr. J, George Gervin, Billy Cunningham—but Gilmore, the strongest person many people ever met, was among the best. He averaged 22.3 points and 17.7 rebounds per game over five

ABA seasons. The term for that is dominance. But it's his style people remember. The pork chop sideburns and Fu Manchu mustache, the vertiginous afro, short-shorts, and candy-colored shoes—the man was a relic of the psychedelic age.

Four ABA teams were absorbed by the NBA when the leagues merged in 1976. The players on the other teams were dispersed by draft. The Bulls said they would agree to the terms only if they were allowed to pick first, meaning only if they got Gilmore. When he arrived in Chicago, he brought the excitement, freedom, and glamor of the defunct league. For many years, Gilmore was the only reason to watch the Bulls. We embraced him like a life preserver at sea. But as soon as the team got good, Gilmore got old. He was traded, then came back. He was still an inside presence in 1987, but had lost his shooting touch. The exuberance was gone and his hair cut short, a Samson-like shearing.

Krause promised Gilmore he would start, but as the season went on, he played less and less. He lost his spot to Dave Corzine, a moderately effective white center. It was humiliating. Artis sat in the locker room after games, long legs stretched before him, staring at his unscuffed size-14 shoes. "Exciting statistics, huh?" he told a reporter. "Two points in twenty minutes. That's as many points and rebounds as you'd get from a dead man."

The sad opera reached its conclusion in December 1987, when Krause released Gilmore. The Bulls were in Manhattan, having played the Knicks at Madison Square Garden. Artis packed his gear and left without telling anyone. A reporter saw him in the street, behind the collar of his fur coat, hailing a cab as the snow fell. It was pathetic not because it was unusual, nor because he'd once been great, but because, in one way or another, it's the end that awaits everyone.

Gilmore was not the first, nor the last. The Bulls were ditching every kind of veteran. In 1985, point guard Ennis Whatley was cut to make way for John Paxson, a 23-year-old Notre Dame grad Krause poached from the Spurs. Jordan came to trust Paxson more than anyone else on the floor. It was his discipline, how hard Paxson worked, that impressed the captain. Paxson played every scrimmage as if it were Game 7. And never shied away from the big shot. Even some great players blink in the bright lights of the key moment. Not Paxson. He always wanted the ball.

Because of the relatively small size of NBA rosters, a single draft can make the difference. If you look into the backstory of most basketball dynasties, you'll often find a single draft or trade that put the pieces in place. NBA teams advance not by accretion but by sudden leap. It was not Bird's debut that marked the rebirth of the Celtics, but the 1980 draft-trade that added McHale and Parish. It was not Isiah Thomas's acquisition that turned around the Pistons, but the 1986 draft that added John Salley and Dennis Rodman. The arrival of Michael Jordan in 1984 made the Bulls interesting, but it was the 1987 draft, in which Krause selected both Scottie Pippen and Horace Grant, that would make them a contender.

Pippen's story is famous. "His rise to the NBA reads like a fairy tale," Phil Jackson said. "He grew up the youngest of twelve children in Hamburg, Arkansas, a sleepy rural town where his father worked in a paper mill. When Scottie was a teenager, his father was incapacitated by a stroke, and the family had to get by on his disability payments."

"All of a sudden, Dad dropped his plate and slumped toward the edge of the sofa," Pippen wrote in his memoir, *Unguarded*. "A deranged look was in his eyes and he was throwing up, food coming out of his nostrils. I didn't know what to do. Kim, who had brought him his dinner, ran out to have a neighbor go to the church to find Mom, who made it home before the ambulance arrived. Dad was having a stroke on the right side of his body. Somehow I assumed he would be fine. I was too young to understand what a stroke can do to a person. He would never be able to walk, or really speak again."

From that moment, Pippen poured himself into basketball.

The playground and the high school gym were where he went to escape. He narrowed his plans down to just one—reach the NBA. "He was a respectable point guard in high school but at only six-one he didn't impress college recruiters," said Phil Jackson. "But his coach believed in him and talked the athletic director at the University of Central Arkansas into giving him educational aid and a job as the basketball team's equipment manager."

Then Pippen grew—half a foot between freshman and sophomore years. He was a glorified water boy when he left for the summer; he was the best player in the history of Central Arkansas when he returned. "I would eventually end up around six-foot-seven," said Pippen. "The added size would serve me well. I already possessed the passing skills of a point guard. Now I could employ those skills against smaller defenders. If guys doubled me, I would be able to see above them and easily spot the open man."

Central Arkansas competed in the NAIA, an athletic division for small schools, which kept him hidden from most pro scouts. You were not going to see Pippen on ESPN, or in a nationally televised tournament. The coach at Central Arkansas, worried his prodigy would be overlooked, recorded a video and sent it to Marty Blake, a friend who worked for the NBA. Blake, who made a hobby of connecting overlooked prospects with general managers, studied the tape, then sent it on to Jerry Krause along with a scouting report on Pippen: *Can play point and off guard and point forward . . . great 3 pt college range . . . can handle ball . . . has ability to become a star if he can handle the pressure . . . has a variety of big-time skills.*

Krause went to see Pippen a few weeks later. It was love at first sight. Ghoulish as it sounds, the GM had an ideal basketball body in mind. Long legs and big hands, big feet, long fingers, and long arms—Pippen had it all. Even his face was long. High cheekbones and aquiline nose, big dark eyes and long eyelashes. A face out of time, the face of an Egyptian pharaoh.

"You said he had long arms!" Krause told Blake. "They're freaking down to here!"

"Krause saw Scottie early, and tried to keep him a secret, but word leaked," Pete Babcock told me. "Pippen played in a college tournament in Portsmouth, Virginia, and everybody got to see him. He was up against great players, and still jumped out."

The Bulls had the tenth pick in the 1987 draft. That seemed like it would be enough to get Pippen, but after the Portsmouth tournament, Krause wasn't so sure. In a last-minute panic, he arranged a three-way trade that in essence gave the Bulls two first round picks. Using Seattle as a proxy—the Sonics agreed to draft Pippen, then trade him to the Bulls—Krause acquired Scottie, who went fifth, then took Horace Grant tenth overall.

Horace Grant was another surprise. Krause took him at the insistence of Johnny Bach, who'd spotted Horace on film while scouting a different player. A 6'10" forward from Clemson University, Grant would give the Bulls a physical presence under the basket. (He'd take over Oakley's spot when Oakley was traded to the Knicks in the summer of 1988.)

Jordan liked to test rookies. He teased Pippen, who never really felt comfortable with the scale of MJ's celebrity. It was like living ten feet from the sun. "You'd go to the locker room and Jordan would be talking to Jesse Jackson or Kid 'n Play and Pippen would be alone at his locker, staring into space," Jack McCallum, who covered the NBA for *Sports Illustrated* in the 1980s, told me. "That was a big part of adjusting to the NBA for Pippen: just finding a place in Jordan's world."

Jordan eventually befriended Pippen—he gave Scottie a set of Wilson golf clubs his rookie year—but never really accepted Grant, who grew up in Augusta, Georgia, which, to Jordan, made him a hayseed and a rube. Grant was a good player who could've been great if not for a fatal flaw: the sin of pride. He accepted that he'd never be top dog in Chicago, but wanted to be number two. In the early 1990s, when it became obvious it would be Michael and Scottie—the newspapers called them Batman and Robin— Horace began to act out. He eventually demanded a trade. In the meantime, and it was a long meantime, Grant, along with Oakley, gave the Bulls new power under the hoop. Grant became even better when an assistant noticed him squinting while taking a jumper. When he began wearing glasses, Horace became a shooting threat from the outside.

The Bulls were a young team in 1987–88, nascent, in ascendance. They were in fact the future of the NBA, even if no one but Krause and Jordan saw it. To see it, you just had to step back and examine the progress they'd already made. A team recently dismissed as Michael and the Jordanaires had become a fully functioning unit. The Bulls "still had a few holes," said Phil Jackson. "Their center, Davie Corzine, was not that quick or skilled on the boards, and their six-eleven forward Brad Sellers had chronic injury problems. But they had a strong power forward, Charles Oakley; a solid outside shooter, John Paxson; and two promising rookie forwards, Scottie Pippen and Horace Grant, which [Johnny] Bach called 'the Dobermans' because they were fast and aggressive enough to play a smothering pressure defense. The star, of course, was Michael Jordan, who had blossomed into the most transcendent player in the game."

For the Bulls, the seemingly insurmountable obstacle was the Pistons. "We knew that, to beat the Bulls, we only had to stop Jordan," Earl Cureton, who played on the Pistons in the 1980s, told me. "And, if we couldn't stop him all at once, we'd do it play by play, pounding on him till he quit. Put Michael on the ground every time he gets inside—that was our plan. Foul him hard, knockdown, drag-out basketball. All night, make Michael pay a price. That's how we beat the Bulls."

"Our nemesis, the Detroit Pistons, came up with an effective scheme called the Jordan Rules," Phil Jackson said. "[It] involved having three or more players switch off and close in on Michael whenever he made a move to the hoop."

The Jordan Rules depended on Pistons guard Joe Dumars, who had turned himself into a specialist: a Jordan-stopper. Dumars covered Jordan one-on-one for the first three quarters of a game—he tried to make Michael go left, to his weaker hand—then brought in reinforcements late, a second or even a third defender who did not let Jordan operate in the paint. When Jordan started looking for help, his teammates, who'd hardly shot all game, were cold and ineffective.

Forced to find a solution to the Pistons, the Bulls became a better team. "We benefited from those battles," said Brad Sellers, who was serving as mayor of his Ohio hometown, Warrensville, when we spoke. "You bang your head against a wall for only so long before you either improve or die."

"We should've paid them a tribute," said Bill Cartwright, who reached Chicago via trade in 1988. Cartwright was in his office at the University of San Francisco when we talked. He's old and gray now, but still moves like an athlete. "We had to get strong to overcome Detroit. They paved the way for the kind of game we learned to play."

Cartwright paused a moment, then added, "It was like overcoming a monster."

Sam Vincent, a shooting guard who spent eight years in the league, was traded from the Celtics to the Sonics, then from the Sonics to the Bulls, arriving in Chicago in the middle of the 1987–88 season. In this way, he got to know the Pistons from the perspective of both Boston Garden and Chicago Stadium. "Experience, disappointment, and depth is what Detroit had over Chicago," he told me. "The Pistons got their experience in the course of getting beat up by the Celtics. Those nasty battles were a refiner's fire. It made them strong and took them to the top, where they stayed until the Bulls emerged from the same fire. That's how the league has always worked: Power teaches power, badass unseats badass, king wipes out king."

"Detroit had to get tough like Boston to beat Boston," he added. "They had to learn to play the same kind of mean, hardnosed game to reach the next level."

Charles Davis, who was with the Bulls in the fiercest years of the rivalry, cursed every time I mentioned the Pistons. "It's not that the Pistons were a little dirty," he said. "It's that they were filthy dirty. Like someone goes for a layup, they'd knock that person out of the air. Like someone drives for the basket, they'd shove that person into the stanchion, then step on him when he's down. Some of things they did weren't even basketball."

The Pistons also happened to be great. "We had everything," Rodman said. "Power, finesse, *and* brains. We could beat the ugly shit out of the other team, or play pretty. It didn't matter. Pick how you want to lose, because we didn't care how we beat you."

About fifteen years ago, Charles Oakley and Michael Jordan went, with a handful of friends, to Churchill Downs in Louisville to see the Kentucky Derby. Jordan dressed like a gangster in a beige-and-white candy-striped suit, white shirt, gold tie, white shoes with thick soles. He carried a cigar, sometimes in his mouth, sometimes between the fingers of his right hand. He was talking preliminaries and odds when his crew happened on another crew, this one centered by John Salley and Dr. J and including the actor Chris Tucker and the comedian Dave Chappelle.

The groups met and mingled, admired, confronted. Salley wore a linen suit with a white shirt and a modest tie. He had one cigar in his hand and another tucked, with his sunglasses, in his breast pocket. He towered over everyone, in a panama hat with a rust-colored band. Chris Tucker wore electric blue—suit, tie, shirt, belt. The toes of his shoes were pointy. Dr. J wore a fedora and a bolo tie. You'd have half expected them to break into song. The PA system announced the names of horses and trainers. Mint juleps went by in the crowd.

Salley, who'd played with and against Michael in the NBA, leaned close to Jordan, smiled, and, in the way of an old warrior sharing a joke at the end of a long day, gave MJ a little friendly ribbing. "At twenty-seven years old," Salley told Jordan, "Kobe Bryant would've given you the business."

And then, out of nowhere, like a bolt from the Kentucky blue, WHAM!

Oakley, a decade past retirement, gray, gimpy, and old, threw a gym-strength uppercut into Salley's sternum, knocking the wind out of the seven-footer, doubling him over. Hands on knees, linen suit and all, he struggled to get his breath.

"Oakley's been wanting to hit me since the eighties," Salley said on *The Dan Le Batard Show with Stugotz* podcast. "But man, he hit me with everything he could. I had a suit on, too. And I wasn't going to stand back up and fight him. I'm a karate man. I bruise on the inside."

Oakley denied it. Not that he hit Salley at the Kentucky Derby, which he joyfully owns, but that it was because Salley trash-talked Jordan. "I definitely hit him because he said something I didn't like," Oakley explained, "but it had nothing to do with Michael and Kobe."

Whatever it was must've been important, but Oakley can't remember. The point here is that Oakley was falling, as you fall into a familiar routine, back into his first and most satisfying role in the NBA—protecting Jordan from a Piston.

Jerry Krause never had to state the role explicitly, nor include it in a contract, but it was clear what the GM wanted when he told Oakley that his job was to rebound, create space, and protect the marquee players. For Oakley, this role went from professional to personal early in his first season in Chicago, when he came to see Jordan as something more than a teammate. They were brothers, and remained so even after Oakley was traded to the Knicks.

A basketball team is a family, a collective, a series of alliances, relationships, rivalries, and triangles. Horace Grant loved Scottie

Pippen, who loved Michael Jordan, who also loved Michael Jordan. If you look closely, you'll discover a father figure on most teams—this is usually the coach, though not always—as well as an oldest brother, a middle child, a youngest, a stepsibling, a black sheep, and an overnight guest. Imagine the great teams of the 1987–88 season settled not in arenas but in houses on the same street. The Celtics are the faded aristocrats, a family that had money and lost it, that has only its memory, honor, tradition, and titles to support it. The Lakers are the flashy millionaires, the rock-and-roll gang of free-spending, charismatic superstars. That driveway is all Porsches and Lamborghinis. The Pistons live in the ruined Victorian at the top of the cul-de-sac. The house looks haunted with its rotting porch and crooked gables, with its crabgrass-choked yard. There is a Corvette on blocks in that driveway; two men in greasy muscle shirts stand over the engine, conferring. The rooms of the house are filled with bad boys and ne'er-do-wells, truants and hard cases you secretly admire. The lights burn all night. People come and go. The music never stops.

The Bulls live in a new house built on the ruins of a teardown. It's sleek and modern, but not yet finished. The family is young, with lots of little kids. Michael is the hope and pride of the family, which makes him a target for bullies, which is why the father has asked the tough little brother, Oakley, to look out for him. *Watch out for one another, no matter what the circumstances. If I ever heard you didn't stick up for one another, you shouldn't bother coming home.*

For Oakley, who was twenty-two when he arrived in Chicago, mission one was get to know the team, which meant get to know Jordan. Oakley rented a house just down the street from MJ in Northbrook. It turns out they had a lot in common. They were both little brothers at the start of long NBA careers. Jordan would spend fifteen seasons in the league. For Oakley, it would be nineteen. They were both low-key off-court, high-key on. They were obsessed with surviving and thriving and lasting, which meant steering clear of the usual traps. Both were terrified of drugs, use of which was rampant in the 1980s NBA. For Oakley, that fear came out of his childhood, what he had seen in Cleveland. For Jordan, it came from watching his favorite player—David Thompson at NC State—shorten his career with blow.

The Bulls' roster was riddled with addicts back then. There were temptations in every hotel lobby, where dealers awaited their marks. "The NBA had a serious drug problem when I got to the league," Oakley writes in *The Last Enforcer*. "In the early 1980s, *The Washington Post* estimated that 40 to 75 percent of the league was using cocaine, and that maybe 10 percent were freebasing."

Jordan and Oakley took refuge in each other. "I only played with Michael for three seasons in Chicago, but I probably went to dinner with him eighty times," said Oakley.

They'd have room service on the road, play cards, watch a movie. Jordan liked Westerns, especially *The Outlaw Josey Wales*. They spent hours at Jordan's house during home stands, lifting weights, playing hoops, or just hanging out.

"[Jordan's] basement had a hot tub and a pool table that could be converted for ping-pong," Wright Thompson wrote in *ESPN* magazine in 2014. "They'd play for hours, listening over and over to the first Whitney Houston album.

"James Jordan had remodeled the basement for his son. Did all the work himself, because he'd never let Michael pay for something he could do on his own," Thompson continues. "The first winter, while Michael was out of town for the All-Star game, his pipes froze. His dad ripped out the walls, replacing the pipes himself, patching and repainting when he finished."

Jordan and Oakley had a game day routine. Oak, a skilled amateur cook, would make himself what he considered a healthy breakfast ten hours before tipoff. Jordan preferred fast food, Egg McMuffins by the handful. Three hours before tip, they'd eat again. "I ate steak before most games," Oakley writes, "but Michael literally had steak before 100 percent of his games. And before 90 percent of our practices, he ate McDonald's breakfast."

They'd drive into the city together—sometimes you'd see them, MJ and Oak, seats pushed all the way back, weaving in and out of traffic on the Edens Expressway on their way to Chicago Stadium, the Madhouse on Madison. Fans would see them, flash their lights, wave. Jordan would nod, then streak past. If they tripped a radar gun, the cop would eat it. No one was going to stop Jordan on his way to the arena.

They'd change into sweats at the stadium, stretch, warm up, cycle through the layup line, go back to the locker room, listen to what Doug Collins had to say—even pre-game, he would be in a lather, pushing too hard—then sit with eyes closed as the seconds ticked down.

The arena was filled when they went back out. The players gathered in a circle at the edge of the tunnel. They put their hands in. Jordan looked at each of them, then shouted a simple question: "What time is it?" The answer came in unison, a collective roar: "GAME TIME!"

PISTONS AT BULLS

January 16, 1988. The Bulls and Pistons had already played each other twice that season. Detroit won both games but needed overtime to do it. Each time, they stuck to their simple strategy: Goad Jordan into losing his cool. "Those games were getting harder and harder to win," said Detroit guard Vinnie Johnson. "We were better than the Bulls, but we had a sense that they were always gaining on us."

The Pistons had two top scorers in 1987–88, each of whom considered himself the leader and the star. Two leaders usually means big points and bad trouble. There was the charming, approachable Isiah Thomas, and opposite him was the mercurial, aloof Adrian Dantley, a future Hall of Famer and a basketball vagabond. Dantley would play for seven different teams by the end of his seventeen-year NBA career. It was the aloofness, silences, and rages—he just couldn't stick. However much he was given, he demanded more. More minutes, more attention, more respect. He needed the ball in the fourth quarter. He needed the last shot. He'd wave his hands and scream when he was open. In the midst of the ultimate team game, Dantley, with his sharp, intelligent face and socks pulled high, was all alone. In the end, he'd blame Isiah for the difference between what he wanted and what he got.

By January 1988, the Pistons were already playing like the team that could spoil L.A.'s hopes for a repeat. It was Laimbeer at center, Dantley and Mahorn at forward, Dumars and Thomas at guard. (Recalling that lineup, Oakley says, "Isiah Thomas, Joe Dumars, Adrian Dantley, Vinnie Johnson, Rick Mahorn, John Salley, and Dennis Rodman. That's a lot of talent. They also had Bill Laimbeer, who was an asshole.") The Bulls were a work in progress by comparison, with Corzine at center, Oakley and Sellers at forward, Sparrow and Jordan at guard. Only Jordan would remain in the starting lineup the next year. Watching the 1987–88 Bulls today, you understand what Buddhists mean by Impermanence. *See this world and its people? Close your eyes, turn around twice, and look again. It's all gone.*

In those days, before the ascendance of the 3-point shot and the new rules against interference, the most exciting action took place under the basket, where at times half a dozen players battled for position, put-backs, rebounds. It could be hard to see exactly what was going on in there—amid the elbows, hands, and legs. Faces went by like clothes in a laundromat washing machine. Under the basket, tempers flared, people got hurt. For bruisers like Oakley and Rodman, the temper and tumble, and not the scoring, was the game.

Jordan hung just outside the paint, waiting for the ball, which he knew would come. The ball loved him and wanted to be in his hands. He grabbed it, took two strides, and was approaching the rim in the air, calculating the best way to finish. He was just as riveting without the ball, bent at the waist, fingers grazing the floor, grounded by the touch of varnish. There had never been an NBA player with that kind of charisma and focus. You were compelled to go to your driveway or local park and start shooting around after you watched him play. He changed the way kids in the playgrounds moved. Soon everyone was crouching low, and loping.

And it wasn't just the way he went up for a shot. It was how he dressed, how he carried himself. His influence on fashion was enormous. Basketball players had always worn short-shorts. You could see knee, thigh, hamstring. When a player like Dr. J stretched out in the air, you feared you might see too much. Jordan began like that too. He wore short-shorts in 1984, 1985, 1986. And had hair. When the hair began to go, rather than cling to the remnant, he shaved and waxed his skull into the aerodynamic dome that made him look futuristic. It was Michael Jordan who made being bald kind of cool. Then came the oversized shorts—baggy, cut just above the knee. Some of the players who at first made fun of MJ's giant shorts were soon wearing their own shorts the same way. That's the power of style—you don't want to do it, but can't help yourself. See bell-bottoms. See moon boots. See Joe Namath's fur duster. By 1990, it was John Stockton, the last player in the NBA still wearing short-shorts, who was being mocked. Short-shorts vanished from the inventories of Banana Republic and the Gap. By 1994, we were all dressing like Mike. According to David Halberstam, Jordan wore oversized shorts because he had his lucky pair underneath, the sky blue UNC short-shorts he'd been wearing when he hit the game winner at the NCAA Final.

The oversized shorts irritated old-timers like Dick Motta, a former Bulls coach who was announcing the Bulls–Pistons game on WGN that January. "How can a guy with pants that long be a good player?" Motta asked co-announcer Johnny Kerr. A moment later, when Jordan hit a beautiful fadeaway, Kerr said, "He can wear his shorts however he wants."

Isiah elevated his game whenever he played Jordan. It was as if he were battling not just for the win but for the love of Chicago. Zeke grew up a mile from the stadium. He considered the fans his people. He seemed to resent Jordan less as a player than as a good-time Charlie stealing his hometown's heart. Isiah was a captain on the Pistons, so it was his energy—the energy of the jilted—that raised the temperature whenever the Pistons played at Chicago Stadium. You saw the anger and sense of aggrievement in the rabbit and kidney punches under the hoop, in the extra shove or taunt. The referees might miss it, but the fans—18,000 plus—never did. Boos rained down each time Thomas or Laimbeer got the ball.

When the starters began to give way to the backups midway through the first quarter, the Bulls were ahead by 5. Rory Sparrow, Brad Sellers, and Charles Oakley were replaced by Scottie Pippen, Horace Grant, and John Paxson—a glimpse of the future. The energy flagged whenever Jordan checked out, not just on the floor but in the arena. That was when the spectators went to the bathroom or concession stand. Who wants to see the Jordanaires without Elvis? It was also when the Bulls' weaknesses became painfully evident. They only had one dependable way to score in 1987–88, one engine. When Jordan sat down, even the other Bulls stopped caring.

"Jordan's teammates were often just as enchanted [with him] as the fans," Phil Jackson said. "[Doug] Collins devised dozens of plays to get the rest of the team involved in the action; in fact, he had so many he was given the name Play-a-Day Collins. That helped, but when push came to shove, the other players usually faded into the background and waited for Michael to perform another miracle. Unfortunately this mode of attack, which assistant coach Johnny Bach dubbed the 'archangel offense,' was so one-dimensional, the better defensive teams had little difficulty shutting it down."

The Pistons seized the initiative against the backups, forcing Collins to send Jordan back into the game before he'd had time to rest. You felt the change as soon Michael returned. He cut to the basket without the ball, leapt, turned, and there it was, waiting. He plucked the ball out of the air, drew it back, and slammed it through.

The score was tied at 48 at halftime.

Pistons coach Chuck Daly made adjustments during the break. Jordan was played much more aggressively in the third quarter, hammered whenever he got the ball, knocked on his ass, tripped to his hands, checked into the seats. He got up every time, and scored. But his anger, and that of his teammates, began to build. It was palpable. It hung like a thunderhead, roiling and black, with lightning inside. It broke five minutes into the quarter.

Brad Sellers shot and missed. Jordan got the rebound and drove the basket. Rick Mahorn, the most brutal of Detroit's goons, grabbed Michael around the waist, spun him in a circle, and threw him to the floor. Every whistle blew. Michael got to his feet and charged Mahorn. Oakley, who'd been battling Mahorn—"He slammed me in the side early and I told him, 'You're not going to get away with that the whole game,'" Oakley said—pushed Jordan aside and went at Mahorn himself. "When he slung Michael down, I said, 'That's it.' I had to let him know he couldn't take out our number one player."

Mahorn shoved Oakley, who hit the Piston with a forearm to the neck. The benches cleared, the crowd was up. As Mahorn and Oakley brawled, Doug Collins, who'd already sweat through his blazer, ran out and tried to get Mahorn in a headlock. A foot shorter and a hundred pounds lighter than Mahorn, Collins later said he'd felt like a parent racing into a fire to save his child. Mahorn tossed Collins onto the announcer's table, where Johnny

Kerr caught him, stood him on his feet, and pushed him back onto the floor, where he went after Mahorn again, getting him around the shoulders this time, pulling him away from Oakley. The *Detroit Free Press* described Collins's dash into the melee as "a brave but foolish act." Mahorn hit Collins with a quick jab, then threw him into the scorer's table—"like a rag doll," Oakley said. It was like a fight in a Burt Reynolds movie.

Assistants and players from both teams—including Phil Jackson and Johnny Bach—came out to separate the players. Oakley wiped blood from his face. Mahorn needed four stiches to close a cut on his wrist. As the referees gave out penalties, fans rained down the souvenir memo books that had been given out at the front gate.

"Look at Collins!" said Johnny Kerr. "He's got a little mouse under his eye."

Isiah Thomas stood back, folded his arms, and laughed.

Chicago.

Mahorn and Oakley were ejected. Jordan was awarded two free throws and hit both. The energy changed. The game went from tense to ugly. The storm had come, but the air had not cooled.

"The weak of heart should go home," said Motta. "I mean the players. I love this. This is great. I don't like to see the fighting, but I love to see how the players play after the fighting."

Bulls fans still refer to this as "the Fight Game." It's remembered because it was emblematic. It typified the battle the Bulls and the Pistons waged in those years. The Bulls were good in 1987–88. The Pistons were better. Good would have to become great before the Bulls could ascend.

Laimbeer fouled out in the fourth. He slammed the ball down when the whistle blew. He looked like he would heave it into the stands, reconsidered, handed it to the ref, and walked off beneath a shower of abuse.

Jordan stayed in till the very end—the Bulls won 115–99—

recording his fifth triple-double of the season (double digits in points, assists, and rebounds). He ended the game with a classic MJ move, a gift for the fans. Sparrow beat Dumars, then passed to Jordan, who jumped with his back to the basket. Legs bicycling, he tossed the ball up and over his shoulder without looking. It touched the glass and dropped in.

Asked after the game what he thought the Pistons had in mind in the third, Jordan said, "I think they were deliberately trying to hurt me.

"Detroit thinks they can intimidate," he went on. "I understand [Mahorn] had to stop me, but not to where he had to throw me to the floor not knowing if I'd get hurt."

Penalties were handed out by the league office the next day. Mahorn was suspended for a game and fined $5,000. Oakley was fined $2,000. Collins was fined $1,500.

Asked to comment, Laimbeer, who had a tendency to look over the heads of reporters and respond to questions with a single word, such as "No" or "Next," said, "I think the Bulls are paranoid."

Detroit was the only franchise in the NBA with its own plane in 1987–88. This was due to the largesse of their owner, automotive industry tycoon Bill Davidson. While other clubs had to stay over after road games, then leave on the first flight out in the morning, which usually meant a 4:00 or 5:00 A.M. wake-up call, the Pistons, having exited on their own jet, got to sleep late the next morning. It was a real advantage. Nothing, not even human growth hormone, is as restorative as sleep. In addition to being the nastiest team in the league in 1987–88, the Pistons were the best rested.

Players usually dozed on the plane, but they stayed up talking when they left Chicago after the fight. The Pistons were on their way to Denver to play the Nuggets. At that moment, Detroit's record was 21–11, putting them behind the Celtics in the Eastern Conference. An assistant coach had grabbed the early editions of the morning papers at the airport. BULLS KO PISTONS IN SLUGFEST, read the *Chicago Tribune*. OAKLEY-MAHORN FIGHT, JORDAN TRIPLE DOUBLE SPARK ROUT. According to the *Detroit Free Press,* ANGRY JORDAN ACCUSES PISTONS OF DIRTY PLAY.

"Jordan called us the dirtiest team in basketball," Isiah said later. "He said that we intentionally tried to hurt people. We'd been labeled a dirty team before, so that was nothing really new. Red Auerbach had said the same type of things as Michael Jordan. Now, Red's a pretty smart individual, and he was planting the seed in people's minds that Laimbeer and Mahorn were two of the dirtiest players in the game." But Jordan saying it was different— a player is not an executive; a player should know better. That's what angered the Pistons.

Isiah said that Jordan—the NBA's golden boy—victimized the Pistons with "stereotyping and labeling." Pegged them as thugs, ostracized them from colleagues, referees, fans. Intentional or not, Jordan's language made Detroit's success seem illegitimate, undeserved; but rather than fight the label, Isiah and the Pistons decided to embrace it. *They want a villain? Fine. Let's be the best villain this league has ever seen.*

As a franchise, the Pistons had never really had an identity. It had been a mediocre organization that was mediocre for decades. It was Isiah's ne'er-do-wells who finally put Detroit on the NBA map. "The way I saw it, we could be like the old Oakland Raiders," Isiah explained. "They had all the characters on their team, were a bunch of misfit guys grouped together. That's the same portrait that had been painted of us: a bunch of crazies assembled on one team. The implication was that none of us really belonged, that our locker room was a padded cell, that Chuck Daly was coaching in an insane asylum."

Before the plane landed, the Pistons had decided to assume the identity.

"We adopted a line from *Scarface,* because I love Al Pacino," said Isiah. "In that movie, Al Pacino was sitting in a restaurant eating dinner, just after he'd cursed out the waitress and everyone else in the place and made a fool of himself. He then said, 'Say hello to the bad guy, because you'll never see another bad guy like me.' For the first few games [after Chicago], we'd walk onto the court and get into our huddle, and we'd all say, 'Say hello to the Bad Boys, because you ain't ever going to see Bad Boys like us again.'"

It was a self-christening that etched the Pistons in memory, immortalized them as legendary heavies. ("The outcasts, the displaced of America, found a champion in our team," said Isiah.) It was the kind of prophecy people call self-fulfilling. Players, having tagged themselves as Bad Boys, felt honor bound to live up to the label. Fans wanted it, opponents expected it. When Rodman delivered a hard foul, when Laimbeer threw an elbow, when Mahorn clotheslined a high-flying star, the Pistons were doing just what you'd expect from the Bad Boys. They became a different team as a result. You wear the costume, you become the mask.

THE LAKERS

The 1988 All-Star Game was held in Chicago on one of the coldest weekends of the year. The players who'd been sent from each team—Kareem, Worthy, and Magic from the Lakers; Bird, Ainge, and McHale from the Celtics—rejoined their own clubs with horror stories about the conditions. "When you spit, the spit would freeze before it hit that ground," Danny Ainge told Dennis Johnson. More than just an exhibition, the All-Star Game is the seasonal hinge in the NBA. It's the midpoint, the last moment for an underachieving club to get it together. The playoffs loom. This is when teams focus and find their identity, when the coach makes a difference—how hard will he push?—when the standings start to matter and the leaders start to ignore injuries, the bruises and muscle strains, to "play through" in an effort to win those close road games that will put their side in position for a deep run. Everything that happened before can seem like a prelude.

The real season starts here.

The Celtics had extended their lead in the Eastern Conference to thirteen games by February. The New Jersey Nets, in last place in the conference, were twenty-three games behind.

The Atlanta Hawks still led in the Central Division, but the Pistons, having begun to make their move, were just a half game back. From top to bottom, this division was the most competitive in the league, with the Bulls a half game behind the Pistons, and the Cavaliers a game behind the Bulls. The last-place Bucks were only four games behind the first-place Hawks. Just about everything was still up for grabs.

Dallas, led by Mark Aguirre, who averaged a Jordan-like 25 points a game that season, held the top spot in the Midwest Division, with the Rockets, the Nuggets, and the Jazz close behind.

The Lakers, twelve games ahead of their closest pursuer in the Pacific Division, had started the season on a roll and never looked back. They had two separate seven-game winning streaks between January and late February, and people were already speaking of them as a team that would not only repeat as champions—as per Pat Riley's guarantee—but sweep the playoffs.

They had lost three games in a row only once all year—to Portland, Milwaukee, Cleveland—and that was in November. Otherwise, they never lost more than twice in a row, and hardly did that. They'd win fifteen straight in December and ten straight in February. The arenas of even the lowliest teams sold out when the Lakers came to town—this was Showtime, the greatest team of the age at the peak of its function.

Only a handful of teams have ever been that dominant: the 1971–72 Lakers—with Jerry West, Elgin Baylor, and Wilt

Chamberlain—who between November and January won thirty-three games in a row (still a record), then beat the Knicks in the finals; the 1985–86 Celtics—Bird, McHale, Parish, Walton—who won sixty-seven regular season games, then blew through the postseason; the 1995–96 Bulls, who finished 72–10, then went 15–3 in the playoffs to win the franchise's fourth NBA title. The 2016–17 Golden State Warriors won more games than those Bulls, but lost in the finals, which disqualifies them from the all-time list.

And yet, despite the Lakers' dominance in 1987–88, Pat Riley, who had dreams of leading this team to three, four, five straight titles, kept pushing and pushing, driving his players to operate at breakneck speed. He was especially concerned about midwinter, January and February, which he referred to as "the watch-out months." It's not just the games but the travel that gets teams down, the early mornings and rowdy fans on the road, the heckling and reporters. "The flights seem longer in January and February," said Riley. "The practices seem tougher. Everybody's tired. They call it the Dog Days in the NBA. A leading contender can get burned during the Dog Days—it happens every year."

But there was something indomitable about the Lakers in 1987–88. It was not just that they won, but the way they did it—like spokes turning around a hub, players spinning around the all-time-great center, Kareem. It was beautiful partly because it resonated with franchise history, the Lakers having invented the role of the modern big man. It did not even start in L.A., the city that embodied Showtime, but in the Lakers' original home, Minneapolis, Minnesota, the land of ten thousand lakes.

The Lakers as we know them appeared with the arrival of the game's original athletic center, George Mikan, a 6'10" DePaul standout and forerunner of Wilt, Kareem, and Shaq. Mikan, who debuted in 1948, averaged 23 points a game in an era when an entire team rarely scored more than 60. He was even better on defense. Positioning himself under the hoop, he'd reject anything that came close. It's on account of Mikan that the NBA banned goaltending—you can't interfere with a ball on its way down.

He played for seven seasons and led the Lakers to the championship in five of them. When he retired in 1956, the pain of the hangover—the city had been drunk on winning—encouraged the Lakers, in the way of the brokenhearted moving West to start a new life, to relocate to Los Angeles.

Jack Kent Cooke, who bought the franchise for five million dollars in 1965, built a new arena for the team, the Forum in Inglewood, a nondescript neighborhood near the airport. It was designed in emulation of the Roman Forum, a circular façade ringed by columns. The interior, built without resort to stanchions or beams, was considered an architectural wonder. There were no bad seats in the Fabulous Forum.

Impatient to return his team to Mikan-era glory, Jack Kent Cooke resorted to free agency. He poached Wilt Chamberlain from the Philadelphia 76ers in 1968, paying the seven-footer $250,000 a year after taxes, a record at the time. In 1972 the Lakers, with Jerry West and Gail Goodrich at guard and Chamberlain at center, won the franchise's first championship in twenty years.

The retirements of Elgin Baylor, Wilt Chamberlain, and Jerry West sent Kent Cooke back to the open market, where, in 1975, he poached Kareem Abdul-Jabbar from Milwaukee. Having been a star at UCLA, Kareem was, in a sense, returning home. He belonged in L.A. and personified L.A. Like the city, everything about him was oversized and romantic. A twelve-pound, eleven-ounce newborn named Ferdinand Lewis Alcindor at birth, he grew up in the Dyckman Street projects in Inwood in northern Manhattan. For him, size was destiny. He ended up on the court not because he loved basketball—he loved jazz, he played basketball—but because that's what you do with a colossus. "I was nine years old and 5 feet 4 inches tall and the pattern of my life was set," Kareem wrote in his memoir, *Giant Steps*. "I operated on a cycle, and the cycle was based on the basketball season. All life revolves around it, like a biological clock."

His height both isolated and distinguished him. "I'd always been a minority of one," he said. "Very tall. Black. Catholic. Ever since childhood I had this ability to draw into myself and be perfectly contented."

A curiosity in middle school, a phenom in high school. He played for Power Memorial Academy in New York's Catholic school league. He was recruited by every college with a basketball program in the country. He chose UCLA because he wanted to put distance between himself and the racism of his childhood. (Once, trying to "motivate him," Kareem's high school coach told him to stop "acting like a [n-word].") Having been trained by UCLA's legendary coach John Wooden, he led the Bruins to multiple NCAA championships. Meanwhile, the culture on campus opened his eyes to the larger world. At UCLA he read writers who changed his life: Saint Augustine, Kierkegaard, Camus. He experimented with marijuana and LSD. "There were jet-stream trails behind everything that moved—my hand, my friend's whole body, cars that passed us on the road—and we rushed and tripped and somehow found more than an earthly significance to it all," he wrote of his first acid experience. "We sat on rocks high above Los Angeles and wondered aloud among ourselves where the sun came from, what life really meant . . . race, the difference between black and white, cosmic realities, cosmic myths." He became politically conscious in college, demonstrated for civil rights and against the Vietnam War, read *The Autobiography of Malcolm X* and the Koran, converted to Islam, and changed his name. He refused to try out for the United States men's basketball team for the 1968 Summer Olympics. Threatened with backlash, he issued a statement: "I was born in a racist country. I laid my life on the line when I was born. I don't have anything to lose."

Listed at 7'2", Kareem was closer to 7'4". He'd always been

embarrassed by his height, painfully aware of his uniqueness even as, jammed in the front seat of an Alfa Romeo, he zoomed up the Pacific Coast Highway listening to jazz. The Bucks took him with the first overall pick in 1969. Paired with Hall of Fame guard Oscar Robertson—the Big O—Kareem won MVPs, scoring titles, and a championship. But he felt like a stranger in Milwaukee, cold, lonely, different.

L.A. welcomed him back like a prodigal son, a brilliant and beloved West Coast eccentric. He studied Arabic and collected Oriental rugs, suffered migraines, refused to give autographs, and blew off fans. A devotee of martial arts, he appeared in the strangest fight scene in movie history. In *Game of Death,* the 7'4" Kareem battles the 5'6" Bruce Lee in a shuttered room at the end of time. He appeared in other movies and shows: *Mannix, Man from Atlantis, Tales from the Dark Side, 21 Jump Street.*

Then, in 1979, Jack Kent Cooke sold the franchise to Jerry Buss, who used his first draft pick on Earvin Johnson. Magic added speed and youth to the roster, took the pressure off Kareem, and made everyone better. Kareem won his first title as a Laker in Magic's rookie year. It was the press that dubbed the offense "Showtime." The team embodied the city as it imagined itself: fast and glamorous, always on the move, always closing a deal and rolling out the red carpet. It was not enough for Jerry Buss to win. He wanted to win with style. To him, basketball was less sport than entertainment. It was his tenure that gave the world the Laker Girls and the Forum Club, the after-hours nightspot he'd opened in the arena. At Chicago Stadium, courtside seats were occupied by businessmen. It was politicians in Boston, mobsters in Detroit. In L.A., it was—and always will be—movie stars.

Jerry Buss hired Pat Riley to coach in 1981. A former Laker who'd grown up in Schenectady, New York, Riley remade himself from scrubby dead-end kid to *GQ* cover model, with his trademark slicked-back hair and bespoke suits. But there was always a hard core to Riley, steel beneath the silk. He wrote about his last meeting with his father, a broken-down minor league baseball coach. It was at the end of a wedding. "As he was pulling away, my father stuck his head out of the window of the car. It was a red 1965 Chevrolet Caprice with primer spots on the fenders. He looked at me and said, 'Just remember what I taught you: "Somewhere, someplace, sometime you're going to have to plant your feet, make a stand, and kick some ass. And when that time comes, you do it."' That was the last time I ever saw him. He died of a heart attack shortly afterward."

Lakers general manager Jerry West made the trades and picks that surrounded Kareem and Magic with the pieces that turned their title team into a dynasty.

Michael Cooper was drafted in the third round in 1978. He would become one of the best defenders in the NBA. In the 1980s, it was his mission to shut down Bird. Reporters called him "Larry's Shadow." He said he had 130 Celtics videos at home. He studied them, searching Bird for weaknesses. His wife complained publicly when Cooper brought those videos on vacation to Italy. While she was visiting the Sistine Chapel, he was in the room watching Bird.

Kurt Rambis arrived as a free agent in 1981. He'd become a folk hero in L.A. by the end of his first season at the Forum— because he looked like the common man when the common man imagined himself in the game. A 6'8" nerdy white guy with shaggy hair and chunky glasses, he was a surprisingly nimble power forward. He'd spent his childhood in Cupertino, California, where he learned to play in the wind and rain. He was strong and effective but also embarrassed by his size, his ungainliness. He hated that he needed glasses and hated that, because his rough play almost always resulted in the breaking of those glasses, his father insisted he wear the indestructible Buddy Holly frames that made him an object of derision in school.

He played at Santa Clara University, where he was an oddball standout. The Knicks, with their tradition of turning gangly white guys (see Phil Jackson) into role players, took him in the third round in 1980. Believing he'd do little more than watch from the bench in the NBA, and being of Greek extraction, Rambis played for AEK Athens in the Greek league instead.

Jerry West began calling only after Laker power forward Mitch Kupchak suffered what was thought to be a career-ending injury. *We need you, Kurt! This is your shot!* Rambis played his first game in purple and gold in November 1981. The shaggy hair, cop mustache, wild eyes behind thick frames—how could you not love Kurt Rambis? According to *The Philadelphia Inquirer,* he "looked like Clark Kent, rebounded like Superman, and shot like Lois Lane."

Rambis had intangibles that could not be measured. He played his best when it mattered most. He lifted up his team. He served as locker room friend and late-night confidant. The glue that binds the boys together—there's no stat for that, but without that kind of player on your team, you won't win.

Laker fans began to dress like Rambis at home games. They called themselves the Superman Fan Club. Rambis hated it. He soured whenever he looked into the faces of all those doppelgängers. He asked the Lakers PR guy to set a meeting. He intended to ask the club members to cut it out, stop dressing like that. "I thought they were mocking me," he explained. "I thought they were teasing me. But when I walked through the door"—he met the club members in the Forum Club—"you would have thought Jesus Christ himself had walked in. I mean, these guys actually liked me. They were just so complimentary. They weren't mocking me at all. They just enjoyed my style and what I did for the team. They were such huge fans that I quickly changed course and said, 'Thank you guys very much.'"

Rambis's peak Laker years came between 1984 and 1986, when he started 120 games and played a key role on a team some consider the best ever. But he's remembered less for something he did than for something that was done to him. Game 4 of the

1984 Finals. The Lakers were running the Celtics into the ground. Boston coach K. C. Jones called on his players to step up—don't just let them embarrass you like this! Rambis got the ball on a fast break. He had one man to beat, McHale. Instead of conceding the basket—there was no legal way to stop it—McHale clotheslined Rambis; he became a truck speeding under a low bridge. His legs came out, his body went flying. This was a characteristic moment of the great rivalry. The Celtics, playing that hard-nosed Eastern Conference basketball, got into the Lakers' heads with this play, taking them out of their game and changing the direction of the series, which Boston went on to win in seven games. "K. C. kept saying he was tired of all the layups," McHale explained. "He wanted us to do something. L.A. started the game doing what they always do, running up and down. So I stopped it. My only regret is that it wasn't Worthy or Magic or someone better. It just happened to be Kurt Rambis."

James Worthy, who would become a top player of the era, was taken first overall in the 1982 draft. "[Magic] can push the ball up the court at an incredible tempo but he needed someone even faster to break for the wing and fly," said Riley. That was Worthy, "the fastest man of his size in the NBA. In terms of finishing the fast break creatively and swiftly and deceptively, no one compares."

In 1983, Jerry West traded All-Star Norm Nixon for Byron Scott, who grew up just a few miles from the Forum. Scott struggled for a time in L.A., but eventually found his footing. "His weaknesses were more emotional and attitudinal than anything," said Riley. "He arrived as a rookie in a pressure situation. Management dumped Norm Nixon, a veteran, to bring in Byron. The general public didn't know that trouble had been festering on the team because Nixon couldn't come to terms with being less of a star than Earvin."

Power forward A. C. Green was selected in the first round of the 1985 draft. He would soon replace Kurt Rambis, who, be-loved or no, could not match Green's skills. "[Green] came from Oregon State, under coach Ralph Miller, where they emphasize teamwork and fundamentals," said Riley. "Like Earvin Johnson, A.C. arrived already understanding how to play unselfish basket-ball. The footwork and fundamentals were all perfect. And he was blessed with a young six-nine, 230-pound body that could propel itself up and down the court all night long."

In 1986, Jerry West sent a first round pick and two veterans to San Antonio for Mychal Thompson (father of Klay), a big man to back up Kareem and serve as a Kevin McHale shutdown artist. Having played with McHale at the University of Minnesota, Thompson knew all his tricks.

Wes Matthews, a first-rounder in the 1980 draft who proved a bit of a bust—he played for half a dozen NBA teams in as many years—arrived as a free agent the same year. Matthews, who grew up in Bridgeport, Connecticut, was a calculated risk. "His past record included insubordination and drug problems," said Riley. "But he also had brilliance. He could be fearless against anybody. In the first round of the '85–'86 playoffs Wes tagged us for over 90 points over three games. Wes was the kind of whippet guard a fast-breaking team needs."

"They wanted a backup for Magic and I had nailed them in the playoffs," Matthews told me. "It was a no-brainer when they called. I said, 'Hey, I'm on my way.' It was a dream. To this day I love Pat Riley, and appreciate Magic and the fellas for allowing me to be a part of that. I knew Magic from playing against him in col-lege. We used to go at each other. I'd played against Mychal Thompson in Minnesota. So I was familiar with the guys, and they welcomed me. They said, 'Just handle your business and you'll be all right.' And also: 'Get your ring size measured, 'cuz we're going for gold.'"

When people speak of Showtime, it's this roster they have in mind. Though many basketball veterans consider the '85 Celtics the best ever, others, like coach George Karl, laugh at the notion. "Are you kidding? The Lakers were better in '86, '87, and '88. They had so many ways to beat you. Byron Scott and Magic Johnson and James Worthy all on one team? It wasn't fair."

A chorus of other veterans and experts agree with Karl.

"Kareem underneath, Magic at point guard, smallest guy on the floor was probably Scott and he was six-foot-five—how do you stop that?" asked Duke legend Johnny Dawkins.

"Those Lakers beat the '91 Pistons, the '85 Celtics, the '95 Bulls, anyone," Trail Blazers All-Star Terry Porter told me.

"Kareem, Worthy, Magic? As good as Jordan was, he never had teammates like that," said Sam Perkins. "He had Scottie, but there never really was a bona fide third player. The Lakers had four Hall of Famers in the same lineup."

"We were all business," Wes Matthews went on. "That was the beauty, it was business and also fun. Showtime. That was our motto: 'Put on a show and get out of town.' From the outside it was like, 'Damn, how do you beat these dudes?' I had a chance to play against them when I was with the Spurs. I averaged thirty-three in the playoffs, but they still kicked our butts. They were full of weapons. And loved each other. And played for each other. And wanted to maintain the legacy of all the previous championships. It's a rich tradition. The Lakers don't have seventeen titles for no reason. Riley's motto was: 'We take care of what we take care of and don't worry about anybody else.'"

"It was a beautiful time," said Magic. "We had graceful players. Kareem with his skyhook. James with his floaters and finger rolls. Byron with his beautiful jump shot. Michael Cooper with the defense he played and the alley-oop from Coop-a-loop."

The Lakers appeared in eight finals in the 1980s. They lost three, falling to the 76ers, the Celtics, and the Pistons. But they won five, defeating the 76ers (twice), the Celtics (twice), and the Pistons. In 1987, they beat Boston in six games. It was in the locker room after that game that Pat Riley made the repeat guarantee that haunted the 1987–88 Lakers.

Asked to comment on their coach's promise, the players—Worthy, Magic, Kareem—laughed, then choked on their laughter. The championship celebration, trophy kissing and champagne chugging, is a ritual performed for the cameras. It's also a genuine expression of accomplishment and relief. It's about finishing, getting out from under, escaping the grinding expectations of coaches and fans, the fear of making a decisive blunder. For a few weeks, you are free of all that pressure, or should be. But Riley's guarantee put the Lakers right back in the spotlight. Instead of being asked how they'd celebrate, they found themselves being asked if they could do it all again. Most of the Lakers forgave the coach, figuring it had been a champagne-induced lapse. But this was not the case.

No team had repeated as NBA champions in nearly twenty years. It was a trick many considered impossible to turn in the modern era. Victory carried too many seeds of defeat. Players lost their focus after winning a title, became distracted by parties, vainglory, desire. "I call it 'the disease of more,'" said Riley. "People start thinking, 'I'm really the key ingredient. It was my quality minutes off the bench,' or 'It was my brilliant coaching,' or 'It was my outstanding defense.' People who'd been quiet during the lean years suddenly want more money, more playing time, more recognition. And they get aggressive and jealous about pulling in their 'more.'" And meanwhile, just as the defending champions are losing focus, other clubs, having adjusted and improved to overcome the winners, return with renewed energy and purpose.

Every game the Lakers played in 1987–88, even the seemingly

meaningless early season games, was played with unsettling intensity. Issuing the guarantee was Riley's way of forcing his team to focus. "I made a conscious decision to put myself on the line for the upcoming season," he wrote in the diary he published as a book after that season. "While I was still soaked in champagne from head to shoes after our Game Six win over Boston, reporters whipped out their notepads and extended their microphones to ask if the Lakers could possibly win two championships in a row. I looked right at them and answered, 'I guarantee you we're going to repeat next year!' My statement was well thought out. I wrote it a week before we took the trophy. I went out on a limb because we have gotten to a point in maturity, talent and emotional commitment where we have a terrific chance of winning consecutive championships."

A team can't merely be as good as they were if they want to repeat—they have to be better, work harder, and sacrifice more, which is a hard sell to players suffering from "the disease of more." The Lakers preseason practices were tougher in 1987 than they'd been in 1986. Riley wanted his team to play faster. "The first thing we developed in the summer was a resolve to throw our quickness at people, to gamble that our style could prevail," he wrote. "Let small and quick go after slow and big and see who can beat who first."

The 1987–88 Lakers were 35–8 at the All-Star Break, far ahead of their closest competitor. Riley pushed them in February, when even great clubs lose focus.

Of course, the Lakers never had trouble focusing when it came to the Pistons, because the Pistons could physically hurt you. Los Angeles had won thirty of thirty-three games when the Pistons, riding a winning streak of their own, came into town in February 1988. There was always something personal about these matchups. Magic had mentored Isiah. They were close friends. Isiah often stayed at Magic's house when he visited L.A. They played one-on-one in the summer. They talked each other through setbacks. It was not Mary Thomas or Lord Henry that Zeke called when Larry Bird picked off his pass at the end of Game 5 in 1987. It was Magic.

It pained Magic to see Isiah playing with a goon squad—*That's not your game, Zeke*—especially Laimbeer, the rich kid whom the L.A. *Times* called the "downhome heavy from Palos Verdes High School."

"We hated Laimbeer because Laimbeer was a dirty dude," Wes Matthews told me. "OK. I won't say dirty. Physical. He played physical. And that was basketball back then. Right now, the fouls Laimbeer committed would get him suspended. And Mahorn! He was clotheslining people. They'd suspend him for a season. Then it was still 'No blood, no foul.' Get up and let's go, and then when that dude comes down the lane, you pay him back with his own money. When the Pistons showed up at the Forum, we geared up because we knew it was going to be old-school basketball."

PISTONS AT LAKERS

February 21, 1988. The Lakers did not approach the game with the same discipline as the Pistons. Most of the team had been out late the night before. This was the age of the never-ending party in L.A., the bathroom rendezvous, the tequila shot, the cocaine baggie, the line inhaled off the stripper's back.

After home games, the players went straight from the press conference to the Forum Club. To join your teammates at the Forum Club was to be sociable, part of the family. To give it a skip, as Kareem did—Kareem was older, wiser, and could do whatever the hell he wanted—was to make a statement, not merely of unwillingness but of judgment.

Are you too good to party with us?

The Forum Club was filled with Hollywood types, starlets and producers, drug dealers, low-level criminals and lizards, by the time the players began turning up at around 11:00 P.M. Magic and Worthy. Scott. Rambis. Cooper. They arrived in twos and threes, celebrities who burned even brighter than the film stars. They stood over the bar, scanning—*Who is here? What will happen tonight?*—or sank into a table in back, looking out from the shadows, stingrays in the cool of the reef.

Magic had married his college sweetheart, Cookie Kelly, but, as they say in the underworld, marriage is an institution. What happened in the bars and apartments and hotel rooms was really just another sport, outside and exempt, arms and legs, morning light in the window, the quickest way to let off the heat of battle. It's how Magic came down from the high of the game. If you don't break your fall with some kind of stimulant, you'll burn up on re-entry.

Magic was friends with players across the NBA. He was admired by everyone, even opposing coaches, who whispered to him in the handshake line. He'd been taken under wing by grumpy old Kareem when he—Magic—was a rookie. *What does this young blood want from me?* In his ninth season, he sought to do the same for the young men on the Lakers roster. He made a special project of A. C. Green, the 6'9" power forward Jerry West drafted twenty-third overall in 1985. Green was twenty-two when he arrived at camp, boyish and happy with that big smile, the sort that crumpled his face and made his eyes disappear.

Green would be L.A.'s answer to McHale in Boston and Mahorn in Detroit, but there was something funny about him. Mahorn was a hard case—the dirtiest player in the league. McHale was stoical and fierce—a lumberman from Minnesota's Iron Range. Green, who would fight them all to a standstill beneath the hoop, was more like Mr. Perfect. A devout Christian, a strict textualist—if it was in the Bible, he believed it—he came into the league a self-proclaimed virgin. He had not done it, and would not, until married. Nor touch drugs. Nor drink alcohol. He actually stepped away when the team sprayed champagne around the locker room, lest some touch his lips and change his life.

It's funny that he ended up in L.A.—Salt Lake City would've made more sense—on the favorite team of some of the nation's biggest sinners (see: Jack Nicholson). A young man intent on keeping his virtue had been dropped into the middle of the biggest party of the 1980s. And still he'd go to the Forum Club and sit with his juice or water, because that's what was expected. Stay with the team, no matter the temptation. And it's what Magic wanted. Even the sober must bond. It was a source of entertainment for other players. They'd find the hottest woman in the room, give her two shots of vodka, and send her over to sit on A.C.'s lap and test his faith.

But A. C. Green was a rock and would remain true throughout his sixteen-year career. Some believed it was the secret of his strength. By depriving himself, he channeled all that bottled-up energy into his game. As Mickey told Rocky, "Women weaken legs."

Pressed to comment on his virginity, Green spoke not of the game, nor even of God, but of discipline. "You need to have self-respect, values, and virtue in your life."

When asked how his on-court ferocity—he was a bad man in the paint—jibed with his beliefs, he smiled and said, "I'm gonna hit, and I'm gonna hit, and I'm gonna hit. I learned that from reading the Old Testament.

"Jesus as a basketball player would have been unstoppable on the court."

The Pistons had not won in the Forum in three years by the winter of 1988. Isiah blamed the lure of Hollywood. There were three bars and five celebrities in Detroit, and everything was closed by 2:00 A.M. The Pistons were like kids in a candy store in L.A. Dan Tana's. The Viper Room. The Sunset Strip. John Salley hung out with Arsenio Hall. Dennis Rodman partied at Danceteria. Isiah, who understood the importance of this matchup, set a team curfew the night before the game in February 1988. In your hotel room with door locked by eleven. Lights out by midnight.

Isiah took control on Detroit's first possession. He was smaller than the other players on the floor, shiftier, meaner, more determined. He was also better-looking, too adorable for his playing style. The ferocity caught you by surprise. There's nothing more terrifying than a killer with a sweet smile. He made eight straight shots in the first quarter that night, quieting the Forum. But Byron Scott kept L.A. close. Whenever Isiah hit, Scott hit back. Isiah hit a one-handed runner. Scott hit a fadeaway. It went back and forth like that for ten minutes. Even so, the Pistons led by 8 at the end of the first quarter.

Rick Mahorn bowled his way into the paint to start the second quarter, finishing with a deft move, reminding you that, in the NBA, even the bruisers are magicians. Big beefy Mahorn was neatly groomed, with a part carved in his close-cropped hair. His thin little mustache made him look like a Jazz Age gangster. The announcers talked about his weight. In 1986, when Mahorn asked Pistons GM Jack McCloskey why he wasn't playing, McCloskey said, "Why? Because look at yourself! You're fat!" Mahorn dropped twenty-five pounds in the off-season and recovered his place in the starting lineup.

Kareem, who'd been on the bench, pads on his knees, knees around his ears, eyes remote behind thick goggles, stood stiffly, stretched, then went to the scorer's table to check in. The crowd cheered. Kareem was appreciated not just as a Laker but as the oldest player in the NBA, a living relic, history captured in a single career. In his rookie season, he played against Earl Monroe, Jerry Sloan, Elgin Baylor. In his twilight, he faced a new generation of

centers—Hakeem Olajuwon, Patrick Ewing, Ralph Sampson—
which meant answering a question known to only that handful of
athletes who were durable as well as great: How do you maintain
your sense of dignity while growing old in public?

Nothing brings fans closer to an athlete than watching him
struggle with mortality, watching him adapt and improvise a place
for himself in the game. Not only does such a player illustrate
time, connecting the league as it was to the league as it's become;
he dramatizes the human condition. The pro athlete dies twice,
once like everyone else and once when, still relatively young, he
must give up the only life he's ever known.

Kareem was forty-one in 1988, but already looked like Methu-
selah. His shoulders slumped, his head hung. Yet he found ways
to contribute. He played fewer minutes, stayed out of scrums, and
gave the unimportant skirmishes a miss, but, now and then, by
picking his spots and focusing on details, he'd make a key shot or
assist. He never put himself in a position to look bad, embarrassment being everyone's great fear. He felt the drift of the game, its
ebb and flood tides. Some moments matter more than others. He
might vanish for a quarter only to emerge with a crucial steal late.
"Certain things have slipped, like the ability to go after a rebound
two to three times in a row, or the lateral movement," Riley said.
"Don't let those things distract you. [Kareem] can still put the ball
in the hole better than anybody. He's still the most vital force at
the end of a game."

For Kareem, playing Detroit meant dealing with Laimbeer,
the biggest irritant in the league. He hacked Kareem under the
basket that night, tugged his jersey, elbowed his kidneys, stepped
on his feet. At one point, Kareem posted up just outside the paint,
got a pass from Magic, turned, banged Laimbeer with his shoulder, creating space, stepped away, and hit the skyhook. He shouted
at Laimbeer as that shot fell. Laimbeer glared. The men stood
toe-to-toe, yelling. The referee, eighteen inches shorter than either player, held them apart.

Kareem blocked a Joe Dumars shot at the end of the first half, snagged the rebound, held off Isiah, then started a fast break with a pass to Magic. When the Lakers scored, Chuck Daly called time-out. The Pistons were ahead, but the momentum had shifted. That's what basketball is about—mood swings. If you're not on your toes, you're on your heels. Chuck Daly, a chubby man older than most NBA coaches, designed a play to recapture the initiative. Isiah received the inbound and brought the ball up-court. Magic reached for the steal, but Zeke stepped around, faked Worthy, and headed for the basket. He jumped, knee-high, looked for the pass, then, seeing no good options, leaned in and shot. He made the basket and drew a foul. A 3-point play.

The Pistons spread across the floor and began to operate. For the next five minutes, they outran, outjumped, and outhustled L.A. The Lakers were famous for their Showtime speed, but the Pistons suddenly looked younger and faster. For a moment, Magic, Worthy, and Kareem seemed superannuated. You can't teach height. You can't teach speed. But you also can't teach a player to be younger. In the closing moments of the first half, you could hear the tumblers of history. It might be this year or it might be next, but time was running out on one of the game's great dynasties.

The Pistons led by 12 at the break. The third quarter is telling in basketball. It's during halftime that a coach, having seen enough of the other team, is expected to make the adjustments necessary to win.

Pat Riley, composed on the floor, was furious in the locker room. Red-faced, veins throbbing in his neck. The business patois he'd learned on the guru circuit gave way to Schenectady school-yard slang. *What the fuck, you fucking fucks?* Riley knew this game was more important than it seemed. The Pistons were a rising power. The Lakers might face them in the finals. It was important for L.A. to establish dominance and protect their home court. "They must leave here thinking we are unbeatable in the Forum," he said. Asked what he'd told his players at halftime, Riley said he'd told them that "you can't let 'em come into your backyard and give you a backhand."

The Lakers opened the third quarter with an 11–2 run. Just like that, they were within 3 points and had the momentum. The mood in the arena changed, too. During a time-out, Jack Nicholson, wearing a black beret and yellow shades, stepped onto the floor, turned to the crowd, and waved his arms, summoning their energy. Magic and Worthy rode that energy, extending their run to 21–6. When L.A. took the lead, they did it with a fast break. They ran, and, as they ran, it was as if they became young again. The Pistons did their best to simply survive the onslaught. *Let them exhaust themselves, then we'll begin again.* Frustrated, Mahorn lashed out, grabbing and whirling Byron Scott to the floor, just as he'd done to Michael Jordan in Chicago. Players started cursing, shoving. Riley had to be restrained. Mahorn smirked. He'd already tossed one coach over a scorer's table that season—he'd gladly do it again.

A. C. Green, the youngest and strongest Lakers starter, stepped up to play Mahorn. He banged into Mahorn, glared at him, stole from him, scored on him. Green, in his third NBA season, was crucial in the battle against Detroit.

The Pistons somehow hung in, then struck back, tying the score with nine minutes left. The contrasting styles—the Lakers were fancy, the Pistons brutal—made the game exciting. It could not have been any closer. After being tied at 93, the teams were tied six more times. According to Billy Cunningham, the former coach who was announcing the game on TV, Detroit had already achieved their goal. "The Pistons needed to come in here and show they could play with the Lakers on the Lakers' court, that they wouldn't be intimidated and would not back off," he said, "and that's exactly what they've done."

With three minutes to play and the score tied once again, Isiah hit an off-balance runner for his 39th and 40th points. The lead changed hands, then changed hands again. At forty-one seconds, Mychal Thompson scored over Mahorn to put the Lakers ahead by 2. The Forum faithful were on their feet. Jack Nicholson had his binoculars trained on Chuck Daly, who had called time and was talking to his players in a huddle. Daly was sweating, an arm around his captain.

Isiah got the inbound, dribbled across the 3-point line, dodged Scott and Magic, looked for an open man, then, not seeing anyone, went up to take a last-second shot for the win. Just as Zeke started to release the ball, Kareem, appearing from nowhere, reached out and swatted it away.

Block.

Game over.

In the next morning's *Los Angeles Times,* a writer named Scott Ostler said the game proved what he'd already known: "The Lakers are the greatest basketball team of all time."

Bill Laimbeer, asked about the boos that greeted him in his hometown, said, "I have a wife. I am the father of two kids. I live in a nice neighborhood. I have never been arrested. People think I'm this horrible guy, but it doesn't matter. I definitely play ugly basketball, but I'm effective. I don't consider myself an enforcer. My job is to win games for the Detroit Pistons. It doesn't matter how you accomplish your goals, as long as you play within the rules."

THE PISTONS

Charles Oakley, who did not like Dennis Rodman in 1987, liked him even less in 2017 when he ran into him at Jerry Krause's memorial. Rodman was pierced and tattooed. Multicolored hair, eye shadow, mascara. He'd just returned from North Korea, where he'd palled around with dictator Kim Jong Un, whom Rodman characterized as "an awesome guy." When Oakley shook Rodman's hand that day, he came away with a single impression: He reeked of booze.

The drug and alcohol problems that have plagued Rodman since retirement are well known—he's written about them candidly in his *four* autobiographies—but he'd been nothing like that when he arrived in Detroit in 1986. At twenty-five, he was the oldest rookie in the NBA. He was also the most troubled and most immature.

Rodman had few friends growing up, and fewer still in the NBA. In his off-hours, he tended to hang out with white kids who didn't play. Admirers. Camp followers. He glommed on to their families, the sleepover guest who stays for weeks, or until asked to leave. It was as if, through these confused, exhausted families, Rodman sought to taste the typical American life he'd never known.

Rodman befriended a young guy who worked in the Pistons media department in Detroit. They'd confer before games, go to dinner after. Then clubs. When a bouncer spotted Rodman waiting at the back of a line, he'd wave him forward. Dennis refused to cut. He did not want to be treated better, worse, or differently. He just wanted to be like everyone else.

He ordered water at the clubs, then found a corner where he could play pinball. He'd quickly get himself into the bonus. On one quarter, he could go all night. This was Rodman before booze and spectacle. In love with basketball. In love with the team. In love with the coach, Chuck Daly, the father he'd never had.

Dennis drove a pickup truck. It could be seen around the city. He'd show up at the arena many hours before tipoff. Just to hang out, lift weights, shoot around. He was like a kite without a tether, a plaything of the wind. He'd sit at his locker, headphones on, music cranked. Hip-hop—that was the soundtrack of the NBA. But Jordan preferred Whitney Houston. And Rodman preferred Pearl Jam. He acknowledged Eddie Vedder—*Your music is a real inspiration*—on the first page of his first book.

Rodman started thirty-two games in 1987–88, playing his way into importance. By mid-season, he'd become a critical piece of the machine. When the energy of the starters flagged (he came off the bench most nights), he could usually get it going. His entrance—onto the floor, into the party—changed the mood.

He ended his rookie year with his infamous remarks about Bird, a three-time MVP: "He ain't the best player in the NBA, not to me," said Rodman. "He's white. That's the reason he gets the MVP."

When the gaggle of reporters went to Isiah for a comment, Zeke, the veteran and captain, who should have pulled back and tamped down—*Don't listen to Dennis; he's a rookie; he's emotional; he just lost the biggest game of his life*—piled on instead. "I'd have to agree with Rodman," said Isiah behind that slow smile. "If Larry Bird was Black, he'd be just another good player."

Brouhaha and hubbub followed. News segments, editorials, denunciations, all because Isiah had said what half the Black players in the league believed but would never admit. Zeke was forced to apologize to Bird at a press conference; Bird was forced to sit and listen and accept the apology. As Larry walked out, Ira Berkow, a *New York Times* reporter, heard him say, "I just saved the little shit's ass."

When the Pistons arrived at training camp three months later, they came with a single goal: Get back to the Eastern Conference Finals, and win.

The Pistons got off to a rocky start in 1987–88. It was a season of injuries, ups and downs, winning and losing streaks. There were internal battles, mostly about playing time. Isiah yielded minutes as the young players developed—that, he learned, was a key to success in the NBA. It's not about doing more. It's about doing less. But Adrian Dantley, the mercurial frontline scorer, refused to yield. When asked to make way late in close games for Rodman, who was a much better defender, Dantley revolted, stormed out, stormed back, kicked over a basket of towels, stormed out a second time.

It always ended the same way—with Zeke and Adrian screaming at each other. Thomas called Dantley selfish. Dantley said it was being selfish that had made him the NBA's scoring leader twice in the past. Thomas said Dantley needed to see the big picture. Dantley said it was not the big picture he needed—it was the ball. "When I shoot, we win. When I don't shoot, we lose. That's the big picture."

While Dantley was the Pistons' best option in the post, he was not a team player; he was distant, weird. He went off by himself, did his own thing. He vanished as soon as the game was over. And that was how he played, too. Like he was alone on the floor. It created tension on the team, pressure that increased and increased until, in the middle of the next season, Jack McCloskey, having had enough, traded Dantley to Dallas for Mark Aguirre, who, though maybe not quite as gifted as Dantley, would at least listen to Zeke. Most of the Pistons believed Isiah orchestrated the trade, but he denied it. The fact that the Pistons, on the way to their first championship, swapped Zeke's nemesis for one of his oldest friends? Mere coincidence. On Dantley's first trip back to Detroit as a Maverick, he pulled Zeke aside and said, "I know it was you, Isiah. I know you got me traded. And I will pay you back, no matter how long it takes."

Pistons fans did not seem to mind the internal conflicts, the feuds and wild behavior. In fact, they seemed to enjoy them. In their mood swings and neuroses, the Pistons reflected the mood of their city, the former car capital of the world that had fallen on hard times. Detroit, which had once been known for its Gilded Age mansions and robber baron splendor, had by the 1980s become miles and miles of burned-out tenements, vacant lots, and shuttered factories. This was a great city with a proud, boosterish population that had lived to see its greatness fade. The masterpieces in the art museum, the smokestacks above the warehouses, the bridges that crossed the great river, the marble courthouses, the recording studios, and the crumbling dynamos—it was the afterpiece of Motor City's twentieth-century dream. The streets had fallen into chaos, violence, ruin. On some nights, it seemed that only the basketball team held the town together.

As bad as it gets, at least we have the Pistons.

They had regained their form by mid-season, and by spring were the team no one wanted to play. There were so many ways they could beat you. Their defense could pummel you and hold you to 80, or their offense could outrun, outshoot, and beat you even though you'd scored 110.

The Pistons were in first place, one game ahead of the Hawks in the Central Division, 3.5 games ahead of the Bulls. What's more, they'd been built, in the way of Detroit's priciest cars, for comfort as well as speed. The 1987–88 Pistons were the NBA version of an old-time Camaro: luxurious shocks, deep seats, and oversized gas tanks that could take you coast to coast without a refill.

That had been the goal general manager Jack McCloskey, aka Trader Jack, set when he took over in 1979. He wanted a team that could do more than merely compete with the behemoths on the coasts—the Lakers and the Celtics. He wanted a team that could win.

Detroit had been at the bottom of the NBA barrel when McCloskey arrived. They were the Fort Wayne Zollner Pistons— Fred Zollner made auto parts—before moving to Detroit in 1957. They'd had a handful of stars over the years—Dave DeBusschere, Dave Bing—but rarely a good team. Their franchise record as of 1980 was 1,077 wins and 1,422 losses. They'd gone 16–66 the year before McCloskey arrived, one of the worst single-season records in NBA history.

"Jack began to build the Bad Boys as soon as he was hired," Pistons announcer George Blaha told me. "Jack was not shy about work. He was a coal miner's kid from Pennsylvania who played basketball and football at Penn. He played a little pro ball in the Eastern League, then started coaching. He was the head coach at Wake Forest and U. Penn, then worked for the Trail Blazers and the Lakers. Taking over the Pistons, the worst team in the league, meant he'd start with a top-five pick. He ended up with number two, and used it to get Isiah, who'd be the cornerstone."

McCloskey then looked for players who'd work well with Zeke. The league was filled with scouts, but he devised his own system to find undervalued talent. Like any good entrepreneur on a budget, he was out for bargains. Working at a desk in the Pistons executive suite, he rated every prospect in ten categories, assigning 1 to 10 points in each category, numbers he then totaled and averaged. McCloskey circled anyone who rated higher than 80.

It was this system that led McCloskey to Bill Laimbeer, who, short on athleticism but long on hustle, grit, and smarts, was the first Bad Boy to join Isiah in Detroit. These days, Bill Laimbeer, who coaches women's basketball, is a giant sun-reddened white guy, seven feet tall, too heavy for the hotel scale, potbellied and straining every button of his oxford shirt. Much has changed about him over the decades, but his essence remains the same. He still hates reporters, is still irascible, sharp-tongued, and blunt. He still has an alarming tendency to tell you what he *really* thinks: that Michael Jordan was a crybaby who worked the officials; that Kareem had become a shell of himself by 1987–88; that Pat Riley was a stuffed suit topped with a dime-store pomade. Laimbeer still has the same forelock, the same swoop of greasy hair, now gunmetal gray. He still has the same condescending, I-dare-you-to-punch-me-in-the-face look about him.

One might think that the tougher the upbringing, the tougher the player, but Laimbeer grew up privileged. His father was president of Owens-Illinois, a *Fortune* 500 company that manufactures every variation of glass container. Laimbeer once described himself as "the only player in the NBA who makes less than his dad." And yet Laimbeer was as nasty as anyone in the league. The revulsion with which old-timers still receive his name testifies to that. They hate him because he was rich *and* mean, pampered *and* nasty, the NBA's version of a Van Patten bully. Maybe it had to do with his size, how much bigger and heavier he was than anyone else on the playground. Maybe girls recoiled. Maybe teachers were intimidated. Maybe he looked in a mirror and saw a monster looking back and decided to embrace it. At seventeen, he was cast in the TV show *Land of the Lost* as a Sleestak, a reptilian/humanoid creature who crushes and kills in the time of dinosaurs.

He played at Notre Dame, where he developed into a rebounder with a shooting touch. It set Laimbeer apart from other big men—he could reliably hit from twelve feet. He was listed at center, but did not play it conventionally. "Call him what you want, but the position is how you play," Rudy Tomjanovich told me. "Laimbeer was called a center but he played at the top of the key. By doing that, and because he could hit that outside shot, he pulled the other center out, which opened space for the forwards and guards underneath."

"He was a precursor to the modern outside-shooting big man," *The Boston Globe*'s Bob Ryan told me. "He was a seven-footer who wanted nothing to do with the ball. We used to kid him and say, 'Why don't you buy some moves this summer.' But all he did in the summer was play golf. But he could really hit that twelve-foot shot."

Laimbeer was drafted by the Cavaliers in the third round in 1979. He played in Europe and in Cleveland before McCloskey traded for him in 1981. Laimbeer was brought in to balance Isiah, put size in the lineup—score, rebound, and protect the captain. Scott Hastings, who was traded to the Pistons in 1989, was briefed on the big man's task in Detroit soon after he arrived. "Laimbeer took David Greenwood and me to dinner," Hastings said. "He's sitting alone on one side of the table, like he's the Godfather, and he's telling us about how the Pistons protect their guards. He was like, 'If somebody puts one of our guards on their back, we put one of their guards on the bench.'"

Laimbeer was a fan favorite in Detroit and a Bond villain everywhere else. He was, by consensus, the most hated player in the NBA. "The biggest jerk ever" is how Sam Perkins described him. "He would do all the things you were taught to never do. He would get the rebound and spread his elbows so you'd get hit with them. Who does that? But it worked. I mean, he really took you out of the game mentally. Once he did something to me and I threw the ball at him, and for a moment I thought it was just me and him out there and I was going to kick his ass. I forgot there were referees, a game to win. I threw the ball at him as hard as I could. Then I realized, 'That's what this asshole wants.' And I checked myself, and he stuck his tongue out at me like a spoiled kid."

"I give Laimbeer credit for maximizing what little talent he had," Dave Corzine told me. "He got the most out of the least and played a key role on those great teams. He fit in. And led. And set a good screen for Isiah. And was a good perimeter shooter. If Isiah or Dumars or any of those guys were double-teamed, it meant Laimbeer was open, and he'd hit that open outside shot."

"Some people call him a dirty player," said Magic Johnson. "To me, he's a cheap-shot artist. Fouling is one thing, but Laimbeer tries to punish you at the end of the foul. He'll smack a guy on the head or push him all the way to the floor so he'll hit the ground harder."

With the core in place, McCloskey shopped for specialists, sharpshooters, rebounders, and the sort of high-energy players that could be injected into a game like adrenaline when the starting five flagged.

Vinnie Johnson was added in the middle of the 1981–82 season. A two-time Baylor All-American, Vinnie was taken by the SuperSonics just behind Magic in the 1979 draft. Though VJ struggled in Seattle, McCloskey still had him rated high on his chart. There were so many ways Vinnie could score: on the drive, with a jumper from fifteen feet, off the pick-and-roll. Danny Ainge nicknamed him "the Microwave" because he got so hot so fast.

Joe Dumars, whom McCloskey had spotted at a college tournament where he'd gone to scout another player—"In the first two minutes, he made a great move," said McCloskey, "and I turned to someone and said, 'Hell, this kid can play'"—arrived via the 1985 draft. Though Dumars had been a top scorer in college, McCloskey wanted him as a wingman to Isiah. Pass. Set picks. Lock down the other team's top guard. It was Dumars, not Thomas, who was called on to stop John Stockton, Magic Johnson, Clyde Drexler. When designing the Jordan Rules, Pistons defensive coach Ron Rothstein made every Piston watch film of Dumars, then said, "Do that."

Power forward Rick Mahorn, most feared of the Bad Boys, was acquired by trade before the 1985–86 season. He'd come out of the tough basketball scene in Hartford, Connecticut, then gooned it up for five NBA seasons as a Washington Bullet. The 6'10", 240-pound Mahorn made up for his lack of skill by infuriating and entangling more gifted opponents. He was a practiced practitioner of a sly trick called "pull the chair." He'd play McHale incredibly tight and then, when McHale leaned back to create space, jump away, which usually sent McHale reeling.

"To beat the Celtics, we needed size," said Ron Rothstein. Currently broadcasting Heat games, Rothstein was in Miami preparing for the 2021 NBA Playoffs when we spoke. "Boston had that huge forward line," he explained. "They could all shoot, they could all post up. Bird was one of the greatest passers of all time. We needed size and presence to compete with that. Mahorn was perfect for the task, especially when teamed with Laimbeer."

Here was the beauty of McCloskey's project: You could see the design in every acquisition, draft, trade. The GM was after redundancy, a second team that would be just as good as the first. It was his great innovation, and what made the Pistons so hard to beat.

An underdog oddball team made of spare parts like the Pistons needed an oddball underdog coach, which is exactly what

McCloskey found in Chuck Daly. Unlike Pat Riley, who went straight from active roster to announcers' booth to sideline—he was just thirty-six when Jerry Buss hired him to coach the Lakers—Daly, having climbed through the ranks, was old when he reached the NBA.

He started as a high school coach in Pennsylvania in the 1950s. Asked to describe his experience leading the Punxsutawney Woodchucks ("the Punxsy Chucks"), he said, "Have you ever seen the movie *Hoosiers*?" He learned how to innovate in the lean years, make do. He deflated basketballs and refilled them with sawdust in Punxsutawney, then made his players scrimmage with those balls—this taught them to move up the court without dribbling. He made them play blindfolded. He tied their strong hand behind their backs and made them spend a day or even a week using only their weak hand. He was a coaching legend in the public school ranks. He could be seen outside the hotel the night before the state tournament, walking at two or three in the morning, previewing every play in his head. He never went anywhere without a history book. He underlined biographies of Churchill, Roosevelt, Patton. He read passages to his players. He believed there was something to be learned from every great leader.

He ascended—first to the college level, then the NBA. He did a short, embarrassing stint in Cleveland before McCloskey, who'd coached with Daly at Penn, gave him a second chance in Detroit. "I saw him in his college days and knew that he was a motivator," McCloskey explained. "I knew he had good communication skills."

Daly was fifty-three when he took over the Pistons. He had the aura of the late bloomer, which was perfect for Detroit—a place of second chances, where players like Laimbeer and Vinnie Johnson got a new lease on life.

The history-making acquisition for the Pistons came in 1986, when Jack McCloskey got John Salley and Dennis Rodman in a single draft.

First, John Salley.

Detroit took him in the first round with the eleventh pick overall in 1986. Tall and athletic, Salley could play forward or center. He got up and down the court as fast as anyone. A star at Canarsie High School in Brooklyn, then at Georgia Tech, he would have gone in the first round of any draft. His talent was easy to recognize. Six-eleven, 230 pounds—scouts called him supple, lithe. If Mahorn was a pipe, Salley was a pipe cleaner, sharp, bendable, and tough. To the fans, he was "Spider."

Here's the strange part: Although John Salley was Jack McCloskey's first pick in 1986, he was not his first choice. Dennis Rodman was his first choice, but McCloskey knew he wouldn't need a top pick to get Rodman. Dennis had come into his body and game off the radar, a scout's dream of buried treasure. He grew up on the wrong side of the highway in Dallas. He was one of the many offspring of the aptly named Philander Rodman, who only made a serious effort to meet his son after Dennis had become rich and famous. Rodman had been a pipsqueak in high school, a bully magnet, taunted because he was small and strange. "I was just a kid from the projects too skinny or too funny-looking to be taken seriously," he wrote in his memoir *Bad as I Wanna Be.*

He shimmied when he played pinball—that's why they called him "the Worm." And that's how he played hoops, too—all shimmy and hustle. His sisters were basketball stars in college, but he was too small for high school varsity. He quit the JV team, but not the game. He played in the park near his house. He was 5'7" senior year, a jug-eared goofball seemingly destined for nothing good. He worked a variety of jobs after graduation, cleaned cars at the Oldsmobile dealership, did yard work and construction, and was a janitor at the Dallas airport. Late one night, the concourse deserted, the departures board showing the names of cities he'd seemingly never visit, Dennis squeezed his hand through a jewelry store security grate and stole fifteen watches. Easily identified, he confessed, returned the watches, was fired and arrested, but the charges were dropped. He was a kid who'd made a stupid mistake and deserved a second chance.

Then Rodman's life began to change. He grew ten inches in one year. He grew so fast you could almost hear it. He was the talk of the playground. He still operated with that wild, little-man chip on his shoulder, only now he was not so little. As with Jordan and Pippen, growing late turned out to be a blessing.

He was recruited by a coach at Southeastern Oklahoma, a Division II program. He became a small-school star, but there were issues. He could be hard to control, was a showoff, pumped his fist when he scored, played to the kids in the stands. He was a flake. He played dirty. He said he enjoyed pain and never felt more alive than when his mouth was filled with blood. He wasn't a natural shooter. And he was old. Isiah had been twenty going into his rookie year in Detroit. Rodman would be twenty-five.

McCloskey started taking Rodman seriously after the Portsmouth Invitational Tournament. Rather than vanish amid top D-1 prospects, Rodman emerged. Several NBA scouts noticed. They penciled his name on their draft sheets, which, when Rodman underperformed at a handful of later tournaments, they then erased. McCloskey sent a scout to investigate, find out what the hell had happened to the kid. As it turned out, Rodman suffered from seasonal allergies, had asthma. He'd played at Portsmouth in the winter, before the pollen flew. His lungs had been clear, and he'd excelled. He was wheezing and going half-speed by the time he reached the spring tournaments. He'd never seen a doctor or tried an inhaler.

McCloskey drafted Rodman in the second round in 1985, took him to an allergist, got him fixed with a canister of albuterol, then introduced him to the media and fans.

"I made news right away," Rodman said. "The day I signed my contract, I hyperventilated and had to see the team doctor."

Rodman became a kind of mascot in Detroit, a tension-breaking eccentric.

"He was the court jester," said Phil Jackson, who coached Rodman's late-career second act with the Bulls. "Dennis had a way of getting everybody to lighten up when things were tense."

Rodman loved his Detroit teammates in the way of family and he loved his coach in the way of a father. "I was a raw player, full of wild energy, and Chuck Daly was a teacher," Rodman said. "I used to call him 'God' and mean it."

Rodman identified a niche for himself, then worked filling that niche into an art. He decided early in his career to make himself into the greatest rebounder—an all-important, unglamorous part of the game—in NBA history. "I never want to score," he said. "I want to rebound. I want to break the record for most consecutive years leading the league in rebounding. If I do that, they'll have to say I was one of the best who ever played."

Watching Rodman rebound was exciting. He'd go up again and again. If he could not control the ball, he'd tip it into the air and try again. "I've got a quick jump—one of the quickest," he said. "I can get down on the floor and back up in the air faster than a pogo stick. Most people think you have to jump high to get a rebound, but jumping quickly is more important. I can jump and tip, jump and tip, jump and tip—boom! boom! boom!— three times in the time it takes the other guy to jump once."

Sitting courtside was dangerous at a Pistons game. Rodman would often bound off the floor and into the laps of spectators. He knocked a lady out cold in San Antonio. He kicked a cameraman in Chicago.

"I was physical like Mahorn and Laimbeer, but I was faster than shit and could guard anybody in the league," Rodman said. "I was like a new product, something the NBA had never seen before."

By the spring of 1988, Jack McCloskey's rebuild was nearly complete.

The resulting team was eccentric and wild, and had been designed to humble the fancy teams on the coasts. Their starters were good, but their depth was what made them dangerous. Most NBA teams carry six to eight genuine NBA players. Detroit carried nine. Players who would have started elsewhere agreed to come off the bench in Detroit. That's why none of them averaged more than 20 points a game in 1987–88. The scoring was distributed across the entire lineup, which made them unique. When you played Detroit, you were playing not one but two starting teams. The second, with Rodman and Salley, was arguably better than the first. The advantage was obvious late in games, when the Lakers or Celtics starters had to rest and the subs found themselves battling the league's best young squad. Many coaches responded by keeping their starters on the floor—Jordan often played the full forty-eight minutes against Detroit—which left them exhausted in the clutch. What's more, whereas an injury might end a title run for the Lakers or Celtics, the Pistons had been built with duplication. Just like the Detroit assembly line: Snap a fan belt, pop in a replacement.

The NBA had changed its rules in 1977–78, allowing teams to roster only eleven players: two full units of five, plus a backup. The owners liked this because it kept down costs. The players hated it because it deprived twenty-two athletes of jobs. In 1982, the league, flush with the cash generated by the Bird vs. Magic rivalry, went back to the old rule, allowing for a second sub, the fabled "twelfth man."

You might think the twelfth man, the last person on the bench, would be the least valuable player. *Wrong!* In fact, the twelfth man often filled a unique role. He was a specialist, with a very particular function. Asked to describe the quality that made a good twelfth man, NBA executive Pat Williams said, "A good sitter. You don't want an impatient, troublesome guy down there," he explained. "The guy's not a factor in most situations, but you want someone who understands what his role is."

The twelfth man might be a project, someone still developing, learning the trade. He might be of particular use during practice, able to challenge and sharpen the big man. He might be comic relief, a mascot, a high-energy perspective-giver who keeps the stars loose. He might say things like, "Hey, guys, it's just one game." Or: "Hey, guys, it's just a walnut in the batter of life."

Journeyman Chuck Nevitt played the role for the 1987–88 Pistons. He grew up in Marietta, Georgia. He got his height from his parents. His father, a professor at Mercer college, was 6'7". His mother, a nurse, was over six feet. She scolded Chuck whenever he brought home a short date. "I once dated a girl who was 5'3" and my mother lectured me on all the tall girls who were sitting home alone, waiting for someone taller to come along, and here I was with a girl who was two feet shorter," said Nevitt.

This quote appeared in a Steve Wulf *Sports Illustrated* story, which, in paying homage to the NBA's overlooked twelfth man, featured Nevitt as the most colorful of them. "Fans may giggle at first sight of his pipe-cleaner physique," wrote Wulf, "but if they watch him cheer his teammates on, watch him high- and low-five the ball boys, watch him listen intently to the coach during time-outs, watch him join the crowd in the Wave, they know that Chuck Nevitt is more than just the longest standing joke in the NBA. He is a genuine folk hero."

Nevitt was seven feet tall by the end of high school, but did not play hoops. The growing pains were so intense he could hardly walk. He sat on the bench most of college, starting only his senior year at NC State, where he played for Jim Valvano. He averaged 3 points a game. The Rockets took him on a whim in the third round. The player they'd wanted was gone, and there he was—a beanstalk who could touch the rim without jumping.

At 7'5", Nevitt was the tallest player in the NBA, a distinction he'd maintain until 1985, when the Bullets drafted the 7'7" Manute Bol.

He played for the Rockets and the Lakers before signing with the Pistons. Teams kept him around because he was funny, people loved him, and his jokes lightened the atmosphere. Then teams would cut him because, at the end of the day, he was not a great player. "Chuck gets waived as soon as he runs out of jokes," said Jazz forward Thurl Bailey.

His extreme height also made you see every other player on the floor differently. Just about all of them, save the exceptions (Isiah, Michael) were halfway to being freakish. Monstrously tall, enormous wingspans, and out of all proportion. Nevitt was merely the extreme of the extreme. Seven-five but only 225 pounds. He wore jeans with a 38-inch waist. The man was less sculpture than line.

The Lakers liked him because he was a traffic cone for Kareem to play against in practice. And colorful. Between NBA stints, he worked at a big-and-tall men's shop in Houston called the King Size Company. Asked about Nevitt's effectiveness as a salesman, supervisor Clovis Goodwill said, "He did OK. He'd tell the customers corny jokes, and if he had them laughing, I knew he had a sale."

He designed and printed pamphlets that he sent around to basketball teams when he was looking for a spot. These showed Nevitt covering future NBA Hall of Famer Ralph Sampson (number 50) over the words: *If you don't recognize No. 50, you don't follow pro basketball very closely. He's the incomparable Ralph Sampson. But how about the guy hovering over him, blocking the shot? Do you know him? After all, Sampson is 7'4". Not a lot of folks make him eat the ball.*

The Lakers kept Nevitt around even after they cut him from the active roster. They sent him to a mall to sell tickets and featured him at events. PR director Josh Rosenfeld said: "Basically, what Chuck did was get things off the top shelf for me."

When the Lakers cut ties in the middle of the 1986 season—he won two championship rings in L.A.—several players went to break the news in person. "Kurt Rambis and Ronnie Lester and some other guys and I went to his room to make sure he was OK," Mitch Kupchak said. "We went to cheer him up, and pretty soon he was cheering us up. But you know, maybe if he wasn't so nice, he'd be a better player. Sometimes I wanted him to get mad, get meaner. It's a double-edged sword. He's a good guy to have on a club because he's so nice, but his niceness makes him expendable."

Jack McCloskey noticed Nevitt when he was at NC State. "During a time-out I always watch the huddle to see how the players relate to the coach," McCloskey explained. "This guy in back of the team was leaning way over, listening intently. I thought to myself, 'There's a dedicated player. He's standing on a chair to hear his coach.' But when the huddle broke up, there was no chair! I couldn't believe it. He was so big."

Nevitt was a tension-reliever in the Pistons locker room in 1987–88. He cut the bitterness, subdued the toxic rivalries. Though he only appeared in seventeen games, he became a Motown favorite. A pizza place offered a promotion: a free pie for every shot Nevitt blocked. (Pizzas were given away just three times that season.) People called him "the Human Victory Cigar," a wink to Red Auerbach. If he was on the floor, it meant the game was over.

BULLS AT PISTONS

April 3, 1988. It was the last time the teams would meet before the playoffs. Each club came in wanting to set a tone. The Pistons remained dominant, the Bulls were ascending. Chicago needed to prove they could beat Detroit in Detroit; the Pistons needed to shut that down before the Bulls got any bright ideas. They'd played five times that season. Detroit had won four of those games, but all of them had been competitive, mean, and violent.

This was the Pistons' last year in the Silverdome, the strangest arena in the NBA. Thirty miles outside Detroit, amid the abandoned cars and cattails of Pontiac, Michigan, the Silverdome had been state-of-the-art circa 1975. Sitting courtside was like watching an old sci-fi film. The roof was made of Teflon. When the sun beat down, the air inside turned silvery. The dome sagged in the snow and snapped in the wind. It collapsed twice, the first time in 1985.

It had been designed for mass spectacles. The nearly 100,000 people who gathered beneath the dome to take Communion from the Pope in September 1987 set a record that was broken a few weeks later by the even larger crowd that came to see WrestleMania III. When the Lions played football there, 80,000 people crammed inside. Basketball, with its junior-high-school-like gym floor, seemed lost in all that immensity. The arena was divided in half when the Pistons played. The floor was set on one side of the football field and surrounded by temporary seats. Behind them, a massive curtain hung down the center, creating a sense of intimacy. "Detroit is a workingman's town, which means a lot of people wouldn't have been able to afford seats in a typical NBA stadium," said George Blaha. "But everyone could afford a ticket to the Silverdome. Some Pistons games drew over sixty thousand."

The Silverdome was at once overwhelming and intimate. It was the regulars, the hecklers and know-it-all buffoons, that made it feel like home. Leon "the Barber" Bradley, bearded in a Pistons jacket and baseball hat—he actually did cut hair for a living—was the most notorious. He occupied a seat behind the Detroit bench until the night a ref, hearing the Barber but thinking it was Pistons coach Dick Vitale—Vitale coached Detroit before Chuck Daly—threw Vitale out of the game.

The Pistons moved Leon to a new spot behind the visitors' bench, where he came to the attention of every opposition player in the league. Not content to comment on a particular game, Leon did research, dug up gossip, litanies of past failures, which he trumpeted from first tick to last. He was featured in an L.A. *Times* article headlined DOES 1ST AMENDMENT PROTECT A NASTY FAN? "Leon gets on athletes the way white gets on rice," according to the reporter. "He has a seat right behind the visiting team, and amuses himself for two hours or more by insulting them in ways Don Rickles never imagined."

Some players wanted to kill Leon. Others were amused. The season is long and life can be boring; value entertainment where you find it. Larry Bird wasn't the only Celtic who looked forward to seeing Leon in Detroit. Dennis Johnson covered his face in a towel to hide his laughter whenever Leon the Barber sounded off on his teammates.

And it wasn't just the hecklers that distinguished the Silverdome. It was all the promotions. "Marathon Oil had giveaway nights," Pistons assistant coach Ron Rothstein told me. "If you bought two or more tickets, they gave you two gallons of gasoline. You went behind that big curtain to pick it up. On those nights, the whole arena reeked."

The Bulls arrived with their best record in thirteen seasons: 43–29. The Pistons, at 46–24, were even better. Isiah spent most of the first quarter passing. He used the start of every game to size up his teammates, figure out who was hot. He could tell just by the way a player carried himself if he was feeling it. Having so many weapons meant someone was always in the groove. Having identified him—Dantley? Laimbeer? Dumars?—Isiah would get that player the ball. If no one had a hot hand, Isiah took it himself. On such nights, he might score 20, 25, 30. It's not that he couldn't have matched Jordan or Bird in scoring. It's that he didn't want to—it wouldn't have been in the best interest of the team.

Statisticians will tell you that there's no such thing as a hot hand, that it's a myth, that all the numbers balance out in the end. It's not about moods or magic—it's about data. The past predicts the future. But Isiah and every other great shooter believed in the hot hand, because they'd experienced it. On some nights with the game on the line, you'd give the ball to Jerry Sichting instead of Larry Bird, because Jerry Sichting had the hot hand.

Joe Dumars had the hot hand in the first minutes on April 3, 1988. Jordan played Dumars tight, talked trash, and swatted at the ball, but none of that matters when you've got the hot hand. The Bulls started sloppy, missing open men, missing open shots. Doug Collins called an early time-out. The announcers said the Bulls were jet-lagged. They'd flown in from Seattle the night before; then, in addition to the two-hour time difference, daylight saving time had kicked in. This, according to Billy Cunningham on CBS, is why Jordan and Oakley looked flat. "We think of them as indestructible," he said, "but these are people and people get tired."

When Detroit went on a 7–0 run, Collins pulled his starters—all except for Jordan—and sent in the rookies. Grant replaced Oakley. Pippen replaced Sellers. Scottie had had a good start to his rookie season, then faded. Collins had wanted to start Pippen ahead of Sellers, but Pippen's mistakes made it impossible. He threw errant passes, put up air balls, took low-percentage shots. He had the athleticism and skill, but his head was all wrong. Even the most gifted rookie will lack the confidence that comes with experience, the knowledge that accrues after playing night after night against the best players in the world. Being a good pro does not just mean having the occasional good game—anyone can excel when they have the hot hand—but finding ways to contribute even when not feeling it.

Pippen missed several shots as soon as he entered, threw an errant pass, was clobbered underneath by Mahorn. Horace Grant made mistakes too, but this had less to do with confidence than vision. He was not yet wearing the prescription goggles that would later characterize him, and his eyesight was a liability. The refs, the coaches, the players—it was all a blur. Grant was fouled, went to the line, and missed both free throws because he could not see. He made a great play underneath, put the ball off the glass, but stepped out of bounds. Because he could not see.

Jordan was off too. One of his jumpers clanked off the rim. Another bounced off the top of the backboard. Michael was in the process of finding his range. When Jordan made a jumper halfway through the first, CBS announcer Billy Cunningham said, as if to himself, "Uh-oh. He's got it." By making shots from the outside, Jordan opened up the inside, then began driving and scoring underneath, too. He had 18 points after twelve minutes, then started the second quarter on the bench to save his legs. This gave the Pistons bench room to operate.

Detroit's second team had a new leader, the 7'1" center James Edwards, who'd arrived via trade from Phoenix earlier that month. Pistons fans called him "Buddha" on account of his handlebar mustache and peaceful countenance. He was thirty-two, old in basketball terms, but having just lost eleven straight games with the Suns before he was traded, Edwards was energized by the chance to play for a contender. He'd been a skill player for Phoenix, but that changed after Laimbeer took him to dinner and explained the gig. "He didn't have a reputation for being a tough guy in Phoenix," Rothstein told me. "He was finesse, but, after he'd been with us maybe a week, I saw him in practice, and it was like he'd become a new guy. There was a loose ball and he blew two or three guys out of the way going for it. I went up to him after and said, 'Hey, Buddha, when's the last time you went to the floor after a loose ball in practice?' He said, 'Coach, I've been here two weeks, seen how they play, and figured I'd better join up.'"

He had an excellent shooting touch and was skilled in the post. He gave the Pistons a legitimate inside scoring presence. Daly had expected Salley to fill that role underneath, but Salley was better on the run. It was Buddha who'd take McHale and Abdul-Jabbar to the hole. He played especially well when teamed up with Daly's sixth man, Vinnie Johnson. Once they started working the pick-and-roll, Doug Collins had to send Jordan back in. Michael took the ball to the hoop as soon as he was back on the floor. He jumped, was fouled, made the shot, made the free throw.

Jordan was Chicago's shooting guard, while Sam Vincent, who'd arrived in Chicago from Seattle mid-season, was at point guard. Michael played with three different point guards that season—Rory Sparrow, John Paxson, Sam Vincent—which tells you that Doug Collins was still searching. He'd eventually settle on Paxson—because he was solid, hit the big shot, and worked well with Jordan. You saw this at the end of the first half, when Jordan, swarmed by Pistons, went up, faked a jumper, then threw a no-look crosscourt pass to Paxson, who hit a 3 at the buzzer.

The Bulls were down 66–63 at the break.

Laimbeer hit a fifteen-footer to start the third. Pippen continued to struggle. He was called for goaltending, then dribbled off his foot. Watching Scottie flail was painful for loyalists, but it made him seem human, relatable. Jordan was a prodigy. There was never a season when he was not an All-Star. The stories of his youth are like the stories of baby Moses: He could walk at two weeks, trash-talk at five. Pippen was tortured and flawed in comparison. His gifts did not save him from suffering. He was maddened by his mind, the nit-picking internal monologue. He was sensitive and easily wounded, an exposed wire. The times when he came up short, when he seemed fragile, made us love him even more. Despite the famous ad campaign, no one can really "Be Like Mike" because Mike was from another planet. There was greatness in Pippen too, but it was a kind of greatness you could almost imagine for yourself.

Dumars was the only player in the NBA who could stymie Jordan. He didn't stop Michael so much as direct him to less productive places on the floor. Whenever they faced the Bulls, Dumars was uncharacteristically active on offense, forcing Jordan to cover him on defense, tiring him out. He wanted to get Jordan into foul trouble. And it usually worked. Jordan performed significantly worse against the Pistons than any other team. A 53 percent shooter in 1987–88, he shot just 34 percent against Detroit.

Of course, there were games when it didn't matter who covered Jordan. He had 34 points by the beginning of the third quarter on April 3, 1988. For a time, he'd gone back and forth—call-and-response—with Isiah. The duel ended with Jordan driving to the basket. He leapt eight feet from the hoop, closed on the rim in the air, tongue out. Those were points 40 and 41 for Jordan. It was the fourteenth time he'd scored more than 40 that season.

Rodman was watching impatiently from the bench, bouncing his knee, looking imploringly at Daly, who finally waved him over. Dennis checked in with the score tied at 90. Rodman platooned with Dantley that season. Dantley played when the Pistons needed points. Rodman played when the Pistons needed defense. "I didn't play much. That killed me," Rodman said. "When I did get on the floor, I was wild. I wanted to do everything at once and show them all I needed to play."

Rodman immediately put up a dumb, off-target 3-pointer.

"That's a terrible low-percentage shot," said Billy Cunningham, "but it's not really a shot. It's a message. It's Rodman telling Chuck Daly he's pissed off."

Just about every starter on both teams was in foul trouble by the end of the fourth. When a journeymen named Granville Waiters checked in for Chicago, announcer Dick Stockton described him as old and bald, a garbage-time player. But with Waiters on the floor, the Bulls were able to run a defensive play that would come to characterize the team: "the trap." If Jordan and Waiters caught a Piston alone with the ball in the back court—it was rare for teams to pressure full court—they'd close the trap, circling and surrounding the ball carrier, making it nearly impossible for him to find a passing lane. Ideally the trapped man would turn the ball over or be forced to call a time-out. But it was risky. Running the trap meant leaving someone open. The gamble was that the ball carrier would be too confused and obstructed to find the open man. When successful, the trap was especially gratifying, a game within a game—a game of keep-away. But it was only moderately successful against the Pistons in 1987–88. Detroit was too athletic to be stopped by Granville Waiters.

The Bulls were up by 3 with five minutes left. Rodman got three rebounds on a single possession, frustrating the Bulls, taking them out of their game. Collins called time-out. The crowd roared. There were barbs in the noise, taunts. The Teflon dome shuddered in the wind. Collins's sweat dripped onto the wipe-board, turning his play into a smudge.

Aw hell, just get the ball to Michael.

The Pistons led by a point with two minutes left. Jordan went for the hoop and was fouled as soon as he stepped into the paint. He made one of two free throws—Jordan's 57th point—tying the game at 110.

Chuck Daly called a time-out. He drew up a play. Isiah got the inbound at the top of the key, dribbled back and forth, watching the seconds bleed away—*9, 8, 7*—and threw to Laimbeer, who, seeing the defense close, hurried a pass, which was stolen by Brad Sellers, who got the ball to Jordan, who Laimbeer pulled down at midcourt. Two free throws. Jordan hit both.

Game over.

CBS reporter Pat O'Brien put a microphone in MJ's face less than a minute later.

"Do you know how many points you scored?"

"No. The win! The win is all we wanted."

THE PLAYOFFS

The 1987–88 NBA Playoffs opened in four cities on April 28, followed by four more cities on April 29. Sixteen teams competed: the Lakers, Spurs, Trail Blazers, Jazz, Mavericks, Rockets, Nuggets, and SuperSonics in the West; the Celtics, Knicks, Hawks, Bucks, Bulls, Cavaliers, Pistons, and Bullets in the East. It was best of five in round one, best of seven thereafter. To be champion, a team had to win four series and a minimum of fifteen postseason games.

It took the Bulls—who opened their first round in a deliriously jam-packed Chicago Stadium—the full five to beat Cleveland, a team that would have excelled in any other era. By Game 5, Scottie Pippen, the rookie who'd spent the season coming off the bench, was starting, having earned a spot he'd retain for a generation. In this way alone, the series was significant. By the end, the Bulls, who closed Game 5 with Jordan, Pippen, Grant, Paxson, and Oakley on the floor, were four-fifths of the way to the lineup that would win three straight titles.

It likewise took the Pistons the full five to defeat the Bullets, which was just the sort of veteran team—Bernard King, Moses Malone—that can surprise you. One bad quarter, one lapse in concentration, and it's over. Asked what he'd learned from the series, Laimbeer said, "That every game is a bitch."

The Bulls faced the Pistons in the second round, but the series did not quite live up to expectations. The Bulls, though well on their way, were still not ready. It wasn't just size and speed they lacked, it was maturity. The Pistons goaded, taunted, heckled, and fouled, and the Bulls fell for it every time, forgetting their game plan, losing their composure, and being suckered into the pit, which is just where Detroit wanted them.

As Mike Tyson said, "Everyone has a plan until they get punched in the mouth."

"The Pistons' primary objective was to throw us off our game by raising the level of violence on the floor," said Phil Jackson. "They pounded away at our players ruthlessly, pushing, shoving, sometimes even headbutting, to provoke them into retaliating. As soon as that happened, the battle was over. Anger was the Bulls' real enemy, not the Pistons."

"We would target players," said Rodman. "It was almost like a football mentality. Our strength was intimidating guys, taking them out of their game so we could run the game the way we wanted it to be run."

It was clear by the end of Game 1, which the Pistons took 93–82, that the Bulls were still missing a few key pieces, a solid inside presence most notably. This would eventually be center Bill Cartwright, who arrived the following year from the Knicks in a trade for Charles Oakley. With Dave Corzine guarding Rodman or Salley, Detroit might get four or five offensive rebounds on a single possession in 1987–88. It was like watching a kid playing against a grown-up.

Jordan made a point of not shooting in the first quarter of Game 2 at the Silverdome. He wanted to get his teammates going, which would take pressure off him in turn, giving him room to operate. Jordan hit 90 percent of his shots that night, collecting 36 points and basically winning the game by himself.

Final Score: Chicago 105, Detroit 95.

Isiah said Game 3 would be the crucible of the series, even the season. It was time to shut down the Jordan Show and seize fate by the neck. Zeke showed up for the travel-day practice carrying a stack of Chicago newspapers: "Have you all seen what they're calling us?" The Windy City columnists believed that, with their Game 2 win, the Bulls had broken Detroit's spirit.

A storm blew through Chicago early in Game 3, a freak system that came from the West. The sky turned black at midday. Streetlamps with sensors flicked on across the Loop. The thunder came with the lightning; the beast was right on top of you. Rain poured down. Upper Wacker Drive was a snarl. Lower Wacker Drive filled up like a bowl. A bartender stood in the window of the Billy Goat Tavern, looking out. When the wind arrived, it hit the skyscrapers like an open hand. The storm warning was up-graded first to a tornado watch, then to a tornado warning. People scurried for cover on Michigan Avenue and State Street. The gusts turned umbrellas inside out. Even people inside the stadium could feel the storm. The broadcast was knocked briefly off the air, but the game continued, meaning, for a time, that only those in attendance knew what was happening. To them, the weather was too perfect, a pathetic fallacy, the outer world reflecting the gloom felt by every fan who watched the Pistons descend on the Bulls with renewed focus.

Bill Laimbeer fed on dark energy. He was a Bond villain, a heel. He hit a shot from the top of the key, pumped his fist, then caught Jordan with a quick, dirty hip check as the Bulls were run-ning up-court. Jordan reeled, turned, and charged at Laimbeer.

From that moment, Jordan, who later said Laimbeer had hit him "in the balls," forgot the mission, lost his composure, timing, and shot.

"It distracted us," said Doug Collins. "And we never recovered."

The Bulls scored just 79 points that night, their worst performance of the postseason. Having come for a coronation, Chicago fans witnessed a funeral.

What followed seemed inevitable: a desultory performance in Game 4—the Bulls did even worse, scoring just 77 points—followed by the Bulls' final loss of the season in Game 5 in Detroit. What people remember is Michael and Isiah going up for a rebound in the third quarter. Michael caught Isiah with an elbow in the head. Isiah was unconscious before he hit the ground. For a moment, the game continued around him. Then the whistles blew. Trainers and coaches came running. Detroit assistant Ron Rothstein waved smelling salts under Zeke's nose. His eyes opened. In them, you recognized fundamental questions: *Who am I? Why am I here?* His vision cleared; he got up and stumbled off. They said he was done for the night. He went to the locker room, found the door locked, and so, not knowing where else to go, returned to the bench. The announcer said he'd come back not to play but only to support his team. Then, a minute later, the same announcer said he would play but only if absolutely necessary. A few minutes after that, he was out on the floor. The Bulls were rallying. Zeke was told to stanch the bleeding.

Bulls fans dismiss Isiah Thomas as a whiner, a flopper prone to bitching and complaining, like the rest of the Bad Boy Pistons. But I've never bought this because I actually watched Isiah play. There was no one grittier, tougher, or more willing to sacrifice his body and well-being to the cause. As a regular-sized person in a big man's game, he swallowed more than an adult portion of abuse, was knocked down, knocked out, and stepped on but almost always came back, reenergized, angry, and ready to play.

What he did that afternoon at the Silverdome is proof. At 1:55, he was out cold in the paint. At 2:10, he was pulling on the bolted locker room door. At 2:30 he was back in the game, carrying his team across the finish line.

The Bulls were within a basket when Zeke returned. Five minutes later, when he checked back out, they were finished. He'd scored 9 consecutive points in three minutes to end Chicago's season.

Boston had blown through the Knicks in the first round, then met the Atlanta Hawks just as the Hawks were hitting their stride. Detroit—whom the Celtics would face if they reached the conference finals—had to watch and wait.

Boston crushed Atlanta in Game 1 at Boston Garden, with the front line—Bird, Parish, McHale—combining for 85 points. They did the same in Game 2. Then, on the way to Atlanta, seemingly every Celtic caught a cold. In addition to cortisone, the doctor was shooting players full of antibiotics. The ball looked like it weighed a hundred pounds in Bird's hands at the Omni Coliseum in Game 3. He played forty minutes and led Boston with 22 points, but the numbers give the wrong impression—he belonged in bed. The Celtics, having sneezed themselves into a stupor, lost three out of the next four games, setting up a Game 7 in Boston Garden that some consider the greatest game ever played.

"The game started, and even though the crowd was crazy, I remember it being quiet," Atlanta guard Tree Rollins said. "I could hear sneakers screeching on the floor. I could hear coaches screaming out plays. I could hear my teammates talking on offense and defense. That was the highest level of concentration I attained as a player."

Kevin McHale scored 33 points that night. Doc Rivers collected 16 points and 18 assists. Danny Ainge hit two big 3s late. But Bird vs. Wilkins was the show.

"We were running downcourt, me, Bird, and Kevin Willis," recalled Wilkins, who was shooting hoops behind his house in suburban Georgia as he told me this story decades later. "Kevin reaches across to me and says, 'Don't let that son of a gun score any more, man.' And I'm like, 'Shut up. He can hear you!' And I look over, and Bird's eyes are like *this* big. I knew it was on after that. Those are the words that woke him up. That's really when the shoot-out began."

"My mindset in the playoffs was you play, see how the game is going, figure out what your team needs, and do that," said Bird. "We were rolling early and I was just trying to feel out the game. Dominique was scoring and I just watched. Then, in the fourth, I got hot. That's when Dominique and me started matching basket for basket."

"Bird was hitting impossible shots," said Willis. "Dominique, he was not going to be shown up, especially in a big game. So it became a show. Even though we were in the game, we were really just watching the show."

"It was like HORSE," said Atlanta forward Cliff Levingston. "Bird makes this shot off the glass. Dominique comes down— off the glass. Bird goes all net. Dominique goes all net. Larry gets a layup. Dominique gets a layup.

"Larry would tell you where he was going to shoot the ball, and how he was going to shoot it," Levingston continued. "He would take you all over the floor, setting picks, coming back, and next thing you know, you look up and he's on his favorite spot and you're like, 'Oh no!'"

The Lakers had gathered in Magic Johnson's mansion in Bel Air to watch the game on TV. They were hooting and hollering every basket.

Byron Scott said Atlanta would win; Wilkins was just too hot.

"No, no," said Magic. "Don't underestimate my boy Larry!"

Bird won the game and the series on the last shot: a 3-pointer taken a foot away from Atlanta's bench.

According to Albert Einstein, if you get in a spaceship and travel as far as you can in one direction, you'll eventually return to the place from which you started. This is something like what happened to the Pistons between June 3, 1987, when they were closed out by the Celtics in Game 7 of the Eastern Conference Finals, and May 25, 1988, when they returned to Boston for Game 1 of the same round, only now improved by the experience and humiliation of defeat.

At this point in the season, the Pistons' depth posed a huge problem for Boston and their comparatively shallow, and aging, roster. That year, when Boston pulled their starters for a rest, the Pistons' second team, which included two future Hall of Famers and four All-Stars, ran up the score, forcing Celtics coach K. C. Jones to return his starters to the floor before they were ready, further stressing what was already a roster of beat-up old men. "They were as deep as any team in the league, and had players who could really play defense," said Bird. "They had nine legitimate NBA players. We were basically in trouble from the word go."

"By 1987–88, we were no longer the team we had been," Danny Ainge told me. "It was injury, it was having laid it on the line year after year. McHale was not the player he had been, and neither was Bird. It was his back, his whole body. And then, just when you thought help was coming in the form of Len Bias . . . Well, you know. After that, it was just us and eternity."

The Pistons took Game 1 at Boston Garden, stealing home court advantage, which Boston had worked for all season. The Celtics won Game 2, but it took double overtime. Bird was cold from the start; experts wondered if he'd been depleted in the Game 7 shoot-out against the Hawks. But McHale rose to the occasion. Appearing mechanical and stiff, McHale resembled the Iron Giant and seemed to play the way my father did in our driveway when he got home from work, in his loafers and suit, jacket off, sleeves rolled, change jingling as he lumbered to the hoop. He'd turn his back to the basket eight feet out, use his butt to push me aside, then grunt as he hit the hook. While McHale may have seemed more Tin Man than Wizard, if you looked closely, you'd see that his footwork was complicated, well practiced, mesmerizing. He was arguably the best post-up player in the NBA. Once he got a defender one-on-one, there were a dozen ways he could finish. He scored 32 points in Game 1 and 15 points in Game 2, and averaged over 30 a night in the series. He forced Game 2 into a second overtime when a pass meant for Bird went askew and found him at the 3-point line, where McHale hit his first trey in over a decade to tie the score.

By Game 3, which the Pistons won at home, it was clear that Bird was in a slump. It's the biggest fear of athletes, painters, musicians, and every kind of artist. A shooter in a slump is a person who discovers his key no longer fits his lock and he can't get in to his own house. Until he finds the groove, he won't know how to be who he was. "Slump." Merely speaking the word aloud is bad luck. That's why players hate to be asked about their shooting woes. If you are asked about it, you think about it, and if you think about it, you're finished.

No one knows what causes a slump. Maybe it's bad luck, or loss of concentration, or a malady of the heart. Maybe it's the moon moving into the seventh house. Maybe it's exhaustion. Boston's series against the Hawks was tiring, the victory Pyrrhic. Bird especially had been spent like cash. Or maybe it was Detroit's defense. That's what Bird believed. It wasn't his age, he said, or his state of mind. It was Dennis Rodman and John Salley. "We send Rodman in to body him up," Chuck Daly explained. "We don't even let him turn around with the ball. We don't even let him get his hands on it."

"I'm doing *something* wrong," Bird told reporters. "I start out and hit a couple of shots early, then, after that, I lose my rhythm. My confidence is not where it was in my last game against Atlanta. Sometimes you leave your confidence on the practice court."

Bird thought a moment, then said, "There's nothing wrong with me. Stop asking. Stop looking. I'm fine."

Daly suggested that Bird was playing possum, hanging back, waiting for his moment. That was his aura, the fear Bird struck in opposing coaches. Even if he appeared out of sync, they worried it was part of a plan. "Larry Bird is a time bomb," Daly said. "We're waiting for him to go off."

Bird continued to miss in Game 3, going six for seventeen. McHale did his best to carry Boston, but it wasn't enough. The Celtics faded late, which is the way with rickety dynasties. The heart is there, but the legs turn to jelly.

Boston squeaked past Detroit in Game 4. The fact that Laimbeer, whom every Celtic loathed, passed up what would've been a game-winning shot at the end, was all Bird wanted to talk about in the locker room. "Even if I'd been oh for three hundred, I'd have taken that shot," he said. "But I knew there was no way he was going to take it. It just isn't in Laimbeer's makeup."

Here's the last marker of the quality dynasty: Even when old, especially when old, they're nearly impossible to close out. Detroit won Game 5 in Boston and clinched in Game 6 at home, but, on both occasions, needed overtime to do it.

Four overtimes in six games.

Rodman got into a brawl with Boston backup Brad Lohaus with eight minutes left in Game 6. Detroit was leading by 12. Referee Earl Strom, known by his characteristic whistle, raced over, hands in the air: *tweet*-pause-*tweet-tweet-tweet!* Players from both benches ran onto the floor, where they were met by the Detroit police. Rodman and Lohaus were ejected. Rodman ran screaming into the tunnel.

Lohaus left to boos, a cacophony that resolved into a chant:

"Boston sucks! Boston sucks! Boston sucks!"

Bird, McHale, and Ainge left the floor with eight seconds to go. Pulling Isiah aside on his way out, McHale said, "Don't be satisfied with just getting to the finals. Win it! They don't like to play physical out there. Go right at them. You guys are really good."

The Lakers swept the Spurs in the first round, which was the only break they caught in the 1988 playoffs. From then on, every Laker series went the distance, the full seven; before it was over, L.A. would play twenty-four postseason games, a record at the time. (The Celtics appeared in twenty-six postseason games in 2008.)

Pat Riley never lost sight of his goal: *Repeat as champions.* The promise hung over the team, set the tempo, was the heartbeat of the playoffs. Fear of failure is a stronger motivator than the prospect of success. It's wonderful to win, but it's an embarrassment to lose. Because of Riley's guarantee, the Lakers could seem less like they were running to something than like they were running from something; not toward the title, but away from humiliation.

They faced the Utah Jazz in the second round, which meant John Stockton and Karl Malone and coach Frank Layden, a Brooklyn-born genius of comical leadership. When reminded of Riley's guarantee of a repeat, Layden said, "I agree with him. That team is awesome." After being blown out in Game 1, Layden said, "I honestly don't see how we can win a single game." When the Jazz surprised the Lakers in Game 2, Layden said, "You just saw Tommy Lasorda strike out Babe Ruth." After a heartbreaking loss in Game 5, Layden refused to talk to the press. A reporter hung a sign on Utah's locker room door: CLOSED TILL CHRISTMAS. It came down to Game 7, which the Lakers won 109–98 at the Forum.

It took the Lakers seven more to dispatch the Dallas Mavericks. For me, the great moment of that series came not on the floor but at a press conference. Magic Johnson was talking to reporters after the Lakers' Game 4 loss in Dallas. Mark Aguirre, who'd vacationed with Magic and Zeke in Hawaii during the off-season, appeared beside the podium with a stack of eight-by-ten Magic Johnson glossies.

He wanted them autographed.

"Is this for real?" asked Magic, who took the pictures and started signing.

"Do that one for Shirley," whispered Aguirre.

Aguirre kissed Magic on both cheeks, then said, "See you in L.A."

Magic arrived at the Forum hours before the start of Game 7. He was nervous, believing anything could happen in a double elimination contest. "It's not just that I thought we *could* lose," he said later. "It's that, at two or three A.M. the night before, lying awake in bed, I was certain we would lose."

He put on his sweats and walked around the empty arena. He was working the problem as he walked. He credited the Mavs' success to a single player, their center Roy Tarpley. He was so young and strong. None of the Lakers had been able to stop him. Assigning the task to Kareem seemed like elder abuse.

Magic was waiting to talk to Coach Riley when he arrived.

"Earvin challenged me," Riley said. "He told me that he wanted to play Tarpley."

Magic: "Exact words? I told him that, if he wanted to keep Tarpley under ten rebounds, let me play him."

Magic had 24 points, 11 assists, and 9 rebounds that night. And he held Tarpley to 7 rebounds. He did it by battling for position, fighting for every loose ball. "That's why my lower back is killing me," said Magic. "He beat me up. I boxed him out, but he made me pay for it."

THE FINALS

For many, a Pistons vs. Lakers final seemed like an Isiah vs. Magic final. They'd been friends since they were kids. Fellow high school standouts in the Midwest, they'd first met in dimly lit gyms and on the sidelines of all-star tournaments. Magic advised the younger Isiah on the big transitions—from high school to college, from amateur to pro. He mentored Zeke, vacationed with Zeke, schooled Zeke in games of one-on-one played behind Magic's mansion in the shadow of the San Gabriel Mountains.

Magic taught Zeke how to order food, how to eat sushi, how to tip a waiter, and how to tie a Windsor knot. He taught him how to win and taught him how to lose. He celebrated his successes and put his failures in perspective. He talked him down when he'd screwed the pooch. He wanted the best for his friend. He'd often said he couldn't wait for Isiah to become an NBA champion. *You can't imagine what it's like,* he told Isiah. *You don't know until it happens.* But now, if he was being honest with himself, he had to admit that the only thing worse than losing in the finals might be losing in the finals to Isiah, which would be like losing to your little brother. For the first time in their friendship, they'd face each other in a zero-sum game. Here's what that meant to Magic: *For me to be happy, my friend must suffer.*

The press made a careful study of the relationship. There were similarities and differences. Magic and Zeke were both finesse players and team leaders who could contribute without scoring. Both were characterized by their contagious smiles. Both were Midwesterners, and both played point guard. Whereas Magic was too big for the position, Isiah was too small. It was only determination, that Nietzschean will, that let Zeke play as big as anyone. Magic seemed genuine, like a truly good guy, a perfect representative of Hollywood and the Showtime Lakers. Isiah was not like that. Isiah smiled but the smile was a mask. It hid more than it revealed. He'd cut you to ribbons and leave you bleeding on the floor, in which case the smile only added to the pain. He seemed disingenuous, a perfect representative of post-industrial Detroit and the Bad Boy Pistons. Though they vacationed together, talked into the night on the phone, and played HORSE on Magic's palm-fringed Bel Air court, neither lost sight of the goal: Bury the other man and walk away with the crown.

They met at center court before every game of the finals, exchanged pleasantries, then kissed—lips to cheek, Parisian style. The kisses grew increasingly perfunctory as the series developed and the bad blood flowed, but never stopped. Their teammates razzed them—*Don't kiss the enemy before battle!*—but Magic and Isiah were determined to prove they could remain civil without sacrificing the edge. But the tensions that would eventually end the friendship were already evident by 1988. Magic resented the way Isiah, backing up Rodman after the loss in the 1987 playoffs, claimed that Bird's stature in the league was due only to his race. In belittling Magic's great rival, he was diminishing Magic. Ali isn't Ali if Frazier is "just another good player." And, by bringing race into it, Isiah was undermining all the work Magic had done to move the NBA from the fringe to the mainstream.

The L.A. media belittled Isiah and the Pistons in comparison to Magic and the Lakers. On the morning of Game 1, the L.A. *Times* sports section, which predicted a Lakers win in five games, was headlined: IT'S MAGIC VERSUS HIS LITTLE BUDDY, POCKET MAGIC.

According to CBS commentator Brent Musburger, the Pistons would be challenged not just by the Lakers but by the blinding awesomeness of the Hollywood Scene, the glitz of the Fabulous Forum, the nightlife temptations and courtside celebrities. How could a hick like Dennis Rodman focus with Farrah Fawcett sitting right there? How could John Salley from Canarsie, Brooklyn—that's the weeds, out where the mob dumps bodies— play beneath a bleacher full of faces from TV? "I met Sam Kinison!" Salley said after Game 1. "I met Billy Crystal! And Arsenio Hall! I love this town. Billy Crystal was sitting two rows from our bench, and I was like, 'Hey, what's up, Billy Crystal?' He was sitting with Garry Shandling, the white guy with the big lips."

When Musburger ran through story lines before the opening tip, it sounded like a *Sopranos* recap: "Let's start with the Lakers. Without a doubt, they are the team of the eighties. They have won four championships. The drive for five is only four victories away. And there is another goal for this team. If they win this one, they will become the first team since the Celtics in '68 and '69 to win back-to-back NBA championships. For Detroit, the issue is one of emotion. Did they [already] achieve their goal by beating Boston? Or can they climb back emotionally and recapture that spirit against the Lakers?"

GAME 1

At the start of the game the Pistons, gathered around Chuck Daly beside their bench, let out a communal cheer, then ran onto the floor. Laimbeer came out with his head down. The Forum was a few miles from his high school. He returned with an air of defiance and played angry from the first minute. Predictions that the Lakers would win the series in five games, or even in a sweep, infuriated Laimbeer.

Detroit had played a half-court game against the Celtics, but Chuck Daly sent his team into Game 1 with a different plan. The Lakers were known for speed, but the Pistons were younger and just as fast. They came out running, meeting speed with speed on one end and wrenching defensive pressure on the other, employing a full-court press early. The Pistons were like an upstart nation trying to shock a superpower with a quick surprise, a blitzkrieg. Hit 'em with everything, and see what happens.

Laimbeer battling Abdul-Jabbar was a matchup that would define the series. Laimbeer did his best to muscle Abdul-Jabbar, who was four inches taller. On play after play, you'd see Kareem, back to the hoop, leaning against Laimbeer's forearm. "I can't block him," Laimbeer explained, "so I just try to push him into no-man's-land and hope he misses when he shoots."

Kareem went one for eight in Game 1. Everything else worked for Detroit too. Dumars hit his jump shots. Isiah set the tempo and drove the lane. Laimbeer was perfect from the outside. Dantley was having what Isiah described as "his best game as a pro."

"During the season we had given [Dantley] the nickname 'Teacher' because he so often takes his opponent to school," Isiah explained. Well, he schooled the hell out of the Lakers that night, Isiah said, making fourteen of sixteen field goals and scoring 34 points.

The Pistons started the game with an 8–0 run, sucking the energy out of the Forum. Even the Laker Girls looked flat. At one point, Worthy collided with Laimbeer and fell, landing on his hip. Worthy's howl of pain could be heard in the upper level.

Then the starters gave way to the second teams. The Lakers had a good second team—Mychal Thompson, Wes Matthews, Kurt Rambis—but Detroit's was better. Edwards, Salley, Rodman, Vinnie Johnson. No one in the league could match that bench.

As often happened, Vinnie Johnson—"the Microwave"— caught fire as soon as he entered the game. On such nights, it looked like he was just having fun, like he was back in Brooklyn where he used to ride his bike for miles in search of a game. He stayed on when the starters returned. He dished the ball cross-court to Laimbeer, who hit a 3-pointer from the corner. Perhaps because there were only four seconds left in the half, Kareem in-bounded lackadaisically. Isiah picked off the pass, turned, and jumped, releasing a rainbow that dropped for another 3 as the horn blew. Six points in seven seconds. Detroit went into the locker room with a 17-point lead.

Worthy was back for the second half, which made a big differ-ence. The Pistons had trouble containing Worthy's mix of power, intelligence, and speed. It was only his retiring nature, his life in the shadows—first of Jordan at UNC, and then of Magic in L.A.— that kept Worthy from being rated among the top twenty-five to ever play. He might have paled a bit in the regular season—he tended to fade in the Dog Days of January and February—but played his best, and about as well as anyone has ever played, in the playoffs, when it mattered most, a classic mark of excellence. Great teams need at least two great players. The second of those two usually dims in proximity. For the Bulls, that was Pippen. For the Celtics, it was McHale. For the Lakers, it was Worthy. Without "Big Game James," Magic does not become Magic, and L.A. is not Showtime.

The Pistons continued to win the hustle plays. Rodman blocked shots. Isiah scored over and under Byron Scott. Vinnie Johnson torched Lakers guard Michael Cooper, whom many, in-cluding Bird, considered the best defender in the league. "I think the Lakers need a little nudge, a scare, before they can get their game going," announcer Dick Stockton said on CBS. "Maybe that's the function of this game. To scare the Lakers. The way of the format, if they don't get it together, they might never get back to the Forum."

The arena had emptied by the end of the fourth quarter—that's L.A. too.

"The Pistons have done to the Lakers what they did to the Celtics," Dick Stockton said. "They landed the first blow and shocked the world champions."

Final Score: Detroit 105, L.A. 93.

"We are for real," Adrian Dantley said after the game. "Everyone was expecting us to lose in four or five. We got guys that are hungry, we got some character. We know they are favored, but we gonna give them a fight."

GAME 2

The Detroit locker room was raucous. John Salley had gotten hold of a camcorder and was filming everything. He lingered on Laimbeer, who'd cornered the sports guy from L.A.'s Channel 9, who had picked the Pistons to lose in four. Laimbeer had backed the poor man into his locker stall, among the practice jerseys, Tiger Balm, jockstraps, and gigantic shoes. Towering over the reporter, with a finger in his face, Laimbeer demanded "a formal apology to the team and the people of Detroit, right here, in front of the camera"—Salley's camera—"so we can all see what a jerk you are." The reporter seemed confused and scared. He looked at Laimbeer to see if he was joking, raised his hands in surrender, and said, "I apologize, O great city of Detroit."

Ten minutes before tipoff, Chuck Daly kicked out the press and talked to his team. He spoke with head down, improvising. "Yes, we did what needed to be done in the first game, but the Lakers are dangerous. You have poked the bear. Not only do the Lakers want to beat you. Now they want to humiliate you. They want to embarrass you in front of your friends and family. And they can. They're good enough. Don't let them do it. Let's get them now, when they're still stunned and confused. Never forget: The team you're playing is a great team."

This would turn out to be the theme of Game 2. If the first game had been about the Pistons shocking the Lakers, the second was the sequel, the middle volume of a trilogy that appears under the title *The Empire Strikes Back*.

Magic and Isiah met at center court before tipoff for their kiss. Lakers announcer Chick Hearn called it as if calling a pick-and-roll: "Isiah goes up! He's got Magic by the shoulders! He's pulling him in! And here it comes. Ladies and gentlemen: the kiss!" Meanwhile, Billy Cunningham was explaining the significance of L.A.'s Game 1 loss on CBS: "The Pistons now know they can in fact beat the Lakers at the Forum."

Kareem missed a skyhook on L.A.'s first possession. Then shot and missed again. Then again. He'd been off in Game 1 and spent most of the second half on the bench, head in hands, sad-eyed, moping. Riley wanted to get him going early in Game 2, hence all the wayward skyhooks. *Keep shooting till you find the groove,* Riley told him. At this point in his career, Kareem could not single-handedly win a game for the Lakers, but he was still essential. Showtime was built around the big man—the players turned around Kareem like planets around a sun. He took up space, collected rebounds, put back wayward shots, and intimidated by his presence. When he was off, everyone played worse. He was just one of those guys: You did not necessarily notice him when he was going good, but you could not miss it when he was going bad. When he finally hit the skyhook on his fifth attempt, you could see his shoulders lift.

The Pistons started out even colder. Dumars and Laimbeer missed shots. Isiah lost the dribble. Detroit scored just 1 point in the first five minutes. Chuck Daly paced the sideline in a double-breasted suit. He "dresses in silk," said Dick Stockton, "but speaks in denim."

Twenty-six-year-old Lakers guard Byron Scott, who led L.A. in scoring in the regular season, started making shots in the first quarter. Treys—one, two, three, just like that. He hung in the air after he released, arms extended, eyes tight with concentration.

Magic looked beleaguered in comparison, jersey loose on his shoulders, a brace on each knee, face gaunt and haggard. He was recovering from the flu. Advised to skip the game by his doctor, he played anyway. He'd lost eight pounds in a week and looked skinnier than he had in years. *If he can shake the lethargy*, Billy Cunningham said on CBS, *the flu might turn out to be a blessing in disguise.* He started running in the second quarter, passing and driving the lane, using his speed to open up the defense.

Chuck Daly was screaming on the Detroit bench, venting his rage on a single player. It was Chuck Nevitt, the Pistons' twelfth man, the stand-up comedian and 7'5" human exclamation point.

How can you get in trouble when you don't play?

Nevitt had been caught by a TV camera chatting, during the game, with Billy Crystal. Nevitt later said it was the biggest mistake of his career, but it's so hard to refuse a movie star. "Billy just wanted to know a couple of nicknames of guys on our team," Nevitt explained. "Like 'Toad' for Rick Mahorn and 'Buddha' for James Edwards. And I didn't want to be rude."

"What the hell are you doing? Giving him our game plan?" Daly asked Nevitt. "You don't see me talking to Jack Nicholson. Pay attention!"

When Daly needed an answer for Magic and Worthy, he looked to the bench and signaled to Rodman. Dennis limbered up on the sideline, long legs stretched before him, head down, pulling on his toes, then checked in and went to work under the basket. Operating via an intricate geometry, Rodman would corral three or four straight rebounds. At times, it seemed as if the Lakers would never get the ball.

Magic and Kareem battled the lunatic, but they looked tired.

Late in the second quarter, Rodman switched to cover Worthy, who'd been hitting his shots. That's how Rodman was used most of his career: Figure out who is hot, put Dennis in his face. His strategy was simple. If a player was converting from a particular spot, Rodman beat him to that spot, then held his ground. You could not stop looking at him. The jug ears, the amused grin, the way he walked—on the balls of his feet, like a dancer. There was an oddball magnetism in every Wormy gesture. When necessary, he'd foul. Sometimes he'd foul hard. The refs had to pay extra attention, and as a result he'd sometimes get called for things he didn't do. He'd never argue when this happened. He'd smile, turn away, then chew on the top of his jersey.

But Rodman could not cover everyone. When Worthy was tied up, he got the ball to Kareem, who, as per Riley's plan, had established the skyhook. He scored 11 points in the first half. The Lakers led by 10 at the break. Kareem started the third quarter by hitting another skyhook. "He can't do it every night," said Cunningham, "but, when there is a big game like this one, Kareem responds."

The Lakers ran, the Pistons hung on. Dumars hit a jumper off the glass to put Detroit within 4 at the start of the fourth. Magic could be heard yelling at his teammates during a time-out: "Come on, now! Remember who we are!"

But the Lakers had no answer for Rodman, who snagged and put back an offensive rebound to tie the game with eight minutes left. The Lakers almost seemed offended. As if they'd been lied to. The Pistons were not supposed to be *this* good. Here was the goal: Get possession, run the break, score 2. Here was the problem: Detroit kept winning the rebounds, or at least contesting them, turning every loose ball into a battle, which made it impossible to run. What's more, the Pistons, especially Dantley, a master of the art, were drawing an inordinate number of fouls, which meant the Lakers usually started with an inbound pass, giving Detroit time to set up at their own end, making it impossible to run the break.

Riley called a time-out with five minutes left. Randy New-man's "I Love L.A." blasted from the PA system. The lyrics—"Rollin' down the Imperial Highway/ With a big nasty redhead at my side"—amped the crowd, who cheered the song, cheered their city, life, and team, a cheer that seemed to pick up and carry the Lakers back out onto the court, where they caught and rode that energy.

The Pistons stood stubbornly in the face of the breaking wave, and the result was an electric finish, these two great dynasties ex-changing blows. It seemed less a matter of who would win than who would refuse to lose. According to the Pistons, the decisive moment came with two minutes left. Detroit was 3 points behind. The Lakers had the ball. There was one second left on the shot clock. Kareem threw up a desperate skyhook. It came up short. Air ball. Detroit's possession. Isiah threw a strike to Rodman, who was all alone up-court, far behind the defense. You could see the gears turning in his head. How will I finish? What kind of statement will I make? "I was going to do *something*," he said later. "A three-sixty? A one-eighty? I don't know. Something!" But a whistle blew before Rodman could make his move. The referee said Kareem's shot had grazed the rim, giving the Lakers a fresh shot clock. Rodman smiled as he handed back the ball, but you knew what he was thinking.

"That ball was so beyond the rim it was out of the building," Daly said later.

Riley smirked at this: "I think Chuck needs new glasses to go with his fancy new suit."

The Lakers scored on the extra possession, meaning the blown call resulted in a 4-point swing that decided Game 2.

Final Score: L.A. 108, Detroit 96.

The Lakers had answered the Pistons' opening blow with a gritty, stubborn performance that not only knotted the series but suggested it would be a battle, a war of attrition; the winner would almost certainly be the side willing to suffer more.

On one of the game's last plays, 175-pound Isiah Thomas, who'd gone up to contest a shot, collided with 205-pound Byron Scott. You could hear the sickening thump. Isiah dropped like a sparrow. He got up slowly, biting his lip. This was Isiah's first injury of the finals, but not his last.

GAME 3

It was the first game of the finals in Michigan, which made it special for Magic. Michigan would always be his home. He'd given tickets to family and friends. His father, who'd never seen him in the playoffs—Earvin Sr. was afraid to fly—was seated just behind the Lakers bench. Forty thousand people were crammed into the Silverdome at tipoff, an NBA Playoffs record.

Earl Strom, the game's most storied referee—he kicked Red Auerbach out of an All-Star Game in 1967; he punched out a fan in Denver in 1970—was in charge of the officiating crew. You noticed his silver hair and hard face. He called for the opening tip with his characteristic whistle—*tweet*-pause-*tweet-tweet-tweet*—and the game began.

Kareem hit his first shot. Then Dantley scored. Then Scott. Then Dantley again. Then Magic. Then Laimbeer. Then A. C. Green. Then Isiah, going end to end, bobbing and turning like a stick in whitewater rapids. Zeke was reminding the Lakers that this was the Pistons' house, but the Lakers didn't care. Running and scoring, they gained confidence with each play.

Fans and analysts talk about home court advantage, but it can be a relief for a team—especially a team burdened with history and the guarantee made by their coach—to go on the road, where there is no past, no movie stars, no Forum Club, and where there are only the teammates who stand beside you in the paint. Hotel instead of house. Bus instead of car. Game 3 was about the Lakers getting away from Hollywood and out into the country where they could remember who the hell they were: *Showtime!*

Chuck Daly seemed to shrink into himself on the sideline, registering each Magic-to-Worthy fast break like a physical blow. He looked at the scoreboard, then at his team, then signaled his bench. Time for the cavalry. Rodman was chewing gum and blowing bubbles, which seemed to carry his thoughts: *Kill, kill, kill.* It's not only that you felt the energy change when Rodman checked in; you heard it. Los Angeles players who'd been going about their business quietly began shouting and cursing. The Worm was trailed by profanity. *Move your ass, shithead! . . . Fuck off, Rodman! . . . Back up, you fucking asshole!*

The Lakers led 23–21 at the end of the first quarter.

The Pistons started their bench in the second quarter with the exception of Isiah, who stayed on the floor, determined to mark his presence, which he did less by scoring than by setting up his teammates—Vinnie, Salley, Buddha. Riley told the press that he was less concerned with Detroit's starting five—who he believed were no match for his first team—than with their bench. He respected Dantley and Thomas, but worried about Edwards, Salley, and Rodman. Their appearance in the second quarter, just as the game was settling into a rhythm, changed everything. Edwards, unlike Laimbeer, could post up Kareem. Salley, with those freakishly long arms, could reach from what seemed like the stands to swat the ball away from Worthy. Rodman, with his eccentric intensity, could drive even the most coolheaded Laker to distraction.

Riley had studied every matchup on film. He showed highlights to Mychal Thompson and Michael Cooper before Game 3. "You see what's happening here," said the coach. "Edwards has you mesmerized. You're just standing there watching him."

Michael Cooper was a special kind of disappointment. The best defender on the Lakers, he'd lost his shooting touch—he was clanking every 3-point attempt, yielding long rebounds that Rodman and Salley turned into fast breaks. And that slump, which should have been contained to offense, had put him into a funk that bled into his defense. He was moping, playing tight. For long stretches, the Lakers were being carried by two players, Worthy and Magic. And it wasn't enough, not when playing this nine-headed beast.

The crowd—40,000 strong—roared like a diesel engine on an inky black night. The Pistons fed on the energy, which, now and then, tipped toward disorder. Isiah Thomas and Michael Cooper chased a loose ball into the stands. They fell across the court-side seats, where they were surrounded by fans. A group of men holding tall frosty malts stood the players on their feet and pushed them back out.

The Lakers led by a point at halftime. This was the first truly intense game of what would become one of the most intense finals ever played. There was a spirit, a determination. It was as if the players and coaches suddenly realized that this series was going to be a battle. Not four games, or six—it was going all the way.

The Lakers had come into the finals believing in their destiny, in the myth Pat Riley had wound around them like twine. They knew they would win, because that's what history wanted. The repeat was the best story the game could tell. Then came Game 1, when the Pistons not only beat the Lakers but beat them up. Even Game 2 went to the wire. The Lakers had nearly been swept at the Forum, which convinced Detroit that they could win, which changed the way both teams played. This is when the Lakers, having looked into the buzz saw and seen their own demise, took the time to stop, regroup, and start again.

When L.A. took the floor in the second half of Game 3, they were a different team. A. C. Green, who'd been ineffective, began battling Detroit's front line under the basket. Blocked Rodman. Blocked Salley. Blocked Laimbeer and threw him to the floor. Laimbeer looked to Earl Strom for the foul and Strom just stared: *Live by the cheap shot, die by the cheap shot.* The Lakers took over with speed and finesse, touch passes and dunks. Magic pulled every lever. Worthy rushed from the wing. Scott, Kareem, Cooper—

everyone contributed. Los Angeles outscored Detroit 31–18 in the third quarter of Game 3, then continued to push the pace.

Led by Rodman and Thomas, the Pistons staged a comeback in the fourth. Isiah tried to close the gap himself, scoring half his points in the second half. But it wasn't enough. Chuck Daly stormed on the sideline, pompadour flying. He yelled at his players and yelled at Earl Strom. When he ran onto the floor, Strom threw him out with a heave. The crowd booed as Daly made the walk of shame—across the floor, arms swinging, charcoal-gray double-breasted jacket neatly buttoned.

Fans sent down a shower of beer cups and wrappers.

"I'd like to get one of those idiots down here and throw something at *them*," Billy Cunningham said.

Kareem, who'd been taken out when it seemed the Lakers had the game in hand, turned and glared at the spectators in the way of a teacher who'd been hit in the neck with a spitball. He looked disappointed, as if he'd expected better.

Final Score: Lakers 99, Pistons 86.

The Lakers played as if they were ten years younger that night. "[The Pistons] finally saw the real Lakers," said Billy Cunningham. "They have to come back and be ready to compete with *that* team."

The Lakers seemed less ebullient than relieved after the buzzer.

"We finally played the game we wanted to play," said Magic.

"They've made a lot of statements in the press," said Worthy. "We read that. We heard that. That was incentive to us. We're the champions, and we remain the champions until someone takes that away."

GAME 4

Pat Riley called Magic out before Game 4. He felt he needed to issue a challenge—otherwise his team might settle back and lose momentum. That's the job of a coach in the playoffs: Read the mood, press the buttons. Magic was having a great series, which did not matter. Riley knew what he had to do. As the team listened, he told Magic he was sick and tired of his love affair with Isiah. "At some point," said Riley, "you will have to make a choice between your buddy and your team. Here's my question: Will you have the guts to put Isiah on the floor when the time comes?

"We are waiting for you to prove your loyalty."

In the Pistons locker room, Isiah was thinking less about the Lakers than about his own life—his back, which he'd bruised in his collision with Byron Scott in Game 2; and his wife, who, according to Chuck Daly, was "about ten months pregnant."

"I don't know who walks worse right now, Zeke or his wife," said Daly.

"Game Four is pivotal," Laimbeer told the *Detroit Free Press*. "If we lose this one, it'll be very hard to come back in the series. This is a must win."

Isiah and Magic kissed before Game 4, but, if you looked closely, you'd see it was an air-kiss. Over the course of the night, each of them would be called on to choose: Friendship or team?

The Lakers hoped Game 3 had made the Pistons doubt themselves, but the Pistons were maddeningly resilient. They were too dumb to know when they were beat, so they weren't.

Mahorn and Laimbeer double-teamed Abdul-Jabbar early— *Don't let him get established.* Pounded him, whacked him, checked and shoved him when no one was looking. "These guys were more than physical—they were vicious," said Magic. "They tried to intimidate us, take us out of our game. They'd foul, then hit you once more after that. They'd stand over you to make sure you knew who'd done it."

Chuck Daly hardly ever let Magic face the same defender twice in a row. Someone different covered him each time down the floor—Rodman, Dumars, Salley. It threw off and frustrated him. He was still effective but could not get into the groove, that metronomic swing.

On the other side of the court, Detroit was firing on all cylinders. Dantley had complained about not getting the ball in Game 2. He was one of those guys who needs to shoot ten or fifteen times a game; without the ball in his hands, he faded into the wallpaper. So they fed him, and he scored. He led everyone with 27 points that night.

Then, just as Dantley started to tire late in the opening quarter, Vinnie Johnson came off the bench and started hitting. Here was the rule with VJ: If he missed his first two shots, he wouldn't be a factor. If he made his first two, he wouldn't miss again. Oh, the miseries and joys of the streak shooter, who can't hit one minute and can't miss the next! He has higher highs and lower lows than anyone else in the game. When Vinnie sank his first shot, Billy Cunningham said, "If he hits his next . . ." Then, as Cunningham prattled on, Vinnie dropped his second jumper ten seconds after the first, and the announcer said, "Oh, boy! Here we go!"

Pat Riley was kneeling on the sideline, a silken knee on the linoleum, frowning as he watched the game unfold. His hair was shiny black. It was impossible to tell if this was styling gel or sweat. By guaranteeing a repeat, Riley had staked his reputation. Those who make a guarantee and win—Joe Namath before Super Bowl III—become legends. Those who make a guarantee and lose—Patrick Ewing before Game 6 of the 2000 Eastern Conference Finals—become cautionary tales.

Detroit began to pull away at the start of the second quarter. The Pistons' bench outscored the Lakers bench 20–1. For Daly, the biggest concern was the deep bruise on Isiah's back, which made it hard for him to run or jump. Isiah later said he limited himself to set shots—feet on the ground—after the first few minutes. Byron Scott sent Isiah to the floor with an elbow late in the second. Zeke had to roll onto his stomach and push off with his hands to get back to his feet, a detail Riley would notice with interest.

Detroit was up 58–51 at the half.

Whatever chance the Lakers had of coming back vanished in the third, when Worthy and Magic got into foul trouble. Riley blamed ticky-tack calls, which he believed the Pistons got because Daly had complained so bitterly about the officiating after Game 3. In short, while the Lakers had been playing basketball, Chuck Daly had been playing the refs.

The Lakers had been within striking distance when Magic left with his fourth foul. They were down by 18 and the game felt out of reach when he returned in the fourth quarter. He played with an angry passion, like he still expected to win. At times, he seemed to reel like a drunk on the dance floor, looking for a fight. Then he found it. John Salley had just put Detroit up by 20 with a jumper. Magic got the inbound pass, took the ball down the floor, and bounded toward the hoop. Dantley went up for the block. He collided with Magic, knocking him out of bounds. Magic was pointing and yelling when he got to his feet. Then, because the most hated Bad Boy was conveniently at hand, he shoved Laimbeer, who stumbled, recovered, and shoved back. Teammates and officials got between the players.

Isiah, who'd been stretching on the sideline, checked in before the next play. Playing hurt, Thomas had scored 10 points in the last quarter. He feinted, then passed to Dumars. Magic, having fallen for the feint, stepped into Isiah's path, and the men got tangled. They grappled and shoved and even those in the mezzanine could hear Magic screaming at Zeke. Thomas drove to the hoop on the next play. He went through the air with the ball raised before him. Magic went up to contest and caught Isiah with an elbow to the jaw that the L.A. *Times* called "a forearm shiv." Isiah landed on his bruised back, jumped up, and started throwing punches. Laimbeer got between Magic and Isiah. Talking to Zeke over Laimbeer's shoulder, Magic said, "If I get hit, you get hit."

"Riley told Magic he was going to have to prove his loyalty to his coach, teammates, and fans by putting them ahead of our friendship, and I'm afraid that's what happened," Isiah said later.

Each game has a text and a subtext. The text of Game 4: The Pistons *can* run with the Lakers. The subtext: It's the beginning of the end of the most beautiful friendship in basketball.

It was this game, in which Isiah went after one of America's most beloved athletes, that redefined Zeke from adorable point guard who played for Bobby Knight at Indiana to full-on Bad Boy, willing to sacrifice anything to win.

With four minutes left, Jack Nicholson, who had flown from L.A. to be present for the kill, slunk out, incognito in a bright yellow suit and sunglasses.

Final Score: Detroit 111, L.A. 86.

Detroit fans celebrated, running onto the floor after the buzzer. The Lakers had to push and slug their way to the tunnel. Asked what had happened between him and Magic out there, Isiah said, "We're both trying to win a championship, that's what happened."

GAME 5

It was the last game the Pistons would play at the Silverdome. The new arena had been built and was waiting. When its image—the Palace of Auburn Hills—flashed on the scoreboard before tip-off, the crowd booed. It was like seeing an image of your own obsolescence and death. It was like seeing the world as it would be without you.

The Lakers locker room was quiet. It wasn't fear of defeat that shut the players up. It was rage. Pat Riley had put together a reel of dirty Piston plays from the first four games and made everyone watch. These were not the plays that had drawn fouls. These were the cheap shots that had gone unnoticed, sometimes even by the Lakers themselves. Seeing the panoply in sequence—Laimbeer elbowing Abdul-Jabbar when no one was looking; Mahorn stomping on Worthy's foot; Rodman sliding under an in-flight Magic—was infuriating.

Meanwhile, unaware of the indignation across the hall, the Pistons were talking about Isiah, his bruised back and general circumstance. His wife, Lynn, had given birth to the couple's first child, Joshua Thomas, at 7:00 P.M. the night before. The captain was exhausted and overwhelmed.

For Detroit, Game 5 was a hinge. Win here now, and they'd only need a split in L.A. to choke Riley on his own guarantee.

The Lakers came out running. Everything worked for them early; every strike made sparks. Kareem's skyhook dropped. Magic hit from fifteen feet. Detroit did its best to simply survive. Before the fans understood what was happening, the Lakers were up 8–0. Daly called a time-out, but it didn't arrest the fall. Isiah scored the Pistons' first points, hitting a jump shot that made it 13–2, but the Lakers answered. Daly called a second time-out. He circled up his players. Flanked by assistants, he began barking orders, calling for changes to reverse the flow. As long as there is time, there is hope. Something can always be done, storms can be weathered. Never giving up, fighting on—that's what matters. The rest takes care of itself.

Daly moved Dumars to point guard. He knew the minutes that followed would be physical. He called them "hard minutes." He believed Dumars was in better condition to weather those hard minutes than Isiah, who was hobbled and had been slowing the rush. Better to preserve Isiah for the big moments, the sequences that mattered most. This strategy quickly paid off. Zeke, freed from the dribble, began to run through the paint, forcing L.A.'s forwards to cover the smaller, fleeter man. It was in this way that James Worthy picked up his third foul, which forced him to back off.

Then Dumars, mentally occupied by his role as point guard, started shooting without thinking. He found clarity, and with it the rhythm that had been eluding him. Every time he made a basket, the Silverdome public address announcer joyfully cried: "Joe Doooooooooooo-MARS!"

The Pistons chipped away at the lead. Laimbeer made a gutsy rebound at the end of the first, yanking the ball away from A. C. Green and Kareem, wheeling and throwing downcourt to Vinnie Johnson, who, fresh off the bench, finished with the kind of violent dunk you feel in your molars. Detroit was down by just 3 when the horn blew.

Vinnie Johnson was getting stocky in 1988, less like a nail than like a brick. When he got going, players on both teams made space. Everyone wants to win, no one wants to get killed. The momentum shifted when he began to drive the basket. He hit five out of six, scoring 10 points in a row. And drew fouls. Worthy was the best option for L.A., but Riley, wanting to save him for the second half, kept him on the bench. Buddha Edwards, playing in the space opened by Vinnie Johnson, added another 10. Asked about the all-important second-quarter swing, Edwards later said, "Vinnie was the vaccine. I was the booster."

The Pistons began taunting, baiting the Lakers into stupid fouls. The crowd joined in, the rowdies, the hecklers on the floor. Leon the Barber ranted like a shock jock:

"Hey, Magic! Did you forget it's a team game?"

"Kareem! You're too old, Kareem! Go home and sleep. Or are you already doing that?"

"Is that Worthy? The guy they call Big Game James? It should be No Game James."

A. C. Green, having taken a seat alongside Worthy after *his* third foul, became the Barber's primary focus. Virginity, the vows of chastity and sobriety? Has there ever been a richer target for a heckler?

But the Lakers seemed to feed off the nastiness. It woke them up. Magic's game, normally marked by joy, showed evidence of rage. Fed up with Isiah's flailing elbows, he stepped into the lane and knocked his "best friend" to the floor. Isiah lay on his back longer than necessary, smiling at the ceiling—those perfect teeth, those lovely lashes. He hunched over at the free throw line, holding his back, then hit both shots. Detroit was suddenly up by 7. Then Dantley hit, extending the lead to 9.

Have you ever parked at the end of a runway and watched the planes come in? That's what the crowd sounded like, that roar.

Riley called time. He was shouting at his players, but you couldn't hear him. Probably even his players couldn't hear him. He put Worthy back in despite the foul trouble. *What are we saving him for? If we don't stop them now, the fourth quarter won't matter.*

The Lakers looked frazzled in the last minutes of the first half, out of sorts, on the verge of panic. It was Kareem alone, the consummate professional, who kept his cool. He was always at his best in bad times. He set picks, boxed out Pistons, battled for rebounds, drew fouls, made free throws. The jumper he hit just before the horn gave him 18 points for the night. "If it wasn't for Kareem Abdul-Jabbar out there on the floor for the Lakers," Billy Cunningham said, "this game would be over."

"It's just basketball," Pat Riley told Brent Musburger during halftime. "Our job in the third quarter is simple: Play our game, tie the score, go from there."

The Pistons started the third with a 9-point lead. Worthy and Green were back on the floor. Kareem was still clicking—he hit two quick skyhooks, giving him 22 points for the night. Worthy led the rush. Picture him: 6'10", beard and goggles, size-14½ sneakers, running full-out for the basket, steamrolling whoever got in the way. He'd picked up his fourth foul, but Riley let him play.

Daly responded by sending in his second team. Most defenders watch the ball. Dennis Rodman watched the eyes, boring in, as if he could see through the pupils and into the brain. It was unsettling. It was why players would shove Rodman at the end of plays, curse and threaten. *The guy's a weirdo. He looks like he wants to kiss me.*

Lakers backup center Mychal Thompson had his best performance of the finals off the bench in Game 5. He hit several big shots, pulling the Lakers within 6 at the end of the third. But the Pistons were still winning the hustle plays—getting the loose balls, taking the extra jump for the rebound. About some players people say, "He's talented, but doesn't hustle." For players like Rodman and Salley the hustle *was* the talent—the concentration and grit to go all out on every single play.

Detroit was up 90–81 with seven minutes left. A sequence of back-and-forth brilliance, in which Zeke and Magic seemed to go one-on-one, followed. Riley sat on his haunches on the sideline, championship ring on his left hand, rapping the linoleum. A vein in his temple throbbed. You expected it to burst and spew like a fire hose. Isiah drove the basket twenty feet from Riley, spun, and passed to Dumars, who laid the ball in for 2.

"Joe *Dooooooooooooo*-MARS!"

Riley called time-out. The Lakers were down 10 with five minutes left, then down 7 with two minutes left. Rodman fouled out. You want Rodman to foul out—to use every one of those penalties—but not with two minutes still to play. He stomped off the floor. A moment later, he was on the bench, eyes brimming with tears. That he was about to cry is what made Rodman a little scary. It was not a game for him; it was survival. It was not a team for him; it was family. Daly was not a coach for him; he was a father. A coach wants a player to care, but Rodman cared too much. Daly patted him on the back and whispered in his ear.

Magic went for a dunk with just over a minute left. Laimbeer blocked the shot but got the body, sending Magic to the free throw line, where he made one of two. And that was it, the Lakers' last chance to close the gap. By missing that second free throw, Magic let the lead slip out of reach. Los Angeles's starters left the arena with nineteen seconds still on the clock—because of the crowd and the long walk to the tunnel, and "to escape a possible mob scene," as Dick Stockton explained.

Final Score: Pistons 104, Lakers 94.

Game 5 was paradise for the Pistons, almost too blissful to survive. "We're only one win but thousands of miles away from a title," Isiah said knowingly, nervously. "It's right there, but it still feels so elusive."

For the Lakers, it was a moment marked by grim determination. This is where experience comes in—knowing what can be done and how to do it because they'd done it all before. Go home to the Forum, win one game, go from there.

Pat Riley was somber when he spoke to reporters outside the locker room, less game show host—his usual demeanor—than mortician. Black is the color, none is the number—that was Riley's mood. It was not just the prospect of losing. It was the prospect of losing after having made that stupid guarantee. Forget the banner and trophy and locker room filled with champagne. Reputation, legacy—that's what the coach and his players had on the line, the razor-thin difference between being a hero and being a fool.

GAME 6

Isiah's reputation has been diminished by his spotty post-retirement coaching career and by his woeful record in the front office, mostly with the Knicks. He's been fired for poor performance and sued for sexual harassment. In books and movies, especially the Netflix documentary series *The Last Dance,* he was turned into a villain because Michael Jordan was the hero and every hero needs a nemesis. Michael and Magic kept him off the 1992 U.S. Olympic Dream Team. All of this has had the effect of obscuring the memory of a player who was often great and sometimes transcendent. Isiah belongs in the top rank with Bird, Magic, and Michael. It was not just how he played, it was how he played in the most important games. Considering the circumstances,

Isiah's effort in Game 6 of the 1988 finals might be considered the single greatest postseason performance in NBA history. If you erased the rest of his career, all the titles and astonishments, that game alone would be enough to earn him a spot in the pantheon.

But first, before Zeke would have a chance to work his Game 6 miracles, the Pistons had to deal with the mystery surrounding Adrian Dantley's shoe.

The Pistons had flown via private jet—giant men dozing, legs stretched in the aisles, the 727 passing beneath a beneficent yellow moon—to the West Coast forty-eight hours before tipoff. After hotel check-in (the Pistons stayed at the L.A. Airport Marriott) and before morning practice—that's when Dantley realized he was missing a shoe. Normally, no big deal. A typical NBA player has dozens of pairs of Nikes or Adidas or whatever, but one of Dantley's shoes was special. After years of suffering from nearly debilitating back pain, a chiropractor diagnosed AD's problem. One leg was shorter than the other. He'd been cruising around like a car with a deflated tire. The doctor built an orthotic to be worn inside his left sneaker. It leveled Dantley's gait and solved the problem.

Dantley freaked when he realized that shoe was gone. He called the front office and security. He called the cops, who put out a bulletin that was carried on every TV and radio station in Detroit: *Have you seen this sneaker?*

Meanwhile, a die-hard Pistons fan named Steve Craft—he said he'd been going to games since the Bob Lanier days—realized that what he considered an awesome souvenir, the team considered the hottest piece of stolen property in franchise history. To Craft, who was suddenly ranked with Klaus Fuchs (the turncoat who delivered the atomic secrets to Russia), it all seemed like a terrible misunderstanding.

Caught in the delirium that immediately followed Game 5 in the Silverdome, Craft found himself amid a gaggle of reporters. "They rolled up this big door and said, 'Hey, the media can come in,'" Craft explained. "So I looked at my buddies and I said, 'Guess we're going in the locker room.' So we just follow the media and all of a sudden, boom, we were in the locker room with the players getting interviewed."

For Craft, who was living the fantasy of every fan, it was like stumbling into a diorama at the natural history museum. He found himself on the other side of the glass. "It was bizarre," he said. "It was like—surreal. I looked over and saw a stool sitting there next to Isiah Thomas. I went over and sat . . . I was sitting right next to him.

"On the way out, we went by a locker that didn't have a door on the front. It was just a wide open locker and there had to be thirty pairs of shoes in there. So I thought, 'Well, might as well note the occasion with a pair of shoes.' So I just reached in and grabbed a pair of shoes and kept walking like I owned them."

The next afternoon, when Craft realized he was in possession of the MacGuffin, he panicked, called friends, then got up his courage and called the Airport Marriott in Los Angeles, where he knew the Pistons were staying.

He asked to be connected to Adrian Dantley's room.

Rick Mahorn picked up.

Mahorn heard Craft out, then handed the phone to AD.

"This is Adrian."

"Mr. Dantley, I did something really stupid last night. I snuck into the locker room and took a pair of shoes."

". . ."

"I have your orthotics."

Craft pulled out the orthotics—AD said he could keep the shoes—which were put on the next plane to L.A.

Dantley, who met and absolved Craft many years later, was wearing them when he took the floor for the pre-game warm-ups at the Forum.

Saturday afternoon in Inglewood means sunlight and cars, every variety of limo and roadster rolling up to the arena. Jerry Buss, owner of the Lakers, had introduced a new service at the Forum. For twenty bucks, a Laker Girl would wash your vehicle as you watched the game. You'd step out into the golden hour, car gleaming, evening shimmering ahead.

The Pistons locker room was boisterous. Isiah was addressing his teammates, telling them he believed that this was the game to knock off the champs. "Let's do it tonight," he said. "No one knows what will happen in a Game 7."

The Pistons got off to a quick start, were ahead by 6 at the end of the first quarter, and continued to press in the second. The Lakers remained calm. They were following Riley's plan. Don't get drawn in, don't react, don't foul. Let them spend themselves in the first half, then surge in the second. Muhammad Ali called this strategy the "rope-a-dope." George Foreman tires himself out throwing ineffective punches at Ali on the ropes, then, when Foreman stops to catch his breath, Ali unleashes the whirlwind.

For the Lakers, the whirlwind, unleashed in the second quarter, was Magic, Worthy, and Scott on the fast break. That's when L.A. took its first lead. Magic fouled Zeke on Detroit's next possession. Isiah missed the first of two free throws. The crowd laughed and jeered. Isiah looked around, confused.

"I didn't see if Isiah and Magic kissed before this one," Dick Stockton said.

"Oh, yeah, they did," said Billy Cunningham.

Kareem was battling Laimbeer for position underneath. Kareem was winning championships at UCLA when Laimbeer, who grew up a few miles from campus, was in middle school. Standing up against Kareem at the Forum must've felt to Laimbeer like stepping into a black-and-white TV. But Kareem was getting the best of Laimbeer, who went oh for five in Game 6.

The Lakers led 53–46 at halftime.

As he told his teammates before the game, Isiah believed this game was their best shot at the title. And that's how he played—like a man in a hurry, pushing the pace, setting picks, making plays. It was a pleasure to watch him move up the floor, holding off a defender with one hand, controlling the ball with the other. He hit jumpers, runners, fadeaways. Some shots banked in; others went *swish*. If his back was bothering him, it didn't show.

Then disaster struck. There was 5:38 left in the third. Isiah had already scored 24 points. The Pistons were down by 6, but closing. Zeke snagged a long rebound, turned, and raced up the floor beside Dumars. His eyes and body, everything, aimed at the basket—he was an arrow, pointing—but his hands passed the ball to Dumars. The defense and camera crew, having been fooled, stayed with Isiah as Dumars finished with a layup. The Lakers inbounded, but something was wrong. Isiah had fallen to the floor and stayed there. The game continued on without him. Los Angeles hit a basket. Chuck Daly called time-out and called to Isiah, who got to his feet, took a step, then fell.

"I don't think anyone really understands the kind of pain Isiah was experiencing," Laimbeer told me, "or how tough he had to be to do what he did that night."

Here's how it happened: Isiah, after passing to Dumars, stepped on Michael Cooper's foot, rolling his ankle. "Pain shot through my ankle and I collapsed," said Isiah. "I thought it was broken. We were only about fifteen minutes away from an NBA championship."

Chuck Nevitt, the Pistons' twelfth man, hurried out and stood beside Isiah. He talked to him encouragingly, reached down, took his hand. Nevitt held Isiah's hand, a surprisingly sweet gesture. In this moment, Nevitt displayed what made him a vital part of the team, which happened to be the same quality that endangered his long-term prospects. Warmth and compassion. Kindness, which the league reads as softness. It's good to care, but this 7'5" beanpole cared too gently. Isiah reached out, punching Nevitt softly in the leg. A love tap. Zeke was expressing comradeship as well as pain.

The trainer got Isiah on his feet. Zeke left the floor with arms draped around the trainer and Nevitt.

Isiah exited.

Vinnie Johnson entered.

Play resumed.

Zeke's expression on the bench, the body language of the other Pistons—it told you Isiah was done. Yet, somehow, less than two minutes later, he limped back onto the floor. He could put hardly any weight on his right foot. He shambled, dragging the bum stem behind. He wobbled when he ran. "I'd come too far to sit on the sidelines and watch," he said. "Once my ankle was wrapped, I begged our trainer to tell Coach Daly I was ready to go back in. I had to hobble onto the court, but when I got the ball, I blocked out the pain."

Billy Cunningham wondered how effective Isiah could be. Maybe he'll become a liability on the floor; maybe his courage will do the Pistons more harm than good. The answer was not long in coming. Isiah got the ball ten feet from the basket, ducked one defender, jumped another, then released a rainbow that sailed over the outstretched arms of A. C. Green and fell in.

That was the beginning.

Playing on one leg, with a pain you could almost feel, Zeke took over. For ten minutes, he hit everything from everywhere, wild shots, circus shots. He behaved like a man living on borrowed time. He knew his ankle would soon balloon. It was Game 6. Now or never. Isiah was more than a basketball player that night. He was a symbol of perseverance in the face of pain. He was the hero who cuts off his leg to escape the trap. Even Lakers fans began to cheer. This was Hollywood, after all, and this was starting to look like a Hollywood ending. The pain seemed to concentrate Isiah's mind. For him, there was only this moment, and he was living it to the fullest. Isiah scored 21 points in the third, tying the game at 77. He hit a twenty-foot 3-pointer at the buzzer to put Detroit ahead.

The Lakers surged in the fourth. The Pistons had to clutch and grab to slow Magic and Worthy, which got them into foul trouble. Magic conducted the rush, leading his team on a 9–0 run. But the Pistons came back, and were within two possessions with 6:36 left. The Lakers tightened the screws, feeding off the energy of the crowd. When Dantley went up for what looked like an easy bucket, Kareem, moving faster than he had in years, came from nowhere to block the shot, get the ball, and start the fast break.

Rodman crashed into Worthy, who stumbled, hands on hips, goggles askew.

"The Pistons have got to find someone besides Isiah," said Billy Cunningham.

A minute later, when Zeke hit a bank shot for his 40th and 41st points, Cunningham corrected himself, saying, "Maybe they don't."

Michael Cooper poked Isiah in the eye with four minutes left. It was inadvertent, but the whistle blew. Zeke reeled, holding his face, blinking hard. For a moment, everything was blurry, the people in the stands just a smear of color. He saw double—two Rodmans, two Laimbeers—then the picture resolved and he was ready to go.

Dumars received a long outlet pass and missed the shot, but Rodman put it back, drew a foul, and hit the free throw, pulling Detroit to within a point with 3:04 left.

The fact that Rodman, who was just 62 percent from the line that season, hit the free throw when it mattered most, is Rodman in a drop of rain.

Lakers 97, Pistons 96.

These teams had played the entire night, series, and season just to reach this moment, the clutch. The final three minutes might as well have been its own game, season, lifetime.

Dumars stripped Worthy, got the ball up-court to Dantley, who drew a foul and went to the line, where, after going through his intricate routine—four two-handed dribbles; a finger spin; a second, more protracted spin; one more spin—he made both, putting the Pistons ahead by 1 with two minutes to play.

Then Dumars was fouled and hit both free throws. That made it Pistons 102, Lakers 99, with a minute to play. Michael Cooper inbounded to A. C. Green, who found Byron Scott. His jumper put the Lakers within 1, with fifty-two seconds left. Chuck Daly called time. Adrian Dantley inbounded to Laimbeer after the break. Laimbeer passed to Dumars, then freed Dumars with a pick, then floated out to the 3-point line, got a pass from Dumars, turned, and hit Isiah in the corner. Zeke dribbled this way and that, trying to create space, but Michael Cooper clung to him like a burr. Finally, with the shot clock running down, Isiah put up a rainbow that clanked off the rim and into the air, where Worthy corralled it. Turning to the ref, he signaled for time-out.

The Lakers were down by 1, with twenty-seven seconds left.

Riley sent them back to the floor with a set play. Cooper inbounded to Kareem, who passed to Magic, who passed to Scott, who passed back to Kareem, who posted up Laimbeer five feet from the basket. Kareem elevated, arm extended for the skyhook. The ball bounded off the rim and the Pistons had it—the ball and the lead, with fourteen seconds left.

Fourteen seconds from the championship is what the Pistons were thinking, *fourteen seconds from the trophy and parade.* Kill the clock, win the title. They were already celebrating in Detroit. Then you heard it—the whistle. It was the alarm clock that wakes you from a wonderful dream. It was the factory whistle that blows above the coalpits of hell.

The referee said Laimbeer had fouled Abdul-Jabbar on the shot, though, no matter how many times you examine the play, no foul can be found.

"That was not a foul," Bob Ryan, who was covering the game for *The Boston Globe,* told me. "Laimbeer never touched him. But it put Kareem on the line. And changed history."

"Laimbeer was two feet from Kareem," said Rodman. "Then he hit those free throws, and we missed a shot, and they hit another shot, and that was it. They were running all over the place, hugging each other and we were like, 'Motherfuckin' referees,' and throwing shit around the locker room."

The "phantom foul" that cost the Pistons the 1988 NBA championship was the result of a lifetime of good and bad works, the first of which made people trust and respect Kareem, the second of which made people suspect and disdain Laimbeer.

"We were one minute away from winning it all," Dumars said sadly in the locker room.

He was sitting beside Isiah, whose ankle was packed in ice.

GAME 7

In the run-up to Game 7, attention focused on Isiah. What he had done, what he could still do. Would he even be able to play? His ankle had swollen grotesquely. He'd spent twenty hours alternating between heat and ice. Al Davis, the owner of the Los Angeles Raiders, having recognized the Pistons as kindred spirits, sent Isiah to his own team doctors, who treated Zeke with cutting-edge technology, but it didn't help.

The mood in the Detroit locker room was despair giving way to determination. Go out and do your job, fight to the finish, believe you can win regardless; that's the mark of a warrior.

Game 7 was about one thing: survival. Many of the Lakers approached it with the suspicion that the Pistons were the better team, even if they'd not yet realized it. For the Lakers, the task was therefore not just to prevail but to close out a possibly superior squad.

Of course, without Isiah on the floor, the arithmetic changed. Isiah knew it, and that's why he was so determined to play, even if it meant playing on one foot. He'd spent the forty-eight hours between Games 6 and 7 either packed in ice or with his foot in a device meant to bring down the swelling. The fact that none of it worked did not deter Zeke.

Will you play?

Fuck, yeah! This is my whole life right now!

Chuck Daly's job was to find a balance: send Isiah in to boost the team, get from him what could be gotten, but not let his injury slow the rush or gum the works. Daly knew the Lakers were going to test Isiah with speed. Make him hurt. It's a merciless world.

The Lakers arrived at the arena several hours before tipoff. This was their third Game 7 of the postseason, but it was different. Win or lose, this was the last game of the season. If you are still playing after every other team has broken for summer, you have, in a sense, already succeeded.

"We were quiet in the locker room before Game Seven, no talking, just going over everything in our heads as we got dressed," Lakers guard Wes Matthews told me. "Pat Riley comes in a few minutes before the game. He usually had everything written on a board and went to the board and led us through the strategy, the plan, the assignments. But the board was blank before Game Seven. And he just stared at us. I was like, 'Oh shit, what the hell is this right here?' Nobody said a word. He stuck a video in the machine. I wish I had that tape. Highlights from the entire season, everything from the first practice to the drills we'd run the night before. It ended with footage from the 1987 victory parade. Unbelievable; he let the video do the talking. It was like, 'I don't have to say nothing else.' Then he looked at us and said, 'Do you want to give this up?' And we all stood and started shouting."

Riley recalled his pre-game speech this way: "Don't try to win. Just play the game of basketball. Let the winning take care of itself. You've worked for it. You've earned it—now go take it!"

One of the Lakers punched the wall and screamed, "Let's go!"

The team ran through the tunnel into the howl and kaleido-scopic glare of the Forum.

Tickets in the mezzanine were going for $500 apiece. The crowd was energetic, cologne-scented, gold-chained, electric. When they applauded, it sounded like the shore break at Malibu. Once again, it was Earl Strom leading the officiating crew.

The crowd booed when Isiah limped out. His back ached, his eye hurt, his ankle was a balloon.

Kareem won the tip, kicked the ball back to Magic, then ran up the floor hunched like an old man. He set up near the basket, held Mahorn off with his butt, raised his hands, got the pass, turned, shot, and missed. Then Dantley missed. Then Thomas missed. Possession went back and forth, the teams feeling each other out. Isiah was playing at three-quarter speed—every step and pivot drew a grimace. Players on both teams seemed tense. The importance of the moment weighed. They'd need to forget before they could play. "Shots weren't falling," Riley said. "They missed five of their first six, and we missed three out of four."

Then Worthy caught fire. Coming off the best season of his career, he wanted to prove the rightness of his nickname—"Big Game James"—on the biggest stage. You often did not realize how well Worthy was playing until you looked at a stat sheet. Though he was at the top in every category—points, assists, blocks, rebounds—he did it so smoothly it was easy to miss. There was a quietness to his game, a cold competence. He had neither Magic's flash nor Kareem's scale, but he was as effective as anyone on the floor.

Isiah was hustling after loose balls, hitting the occasional out-side shot, but he moved slowly and needed to rest. He couldn't put weight on his right foot. He could hardly run. He'd play just twenty-eight minutes in Game 7. It was one of his great disap-pointments. Meanwhile, Mahorn was missing shots. Laimbeer was missing shots. If one player kept Detroit in the game, it was

Rodman. This postseason had been a coming-out for him, an arrival. You could not escape his brilliance, the effect he had on other players. He dominated under the hoop, drew fouls, and made the otherwise sane Lakers go nuts.

Detroit was up by 2 at the end of the first quarter. The important action was in the paint, where Salley and Rodman battled Kareem and A. C. Green. Those four men shoved, clutched, cursed, rebounded, sweat, and bled. That's where the game was played. When the crowd was quiet, you could hear them grunting and talking trash. It was a meat grinder that now seems like a relic. The logic of the 3-point shot has pulled most of a team's players out to the arc, deforesting the interior. In the NBA, the once all-important inside game has gone the way of the drop kick, the drag bunt, and the whistle-stop presidential campaign.

As good as Rodman and Salley were that night, Worthy was better. He made half a dozen great plays in the first two quarters alone, passes and drives that ended with Big Game James flying to the hoop, arm extended, ball raised before him like a torch. He'd scored 20 by the break, leading the Lakers to a 52–47 halftime lead.

The third quarter is often the difference, and the Lakers did indeed make a statement in its opening minutes: 6'4" Byron Scott dunked over 6'11" Bill Laimbeer, knocked him silly, then stood glaring. This was followed by a shower of Laker shots, then a drive by Worthy, who, fouled by Laimbeer and Dumars, lay on the ground, goggles askew. Worthy hit seven straight shots in the third, as the Lakers tried to finish off Detroit in an ecstatic rush.

The Pistons were obviously frustrated. Laimbeer got into a shoving match with Scott, then with Abdul-Jabbar. Earl Strom blew his whistle—*tweet*-pause-*tweet-tweet-tweet*. He gave Laimbeer a technical. Byron Scott made the free throw, then hit a 3-pointer late in the third, putting the Lakers ahead 70–59. For a moment, it seemed as if the game was over.

But no.

Facing what many considered the greatest NBA team ever, a thousand miles from home, their leader injured, down by 11 with twelve minutes to play—this was when, by battling back instead of giving in, the Pistons demonstrated their grit.

Dumars took over for Isiah at point guard. With seven minutes left, he faked right, drove left, and jumped between Worthy and Green, who knocked him out of the air. He pinwheeled before landing out of bounds. He lay on his stomach, lingering for a moment longer than necessary. If you focused, you could hear him say, as if to himself, "Oh no, World!"

Rodman, battling bigger men for a rebound, knowing he couldn't win straight-up, batted the ball into the air again and again and again, staying with it until everyone else had quit.

The Lakers extended their lead to 13 but the Pistons regrouped and hung in. It felt like they were coiling. When the strike came (a 9–2 Pistons run late in the fourth quarter), it was led by neither Thomas nor Dantley, both of whom were on the bench, but by Rodman and Salley. They ran the floor, "bodied-up," outrebounded, outshot. Next time you looked at the scoreboard, Detroit had pulled to within two possessions with six minutes left.

Kareem and Magic each picked up his fifth foul. Laimbeer hit a jumper to pull Detroit within 4. Riley called time-out. Taking a knee in front of his players, he said, "Fellas, this game is going all the way to the wire. We cannot afford to break down in any offensive or defensive situation now. Don't back off."

With three minutes to go, Kareem pivoted for a skyhook. Rodman, appearing from the mist, from the night fever, blocked it from behind, got the rebound, raced up-court, and scored. 98–96.

"[At that point] Earvin took matters into his own hands," Riley said later. "He brought the ball into the key and shook Rodman loose with a 360-degree spin. Salley shifted off James to help. Earvin's five-foot shot came off the rim. James slapped the ball, attempting to tip it in. It rolled away from the rim. Instantly, on his next jump, James grabbed the ball and banked it in. That was the most vital shot of the entire game, but we couldn't take time to savor it. I yelled to the players, 'Get back! Get back! Turn! Defense!'"

The Lakers led 102–100 with 1:17 to go. You could hear Riley shouting over the din: "Hey, Buck! Get the ball to James." Rodman bodied-up Magic as Magic carried the ball, banging and banging until Earl Strom had no choice but to blow the whistle. *Tweet*-pause-*tweet-tweet-tweet*. Rodman's fifth foul. Magic made one free throw. It was a stupid play but seemed like an example of "Character is destiny." It was Rodman's aggressiveness that kept Detroit in the game; that same aggressiveness threatened to take them out.

The Pistons, down by 5, had the ball with twenty seconds left. Vinnie Johnson shot and missed, but Dumars put back the rebound to cut the lead to 3—a single possession—with fourteen seconds on the clock.

In these situations, there is nothing more dangerous than hope. *If the Pistons think they can beat us, they can.*

Laimbeer fouled Worthy. The Laker fans were on their feet, pressing toward the floor. A shower of trash rained down from the upper tier. Police took positions around the arena.

"I've been to a Who concert and I was at Game Seven," Wes Matthews told me. "Game Seven was louder."

Isiah checked back in. Win or lose, he wanted to be in the game at the end. Worthy missed one of two from the line. Isiah took the inbound, carried the ball up-court, then passed to Laimbeer, who took a long 3-pointer. *Swish*. The Pistons were down by just 1 point, with four seconds left.

The energy at the Forum shifted. The crowd got quiet.

What if we lose?

Magic inbounded, sending the ball down-court to A. C. Green, who was all alone under the basket. His gimme layup iced it. The

Pistons tried to get off another play, but the buzzer sounded. The fans rushed the linoleum. The confetti fell.

Speaking of his legendary Green Bay football team, Vince Lombardi once said, "The Packers never lost a game . . . we just ran out of time."

Reporters jammed the Lakers locker room; champagne flowed; awards were given, then the championship trophy. James Worthy was named Finals MVP. When a reporter asked Pat Riley if he promised a third consecutive title in 1989—the fabled "three-peat"—Kareem stuffed a towel in the coach's mouth.

And yet, something felt a little strange, a little off. "You really had the feeling that the Pistons had been screwed," Jack McCallum told me. "The phantom foul called on Laimbeer in Game Six. All the stuff going on with the crowds and the refs. But, in a way, it didn't matter. By the end of Game Seven, you had the sense that the door had swung shut for L.A. and open for the Pistons. They lost, but you knew they were the better team."

The future belonged to the brash newcomers from the Midwest, first the Pistons, then the Bulls. The moving finger was moving on.

Jerry West, the Lakers' GM, schooled the media, telling them to go down the hall because "there are more stories in a losing locker room than there are in a winning locker room."

"The thing I remember most vividly," Isiah said, "is walking into the shower and seeing Bill Laimbeer on the middle of the shower room floor, water running over his body, slumped over, head down, crying."

POST-GAME

Was the 1987–88 season really the best in NBA history?

I was convinced, but maybe I was wrong. Maybe I'd fallen prey to the common belief that the past is always better than the present, that what we once had is always better than what we have now. Maybe it was no more than a sign of age. I was born in 1968. I was nineteen years old when the events chronicled in this book unfolded. And every sunset is golden when you are nineteen. I remember being carried out of Jazz Fest in New Orleans by friends and thinking, *I love these people and I love this place and I love that tree and I love this hot dog and I love that girl and I love this car and hate only the fact that I will never be this happy again.* Maybe it was less the 1987–88 season that was great than my life at the time.

About ten years ago, I interviewed Lorne Michaels about the history of *Saturday Night Live.* I asked him which *SNL* cast he thought had been the best. He smiled and said, "That's not for you to ask *me.* It's for me to ask *you.* And you know what? Whenever I ask it, people always name the cast that was on the air when they were in high school. That's the cast they knew as kids, and it's always been downhill from there."

Michaels was talking about belatedness, the odd sense that the good times ended a moment before you turned up. Regardless of when you arrived, it was always a moment too late. He was also talking about nostalgia. And its dangers. Dangerous because it prevents you from seeing reality. I was at my best in 1987–88, so, in my mind, that's when the world was at its best too. Maybe my belief in the 1987–88 season is less a rational supposition than a case of mistaken identity. Something was great in 1987–88, but maybe it wasn't the NBA.

I called friends and acquaintances, basketball players, sports-writers, fanatical fans, people involved in the game today and kids just coming up, and asked their opinion: "Which NBA season was the greatest?"

There is no right answer, of course, such things being subjec-tive. If you are a fan, you probably think the year your team won the championship was the best. If you love the 3-point shot, you probably think today's game is superior. If you adhere to the old playground rules, you probably think the game has been cor-rupted by number crunchers and nervous Nellies.

Even so, the dozens of people I queried kept naming the same few seasons:

1976–77. The post-expansion, post-merger NBA. The talent pool was diluted. There were no dynastic teams, but parity made for thrilling competition. The New York Nets were the only team to finish the season with fewer than thirty wins. Kareem won the MVP. Pete Maravich scored the most points. Six of the seven play-off series went six or seven games. The Trail Blazers, led by a young Bill Walton, won the title.

1995–96. Having achieved peak power in Michael Jordan's second iteration—MJ's father had been killed, he'd left the game to play pro baseball, flailed, then returned—the Bulls recorded probably the greatest single season in league history. After finishing 72–10, the team, strengthened by the addition of Dennis Rodman, went 15–3 in the playoffs and won the first of three consecutive championships.

2007–08. Phil Jackson, spreading incense and assigning specific books to specific players—Kobe Bryant got Malcolm Gladwell's *Blink: The Power of Thinking Without Thinking*—was at the helm of the Lakers, his second "team for the ages." Shaquille O'Neal had been traded, leaving Bryant as the sole leader on the floor. This was peak Kobe, the player John Salley had in mind when he told Michael Jordan, "Kobe Bryant would've given you the business." And yet, after overcoming powerful teams in Utah and Dallas, the Lakers fell in a six-game final to the Paul Pierce and Kevin Garnett Celtics. Los Angeles vs. Boston is Pop Rocks and Coke for Boomers.

2015–16. The Golden State Warriors broke the Bulls' regular season record, finishing 73–9. Even so, the level of competition was high throughout. It took Golden State seventy wins to clinch the top playoff seed. The Spurs, led by Tim Duncan and Kawhi Leonard, went 67–15. The postseason was a dogfight that ended with the Warriors battling the Cavaliers, whom LeBron James led to victory in Game 7 after being down three games to one.

But great as all those seasons were, none of that changes my mind about 1987–88. Though I admit each campaign has its merits, that cases can be made, I believe that sports, like music scenes and cultures, experience the occasional golden age that can be objectively recognized. I'm able to accept the 1950s and 1960s as the golden age of baseball—Willie Mays, Mickey Mantle, Stan Musial—even though I'm too young to have seen any of those icons play. I am able to accept that the golden age of hockey—Connor McDavid, Auston Matthews, Nathan MacKinnon—is happening right now. Men's tennis rode a peak from Sampras to Federer. And to me, it seems clear the NBA experienced its peak, a boom that still enriches every player, in the late 1980s, when

Bird and Magic were still great, the Bad Boys (meaning Isiah) were ascending, and the Bulls (meaning Michael) were in the shadows, stage left. And the best of those seasons—because of the talent level, all those future Hall of Famers; because of the personalities, rivalries, and intensities of the game; because of the four dynasties in various states of ascent and descent—was 1987–88. That's the year it all came together. That was the NBA's version of Mickey, Willie, and Stan the Man.

And, as with baseball, it was not just the games but the context in which those games were played. The country we inhabited in 1987 and 1988 was not the country we live in today. There was no Twitter, no Facebook, no Instagram. The TV viewership had not yet splintered. Each city still had its own newspapers, morning shows, and point of view. The best teams played in cities that still felt vibrant and unique, each exhibiting its own neurosis. The fans of each city were each weird in their own ways; fans in Detroit were different from fans in Boston, L.A., or Chicago. And those differences were reflected in the ways the teams played. The Pistons stood for the work ethic and underdog grit of industrial America. Boston was a white city represented by a white team that played a white version of what had become a Black game. Chicago had recovered from the stagflation misery of the 1970s, and its team, like its skyline, stock market, and culinary scene, was young and booming. Los Angeles was the movie industry. It had models, movie stars, cocaine, sex, and fun. Just like the Lakers.

Of course, there was also the quality. It's not just that the best players were great back then. It's that they had style. Magic. Michael. Larry. Isiah. Dennis. Kareem. There hasn't been a collection like that since. And the physicality, the violence of the game, which told you how much the players would suffer to win. And told you something important about the world, too: In the clutch, grit matters as much as talent. It meant something in the 1980s that the Bulls had to stand up to the Pistons as you stand up to a bully before they could become NBA champions. It meant the

Bulls were on a schoolyard quest. That's why, when they finally won in 1991, Michael Jordan fell to the court and cried. It was more than the tension of a game or a series he was releasing. It was the years of battles, all it took to get there, that made the victory so sweet.

To some, the NBA reached its peak only after rules were enacted in the 1990s and aughts that tamed the teams that played like the Bad Boys. Not only did the violent playground style inhibit stars like Magic and Michael, not only did it let the mediocre pummel the superior into acquiescence, it led to career-ending injuries, and pain. The value we placed on toughness back then, on the ability to "play hurt" or "play through," seems wrongheaded to some people today. It robbed players of health, livelihood, humanity. *He's not a piece on a chessboard!* If the game had not been so brutal, they tell you, Isiah Thomas might have lasted another half decade on the floor.

I understand this viewpoint, but don't agree. Maybe it's generational. Members of my cohort grew up during the terrifying last days of the Cold War. We spent much of our time sitting around, waiting to be nuked. Life seemed a brief respite before annihilation, and we admired athletes who offered examples of people who refused to be cautious or submit. McHale posting up with a broken foot. Bird running the floor with a ruined back. Isiah hitting for 25 on one leg in the greatest game of his career. Life comes down to big moments. If you're not on the floor in those moments, then what's the point?

"Guys were hungrier back when I played," said Charles Oakley. "We knew what it meant every night to be on the floor. If you weren't playing, you were showing weakness. You didn't want anyone to see that. If you were at seventy percent, you still played. I think twenty percent of today's guys would be tough enough to play in our era."

Jordan said only four players active in 2015 could have survived in the 1980s: LeBron, Kobe, Duncan, Nowitzki.

Maybe Isiah could have played longer if he'd taken better care of himself, but I doubt he'd have made that trade. It's not longevity we remember, the steady accumulation of seasons. It's the lifetime burning in a single moment.

Time is remorseless. Even the great dynasties fade. In the NBA, they blinked out one by one. First the Celtics, who never recovered from their 1988 defeat to Detroit. Then the Pistons, who lost players to age and lost their edge first to the Bulls, then to time. "When they fell off, they fell off completely," Jack McCallum told me. "It was the injuries. Isiah's body could not hold up. He was too small, and got banged around too much, to play for twenty years.

"Laimbeer and Isiah still bitch that the Pistons are historically underrated," McCallum added. "And I say, 'Hey, you guys, you got a nickname and a documentary. What else do you want?'"

Then the Lakers, who lost Kareem to retirement in 1989, Riley to the Knicks in 1990, and Magic to HIV in 1991. "The Lakers really were the top," said McCallum. "MJ was the best player but the Lakers were the best team, the greatest offense of all time. They could run the floor, or fall into an unstoppable half-court offense with Magic feeding Kareem."

Then Chicago, which won six NBA titles before Jordan left in 1999 to finish his career as a Washington Wizard. The Bulls did not make the playoffs for the next seven seasons.

So what happened to the stars of 1987–88 after they aged out of the game? Well, as with the rest of us, some prospered, some struggled, some lived, some died. Taken in aggregate, the stories of any group of like-aged people—Kareem, the oldest player in this book, was born in 1947; Horace Grant, the youngest, in 1965 —will be a chapter in the story of a generation.

Kurt Rambis cleaned out his locker just days after the Lakers celebrated their 1988 title, the carpet still damp with champagne. He packed his bag and went into the world—first to Charlotte, then Phoenix, then Sacramento, then back to L.A. to end his career where it began. He played in fourteen NBA seasons and retired as one of the most beloved characters in franchise history. *Superman!* He's worked around the league over the years. Head coach, assistant GM. He is currently a senior basketball advisor to the Lakers. More interesting is his second career as an actor, a perk of becoming a folk hero in Hollywood. Almost always playing a guru or a coach, Rambis has appeared in *It's Garry Shandling's Show* (Shandling was at Game 1 of the 1988 finals), *Malcolm & Eddie, Married with Children, Sweet Valley High,* and *7th Heaven,* in which he played Coach Cleary.

When A. C. Green was on TV for any reason other than hoops, it was usually because guests on a show like *Donahue* were discussing his abstinence. Green did in fact remain a virgin for his entire sixteen-season pro career. Let me repeat that: The man did not break his vow of chastity until he was nearly middle-aged. We thought we'd been watching A.C. finish his career with the Miami Heat in 2001, but were really watching *The 38-Year-Old Virgin.* When he did finally indulge—presumably on April 20, 2002, the night after the day he got married—it was reported on the news. "A.C. is the man I have waited for my whole life," Green's bride, Veronique, told reporters. "To know that he has also been faithful in waiting for me is the best wedding present I could ever imagine."

Of course, you never really know what's going on inside a player. You might read their on-court style as an expression of personality, but you'd probably be wrong. Take Celtics center Robert Parish: Fans and teammates called him "Chief" for his demeanor, which he seemed to share with the big Native American in *One Flew over the Cuckoo's Nest*. Stoic, solid, good. Parish said little, but did not have to. His game did the talking. The few times he lashed out, he did so because it's what the code of honor demanded. Hence the shower of blows he rained down on Bill Laimbeer in the 1987 playoffs. Now and then, even a quiet man must act. But appearances can be deceiving. Put another way, there is the game, which was easy for Robert Parish; then there is life, which was hard. Parish has in fact spent the last several decades undoing the legacy—twenty-one seasons, nine All-Star teams, 1,611 games—he built on the court.

He returned home to Louisiana after he retired, where he proceeded to lose all his money. It was his own fault, he said, he'd been too generous with friends. Then he went looking for a job—he wanted to work in the NBA. He said neither Bird nor McHale, both then running teams, returned his calls (Bird has denied this). When talking about Bird, McHale, or Ainge, he is careful to refer to them not as friends, but as acquaintances. He started to sell things. He sold his championship rings: the Hall of Fame ring; the ring that honored him as one of the fifty greatest ever to play.

In the summer of 1995, *Sports Illustrated* ran a story headlined: THE WORST KIND OF COWARD: ALLEGATIONS BY ROBERT PARISH'S FORMER WIFE HAVE CAST A NEW LIGHT ON AN OLD HERO. In it, Parish's ex-wife, Nancy Saad, claimed Parish abused her for years, "beginning when they were dating in 1981 and culminating in a severe beating during the '87 NBA Playoffs that left her hospitalized with head injuries for a week." According to Saad, Parish "kicked her down a flight of stairs when she was eight months pregnant."

"We were in Los Angeles to play the Lakers," Parish explained later. "She came by my hotel and I had a guest. She flips out cause I've got a guest . . . Her intent was to provoke me to do something physically and it succeeded. I take the blame for that, hook, line, and sinker. I'm not going to downplay the domestic violence. I'm not going to downplay that under no circumstance, I regret it. You should never put your hands on a woman, under any circumstances."

This happened at the Airport Marriott in Los Angeles after Game 1 of the 1986–87 finals. The Celtics lost that game to the Lakers 126–113. Parish scored 14 points, but had been contained in the second half. Like I said, you never really know what's going on inside a player.

Dennis Johnson had trouble after his career ended too, but his case was different. He had the sort of post-career trouble not uncommon to pro athletes, child actors, and all those who fall suddenly back to earth. Most players make the transition, some with ease, but a handful burn up on reentry. Overdose. Suicide. The Celtics released DJ in 1990. He knocked around. In 1997, he was jailed in Orange County, Florida, for domestic violence. He'd abused his wife, Donna, whom he met at Pepperdine in 1976 and had been married to for over twenty years. At age forty-three, he began to put his life back together. He worked as an assistant coach on a handful of teams. Bird, who was running the Celtics, hired him as head coach of the Austin Toros, a Celtics affiliate in the NBA's development league. Johnson stepped out of the Austin Convention Center after a practice on February 22, 2007, grabbed his chest, and collapsed. *The New York Times* summed up his life tersely: DENNIS JOHNSON, 52, N.B.A. DEFENSIVE WIZARD, DIES.

Kareem Abdul-Jabbar quit the game for the most traditional reason. Because he'd become woefully, painfully, majestically old. The Lakers celebrated his career in 1988–89, Kareem's twentieth and final season. He was fêted and showered with gifts before road games. He sat imperially, often in a rocking chair that had been dragged to center court, as testimonials were given. Some consider Abdul-Jabbar the best to ever play—more dominant than Michael, Kobe, or LeBron. The people who think this tend to be the people who truly know basketball.

And though he retired, Kareem never really went away. He spent the summer before the 1989–90 season at Laker camp teaching Vlade Divac, his replacement at center, the tricks of the trade. "Very rarely do you get to meet your hero, and, meeting him, come away not disappointed but grateful," Divac told me. "But that was my experience with Kareem. He spent weeks showing me what to expect from NBA centers, how to position myself, make space, shoot that famous hook. It was less like he was coaching me than like he was passing on a tradition."

Kareem always seemed a little older than his years. Because of his height, he often bent like an old man to accommodate smaller people. And this became his attitude, the glacial reserve. Being so tall literally meant being apart, removed by distance, the bird's-eye view. It gave the impression of wisdom, which was complemented by his love of the arcane—jazz, theology, books. It was a role that did not always suit him at twenty or thirty, but he's grown into it. At seventy-five, the author of many books and newspaper opinion pieces, he has become a wise man of pop culture. "With a single petulant blow, [Will Smith] advocated violence, diminished women, insulted the entertainment industry, and perpetuated stereotypes about the Black community," Kareem wrote on his Substack after the 2022 Academy Awards. "Young boys—especially Black boys—watching their movie idol not just hit another man over a joke, but then justify it as him being a superhero-like protector, are now much more prone to follow in his childish footsteps. Perhaps the saddest confirmation of this is the tweet from Smith's child Jaden: 'And That's How We Do It.'"

Though a full decade younger than Kareem, Bill Laimbeer retired just a few years after him. According to the stats, 1994 was Laimbeer's last NBA season, but he hardly played, starting just five games and appearing in only eleven. He was beat-up, chronologically young (thirty-six), but basketball old. The knees, ankles, wrists, and heels—all shot. With every tortured step he currently takes, you picture the clothesline or sucker punch that's probably responsible. As Chicago Bears safety Doug Plank once told me, "Each body has only a certain number of hits it can take." In other words, Laimbeer has given and received more than his fair share of blows, many of them dirty. Yes, his teammates loved him, as did the people of Detroit, but, to the rest of the sports-loving world, he will always be a personification of that Bad Boy nastiness.

In the summer of 1989, when I worked as an intern on Capitol Hill, I spotted several of the Pistons, in suits, walking the marble halls of a House office building. The team, which had just won the first of its back-to-back titles, was going to meet its Michigan congressman, Charles Dingell. I saw Zeke, Dumars, Rodman, and Coach Daly, but my eyes lingered on Laimbeer. For a moment, I understood the mindset of the assassin. I imagined pushing aside the other Pistons and confronting Laimbeer, denouncing him in the name of Bulls Nation, then dropping him with a single punch. *Calm down,* I told myself. *You couldn't reach his face, let alone hurt him.*

Around this same time, Wayne Gretzky, possibly the greatest hockey player ever, was a guest on *The Late Show with David Letterman.* Letterman asked Gretzky who he'd most like to fight in the NHL. Gretzky dismissed the question.

"I am not a fighter," he said. "My job is to score goals."

"But if you had to," Letterman persisted.

Gretzky thought a moment, then said, "Well, if I had to, I'd kind of like to take a swing at that Bill Laimbeer guy."

Laimbeer has spent much of his post-NBA career coaching, mostly in the WNBA. He is revered by his players, which is not hard to believe. Behind all the cheap shots, Laimbeer was a classic overachiever. He played with crazy, passionate intensity because he truly cared. No matter the level or team, he could not stand to lose. (Hence the weeping in the shower after Game 7.) When I talked to him during the quarantine, he was rude, condescending, and entirely focused on the well-being of the members of the Las Vegas Aces, the team he led to a WNBA title in 2021.

Laimbeer was forced to retire before he was ready, and so was Larry Bird. The wounding, wing-clipping of physical decline—that's how most of the great ones bow out. Bird was unique only in that his big injury came not on-court but off. In the summer of 1985, he wrenched his back while shoveling gravel for his mother in French Lick. He was never the same. Many of us remember Bird stretched on the Boston sideline, waiting for the spasms to subside. He signed a contract for the 1992–93 season, but returned the money when he realized he couldn't be effective. He wanted to be remembered as he'd been at his best.

He worked as a Celtics assistant, then took over as head coach of the Indiana Pacers. Bird was a good coach, and soon had the Pacers in contention. In the end, like so many others, he could not get past Michael and the Bulls. The best moment of *The Last Dance* shows Bird, in gray pants and a white button-down, congratulating Jordan in the basement of the United Center in Chicago after Game 7 of the 1998 Eastern Conference Finals.

Bird leans in to hug Jordan, who wears a tan suit with a pocket handkerchief. A microphone picks up the sound of the handshake, followed by Jordan saying, "Enjoy yourself, dog. You bitch. Fuck you. You gave us a run for our money. All right, take care. Now you can work on that golf game of yours."

For most players, their years of retirement are far less interesting than their years in the game. It's like they have two lives: the first is for doing, the second is for remembering what they did. Of course, that's not the case with everyone.

Having first walked onto an NBA court in Chicago in 1985, the age of Reagan, Charles Oakley did not exit until 2004, within sight of Obama. Five cities. Nineteen seasons. He made only one All-Star team, but, as a presence and a personality, his influence was always felt. He was a trash-talker who could back it up. And a world-class rebounder. He recognized his role—he never thought he was going to be top guy, or even guy number two—and played it perfectly, protecting Jordan and building a legacy early in his career, and continuing to protect Jordan and protect his legacy even in retirement. Oakley sometimes did this by running down Patrick Ewing, whom he played beside for ten seasons in New York. According to Oakley, the difference between the Knicks and the Bulls, the difference between six rings and none, was the difference between Jordan and Ewing.

"Michael was the 'it' factor," Oakley explained. "Patrick was just a player."

Oakley blames Ewing for the failure to get over the hump and across the river, where the trophies sit in the shade of the sycamore tree. "If a guy has to question six or seven things out of ten against your leader, that's not good," Oakley said in a *Sports Illustrated* article titled "Charles Oakley Details Why He Won't Forgive Former Knicks Teammate Patrick Ewing." "He was hard to deal with, hard to play with," said Oakley. "A lot of guys might not say that on air, but they say it behind his back . . . I haven't spoken to him, especially after the incident that happened at the Garden and he did not come to my rescue."

This "incident" occurred in 2017, after Oakley, who had publicly criticized Knicks owner James Dolan, got into a shouting match with Dolan at Madison Square Garden. Oakley, gray but still imposing, shoved a security guard, then was swarmed by rent-a-cops and marched out as Knick fans booed. The team released a statement that night: Charles Oakley had been banned from Madison Square Garden for life (the ban has since been lifted).

When Oakley left the Bulls after the 1987–88 season, Scottie Pippen was just beginning to ascend. He'd soon earn his place as number two on the roster, Robin to Jordan's Batman, the sensitive little brother. Pippen suffered a migraine in Game 7 against the Pistons in the 1990 Eastern Conference Finals. And had a tantrum at the end of Game 3 against the Knicks in the 1994 Eastern Conference Semifinals. He hated Jerry Krause, who he felt underpaid and did not appreciate him. When Scottie was going good, he was nearly as effective as Jordan. But he wasn't Jordan. And never would be. And he let that fact define him.

He left the Bulls after the 1998 finals. He wanted to prove he could win without MJ. He played in Houston, then in Portland, where he came to seem like just another player. He returned to the Bulls in 2003, but appeared in just twenty-three games—twenty-three also happened to be Jordan's jersey number; a psychiatrist would find meaning in the coincidence—and averaged fewer than 6 points a game. He retired, then settled in to a mansion in the Chicago suburbs, where he's been a grumpy presence ever since. (Local waiters refer to him as "No Tippin' Pippen.") He took an ambassadorial job with the Bulls, then quit, did this and that, then quit again. Mostly, he broods. His mood soured as Jordan ascended to sainthood, the three miracles identified (63 against Boston in the 1986 playoffs; "the shot!" against Cleveland in 1989; the blizzard of 3-pointers against the Trail Blazers in the 1992 finals), the halo affixed. These days, every word out of Scottie's mouth seems to scream: *What about me?* "Just look at the records," Scottie told a reporter. "Michael did not win a single title before I arrived."

Scottie was stung by *The Last Dance,* which, in turning Jordan into a deity, diminished every other Bull. Pippen, who had in fact been crucial to the team's success, came off as a crybaby. He stopped doing interviews. A withdrawn man, he withdrew still further. He eventually responded in a book of his own, *Unguarded,* which, in its attempt to drop Michael a peg, made Pippen seem defensive and weak, only proving Jordan's point.

Of course, superstars have a tendency to overshadow the accomplishments of less talented colleagues. Some people—like Pippen, like Grant, like Bulls coach Doug Collins—never get over it. There was a real Pete Best quality to Doug Collins's coaching career. He'd been booted from the train a moment before it came into the station. He'd been a key part of Chicago's rise, but gets little credit. While Phil Jackson was lecturing on Zen and the art of basketball, Collins was on the sideline first in Detroit, then in Washington, then in Philadelphia. He never stopped blaming Jackson for pushing him out, snatching his prize. The Bulls were a move or two away when Collins got dumped, but one of those moves was dumping Collins. "Fucking Phil! All that flower-power, Zen-love, peace-and-love bullshit," Collins said. "You know why he wins? Because he's got Michael Jordan. Let's see him take that hippie stuff and try to win in Minnesota." According to *Sun-Times* reporter Rick Telander, Collins pulled one of the Bulls aside before a game in Detroit and said, "The next time he wants to screw me, tell Phil to use Vaseline."

Then Phil Jackson left Chicago. It was this 1998 departure that sparked the general dynasty-ending exodus. Phil, whose departure was followed by those of Jordan, Pippen, and Rodman, went on to lead another dynasty in L.A., where, working with Kobe Bryant and Shaquille O'Neal, he won five more championship rings. Jackson later served as president of basketball operations for the Knicks (2014–2017). You'd see him sitting amid the fans in the lower tier at MSG, taking notes as Carmelo Anthony jogged the floor. Jackson maintained equilibrium even as his Knicks struggled. Through it all, he stayed grateful—for the rings, the players, and the friendships that defined his life, especially with Jordan, who was the best young athlete in the NBA when Jackson arrived in Chicago, and was Elvis Presley when Jackson left.

Jerry Krause, wanting to prove he could tear it all down and build it back up again—that he, not Jordan, Jackson, or Pippen, was the key ingredient—seemed willing, even anxious, to shed the superstars after the sixth Bulls championship.

Asked about Krause's desire to start the rebuild—there was much talk of the Celtics, who, it seemed, stayed with their franchise players a beat too long—Jordan said something like "Rebuilding is overrated. Look at the Cubs. They've been rebuilding for a hundred years."

When the Bulls returned in 1998–99, it was with Brent Barry, Randy Brown, and Dickey Simpkins instead of Michael Jordan, Scottie Pippen, and Dennis Rodman. That team, coached by Tim Floyd instead of Phil Jackson, won just thirteen games. What followed was a fallow for Bulls fans, a million miles wide, a light-year deep. Though the Cubs finally broke their famous curse in 2016, the Bulls are still waiting for that seventh NBA championship.

Krause—he'd been complaining of poor health—left the Bulls in 2003. (He was replaced by John Paxson, who'd stayed on as assistant coach after his retirement in 1994.) Jerry spent the final decade of his career where it began, in baseball. He worked for the Mets, Yankees, Diamondbacks, and White Sox. He was seventy-seven when he died in 2017, a perfect example of the executive as fat man in baggy suit, the actor who never gets proper due because, though he nailed the role, he didn't look the part.

Though he'd hate the fact, Krause's career will always seem

like an asterisk in the big book of Michael Jordan, whose feats read like the legends of Paul Bunyan. Many of his statistical records have been broken, but the legend was never built on stats. It was always about the beauty of the man and the classical arc of his career, which has the resonance of a fairy tale. The arrival from the provinces, stardom in the city, the long struggle with Detroit, the dynasty finally achieved but soured by the death of his father, months in the minor-league baseball wilderness, the glorious return. The man was sui generis, one of a kind. For me, proof of his magnetism came one afternoon courtside at the United Center. I was sitting next to a beautiful woman who would not leave MJ alone. From start to finish, she proclaimed her devotion: "I love you, Michael. I want to marry you, Michael!" In the third quarter, when she screamed, "Michael, I want to have your baby," he turned around, looked at her sadly, and said, "Don't you think you're going a little too far?"

That was Jordan's effect on Chicagoans in the 1980s and '90s—disorienting. He was God. He was Michelangelo's *David,* the perfect man. And knew it, and knowing it became a burden. His last Bulls contract paid him $33.1 million for a single season, which is why he couldn't stay. There was nowhere to go in the city but down. He retired for a second time after winning his sixth NBA championship, then went to work as the chief of basketball operations for the Washington Wizards.

After three seasons in the front office, the old itch returned. Having decided, at age thirty-eight, that he was still better than anyone on the free-agent market, he put himself back on the floor. He played two more seasons as a Wizard. 2001–02. 2002–03. First he was thirty-eight, then he was thirty-nine. He was occasionally great. There were flashes. He averaged 22 a game that first season and made the All-Star team, but it was still a diminishment. He couldn't jump like he had in the 1980s, or hang. In fact, part of the satisfaction of watching the second iteration of MJ— after the first retirement—was watching him reinvent his game around his slightly diminished skills. He became an outside player, a 3-point shooter. He picked his spots. It was an inspiration for every person faced with the riddle of middle age. But he was much more diminished in iteration three. Heavier and slower. Air Jordan had become Terra Firma Jordan.

But by God, he was rich! Having flown commercial in his first seasons in Chicago, Jordan now owns a private jet, a Gulfstream IV painted to look like a sneaker. And is surrounded by bodyguards, who, speaking of MJ on their walkie-talkies, use the code name "Yahweh," the Hebrew's secret, ineffable name for God. He purchased the Charlotte Hornets in 2010, which he's used mostly as an employment agency for his friends. As owner of the Hornets, he's employed several UNC teammates including Joe Wolf and Buzz Peterson, and several NBA pals including Charles Oakley and Doug Collins. But the Hornets have been woeful under Jordan. There's a reason Jerry Krause ignored MJ's thoughts on the draft. In 2023, Jordan agreed to sell the franchise for $3 billion, over ten times what he'd paid. That is, he lost and lost in Charlotte, until he finally won.

Looking back, Jordan seems like a perfect representative of his generation—my generation. Born in 1963, he was the Gen X star. Having grown up in the shadow of the 1960s—assassinations, protests, riots, cities on fire—Jordan shunned politics. I mean, what had all that peace-and-love crap gotten us but high inflation and ruined cities? It made him cynical. When asked in 2020 why he did not involve himself in a heated election in his home state, Jordan said, "Republicans buy sneakers too." This quote has been used to paint him as selfish and retrograde, but it's how a lot of us who grew up in the 1980s felt. Better to go out and play as well as you can than get caught up and distracted by the bullshit.

"It's interesting that [Jordan] came of age in the nineteen-eighties, because he is ruthless, bottom-line, look-out-for-me in ways that are very emblematic of those times," Bomani Jones told *The New Yorker* in 2020:

When you think about Jordan as the figure of the eighties, you've got to remember that he is a black dude in his twenties who was not a fan of rap music. There's all this hip-hop that's played in this documentary [*The Last Dance*], but Michael Jordan is not a dude that's about rap at all. . . . He really does fit more squarely in a nineteen-eighties paradigm. If you think about him through the lens of like, "greed is good," the dedication he had to make the money, the dedication and the fervor with which he did whatever he had to do, that is all in line with the thoughts and ethos of the eighties. LeBron has seemed to live a life that leads him to always want to raise up those around him through his encouragement. He's like the kid in "The Sandlot" who tells his buddy to go to right field and hold his glove up and just stand there, and the ball will get there. Where Jordan is like, If you don't catch the ball, there's going to be hell for you to pay. I question whether Jordan was effective in his technique.

John Salley was nearly the opposite of Jordan. The classic role player. The great athlete who could fit any scheme, play whatever part was needed. Yesterday he was the heel, today he is, well, not the hero but the hero's best friend and ally. He went from the Pistons to the Miami Heat in 1992, then (weird!) to the Bulls, where he came off the bench for the team that won the 1996 finals. Like Rodman, Salley got rings in both Detroit and Chicago. It's amazing how a hated figure becomes beloved when he pulls the same dirty trick for your side. I saw Salley set the nastiest pick ever in 1996. It was clean but brutal. The player who ran into the buzz saw dropped to the floor, then curled up like a ringworm.

Salley has had an equally eventful life outside the game—actor, activist, podcaster, celebrity. He's had parts in dozens of movies, including *Black Dynamite, Nappily Ever After, Bad Boys,* and *Bad Boys II.* I wanted to talk to him for this book, but got no response from his agent, publicist, social media, website, or public email. I finally just typed his name into Gmail, wrote a brief note, and hit Send, hoping to slip by the gate that surrounds every celebrity. I got a response, but not the one I expected. In a way, what I got was better, as it demonstrated the deep penetration made by the NBA teams of that era:

> Hi, I'm John Salley. . . . . . . but not the NBA player John Salley that you are looking for. I am just a 47 YO factory worker from Cleveland, OH.
>
> I get email for him ALL the time.
>
> Good luck,
> The OTHER John Salley

I wrote back:

> Well, as long as I got you, who do you think is the greatest NBA player of all time, and the best team? (What kind of factory?)

He replied:

> Being late teens or early-20's in the 90's, I'd have to give the nod to Michael Jordan and the Chicago Bulls. They were just so dominant. Jordan could take over any game at will. Being from Cleveland, I can never forgive Mr. Jordan for hitting that hanging jumper over Craig Ehlo in the playoffs in 1989. "The Shot". . . . . [Automotive]

Of all the players chronicled in this book, Adrian Dantley has arguably had the most interesting post-basketball career. In ancient China, a wise man, a religious sage, finished with the life of the market, the chaos of the cities, would retire to a hut in the mountains to think about eternity, which is what Dantley did after he left the league—only, this being the modern era, in which the city never ends, he picked out the most humdrum corner of the infinite city and plunged into it.

Following his retirement in 1991 as one of the top scorers in NBA history, following years of coaching, investing, and accumulating, the mercurial man with the orthotic shoe returned to Maryland to work as a middle school crossing guard. Because he likes being around people. Because he considers himself a problem-solver. A kid needs to get to school. Traffic poses a danger. Adrian stops the traffic. The kid proceeds. The problem is solved.

As for the true wackadoo of the era, the most talented of the lunatics . . .

You probably know what happened to Dennis Rodman, because it's still happening.

When the Pistons, giving in to age and the Bulls, began dismantling the remnants of their title team in the early 1990s— general managers do this in the way of an assassin ejecting a spent cartridge while fumbling for another—Rodman was one of the last of the Bad Boys to remain. It was a dangerous time for Dennis. That the team had been his family—Dantley his brother, Daly his father—was the source of his passion. It gave his game the wild intensity that threatened to spin out of control. It caused him to play as if it were more than a game, and turned the normal league mechanics, the contracts and trades, into personal betrayal and disaster. Dantley had been traded, Mahorn let go, Daly had left to coach the Nets (he died of pancreatic cancer in 2009). Rodman dropped into a funk, which turned into a spiral. A security guard found him sleeping in his truck outside the arena with a shotgun in his lap. This was the one moment, he later said, when he considered death as a serious option.

From there, his life became a delirium of becoming, of unmaking and remaking, of falling apart and putting back together. He had skills that would make him an asset to any team, but he was fragile, needy, immature. He played two seasons with the San Antonio Spurs, where he quarreled with the coach and the franchise player, David Robinson. He began dyeing his hair in San

Antonio, covering his body and face with piercings and tattoos. It was his way of maintaining his freedom and expressing his inner nature. He argued with refs and scrapped with opposing forwards. He was hit with personal and technical fouls and booted from games. He'd tear off his jersey, throw it into the stands, and run into the tunnel. If pulled from a game, he'd unlace his sneakers and sit in stocking feet, wiggling his toes on the sideline. His two seasons with the Spurs were so divisive, and he was so unhappy, that for a moment it looked like there might be no place for him in the NBA.

Who was going to take a gamble on this One-eyed Jack, this Suicide King?

Crumbs.

Rodman was perfect for the Bulls. Krause saw it right away. Having lost Horace Grant to Orlando, the Bulls needed inside help. Jordan and Pippen were reluctant at first. Rodman, who had made a habit of tossing Scottie into the stanchions and seats, was a hated figure in Chicagoland.

Krause arranged a meeting, a summit, at which Phil Jackson sounded out Rodman in the living room of his—Phil's—suburban home. If they got along, agreed to terms, and even came to like each other, it's because it was in their interest to do so. Rodman offered the Bulls a way to get back to the finals. The Bulls offered Rodman a way to stay in the NBA. What's more, Rodman admired and even kind of worshipped Jordan. A famous crush. Michael was maybe the only player Rodman respected enough to listen to.

The team that resulted—Michael on the outside, Dennis on the inside, Scottie swinging back and forth between—was maybe the NBA's greatest ever. They did not just win the 1996 championship. They dominated from start to finish. And it was not just skill. It was motivation. Jordan, having been disrespected and taunted and knocked out of the playoffs by Penny Hardaway and the Orlando Magic in 1995, wanted revenge. Rodman wanted to prove himself to Michael and the league, and show he had not been the problem in San Antonio. The Bulls won two additional finals—1997, 1998—almost as an afterthought, as if riding the fumes created by Jordan's return and Rodman's arrival.

But basketball was only part of Rodman's life. There was also the soap opera. He dated Madonna. He dated Carmen Electra. Madonna had his baby, or he had hers, or none of that was true. He married Carmen Electra. His hair became a mood ring, projecting his inner weather. Yellow meant passion, blue meant progress, green meant envy. It was cherry red on Day One of the playoffs. He rode a motorcycle to the game, a Harley, with a friend, Bulls backup Jack Haley, hanging on to the back. He married himself in a ceremony in New York. He stepped out of a horse-drawn carriage wearing a dress. Dennis was the bride.

He could be sentimental and kind. When Jerry Krause's little dog died—a dog that was like a child to the general manager—Dennis was the only player who seemed to understand. He visited Krause, sat with him and cried. He sent flowers. He left when the team dissolved after winning its sixth title in 1998. He played another season for Phil Jackson in L.A., then went to Dallas, where all of a sudden he was old. He played in twelve games for the Mavericks in 1999–2000, then retired, came back, retired again. He was almost forty by then. He continued in the scrub pines of minor league basketball. The Long Beach Jam in L.A. The Fuerza Regia in Monterrey, Mexico. The Orange Crush (for one game) in Orange County, California. The Brighton Bears in England. He wrestled in the WCW, appeared on *Dancing with the Stars* and *Celebrity Apprentice*. He could not quit the spotlight. His ego would not allow it. He hung out with his best friend in North Korea. Of all the great players of his era, Dennis has lived the weirdest and most uniquely American life.

Of course, Rodman would not have succeeded in Detroit without the straight men, the veterans who forgave his trespasses, picked up the on-court slack left by his creativity, and showed him how to win. Isiah was important in this regard, but possibly not as important as the Pistons' soft-spoken number two guard, Joe Dumars, who will always be Joe *Dooooooooooooo*-MARS! He played fourteen seasons in the NBA, all of them in Detroit. And made seven All-Star teams. He was an anomaly for the Pistons, humble, conflict averse, kind—the only gentleman amid that mad pirate crew. He was the first winner of the league's sportsmanship award, now named the Joe Dumars Award, perhaps because it's even harder to keep your head when all around you are losing theirs. He took over as Detroit's head of basketball operations in 2000, fifteen months after he'd played his last game. He proved to be as good in the front office as he'd been on the floor. The Pistons reached six straight Eastern Conference Finals (2003–2008) under Dumars, and won the championship in 2004. When he re-signed in 2014, it was with seventy-three playoff wins. He was portly by then—he shuffles when he walks—but those of us who watched him play will never stop seeing the fit young guard buried beneath the years.

The worst day for many of us who loved the game back then—players, coaches, and fans—was November 7, 1991, when Magic Johnson, standing before cameras and reporters, told the world he had tested positive for HIV. For some, this was the first time AIDS, a terrifying epidemic, seemed real. A great athlete at the height of his power, in good enough shape, or so it seemed, to lead his team on another title run, had been struck down. HIV inevitably led to AIDS in the early 1990s, and AIDS inevitably led to social ostracism accompanied by a withering, painful death.

Magic told his story at the press conference. He'd sat for the annual team physical—for insurance purposes—then set off on a Lakers preseason exhibition tour. He'd been feeling sluggish, under the weather, but no worse, really, than a person might feel in one of the dips, the longueurs, that accompany an active life. Up and down. Funk and spree. Injury and return. The usual cycle of death and rebirth.

A team official reached Magic in Utah. A hotel phone ringing in the night—*Don't answer it.* He was told to return to L.A. No reason given. The doctor was waiting with the team's head of PR. Magic got the diagnosis, which he resisted, then the prognosis— fifteen months, two years?—which he rejected.

I watched the press conference with a dozen other people in the lunchroom of *The New Yorker.* We were stunned when Magic broke the news, and even more stunned when he announced his determination to "beat" the disease.

No one had ever done that.

I heard someone say, "He's delusional."

Then someone else said, "It's shock."

Larry Bird had been driving when he got the news from a basketball official. For a minute, he thought he'd crash. Part of him must have longed for the sound of steel, the breaking glass. He pulled over and reminded himself to breathe. He called Magic as soon as he got home. Magic and Larry had been colleagues and rivals; for much of his career Bird had not allowed himself to think of Johnson as a friend, though they had bonded while shooting a Converse commercial in French Lick in 1986. Being close off-court makes it harder to close out an opponent in the big games. It was only when Magic was ailing that Bird realized what Magic had meant to him. Magic was the great rival and foil of Bird's adult life. Bird loved him.

Magic took calls from many coaches and players in the days that followed. But one person did not call: Isiah. This confused, then infuriated, Magic. There was much gossip around the league about just how Magic had contracted the disease. Magic himself attributed it to "unprotected sex," but for players like Zeke, who grew up in the less than progressive world of the West Side courts, the bigger question was: Who exactly had Magic been having that unprotected sex with? When Magic asked someone to ask someone why Isiah had not called, word came back that Zeke had not called because Zeke believed that Magic was gay— *Only gay men get AIDS.* To Magic, Isiah's rejection, and his misapprehension, was unforgivable. Isiah denies this, but it doesn't matter. This was the last nail, the true end of the Magic and Isiah romance.

Magic retired from the Lakers and announced his intention to battle the disease with the same ferocity he'd brought to the court. His fame and cultural importance gave him access to advanced medical treatment, the cutting-edge and barely tested. As a result, he did not waste away but remained healthy and in fact put on muscle and weight. He was well enough eight months after the diagnosis to be included, with Bird, Jordan, and Pippen, on the basketball team the United States sent to the 1992 Summer Olympics, the Dream Team. Though Chuck Daly coached that team, no Pistons were included. Much is made of the fact that Jordan kept Isiah off the roster, but Magic probably had as much to do with it.

Magic stayed healthy enough to attempt a comeback with the Lakers. His second retirement, which came after forty-three games of the 1995 season, followed a backlash by players concerned about their own health. Considering what was known at the time, this response was not entirely unreasonable. "Look at this, scabs and cuts all over me," Karl Malone told a reporter after a game in Madison Square Garden. "They can't tell you that you're not at risk, and you can't tell me there's one guy in the NBA who hasn't thought about it."

Magic played for a long time, but has been retired even longer, an eventful second life that's included coaching and managing in the NBA, producing documentaries and writing books, turns as an advocate, spokesman, entrepreneur. Probably his most valuable contribution came in the months immediately following the diagnosis, when he served as a kind of ambassador to those suffering the shame of HIV. He met with kids, two of whom were HIV-positive, on a Nickelodeon special. A girl named Hydeia Broadbent cried as she spoke to Magic. "I just want people to know we are normal people," she said.

"You don't have to cry," said Magic, putting his arm around the girl, "because we are normal people. We are. We just want to be treated like that, right? You just want your friends to play with you and call you up and come by and still have sleepovers and things like that, right?"

Magic seemed to repeat the point later, when asked about Karl Malone's comments. He said he'd been hurt by Malone. "It was like a good friend saying we cannot hang out anymore," said Johnson, who could have been talking directly to Isiah.

When night comes, it comes fast.

The Pistons won the championship in 1989 and 1990, were swept by the Bulls in the Eastern Conference Finals in 1991, then were eliminated by the Knicks in the first round of the playoffs in 1992. Having won just forty games in 1993, they did not make the playoffs for the first time in a generation.

Isiah Thomas tore his Achilles tendon on April 19, 1994, and that was that. He was out of the game at thirty-two. Size had been a factor in every part of his career. Considering the style of the era (violent) and the style of his play (into the maw), it's amazing he lasted as long as he did. He was still so young when he retired that it can seem like he's been retired forever. He's started businesses and made investments in his post-playing days, but most of his life has been dedicated to the game. He's been a color commentator, a coach, an executive. Many of his jobs have ended in acrimony. Worst was his stint as head of basketball operations for the Knicks. He made dumb trades in New York, fired good coaches, and left a record of draft-day failure. In 2007, the Knicks paid $11.6 million to settle a claim of sexual harassment that had been brought against Isiah. He was fired in 2008 after the Knicks posted their worst record in the franchise's history, with fifty-nine losses.

As he made his final exit from the Garden, he was met by reporters. Isiah was crestfallen, humiliated. Life can be a walk of shame. He scanned the crowd, looking for a friendly face. His eyes met those of Ira Berkow from *The New York Times*. They'd first met when Isiah was a sophomore at Indiana University. Berkow grew up in the same neighborhood as Isiah—that was the basis of their bond. Zeke's gaze softened when he saw him.

Stepping close, Isiah said, "Hi, Ira, can I have a hug?"

Berkow, feeling the eyes of the other reporters, whispered from the side of his mouth: "Not here, Isiah."

Such episodes have cast a shadow on Zeke the player, as has the acceptance of Michael Jordan as the NBA's GOAT, whose bitter struggle with the Bad Boy Pistons became part of the legend, turning members of that Detroit team—those who dared thwart Michael—into villains. For Isiah, it's a bum rap cemented for another generation by *The Last Dance,* which cast Zeke as the Eternal Foe. What happened to Zeke is like what happened to the Jews when Rome converted to Christianity. What had been a local rivalry between sects—one side of the story—was canonized into an immortal battle between good and evil.

But I remember it differently. Because I was there. Because I saw Isiah play in high school and college. Because I understood what he faced in Detroit, how he sublimated his talent to turn that team around. I admired how he took the weak hand he'd been dealt in Detroit and, with leadership and at tremendous physical cost, turned the team into a back-to-back winner.

"Isiah was prickly, but he really was the best," Berkow told me. "I saw him score 24 points in the fourth quarter against the Knicks at the Garden, then, with the game on the line, go up and reject Patrick Ewing who was like ten feet taller than Isiah, who was maybe five-ten but could dunk like it was nothing. He had what in Chicago we call 'the hops.'"

Consider this book a revisionist history. It's not that I wish to devalue Jordan or Johnson or Bird, all of whom were just as great as people say, but that I aim to return Isiah to the pantheon, where he belongs.

The Athletic's 2022 list of the NBA's all-time best has Michael Jordan ranked first, followed by LeBron James and Kareem Abdul-Jabbar. Magic Johnson is five. Larry Bird is seven. Isiah Thomas is ranked twenty-sixth, behind Jerry West, Steph Curry, and John Stockton. But that's not right. To me, Isiah, based not on numbers but on results, on blood and guts, what he did on the floor and for his team, deserves to be much higher. The third quarter of Game 6 of the 1988 NBA Finals alone should put him in the top ten. His ability to lead, sublimate, rise to the occasion— all unmatched. And the fact that he was, by some accounts, just 5'10" makes him even more impressive. A short man in a land of giants, a Lilliputian among Gullivers, a pebble in a cement mixer. You have to be better when you are smaller. And the shorter you are, the better that better has to be. There have been many mediocre seven-footers in the NBA. Every five-footer who has cracked a starting lineup has been great. Of the seventy-five players named on *The Athletic*'s list, only Isiah is under six feet. Grading on the curve, Zeke was the best of them all.

As for Jordan, we were lucky to have him in the city, the league, the world. I have yet to see another player, in any sport, in his class. At times, it seems like I have spent my entire life watching him. I was in high school when he played his first season with the Bulls in 1984. I was covering the NBA for *Rolling Stone* when he played his last season in 2003. I came across him one morning at the Nets' stadium in the Meadowlands. Alone on the floor, middle-aged but still beautiful, Jordan was shooting free throws. He looked at me when I came through the tunnel. Our eyes met. Then he turned away and made his shot.

The Lakers moved into the Staples Center in downtown L.A. in 1999. The Forum has been refurbished as a concert-only venue. It's like a house where a friend once lived. It's full of memories, but the door is closed and the people inside are strangers.

Boston Garden, Chicago Stadium, and the Pontiac Silverdome have all been torn down. The Celtics play in TD Garden, the Bulls at the United Center—where the site of the old stadium is a parking lot for the new, a fate that reminds me of *The Giving Tree*. It gave us everything, even its body in the end. The Pistons moved to the Palace of Auburn Hills in 1988, then to Little Caesars Arena in midtown Detroit in 2017. The site of the Silverdome has become the location of an Amazon "fulfillment" center. It's Orwellian. The Dome where fans actually were fulfilled has been replaced by a warehouse that offers only the adjective.

I'm not upset the old arenas are gone. I think it's good. The NBA was so special back then. It had the best teams, best players, best rivalries; and the game, too, was at its best. It seems right that the arenas have been demolished, the memories sealed in amber, the very temples where we worshipped ground to dust.

On the desk where I write, I have a brick that was once part of Chicago Stadium. To me, it's a remnant as sacred as the stones of the Western Wall. It conjures the great teams that played in the stadium, the Pistons, Celtics, Lakers, Bulls. The players, too: Bird,

Magic, Isiah, Jordan. It conjures a time when the game was better than it ever had been, or will be. Of course, it might be more than just basketball I am remembering. It might be my childhood, when my parents were young and my life was new and the players I loved were in their prime. It was a time when the games really mattered.

ACKNOWLEDGMENTS

I think we all came out of the COVID-19 quarantine a little crazy, a little wild, and each of us, from world leader to writer, did something different with that stir-craziness. Some of us started wars. Some of us slapped comedians. Some of us bought social media companies. I researched, reported, and wrote this book, not, of course, without the help of a lot of people. So, briefly: I'd like to thank Dan Kirschen at CAA; the many NBA players, executives, and coaches I interviewed, most on the record, a few off; Andy Ward and Marie Pantojan at Random House, who pushed me to dig deeper; Jessica Medoff, my wife and friend, who was a fact-checker at *EW* long ago and returned to the trade to help me nail all this down. Also: Seth Davis, Tom Beller, and Mike Sielski for basketball guidance and early reads. Also: David Lipsky. Ditto my father, Herbie Cohen, who was a basketball coach and, as such, made me love, respect, and at times fear the game. He beat me more often than not in the driveway, even though he played in loafers.

NOTE ON SOURCES

This book was constructed from various documentary strands. There were the games themselves, which I watched either on TV or in person, then watched again on film many years later. There were the books written about the players and seasons and cities and league and sport, the biographies about the players and the memoirs by the players, coaches, and broadcasters. There were the articles, hundreds of them, written by beat reporters in Boston, L.A., Chicago, and Detroit, and the pieces written by writers for *Sports Illustrated, The New York Times, Inside Sport, GQ,* and *Esquire.* There were also interviews; some were done in the past, while I was covering the game for *Rolling Stone, Vanity Fair,* and *Sports Illustrated,* and many more were conducted expressly for this book. I have listed them alphabetically below. A bibliography of books and articles follows.

INTERVIEWS

Joe Abramson   Steve Alford   Pete Babcock
Danny Ainge   Red Auerbach   Thurl Bailey

Shane Battier
Ira Berkow
Bernie Bickerstaff
George Blaha
Shawn Bradley
Hubie Brown
Larry Brown
Bill Cartwright
Dave Checketts
Michael Cooper
Dave Corzine
Bob Costas
Earl Cureton
Charles Davis
Seth Davis
Johnny Dawkins
Chris Dudley
Mike Dunleavy, Sr.
Mark Eaton
Craig Ehlo
Bill Fitch
Mike Fratello
Artis Gilmore
Peter Ginopolis
Jim Gray

Jack Haley
Elvin Hayes
Craig Hodges
Michael Holton
Dennis Johnson
K. C. Jones
Greg Kesler
Larry King
Greg Kite
Larry Krystkowiak
Bill Laimbeer
Jeff Lamp
Wes Matthews
Jack McCallum
Chris Mullin
Ed Nealy
Pat O'Brien
John Paxson
Jeff Pearlman
Will Perdue
Sam Perkins
Ricky Pierce
Terry Porter
Kurt Rambis
Jerry Reinsdorf

Michael Reinsdorf
Doc Rivers
Jimmy Rodgers
Charley Rosen
Ron Rothstein
Bob Ryan
The OTHER
    John Salley
Brad Sellers
Jerry Sichting
Mike Sielski
Jack Sikma
Rory Sparrow
Chuck Swirsky
Rick Telander
Mychal Thompson
Sedale Threatt
Rudy Tomjanovich
Keith Van Horn
Sam Vincent
Jan Volk
Bill Wennington
Dominique Wilkins
Bob Woolf

BIBLIOGRAPHY

BOOKS

Abdul-Jabbar, Kareem, and Peter Knobler. *Giant Steps: The Autobiography of Kareem Abdul-Jabbar.* New York: Bantam, 1983.

Anderson, Sam. *Boom Town: The Fantastical Saga of Oklahoma City, Its Chaotic Founding, Its Apocalyptic Weather, Its Purloined Basketball Team, and the Dream of Becoming a World-Class Metropolis.* New York: Broadway Books, 2016.

Araton, Harvey. *Elevated: The Global Rise of the N.B.A.* Edited and narrated by the *New York Times* staff. Chicago: Triumph Books, 2019.

Auerbach, Red, and John Feinstein. *Let Me Tell You a Story: A Lifetime in the Game.* New York: Little, Brown, 2004.

Barkley, Charles. *I May Be Wrong but I Doubt It.* Edited with an introduction by Michael Wilbon. New York: Random House, 2002.

Bender, Mark. *Trial by Basketball: The Life and Times of Tex Winter.* With a foreword by Phil Jackson. Lenexa, Kan.: Addax Publishing Group, 2000.

Bird, Larry, and Earvin "Magic" Johnson. *When the Game Was Ours.* With Jackie MacMullan. New York: Houghton Mifflin Harcourt, 2009.

Bird, Larry, and Bob Ryan. *Drive: The Story of My Life.* With a foreword by Magic Johnson. New York: Bantam, 1989.

Bogues, Muggsy. *Muggsy: My Life from a Kid in the Projects to the Godfather of Small Ball.* With Jacob Uitti. Chicago: Triumph Books, 2022.

Bondy, Filip. *Tip-Off: How the 1984 NBA Draft Changed Basketball Forever.* New York: Da Capo Press, 2007.

Daly, Chuck. *Daly Life: Every Step a Struggle; Memoirs of a World-Champion Coach.* With Joe Falls. Grand Rapids, Mich.: Masters Press, 1990.

Davis, Seth. *Wooden: A Coach's Life.* New York: St. Martin's Griffin, 2014.

Edwards, Harry. *The Revolt of the Black Athlete,* 50th anniversary ed. Urbana, Ill.: University of Illinois Press, 2018.

Farrell, Perry A. *Tales from the Detroit Pistons.* Champaign, Ill.: Sports Publishing LLC, 2004.

Feinstein, John. *The Punch: One Night, Two Lives, and the Fight That Changed Basketball Forever.* New York: Little, Brown, 2002.

Geoffreys, Clayton. *Scottie Pippen: The Inspiring Story of One of Basketball's Greatest Small Forwards.* Calvintir Books, 2016.

Halberstam, David. *The Breaks of the Game.* New York: Hachette, 1981.

———. *Playing for Keeps: Michael Jordan and the World He Made.* New York: Broadway Books, 1999.

Herring, Chris. *Blood in the Garden: The Flagrant History of the 1990s New York Knicks.* New York: Atria Books, 2022.

Jackson, Phil, and Hugh Delehanty. *Sacred Hoops: Spiritual Lessons of a Hardwood Warrior.* New York: Hachette, 1995.

———. *Eleven Rings: The Soul of Success*. New York: Penguin Books, 2013.

Jackson, Phil, and Charley Rosen. *More Than a Game*. New York: Fireside Books, 2002.

Johnson, Earvin "Magic." *My Life*. With William Novak. New York: Fawcett Books, 1992.

Jones, K. C. *Rebound: The Autobiography of K. C. Jones and an Inside Look at the Champion Boston Celtics*. With Jack Warner. Boston: Quinlan Press, 1986.

Jordan, Michael. *For the Love of the Game: My Story by Michael Jordan*. Edited by Mark Vancil. New York: Crown, 1998.

Kriegel, Mark. *Pistol: The Life of Pete Maravich*. New York: Free Press, 2007.

Lazenby, Roland. *The Show: The Inside Story of the Spectacular Los Angeles Lakers in the Words of Those Who Lived It*. New York: McGraw-Hill, 2006.

———. *Michael Jordan: The Life*. New York: Little, Brown, 2014.

MacMullan, Jackie, Rafe Bartholomew, and Dan Klores. *Basketball: A Love Story*. New York: Broadway Books, 2018.

Massenburg, Tony, and Walt Williams. *Lessons from Lenny: The Journey Beyond a Shooting Star*. Greensboro, Md.: Whyde Range Productions, 2018.

McCallum, Jack. *Unfinished Business: On and Off the Court with the 1990–91 Boston Celtics*. New York: Summit Books, 1992.

———. *Dream Team: How Michael, Magic, Larry, Charles, and the Greatest Team of All Time Conquered the World and Changed the Game Forever*. New York: Ballantine Books, 2012.

McDill, Kent. *Chicago Bulls: If These Walls Could Talk*. With a foreword by Bill Cartwright. Chicago: Triumph Books, 2014.

McPhee, John. *A Sense of Where You Are: Bill Bradley at Princeton*. New York: Farrar, Straus and Giroux, 1965.

Meyers, Christian. *The All-Time Greatest NBA Book: Counting Down the 50 Greatest Teams, the 50 Greatest Playoff Runs by a Player, the 50 Greatest Playoff Moments, and the 100 Greatest Players*. Independently published, 2022.

Naismith, James. *Basketball: Its Origin and Development*. With an introduction by William Baker. Lincoln, Neb.: University of Nebraska Press, 1996.

National Basketball Association. *The Official NBA Encyclopedia*. With a foreword by Michael Jordan. New York: Doubleday, 2000.

Oakley, Charles. *The Last Enforcer: Outrageous Stories from the Life and Times of One of the NBA's Fiercest Competitors*. With Frank Isola. New York: Gallery Books, 2022.

Pearlman, Jeff. *Showtime: Magic, Kareem, Riley, and the Los Angeles Lakers Dynasty of the 1980s*. New York: Gotham Books, 2013.

Pippen, Scottie. *Unguarded*. With Michael Arkush. New York: Atria Books, 2021.

Pluto, Terry. *Loose Balls: The Short, Wild Life of the American Basketball Association*. New York: Simon & Schuster, 1990.

Riley, Pat. *Showtime: Inside the Lakers' Breakthrough Season*. New York: Warner Books, 1988.

———. *The Winner Within: A Life Plan for Team Players*. New York: Berkley Books, 1994.

Rodman, Dennis. *I Should Be Dead by Now: The Wild and Crazy Times of the NBA's Greatest Rebounder of Modern Times*. With Jack Isenhour. New York: Skyhorse Publishing, 2005.

———. *Bad as I Wanna Be*. With Tim Keown. New York: Dell, 1997.

Russell, Bill. *Russell Rules: 11 Lessons on Leadership from the Twentieth Century's Greatest Winner.* With David Falkner. New York: Dutton, 2021.

———. *Go Up for Glory.* With William McSweeny. New York: Dutton, 2021.

———. *Red and Me: My Coach, My Lifelong Friend.* With Alan Steinberg. New York: Harper, 2009.

Schron, Bob, and Kevin Stevens. *The Bird Era: A History of the Boston Celtics 1978–1988.* Boston: Quinlan Press, 1988.

Shaughnessy, Dan. *Wish It Lasted Forever: Life with the Larry Bird Celtics.* New York: Scribner, 2012.

Shields, David. *Black Planet: Facing Race During an NBA Season.* Lincoln, Neb.: University of Nebraska Press, 2006.

Sielski, Mike. *The Rise: Kobe Bryant and the Pursuit of Immortality.* New York: St. Martin's Press, 2022.

Simmons, Bill. *The Book of Basketball: The NBA According to the Sports Guy.* New York: Ballantine Books, 2009.

Smith, Sam. *The Jordan Rules.* New York: Simon & Schuster, 1992.

Stockton, John. *Assisted: An Autobiography.* With Kerry L. Pickett and with a foreword by Karl Malone. Salt Lake City: Shadow Mountain Press, 2013.

Telander, Rick. *In the Year of the Bull: Zen, Air, and the Pursuit of Sacred & Profane Hoops.* New York: Simon & Schuster, 1996.

Thomas, Isiah. *The Fundamentals: 8 Plays for Winning the Games of Business and Life.* New York: HarperCollins, 2001.

———. *Bad Boys!* With Matt Dobek. Grand Rapids, Mich.: Masters Press, 1989.

West, Jerry. *West by West: My Charmed, Tormented Life.* With Jerry Coleman. New York: Little, Brown, 2011.

Whiting, Jim. *The NBA: A History of Hoops: Detroit Pistons.* Mankato, Minn.: Creative Education Paperbacks, 2018.

Basketball: Great Writing About America's Game. Edited by Alexander Wolff and with a foreword by Kareem Abdul-Jabbar. New York: Library of America, 2018.

Zarum, Dave. *NBA 75: The Definitive History.* Richmond Hill, Ont.: Firefly Books, 2020.

SELECTED NEWSPAPER AND MAGAZINE STORIES

Abcarian, Robin. "Coaches Fight Battle of Threads." *Detroit Free Press,* June 15, 1988.

Abdul-Jabbar, Kareem. "Will Smith Did a Bad Bad Thing." Substack, May 28, 2022.

"Ailing Ainge Sent Home." *Boston Globe,* December 5, 1987.

"Ainge's Record Stands at 23." *Boston Globe,* January 27, 1988.

Alamodin, Christian. "John Salley Reveals What Really Happened When Pistons Walked Off Court vs. Bulls in 1991." ClutchPoints, September 16, 2019.

Albom, Mitch. *Detroit Free Press* articles regarding 1987–88 season, eight articles starting January 17, 1988 ("The Plain Truth: There's More to Pistons' Dumars than What Shows on the Surface"), ending June 7, 1988 ("To Beat Lakers, Bust Their Break"). See Authorrichcohen.com for complete listing.

Alter, Marlowe. "Young Bad Boys Shine in Upset Bid. Then Larry Bird Stole the Ball." *Detroit Free Press,* May 26, 2020.

Amico, Sam. "Hot Rod Rose from Scandal to Put His Stamp on Cavs." *Sports Illustrated,* April 23, 2020.

"Angry Jordan Accuses Pistons of Dirty Play." *Chicago Tribune,* January 19, 1988.

Araton, Harvey. "Knicks for the Birds." *Daily News,* November 19, 1987.

———. "Recognized for a Layup, Inducted Too Late: Celtics' Johnson Inducted in Hall of Fame." *New York Times,* August 13, 2010.

Associated Press. "Johnson Is Arrested." October 21, 1997.

Baker, Chris. *Los Angeles Times* articles regarding 1987–88 season, thirteen articles starting May 24, 1988 ("Perkins and Mavericks Suffer Through Game They'd Like to Forget"), ending June 22, 1988 ("Abdul-Jabbar Makes Promise—He'll Return"). See Authorrichcohen.com for complete listing.

"Bird Agrees Jordan MVP." *Boston Globe,* May 26, 1988.

"Bird in Boston." *Boston Globe,* November 21, 1987.

"Bird Wins It at the Buzzer." *Boston Globe,* November 8, 1987.

Blaudschun, Mark. "They Took the Air Out." *Boston Globe,* March 21, 1988.

———. "Big Gun Is Now a Sick Shooter: Bird Loses the Touch in the Trigger Finger." *Boston Globe,* May 29, 1988.

———. "Bird Takes a Seat, then Stands Out." *Boston Globe,* May 31, 1988.

Bonk, Thomas. "Lakers, Mavericks End Up Even." *Los Angeles Times,* June 1, 1988.

Brown, Clifton. *Detroit Free Press* stories regarding 1987–88 NBA season, seventy articles starting November 7, 1987 ("Pistons Win Ugly, 110–99"), ending June 22, 1988 ("Lakers Do It Again: Pistons' Rally Fails, 108–105"). See Authorrichcohen.com for complete listing.

"Bucks Stop Jabbar, Lakers 85–83." *Boston Globe,* December 5, 1987.

Cabot, Mary Kay. "Cavaliers Outlast Bulls." *Chicago Tribune,* January 15, 1988.

Callahan, Gerry. "The Worst Kind of Coward." *Sports Illustrated,* July 31, 1995.

"Celtics Wrap Up East Title." *Boston Globe,* April 20, 1988.

Chotiner, Isaac. "How the N.B.A. Has Changed Since 'The Jordan Rules.'" *New Yorker,* May 17, 2020.

Colthorp, Jason. "Dantley Meets Fan Who Stole His Shoes from Pistons Locker Room in 1988 Finals." ClickOnDetroit.com, February 10, 2022.

"Could Len Bias Have Challenged Michael Jordan?" NBC Sports Chicago, June 18, 2020.

Crouch, Ian. "Dennis Rodman and Diplomatic Dystopia." *New Yorker,* March 4, 2013.

———. "From Bob Ryan to the Players' Tribune: We're Talking About Access." *New Yorker,* October 20, 2014.

———. "On Jordan, 'The Last Dance,' and Activism in the N.B.A. Q&A with Bomani Jones." *New Yorker,* July 20, 2020.

Crowe, Jerry. "Once Again, the Challenge of Bird Brings Out the Best in Cooper." *Los Angeles Times,* December 12, 1987.

Dalton, Kyle. "NBA Hall of Famer Adrian Dantley Earns Less Than $15K Annually and Works as School Crossing Guard." Sportscasting.com, March 24, 2020.

Dodds, Tracy. "Rodman and Pistons Couldn't Quite Hold On." *Los Angeles Times,* June 20, 1988.

Downey, Mike. *Los Angeles Times* stories regarding 1987–88 NBA season, seventeen articles starting October 30, 1985 ("Stan Albeck, Raging Bull of the NBA"), ending June 20, 1988

("Thomas Is Bloody, Not Yet Beaten"). See Authorrichcohen.com for complete listing.

Edes, Gordon. *Los Angeles Times* stories regarding 1987–88 NBA season, fifty-seven articles starting November 11, 1987 ("Lakers Sink Spurs with Late Flourish"), ending June 22, 1988 ("Lakers Repeat Their Title Feat: LA Wins for 5th Time in '80s"). See Authorrichcohen.com for complete listing.

Elderkin, Phil. "Bizarre Route to the N.B.A." *Los Angeles Times,* May 13, 1983.

ESPN editors. "Ranking the Top 74 Individual Seasons in NBA History." ESPN.com, May 4, 2020.

Estrella, Fiel. "The Long and Short of Basketball Shorts Throughout History." *Esquire,* June 13, 2018.

Gladys (Gunderson) Park. Location information on Chicagoparkdistrict.com.

"Goggles for Bird." *Boston Globe,* March 10, 1988.

Goldaper, Sam. "Unsung Nealy Helps the Bulls." *New York Times,* May 28, 1990.

Goldfarb, Aaron. "How Suburban Chicago Became the Unlikeliest Clubbing Scene of the 1980s." InsideHook.com, December 18, 2020.

Goldstein, Richard. "Dennis Johnson, 52, N.B.A. Defensive Wizard, Dies." *New York Times,* February 23, 2007.

———. "Bill Russell, Who Transformed Pro Basketball, Dies at 88." *New York Times,* July 31, 2022.

Greene, Nick. "The 'Tell-All' Book That Claimed Michael Jordan Lost $1.25 Million Playing Golf." *Slate,* May 3, 2020.

Grossfeld, Stan. "Robert Parish Yearns for NBA Coaching Job." *Boston Globe,* January 25, 2013.

Hart, Marla. "Mary Thomas' Story Is a Tale of a Mother's Will." *Chicago Tribune,* December 3, 1989.

"Hawks Steal within Game of the Pistons." *Chicago Tribune,* April 4, 1988.

Hayes, Neil. "Ex-Bull Ed Nealy Selling Cars, but He'd Like to Get Back on Bench." *Chicago Sun-Times,* June 24, 2016.

Heisler, Mark. *Los Angeles Times* stories regarding 1987–88 NBA season, thirteen articles starting February 15, 1988 ("Lakers Get Physical—Celtics Get the Message"), ending June 22, 1988 ("Lakers Repeat Their Title Feat: For Thomas, It's Painful Way to Go"). See Authorrichcohen.com for complete listing.

Hemphill, Lex. "Pistons' Discovery of Inner Peace Was Last Victory." *Salt Lake Tribune,* January 6, 1988.

Hersch, Hank. "NBA Playoffs." *Sports Illustrated,* May 23, 1988.

Holmes, Dan. "Edwards Added a Key Piece to the Championship Runs for the Pistons." VintageDetroit.com, March 20, 2016.

———. "John Long Worked Hard to Make It to the NBA." VintageDetroit.com, April 7, 2018.

Howard, Johnette. *Detroit Free Press* stories regarding 1987–88 NBA season, twenty-six articles starting November 7, 1987 ("Ewing Pointed Rodman to Crucial Interception"), ending June 22, 1988 ("As Leader, Dumars Never Flinched"). See Authorrichcohen .com for complete listing.

"Jordan Wrecks 76ers." *Boston Globe,* November 8, 1987.

Kahn, Howie. "In Praise of the 12th Man." *Grantland,* February 20, 2013.

Kendall, Peter. "Jordan 'Homecoming' Has Tongues Wagging." *Chicago Tribune,* December 24, 1988.

Kirkpatrick, Curry. "Hooray for the Red, White, Black and Blue!" *Sports Illustrated,* July 23, 1984.

Lacy, Eric. "Former Detroit Pistons Bad Boy James 'Buddha' Edwards Says He Misses the Aggressive, Defensive Style of Play the NBA Had 25 Years Ago." Associated Press, March 27, 2014.

"Laimbeer Defies the Pain." *Detroit Free Press,* May 27, 1988.

"Laimbeer's Only Basket Lifts Pistons." *Chicago Tribune,* February 3, 1988.

"Lakers Clinch Best Record." *Boston Globe,* April 20, 1988.

Langlois, Keith. "The Best of Trader Jack." Parts I–X. NBA.com, June 2, 2017.

Lapointe, Joe. *Detroit Free Press* stories regarding 1987–88 NBA season, nine articles starting May 31, 1988 ("The Shot Laimbeer Didn't Take"), ending June 22, 1988 ("Rodman Surprises Even Himself with Shot"). See Authorrichcohen.com for complete listing.

Lincicome, Bernie. *Chicago Tribune* stories regarding 1987–88 NBA season, nine articles starting November 8, 1987 ("Let's Hold Off on Bulls' Title Party"), ending May 16, 1988 ("Besides Jordan, Bulls Punchless"). See Authorrichcohen.com for complete listing.

Lowe, Zach. "The Life and Death of Fandom." *Grantland,* January 30, 2014.

Luhm, Steve. "Shocked Jazz Mourn Their Brightest Star." *Salt Lake Tribune,* January 6, 1988.

MacMullan, Jackie. *Boston Globe* stories regarding NBA, eight articles starting April 30, 1988 ("He Always Rose to the Occasion"), ending February 23, 2007 ("Gang Couldn't Shoot Straight"). See Authorrichcohen.com for complete listing.

Madden, Michael. "It Was in the Bag." *Boston Globe,* May 2, 1988.

———. "Thomas Arrives as Hero." *Boston Globe,* May 27, 1988.

———. "Detroit Fails to Answer Close Call." *Boston Globe,* May 29, 1988.

———. "No Offense, But Celtics Tie Series: In the End, Pistons Off Mark, 79–78." *Boston Globe,* May 30, 1988.

"Magic Tricks Lift Lakers over 76ers." *Chicago Tribune,* March 8, 1988.

Mathur, Ashish. "On *Unguarded* by Scottie Pippen." Sportscasting .com, November 24, 2001.

McCallum, Jack. "The Dread R Word: Pat Riley Has Good Reasons for Asserting that His Lakers Will Become the First NBA Team to Repeat in 19 Years as Champions." *Sports Illustrated,* April 8, 1988.

———. "Tackling a Tough Task: Detroit Had the NBA Title within Its Grip, but L.A. Broke Free to Tie the Playoff Finals at 3–3." *Sports Illustrated,* June 27, 1988.

———. "An Unhappy Ending: Kareem Abdul-Jabbar Didn't Prepare Properly for His Last Season, and It Shows." *Sports Illustrated,* January 23, 1989.

———. "Hub of Emotion: Boston Longs for the Old Powerhouse, but Sad to Say, Larry Bird & Co. Are Simply Not the Same." *Sports Illustrated,* December 11, 1989.

Miss Rosen. "A Portrait of Los Angeles at the Turn of the 1980s." *Huck Mag,* November 11, 2019.

Montville, Leigh. *Sports Illustrated* stories regarding NBA, seven articles starting May 12, 1988 ("Bird Shares Wealth"), ending June 12, 2004 ("Where's the Chief?"). See Authorrichcohen.com for complete listing.

Murray, Jim. "Show Stays on Broadway, Magically." *Los Angeles Times,* June 5, 1988.

Nathan, Alec. "Former NBA Player John 'Hot Rod' Williams Dies at 53." BleacherReport.com, December 11, 2015.

"No Bird, Down by 28, but Celts Win in 2 OT." *Chicago Tribune,* November 19, 1987.

Ostler, Scott. *Los Angeles Times* stories regarding 1987–88 NBA season, twelve articles starting November 11, 1987 ("Spurs, by Winning, Wooing Robinson, Broke Laker Hearts"), ending June 22, 1988 ("Lots of Characters—Even Al Davis—Play Roles in This Fantasy"). See Authorrichcohen.com for complete listing.

Pave, Marvin. *Boston Globe* stories regarding 1987–88 NBA season, five articles starting March 4, 1988 ("The Net Impact: Rude Awakening"), ending May 27, 1988 ("Boston Broken Play Breaks Pistons' Back"). See Authorrichcohen.com for complete listing.

Petzold, Evan. "Remembering the Night Detroit Pistons Dethroned Boston Celtics, Finally Made NBA Finals." *Detroit Free Press,* December 1, 2021.

"Pistons Bounce Bullets." *Boston Globe,* March 21, 1988.

"Pistons Corner: Isiah Fined $3,000 for Initiating Fight." *Detroit Free Press,* December 16, 1987.

"Pistons Missing on All Cylinders." *Boston Globe,* April 20, 1988.

Professor Parquet. "Larry Legend's Last Game." Celticsblog.com, August 18, 2019.

"Remember the Kentucky Colonels." RememberTheABA.com, September 20, 2017.

Remnick, David. "Back in Play." *New Yorker,* May 8, 1995.

Rosa, Francis. "Celtics Get Even; Bruins KO'd." *Boston Globe,* May 31, 1988.

Rushin, Steve. "Give the Kids a Break." *Sports Illustrated,* December 4, 2006.

Ryan, Bob. *Boston Globe* stories regarding 1987–88 NBA season, forty-two articles starting November 7, 1987 ("It's Grand Opening for Celtics, 125–108"), ending May 21, 1988 ("Celtics Stay Alive"). See Authorrichcohen.com for complete listing.

Sakamoto, Bob. *Chicago Tribune* stories regarding 1987–88 NBA season, sixty-six articles starting November 8, 1987 ("Bulls 1st Show a Hit"), ending May 19, 1988 ("Bulls' Best Can't Beat Pistons"). See Authorrichcohen.com for complete listing.

Sandomir, Richard. "Gene Pingatore, 'Hoop Dreams' Documentary Coach, Dies at 82." *New York Times,* July 5, 2019.

Seelye, Katharine Q. "Two Decades of Change Have Boston Sparkling." *New York Times,* January 6, 2014.

Sharp, Drew. "Pistons Are Still East's Best." *Detroit Free Press,* April 20, 1988.

Shaughnessy, Dan. "Celtics Caught by Bulls." *Boston Globe,* November 24, 1987.

———. "Pistons New Local Villains." *Boston Globe,* January 13, 1988.

Simmons, Bill. "The Consequences of Caring." *Grantland,* June 8, 2012.

Smith, Sam. *Chicago Tribune* stories regarding 1987–88 NBA season, five articles starting November 8, 1987 ("Bulls Youth Brigade Takes Debut by Horns"), ending April 29, 1988 ("Cavs' Ehlo Fails to Foul Up Jordan in Bulls' Playoff Opener"). See Authorrichcohen.com for complete listing.

———. "Remembering One of the Greatest All-Star Weekends in NBA History: 1988 in Chicago." NBA.com, February 14, 2020.

———. "1980s and the Chicago Bulls." NBA.com, June 12, 2021.

Solomon, George. "'Jimmy the Greek' Fired by CBS for His Remarks." *Washington Post,* January 17, 1988.

Stern, Marlow. "The NBA's 38-Year-Old Virgin: A. C. Green, the Iron Man with the Iron Will." *Daily Beast,* April 13, 2017.

Thomas, Isiah. "A Friend Who Uses People." *Detroit Free Press,* February 14, 1988.

———. "He Sings High for a 10-Year-Old Boy." *Detroit Free Press,* March 6, 1988.

———. "Trying Hard to Be Popular." *Detroit Free Press,* March 20, 1988.

———. "Two Strikes and Kitty Is Out." *Detroit Free Press,* April 10, 1988.

Thomas, Louisa. " 'The Last Dance' Shows a Michael Jordan You May Know and a Scottie Pippen You Probably Don't." *New Yorker,* April 20, 2020.

Thomas, Mike. "The Los Angeles Lakers Never Trusted the Boston Celtics During the 1984 NBA Finals: 'We Didn't Know Who Was Watching.'" Sportscasting.com, September 13, 2021.

———. "Kurt Rambis Nearly Nixed His Own 'Superman' Fan Club but Quickly Changed Course: 'I Thought They Were Mocking Me.'" Sportscasting.com, December 1, 2021.

———. "Kevin McHale Says He Has Only 1 Regret About Clotheslining Kurt Rambis." Sportscasting.com, March 16, 2022.

Thompson, Wright. "Michael Jordan Has Not Left the Building." *ESPN The Magazine,* February 15, 2013.

Thomsen, Ian. *Boston Globe* stories regarding 1987–88 NBA season, eleven articles starting December 12, 1987 ("Presto! He Stole Celtic Thunder"), ending June 4, 1988 ("Bird Shot Down"). See Authorrichcohen.com for complete listing.

"25th Anniversary of 'the Shot': Michael Jordan's First Legendary Moment." AmericanSportsHistory.com, May 7, 2015.

Vega, Michael. "Nets Stun Celtics." *Boston Globe,* March 3, 1988.

———. "Bird Sleeps on It: Injured Star May Miss Trip." *Boston Globe,* April 22, 1988.

Verdi, Bob. "Laimbeer, the Pistons' Bad Boy, Lambastes the Bulls but Good." *Chicago Tribune,* May 15, 1988.

———. "Bulls' Disastrous Weekend Will Not Be Lost on Collins." *Chicago Tribune,* May 16, 1988.

————. "Bulls Need Better Talent, Memories." *Chicago Tribune,* May 19, 1988.

Vincent, Charlie. *Detroit Free Press* stories regarding 1987–88 NBA season, twenty-three articles starting December 5, 1987 ("Opening Scene Belongs to Rodman and Pistons"), ending June 22, 1988 ("Pistons, Thomas Run Out of Miracles"). See Authorrichcohen.com for complete listing.

Wertheim, Jon. "Tales of Michael Jordan and the 1984 U.S. Olympic Trials." *Sports Illustrated,* April 19, 2020.

Wilbon, Michael. "Laimbeer, Bird Tossed for 4th-Period Fight." *Washington Post,* May 24, 1987.

Wood, Ryan. "The History of the 3-Pointer." USABasketball.com, June 15, 2011.

Wulf, Steve. "A Truly Tall Tale: Chuck Nevitt, the NBA's Funniest Twelfth Man." *Sports Illustrated,* November 7, 1994.

Zeigler, Mark. "The Golfing Yogi: The Man Who Says Michael Jordan Lost $1.2 Million to Him." *San Diego Union-Tribune,* May 10, 2020.

FILMS

Bad Boys (30 for 30). Directed by Zak Levitt, 2014.

Black Magic. Directed by Dan Klores, 2008.

Celtics/Lakers: Best of Enemies (30 for 30). Parts 1–3. Directed by Jim Podhoretz, 2017.

The Dream Team. Directed by Zak Levitt, 2012.

Guru of Go (30 for 30). Directed by Bill Couturié.

Hoop Dreams. Directed by Steve James, 1994.

Hoosiers. Directed by David Anspaugh, 1986.

Kareem: Minority of One. Directed by Aaron Cohen, 2015.

Larry Bird (ESPN Sports Century). Edited by Phil Carruthers, 1999.

Larry Bird: A Basketball Legend. Written by Jim Podhoretz and Larry Weitzman, 1992.

The Last Dance. Ten episodes. Directed by Jason Hehir, 2020.

Magic & Bird: A Courtship of Rivals. Directed by Ezra Edelman, 2010.

A Mother's Courage: The Mary Thomas Story. Directed by John Patterson, 1989.

Rodman: For Better or Worse (30 for 30). Directed by Todd Kapostasy, 2019.

They Call Me Magic. Four episodes. Directed by Rick Famuyiwa, 2022.

Without Bias (30 for 30). Directed by Kirk Fraser, 2009.

INDEX

a manifesto for earth spirituality

one spirit
many peoples

STEPHEN HARROD BUHNER

To Catherine
For the Earth
Stephen Harrod Buhner
4, 2—2001

Roberts Rinehart Publishers

dedication

For Our Ancestors
For Our Children

Published by Roberts Rinehart Publishers, 6309 Monarch Park Place, Niwot, Colorado 80503

Distributed to the trade in the U.S. and Canada by Publishers Group West

Published in the UK and Ireland by Roberts Rinehart Publishers
Trinity House, Charleston Road, Dublin 6, Ireland

International Standard Book Number 1-57098-120-5

Library of Congress Number 97-67696

Manufactured in the United States of America
10 9 8 7 6 5 4 3 2 1

The author extends grateful thanks for permission to reprint the following material:

Killing the White Man's Indian by Fergus Bordewich. Copyright 1996 by Fergus Bordewich. Used by permission of Doubleday, a division of Bantam Doubleday Dell Publishing Group, Inc.

The Kabir Book, versions by Robert Bly. Copyright 1971, 1977 by Robert Bly, copyright 1977 Seventies Press. Reprinted by permission of Beacon Press, Boston.

Infected Christianity by Alan Davies. Copyright 1988 by Alan Davies. Used by permission of McGill-Queens University Press.

Black Elk: Holy Man of the Lakota by Michael Steltenkamp. Copyright 1993 by Michael Steltenkamp. Used by permission of University of Oklahoma Press.

The Sacred Pipe by Joseph Epes Brown. Copyright 1953 by Joseph Epes Brown. Used by permission of University of Oklahoma Press.

Mystical Passion by William McNamara, OCD. Copyright 1977 by William McNamara. Used by permission of Element Books, Inc.

Sweat: The Illustrated History and Description of the Finnish Sauna, Russian Bania, Islamic Hamman, Japanese Mushi-buro, Mexican Temescal and American Indian and Eskimo Sweatlodge by Mikkel Aaland. Copyright 1978 by Mikkel Aaland. Used by permission of Capra Press.

Quotations from Gandhi are reprinted by the kind permission of the Navajivan Trust, Ahmedebad 14, India.

contents

acknowledgments

To the Ancestors of My Body, among whom are:

William Cox: 1580–1655—who was born a member of the *English* nation, who
    worked as a *farmer*, and who died and was buried in *England*

Samuel Winstead: 1670–1726—English, farmer, Virginia

John Burney: 1725–1794—American, farmer and slave owner, North Carolina

John McVay: 1748–1832—Scottish, farmer, Kentucky

Stephen Underdown: 1750–1805—Cherokee, farmer, North Carolina

Johann Siefker: 1768–1840—German, farmer, Germany

Henry Critser: 1793–1877—Bavaria, miller, Indiana

Reverend Colemore Lovelace: 1795–1864—American, Fundamentalist Baptist
    preacher, Kentucky

Elizabeth Lusterheide: 1807–1879—German, midwife and herbalist, Indiana

Rudolph Buhner: 1807–1849—Dutch, farmer, Indiana

Drucilla Bailey: 1809–1875—Irish, farmer, Kentucky

John Henry Buhner: 1830–1864—German, farmer and Union soldier, Tennessee

To the Ancestors of My Spirit, among whom are:

Cecil Gardner Harrod: 1884–1963—adopted great-grandfather, physician

Alberta Harris: ca. 1925–1985—adopted African American mother/aunt, maid

Georgia: ca. 1920–1995—adopted African American mother/aunt, maid

Socrates: 469?–399—Greek philosopher and teacher
Robert A. Heinlein: 1907–1988—American author
Buckminster Fuller: 1895–1983—American thinker and inventor
Mohandas K. Gandhi: 1869–1948—Indian social activist and holy man
Black Elk: 1863–1950—Oglala holy man and Catholic catechist
Galileo: 1564–1642—Italian astronomer
Joan of Arc: 1412–1431—French saint
Theresa of Avila: 1515–1582—Spanish Carmelite mystic
Helen Keller: 1880–1968—American writer and lecturer
Ambrose Bierce: 1842–1914?—American journalist and writer
Mark Twain: 1835–1910—American writer
Aldo Leopold: 1886–1948—American writer and conservationist
Theodore Sturgeon: 1918–1985—American writer
Manuel Cordova Rios: 1887–ca. 1982—Peruvian healer
Frank Herbert: 1920–1986—American writer
Main-gans: ca. 1880–1940—Ojibway holy man and healer
Owl Woman: ca. 1880–1940—Papago holy woman and healer
Thomas Jefferson: 1743–1826—American writer, slave owner, and statesman
Benjamin Franklin: 1706–1790—American writer, inventor, and statesman
Thomas Paine: 1737–1809—American writer and political activist
Edward Abbey: 1927–1989—American writer
Mircea Eliade: ca. 1900–1990—Romanian author and historian of religions
Evelyn Underhill: ca. 1880–1960—English writer
Martin Luther King, Jr.: 1929–1968—Minister and civil rights activist

To the Members of the Nation to Which I Belong, among whom are:
Alice Walker, Barry Lopez, John Seed, Brooke Medicine Eagle, Edward Canda,
Joanna Macy, Delores La Chapelle, Trishuwa, Joan Halifax, Vaclav Havel, Benjamin
Bailey-Buhner, James Lovelock, Malidoma Patrice Somé, Michael Moore, Machelle
Small Wright, Masanobu Fukuoka, Sister Connie Bielecki, Harper Lee, Margaret
Rhode, Bill Mollison, Francesca Garvey, Hilton Silverman, and Carol McGrath

preface

In late 1969 I encountered the sacred for the first time—and that event irrevocably changed the course of my life. My experience was different from any religious experience I had ever heard of, in that it was centered in the powerful sacredness of the Earth itself, something of which I knew nothing. It started me firmly on a journey into what (I eventually learned) is known as Nature mysticism. And as this century, and my own path, has continued to unfold, the application of that kind of religious impulse to the environmental degradation of our times has become more and more apparent to me. In seeing the spread of environmentally unsustainable practices, and reading the increasing number of books on human relationships with the Earth that are being written in response, it seems to me that I am not alone in my experiences, that a great many people are being moved by the sacred power of the Earth. It is as if the human species, feeling the impacts of the greatest environmental devastation our planet has ever

experienced, is being moved by forces long thought to be merely superstitious remnants of an earlier and more primitive time. And this awareness has generated in me a great deal of hope and optimism about our species and the things of which it is capable. But as time has unfolded, I have also begun to notice that there is an increasing backlash to this reemergence of Nature- or Earth-centered spirituality. And that backlash is becoming stronger the more Earth spirituality spreads.

Unhappily, I found that when one touches the sacredness of the Earth, it is inevitable that one also touches, in time, her wounds. The backlash against Earth spirituality is merely a manifestation of those wounds. And it is an inevitable part of the journey into the sacredness of Earth that one must learn how to resolve and begin a healing of those wounds. This book represents, in part, *my* attempts to resolve and begin a healing of those wounds—wounds which lie between us and the Earth and between us as peoples. For myself, in writing this, and for the reader, this book entails an emotional and conceptual journey from the deep ecstatic joy of the sacred to the deep pains of our times. It was not an easy book to write, nor, I suspect, will it be easy to read. But there is a resolution to the environmental conflicts of our times: Out of the destructuring of our world can come another, newer world—one that represents the learnings we have been struggling with as a species. And an essential part of that resolution has been encoded in basic articulations of human contact with the sacredness of the Earth, articulations which have been expressed most strongly by people in hundreds of non-industrial cultures throughout the world. I call it the Indigenous Mind.

STEPHEN BUHNER
VISION MOUNTAIN

part one

the return to the sacred earth

prologue

There was a woman who lived in New York City (once upon a time) who was expecting visitors from France. She was very excited. She cleaned her apartment, made the guest rooms ready, and bought succulent groceries.

When it was time to go to the airport she had the car brought around, carefully threaded her way through traffic, found a parking place (a miracle), greeted them excitedly at the gate, and found room for everyone and their bags in the car.

The French couple and their fourteen-year-old son were filled with the wonder of America and, in heavy accents, remarked with awe on the size of New York City and the bustle with which everyone lived. Their hostess answered their comments and questions as best she could, explaining the city, helping them understand why Americans did things one way and not another, telling them what this building was and what that. Eventually, still talking, they arrived at her apartment.

The porter took the bags from the car and helped them into the elevator, accompanying them on the long ride up. The woman fumbled with her keys, got the locks open, and ushered them all into the apartment's living room. The windows along the south side offered a startling view of the city; the family rushed over to look. She tipped the porter who had carried in the bags while the family made excited comments about the view and the size of the apartment.

She took them on a tour of her home and showed them their bedrooms; they then put away their clothes and showered. All of them gathered afterward in the kitchen to prepare dinner. With everyone helping it was quickly prepared and they soon sat down to a large feast. Their hostess wanted to show them the best of America and had decided on steak and lobster, corn on the cob, fresh bread from the bakery down the street, a huge tossed salad with four kinds of lettuce and ripe red tomatoes and deep orange carrots blended in.

The family had brought a bottle of red wine from France and this they opened and poured into the delicate blue crystal goblets that were usually kept in the cabinet with the fine china. The boy, used to drinking wine at home, was given his own, blended with a little water. To their hostess's questions the parents replied that he was fourteen now and quite capable of drinking wine. When are children in America considered old enough? they wondered. She spent an amusing twenty minutes trying to explain how Americans think, which led to discussions about their respective lives and the different cultures in which they had been raised.

The French couple were enthusiastic. They were especially good storytellers—growing quite animated at particularly funny or sad interludes, interrupting each other, sawing the air with their hands, grabbing onto each other's arms, sharing emotions freely. Their hostess responded, and although more restrained by nature, she began mixing in stories of her own, which, in their own way, were quite as colorful as her guests'. Because of the intimacy, the spontaneous childlike quality of the stories, there grew between them all, even in so short a time, that close bond that sometimes happens between strangers who are getting to know one another.

The talk shifted from the personal past into the present and then to what the family would do here in America. With glowing eyes they spoke of the places they wanted to visit, the things they wanted to see. Occasionally there was a pause as each thought over what had been said.

The dinner was winding down when someone suggested they move to the living room. There, more at ease on the couches, with the lights of the city twinkling in the background, they continued over cups of dark French roast coffee. The talk began to be punctuated by those comfortable silent pauses that occur after good food and rich conversation. Settling into one such period of quiet, into the soft cushions of her couch, with the rich smell of the coffee deep in her lungs, the woman heard the boy clear his throat. She looked up. He met her eyes shyly, smiled, and said, "Tell me, where are the holy places in America? We would like to visit them."

The woman swallowed her sip of coffee and set the cup down, leaned back in the couch. She felt the question, asked in all innocence, push through the surface of her mind and ripple down, penetrating far inside. It found its way to the great quiet place that is far down within each of us and she felt its meaning like some magical efflorescence begin to move through her. In some strange way, at that moment, she seemed to be both inside and outside of her body. She saw the boy looking at her, still with a slight smile on his face, waiting for an answer. She saw the mother and father turning slightly to hear what she would say. She saw herself sitting on the couch and the great lights of the city far out in the velvet darkness of the night.

Her mind seemed to operate with slow clarity. She watched it tasting the meaning of the boy's question as it moved deeper within her in search of an answer. It moved among the years of her life, touching her feelings and memories. She watched it, physically moving among the whorls and ridges of her brain. Looking, looking. Looking for the place where the sacred places of America were located.

Time passed and no nearer an answer, she saw the parents turn fully to look at her. From a far distance she saw herself clear her throat and moisten her lips. She saw her mouth move and say, now, the only thing left inside it.

"I don't know."

This book is the beginning of an answer to the boy's question.[1]

chapter one
the door without a key

Late one evening in San Francisco in 1969, after having
stepped out with some friends to attend a concert, I
found myself standing bemused after stumbling
through a door that had no frame, no lock, and no key.
Standing unmoving on the other side of the door I
could see back through it to where I had come from.
The people, the musicians, everyone all frozen, unmoving. Even the air seemed held in place as if in one
instant all of time had been stopped and I was now
walking outside it, unaffected by its movement. As I
turned from the door to look at what I had stumbled
upon, to try to gather my bearings, I found myself in a
place where my old world, the meanings and directions
of my life as I had known them up until then, meant
no more than a gust of wind on a winter's day.

It is difficult to condense to words an experience
that lies so far outside them. But underneath the foundations of our world lies another, deeper world, and for
some reason I had tripped and fallen into that world, a

world that until that time, was unknown and unsuspected by me. This is my story about it, about what I found there, about what I learned about myself and the Earth. It is a door, through which, I suspect, many people have tripped and fallen in the past thirty years. What each of them has found in that deeper world depends on who they are and why they were called there.

Across from me I could sense a presence so pure and bright to my questing perceptions that had I looked on the sun without the protection of the atmosphere I could not have been more blinded. I quailed before it. I was afraid and yet at the same time it was as if I were starving and not knowing I had been given, for the first time, food to eat. The impact of that which I perceived so near to me was to hear for the first time, to see for the first time, to feel for the first time. All of its presence came flooding in, deep into my quivering soul, and no nook or cranny of myself escaped the flood of its brilliance. I longed to be closer to it—some deep drive inside me drove me to it and yet it burned. It was the first time I felt directly the touch of the sacred.

The brilliant presence seemed to look down from a long, long height and notice me. As its attention focused on me, I quailed again. Never had a gaze so pierced me. I was seen, exposed, opened, unlocked, laid bare. And to me came a deep thrust of *meaning*. In the next few seconds, or three hours, or month— it was as long as a lifetime and as short as a heartbeat—there was between me and that presence an exchange of meaning. Later I interpreted this exchange as sights, sounds, tastes, feelings, and smells—but at that time the directed focus of the sacred poured into me as an essential meaning. I was a container too small for its contents. I was asked, with infinite love and pity (and yet it burned all the same), why I had come.

I did not know and I said so.

"Do you know then, who you are?"

My soul shook inside me. "No."

"Then come and see." A part of that which I saw, and that which I call my Teacher (and which Kabir—the fifteenth-century Indian mystic and poet—calls the Guest), reached for me and lifted me up, out of my body, and said, "Look."

My body stood there, fixed in place like everything else on the other side of that invisible door. Under the irresistible force of that will I looked deep into

the people in the room, the wood of the floor, even the molecules of the air. And each place I looked I could see a living energy, a dancing pattern of light, of the same substance as that which taught me now.

"Touch it," I was told.

Not my hands—which were with my fixed body—but some part of me reached out, went past the surface of the things I was seeing and touched that dancing pattern of light. It slowed in its dance for a minute and looked up at me. I felt a great love coming from it; it greeted me. I greeted it in turn and there was a great joy in that touching.

The presence touched me and once it had my attention it took me to each and every thing in the room, having me touch the dancing light and speak to it. I saw that, indeed, everything was possessed of this sweet and lovely presence, the people, their clothes, the wood of the floor, the windows, the doors of the building, even the air. And when I compared them, the essence that lay at their core was all of the same substance.

The process of seeing and touching went on—hours of time or only seconds, I could not tell. Eventually when all had been seen, that being reached over and touched my eyes. Words as pure as living flame sang in my ears: "So you will always, from this day on, see with them."

"Now come and look at your body." I was lifted up and over to my body. There my spirit floated, hovering off the floor. "Look inside," I was told.

I could see now that there was a core inside where the dancing light, *myself*, resided. Just outside this core was the beginning of layer upon layer of the complexities that I used to give myself a body and the ability to exist in the physical world. Around my spirit (the dancing light that is at the core of all things) there was wrapped a fuzzy gossamer patterning, which I understood to be my psychological body. I could see that it slowed down the impact of information from the universe into manageable bits, and it created time. Further portions of my psychological body specialized in processing the information I received from the universe. Among those specialized portions are the processes I know as feelings. This whole gossamer patterning was then laid inside the physical body to give it shape and form in three-dimensional space. The tendrils of the gossamer patterning infiltrated the physical body and attached in

thousands of different places, the places of physical and psychological inter-face. And deeper than them all was the place where the dancing light resided, and from that place deep inside I could see how it, too, reached out, attaching in thousands of different places to the gossamer patterning that was my psy-chological self and also into the body that was my physical self.

Now my attention was directed to something I had not noticed before. There were various dark places, almost like bruises, here and there in the gos-samer patterning. And when I looked I could see such dark places at various points throughout my body.

"What are they?" I asked.

"Illness. Here—know them."

I was lifted up, taken again to my body, brought into the heart of the darknesses in my body. Each one had a flavor, a taste to it, an identity of its own. I was immersed in each, they were familiar somehow, and they had an intelligence of their own. I was afraid. But I endured until I had met them all. I knew them and they knew me. My demons, my teachers, my illnesses.

I felt a deep sadness come over me.

"You must heal these things in yourself," I was told.

"?"

"I will show you." And there flooded into me each and every thing I would do for many years into the future to fulfill the imperatives I was being given. It was as if ten years of memories, of knowledge, were folded into me in a heartbeat: people I would meet, ways in which I was to train, places I would live, how many years it would take for each period of work. I was overcome. But it did not stop; it continued on. It continued on. It continued on.

There was nothing, I know now, that could have stopped that movement of Spirit, and in spite of the intensity of it, some deep part of me craved it. When at last the flood of knowledge ended there was a brief rest. In that time of silence, that slight pause, what I had been shown echoed and re-echoed within me as if a great bell had been rung and I, standing inside it, felt its rhyth-mic movement ebb and recede in great tides against my spirit.

My teacher touched me again. "Come . . . look."

My attention was directed to the other people. I could see the same kinds

of darkness in their psychological selves, in their bodies, in their spirits as those in me. Some of them were identical to the illnesses I, myself, was suffering from; some were quite different. Into me poured the understanding that, eventually, many years in the future, I would work to heal the darknesses in others—once I had learned how to heal them in myself.

Then my attention was directed to all things of this world. I could see the Earth, the trees, rivers, plants, all living things. In each was that dancing light and when I greeted them, they greeted me in a thousand voices, welcoming me to the world. Each thing of this Earth had, I was shown, its own sacred intelligence, its own *logos*. I found myself irrevocably bonded to them, their voices crying out to me, never to be silent again in this lifetime.

Now my attention was directed to my Teacher. I could see the dancing light, in a fierce, unfettered joy of movement filling up its body. Unconstrained by physical form, it danced undimmed. And I saw it was the same as all the others, only a thousand thousand times brighter and stronger. All that I knew, could conceive of, had been shown was of this I knew, and I bowed before it.

When I looked up again I saw that unfettered light and its reflection in all creation—all together, in harmony—move as if to the beat of a great heart that lay deep, deep below all things. And as I looked I saw the light looking back at me, smiling, welcoming me to the dance in voices a thousand times sweeter than any music I had ever heard. I was swept up in it and I cried out from the joy, almost like pain, of it. Then it crested and began to subside.

With infinite sadness, I knew it was time for me to leave. It was unbearable sorrow—deep grief and a rending. In some manner the assurance came to me that again, in some future time, I would return. Some time . . . sometime. And with that I felt myself put back into my body, there was a gentle push on my shoulder, and I was thrust back through the door that has no frame, no key, and no lock. And I found myself standing in the crowd, hearing the music, wondering what had happened to me and where I had been. I reached up and felt my eyes, which felt the same to my questing fingers. But when I looked at the world I could still see that dancing spirit in all the things around me. My ears seemed the same but I could hear the voices of all life calling out. And if

I looked deeper I could see the dark illness in people's bodies, selves, and spirits. And I could yet reach out and touch that deeper underlying essence of the world.

I felt a great longing to be again where I had been, a drive to return that was greater than anything I had ever known. I looked but I could see no door, no frame, no key, no lock. I noticed then a great bruising to my spirit, to my body, to my emotional self; I had been touched in ways I never had been touched before. I was, I found, very tired.

When I left the concert that night I was not the same person who had started out—I never would be again. Everywhere I went I could see that dancing light at the core of everything. Whenever I looked at it, it slowed a bit and sang out with gladness to me. All around me the voices of the world were raised up until I could hardly hear the voices of my companions. And whenever their voices did get through, whenever I looked at them, I found my eyes invariably looking deeper, finding in them those traces of darkness in their psychological and physical selves that I had been taught how to see. And when they talked to me I could see energetic patterns of communication coming from those dark places, from many areas of the gossamer patternings within them and from many points of their body. I could see these energy flows influencing and shaping the words they used, the forms of communication they chose to send out into the world.

My greatest challenge in the years that followed was learning to differentiate between these deeper communication flows and patternings and the surface communications that people commonly use. My greatest weakness was a lack of emotional maturity, which made it so very difficult to master, with any grace, the gifts I had received.

I found myself responding to the elements in people's deep unconscious that shaped their communications and behavior rather than to the words that floated on top. No other event could have prepared me for the experience I had had; no metaphors could help me explain it; no one in my family could help me. Knowledge of deep experiences of the sacred was almost nonexistent in American society at that time. There were no helping professionals who were competent in the life of the Sacred.

I knew on the one hand that what had happened to me was more real

than anything I had ever experienced before—it was the REAL. My life, charged as it now was by the touch of the sacred, was brighter, more vibrant, more alive. In comparison, my life before was dull and drab. I had no doubt of the reality of what I had felt and experienced. But, on the other hand, I was quite clear that if I told the wrong person, I might find myself labeled psychotic or forcibly medicated. (Talking to God is okay! But when God talks back, Western society begins to get visibly nervous.) This social tension, combined with the deep awe and reverence that the experience had engendered in me, and a sense that premature disclosure of any of it was somehow inappropriate, caused me to wait many years before I told anyone about it. Yet all along the way the living presence that had touched me remained inscribed in my flesh, in the cells of my body, and the memory of it showed me the clear light of my road—the road that I have tried to follow for so long.

When, finally, many years later, I wrote of my experience, my hands shook and the sweat poured off me. Even today, I have not shared it all; some of it cannot be spoken in words; some of it I cannot bring myself to say.

Still, in the years before I spoke of it, I worked on what I had been shown, attempting to harness the capacities I had been given and diligently working on my own personal healing. I focused my training and healing in four areas: the use and development of my mind (primarily the capacity to think, reason, and remember); the healing and understanding of my psychological self (experiencing and training in particular forms of psychotherapy and psychological balancing); the development and healing of my body (going through body movement and deep tissue repatterning and certain physical regimens and training and healing); and the understanding and balanced use of the powers of perception that had been given me (infinite practice and failure, training with knowledgeable teachers, and specializing in the study of transcultural religious experience). And all through my development in these fours areas I was working to bring myself in alignment with the sacred fire that I had felt. I felt its presence each day (to greater and lesser degrees—depending on what I was struggling with in my growth) but within me was a drive to manifest it more and more strongly in myself, to feel it once again in that same degree of purity and power. I wanted to be in that place again.

The work was so hard and I so poorly equipped that I think that had not the love of the sacred been so strong, the memory of its touch so deeply graven on my spirit and body, I could not have continued. I could not have endured the journey that lay before me.

Although the process itself will never be completed, much had been accomplished after eleven years. It was nearly time to begin a more public part of my journey. At that time I had two powerful new experiences of the sacred that were to prove crucial in my development and work. Both of them are integrally connected to the sacredness of the Earth (and the subject of this book) and both of them occurred in 1980 while I was attending a ceremonial Solstice Dance and retreat at Bandolier National Monument in New Mexico.

The spiritual power of New Mexico is phenomenal. The sacred light, which had been my companion for so many years, manifests itself in many forms, each with its own intelligence, power, and knowledge. Many places on the Earth are filled with particularly focused concentrations of this sacredness, and when human beings visit them the sacred light can come into them, fill them up, and rejuvenate them for long periods afterward. This concentration of sacredness was understood by many indigenous tribes and prompted them to set aside certain places as holy. In addition to the sacredness of place, there are kinds of life and types of intelligence (many not recognized by Western science and society) that reside in those places. These beings have their own reasons for existing, their own destinies, and their own unique relationships with humans. They are called by many names (angels and devas among others) and they were well known to the indigenous tribes of the Americas. In New Mexico they are so numerous, and the power of the land is so extreme, that a vibrant, living electricity fills the air. This vibrancy beats upon the consciousness of most Americans and some of it works its way in to where the dimmed and buried self rises up and reaches out to feel its kin-self manifested so strongly in the world. For me, for many years, touching the sacred power of New Mexico's land was almost overwhelming. Like that original vision this trip pulled me into another world and there, awaiting me, were new lessons, new challenges.

The leader of the ceremonial retreat had arranged to have a woman teacher, a member of one of the Indian nations, attend the gathering for several days. I had studied with her once before when she taught at a small gathering in Colorado; I was excited to have another opportunity to learn from her.

Approximately fifty people had come to participate in the ceremonies for the summer solstice. We had spent many days packing in our supplies (about five miles into the national forest), setting up camp, and getting ready for the ceremony. Each part of the process was filled with ceremony and a good deal of hard work. There were latrines to dig, the kitchen to set up, campsites to find and establish, and many meetings so that strangers could become a cohesive community.

During the initial days of our time together there were many ceremonies and experiences that helped us become one group. Some of them were fairly simple, such as extensive drumming and chanting together, talking and sharing of personal goals and intentions for our time together, and teachings by the workshop leader about the nature and context of the ceremonies we were to do. Other activities were more involved. All culminated in the day-long Solstice Dance.

We began the dance as the sun rose above the horizon and continued until it was obscured by the turning of the Earth on the longest day of the year. I danced from sun sight to sun eclipse and to my surprise I was not tired or sore—neither then nor the next day—not ever. I was refreshed, renewed.

These days of ceremony—the intensity and focus of many of them and the intention of the gathering—served to create a special state of mind in us all. We were each experiencing, at ever deepening levels, the sacredness of the Earth; and for some of us, there were times when we slipped into a state of mind in which we experienced the underlying sacredness of our world and the deep communications that are embedded in it. Such outcomes are intentional and natural results of deep ceremonial processes and, indeed, are the orientation of mystical traditions the world over. In many of us there existed a hunger for a restoration of deep meaning in our lives, and such focused ceremony allowed it to occur. So by the time the visiting medicine teacher arrived, everyone was experiencing the fabric of the sacred in a deeper manner than when they had first arrived, myself included.

After she arrived and had rested she met for a while with the workshop leader. She had intended to stay for some time but she said it was now necessary for her to leave that evening. She would stay, however, for a pipe ceremony around the dance circle, and at the appointed time we all gathered.

She stood in the east; in the west stood the ceremonial leader. Filling out the rest of the council circle were the fifty of us. I was standing in the north, not too far from the visiting teacher. The medicine teacher and the ceremonial leader filled their pipes with prayers and ceremony; then they stood up. The pipe woman looked up to the heavens and held up her pipe. In that moment I was transfixed; each moment seemed to last an eternity. The air seemed to sparkle with a living energy of its own and the very ground moved as if alive. She held her pipe bowl in her right hand, the stem lifted to the heavens. In my peripheral vision I noticed a stirring behind her. I moved my eyes from her tall, erect figure and looked. Immediately behind her, in vivid detail, stood another medicine person. He was clothed, like her, in traditional dress, and he stood erect and tall behind her, his hand reaching out, lifting his pipe to the heavens. Behind this holy one, another stood, not quite so distinct, also tall and erect, *his* pipe held up also. And as I looked I saw them standing, each behind the other, far down the line until they grew dim, fuzzy, and indistinct and then faded out altogether, far, far down the line where my sight could not take me. I knew I was seeing in that long, long line of holy ones all the people who had carried that pipe lineage throughout time. The heavy length of years poured over me and caught me up, carrying me along into the depth and richness of the pipe. Then a shuddering sigh shook me and on the edges of my vision I saw a stirring before her. I shifted my eyes toward the front of her body: there, in front of her, stood another holy one, pipe raised to the heavens, and before him, another one, and before her another one. Far, far out in front of her they stretched until they disappeared into the distance of those future times that I cannot see. I looked upon them and I knew that I saw the untold numbers of those who would carry the pipe in other times and other places long after we who were standing there were all dust and long forgotten.

I raised my eyes once again to the medicine woman and then to her pipe. In that moment the power of the pipe entered my body, and a sweetness and

strength and sacredness, unique and different from any I had known before, touched me, called to me, exhorted me. I knew then that this was a ceremony that I would carry for the rest of my life within me.

From that moment I became a pipe carrier although I had not yet smoked the pipe, knew nothing of it with my mind, had not trained in its use at all. For a few seconds only was I swept up into that sacred world but the power of it is with me still. In all the years that I have sat with the pipe, smoked it, and learned from it, the power of that moment has never left me. Even now I feel its touch upon me as I write these words, remembering that time. (Shortly after I returned from this trip a pipe came to me. I would pray with it each morning for seven years before it awakened and told me it was time to begin smoking it.)

But then, the moment shifted and she was just a woman standing there carrying the burden we all carry as human beings. It was as if a great light had shown briefly through her and then had damped down; she seemed smaller and frail. Time began to flow again, people shifted and coughed, and a rustling of movement went through all of us. We all sat and the pipes were lit and passed around the circle. There were so many of us that a pipe would only come to each of us one time. When finally I held it in my hands I felt that I had come home to something that I had always known but had somehow forgotten. I took the pipe and lifted it to my lips and drew the smoke deeply into my body, released it, let it rise to the heavens and Creator. The event shook me. In that moment I felt my body and spirit intermingling with all other life; I felt all of the life web come into balance and a certain ease and community sense were restored to me. Then I passed the pipe to the next person and, in a few moments, the ceremony was complete, the final prayers were said, and people began drifting apart into the groups and isolated clusters that normally make up any gathering of people. The medicine teacher packed up her things and I carried them to her car for her (miles in the dark). We talked a little on the hike but I was still too caught up in the experience to be very sensible.

Over the next few days I was deep in thought. I could feel strong shifts in myself at the deepest levels of my being; I could feel the touch of that sacred being who had come to me so many years before and started me on this journey. It seemed to be standing just behind the scenes, sending the spirit of the

pipe to me, directing these teachings I was receiving—and this gift of the pipe was not to be the last.

Eventually, it would send me one more gift, like all of them so rich that, even in seventeen years, I have touched just the surface of its meaning. The first week of the ceremonial retreat had been focused around the Solstice Dance; the second week was to be focused on a Long Dance at the Shrine of the Mother of the Hunt during the full moon, which necessitated moving our location. We packed up the camp (a huge task for a group of fifty) and began a five-mile hike deeper among the bluffs and forests of Bandolier until we came to the Shrine of the Mother of the Hunt. This shrine is very old, at least 700 years anthropologists say, although the Earth and stones there tell me it is much older. The shrine is a circle of stones. Over the centuries, as people have added more and more stones, the circle has risen to form a low wall broken at one end by a doorway. In the center of the shrine are two large stones resting side by side. Only after looking carefully does one discern that they are in the shape of crouching mountain lions. Because they have been worn down by untold years of weathering, to the casual glance they resemble nothing more than low, oblong stones. Between these two there is a pile of antlers, some obviously quite ancient, some so recent they are still bloody. And mixed with them are shards of pottery, lance points, and arrowheads. It is, in fact, a shrine to a being that is known to tribes all over the world: the Mother who governs the hunt and who will, sometimes, intervene on behalf of humankind when asked to bring her children as food.

As the sun sank below the horizon and the full moon arose, we circled the shrine, entered, and began to dance. This dance, like the Solstice Dance, would last a complete cycle. Instead of beginning with the rise of the sun, however, we would be dancing from the beginning of night until the sun came up again the next morning. Throughout the dance, as the evening progressed, I watched the stone lions grow more and more distinct in the moonlight until it seemed they were newly carved stone, as fresh as the day they were born. As I had during the Solstice Dance, I passed some sort of plateau—even after many hours of dancing I was not tired or even sore.

We all slept late that next day, waking in the afternoon, eating as we were hungry, gathering in small clusters to talk and share. I had been feeling the need

to meet with the workshop leader and at one point, late in the afternoon, I approached her. I caught her eye and said hello. She paused, then motioned me over. I took one step, then another, then walked out of the forest onto the surface of a road I had not noticed before, a road whose existence I had not suspected, which, like the door I had found so many years before, did not exist on any map. The road stretched a long way in front of me.

I halted, disoriented. I looked around and found myself alone. I began to take stock of my surroundings. The road I was standing on was rather narrow and it stretched out so far in front of me that it seemed to taper until it was just a thin ribbon. I could tell that the end of the road was my destination, the place I had been journeying toward all these years. I longed, then, to be there, at the end. And as if I had spoken this thought aloud, an understanding came to me that it was not yet time, that the whole length of the road was to be walked. The purpose of this moment was something else. Again, like my first experience with the sacred, meaning began to flow into me.

I saw that the road I was on was floating in space and there were great worlds to each side of it. At that moment of understanding the experience of those worlds flowed into me: sights, sounds, feelings, tastes, smells, knowledge, and memories. I *knew* those worlds—not all their intricacies but their flavor, nature, depth, complexity, and reality. They were so large that should I enter any one of them there would be more than enough to keep me occupied, interested, learning for lifetimes. The complexity of the worlds, I knew, had the tendency to distract, to become . . . interesting, and, often, knowledge of the road itself would become vague and tenuous. If I should go into one of them I would be distracted by how involved, how deep, it was. I would think it the *only* world.

Each of these places was in fact a unique and distinct world. As I looked more closely I noticed that each world touched upon the road at its edge. If you came to the end of the world you would, invariably, find the road I was now standing upon: the road that threaded its way to that destination down its long, long length. The worlds lay in a long line one after the other on each side of the road—so many choices. They each were a way to the sacred center of all things. Here was the Buddhist world, there the Christian, there the Taoist, there the Lakota, there the Islamic, and so on and on. More worlds and ways than I knew

existed, thousands upon thousands. Understanding dawned on me: I received the knowledge, I took hold of it, I grasped it.

The world that one begins from is determined by a multitude of factors—destiny, personal affinity, birth, lessons to be learned. It—the world—must be followed, understood, completed for particular learnings unique to each soul. But each world that one begins from, no matter its form, if followed with a sincere heart, will lead to the road I stood on, and all lead to the same place in the end. It cannot help but do so. In that moment I knew the great identity that lies at the heart of all religious formulations. I was to walk this Earth path but, in the end I—like those who followed other paths—would come to *the* path on which I now stood. I understood then that all of us who walk this path—no matter in which world—are of one family. And I knew the depth, the beauty, of our diversity. I felt a warm love and deep humor come from that source at the far, far end of the road. Then, in that moment, almost like the closing of a door, my vision of the road and the worlds along its edges was cut off and I found myself back in the forest at Bandolier, the eyes of a teacher upon me. I looked into her deep blue eyes and she nodded. "Ummm," she said, "that was nice."

"Yes, yes, it was," I replied. And then looking again into her eyes, I smiled, turned, and walked back the way I had come. It was time to go home.

In the seventeen years since then I have learned many things about the pipe, have worked with it, carried it, and smoked it, praying with it in one form or another each day of my life. I have learned that it is one of the great and beautiful tools that Creator has given to humans to help them come into balance with all creation, to speak with Creator, and to touch the fabric of the sacred. And I have thought about the glimpse given me of the road we all travel if we decide to go home and the knowledge that the road that calls each of us is no better, no more superior than other roads given to other people. From each of them, on my Earth-centered walk, I have learned something.

Finding the way to the sacred is both the simplest and most difficult thing a person can do. In attempting that journey people begin the act that brings to light the basic essence of their sacredness and of their humanity. It is called by some the mystic way.

chapter two
the mystic way

*A firsthand experience of God, the Absolute Reality, and a
life controlled by the love that that experience awakens:
this is what unites all mystics, Christian and non-
Christian alike; therefore, unity of the human world
depends on the growing number of mystics.*
— WILLIAM McNAMARA, O.C.D. [1]

San Francisco in 1969—the year when an enterprising
thief stole a white polar bear–skin rug and a gold-
headed cane from a house downtown and walked off
with them through the crowded streets in broad daylight. No one noticed. San Francisco in 1969—*everyone*
dressed eccentrically. And it was here in this town that a
door was waiting for me, one without a key, a frame, or
a lock.

I'd come to San Francisco to escape white middle
America. I'd found myself stranded in that boring,
bland, nonculture called American Suburbia. The
houses stretched in insane geometric rows of sameness,

displacing cornfields, farmhouses, and our collective past. The roots of meaning were skin-deep. They went no further than the clothes we all had to have, the car we rode in, the Avon-decorated, bland faces of our mothers, and the absence of our fathers. But a curled wave of immense proportions, climbing unstoppably out of the human psyche, was beginning to grab the nation by the throat and for a few seconds it would shake us all and leave some of us changed forever.

In some past time my mind had made peace with the intolerableness of my life by turning off and shutting down, becoming skin-deep. Who I was and where I was going were thoughts unthought, no more a part of my life than the black experience, American Indians, migrant farmworkers, great art, love, dignity, or strength of human purpose.

I was, of course, in school. "High" school—a term that would come to have, in the 1960s, many meanings. In the beginning it only meant another place where I had to be. Another no-choice in a long line of no-choices. The teachers were as flat and boring and geometrically turned out as the houses we all lived in. No thought, no passion, no deep meaning came out of them and into us to awaken, excite, inflame us into thought, creativity, life. The halls were filled with the dull, plodding backs and fronts of my counterparts rushing between classes to destinations none of us thought about seriously. Lunch was greasy, bad food prepared by licensed dieticians and hair-netted food workers, and among all of us was the tension of unreleased violence and the emerging drive to propagate the species. Neither I nor anyone I knew had been prepared for these changes. The school system was our foster parent and its primary goal was crowd control. The system knew the power of the young when they begin to awaken from their sleep, but we, the young, did not. In nervous unconsciousness we surged toward our individual and collective destinies.

And then the sixties exploded like a cultural atomic bomb. The windstorm of that explosion blew through the collective souls of middle America, carrying with it everything not firmly fastened down. It grabbed me, shook me like a rag doll, and slowly, like many others, I began to wake up. When I finally turned sixteen I filed emancipation papers and moved out—out of town, out of white middle America.

The American Southwest, to those of us from suburbia, lay like a lifeless expanse of baked hell across the southern half of the western United States. Although I was to know it differently in later years, when I first headed across it with little more than the clothes on my back it scared me with its emptiness, heat, and indifferent greenery. A traveling salesman gave me a lift most of the way, dropping me off in Los Angeles. Even in those days the sky over L.A. was dirty and brown, obscuring the nearby hills with the industrial breath of too many people living in too close proximity. I didn't linger. A car stopped in response to my questing thumb. Two young men, in a Volkswagen loaded with a case of Coca-Cola (caffeine *and* sugar, they noted with satisfaction) and their meager belongings, stuffed me in the backseat and carried me up the coast to San Francisco. I didn't linger there either; my destination was Berkeley. My possessions consisted of an old Boy Scout daypack stuffed with a few bits of clothing and fifty dollars in my pocket. It was the first of January 1969.

With a great deal of effort I managed to rent a large walk-in closet for $25 a month just a stone's throw from the university. The People's Park massacre and the Berkeley riots were still fresh enough that the other residents of the apartment, all students at the university, kept gas masks at hand and their pantries filled with canned army rations. The apartment had the air of a place under siege.

It wasn't boring, it wasn't geometrically precise. In Berkeley in 1969 there were Asians, Indians, Blacks, Hispanics, Whites, Lesbians, Gays, Poor People, Rich People, Smart People, Creative People, Dumb People, Angry People, Political People. It was messy—they were all interacting with each other in a noisy, full spectrum of feelings, cultures, backgrounds, hopes, and dreams. As different from suburbia as a Thanksgiving feast from a frozen TV dinner. I couldn't get enough of it.

It was in that time, in that milieu, that I stumbled through that door with no key, no frame, and no lock. And I was not the only one. The sacred center of things was exploding through the world's human cultures like a whirlwind. And we swirled up, blown like down-seeds from the dandelion of the human species by the insistent breath of God. We were being carried this way and that,

some being dropped here, some there, some taking root and growing, some never finding fertile soil in which to grow. But we were being called. Called back to a primal journey, basic and essential to human beings—the journey that mystics have taken for millennia to the source of deep meaning, the source of all things—the human journey to the sacred: the mystic way.

The vacancy left within me from an overreliance on the material world, from the absence of deeper meanings, had been fertile ground for the intrusion of the sacred into my life. Now that I had been touched by it I was struggling to integrate it into my spirit and my heart, but I also wanted to understand it with my mind. I *needed* to understand it with my mind to fulfill the imperatives I had received. So I began to read, to ask questions, to seek. As time went on, I discovered that there were two areas of knowledge that contained the information I needed: the history of mysticism and the accounts of indigenous elders and teachers of the sacredness of the Earth. People, many people, had been this way before me. The map I was working to create, however, needed to have one particular, important difference from those of others. My experience, focused so strongly on the sacredness of the Earth, was of a particular kind of mysticism—nature mysticism. My teacher had been clear: It was not Christian, not Buddhist, not any of the others. It was Earth mysticism.

And it was for this reason that I needed so very much the accounts of indigenous elders and teachers because these traditions had been suppressed or destroyed in my own cultural heritage. (I thought this way, like so many do, in the beginning.) But as time went on I found, to my surprise, that my heritage was other than I had thought. I was not European. Oh, my distant ancestors were—no doubt of it. I was, however, not European—I was a child of this continent. Its blood beat in my veins, its heart in my ears, its rhythms were the song of my life. My body was formed of its soil, my bones of its rocks, my breath of its air. The sacredness I was carrying in me, the work I was here to do, was an expression of this continent, this land. I had to look to those who knew the mystical path but also to those who knew of this continent in particular. Not only had there been a merging of Native and European cultures but a unique spirituality was emerging—a nature mysticism shaped by the fabric of

this continent was coming into being in the children now being born—Indian *and* white. I needed, within myself, to blend both traditions into a unique form of nature mysticism suited for this time and this land and this people. The first task was to understand the mystic way.

the stages of a mystical life

Many people have written about the stages of the mystical life, and in spite of variations in their descriptions, the territory being described and the stages being synthesized are remarkably similar.

Evelyn Underhill, in her book *Mysticism,* examined the personal writings of many of the world's mystics and synthesized the stages of growth they went through. Although her work heavily emphasizes Christian forms of mysticism, it still serves to show the outlines and shape of that road to the Sacred—all mystics travel similar territory.

Underhill identified the stages of the mystical journey and gave them names: Awakening of the Self, Purgation (or Purification) of the Self, Illumination, Dark Night of the Soul, Union with the Divine. Other people have proposed slight variations to her stages. Joseph Epes Brown, anthropologist and historian of religions, defines these stages somewhat differently. Speaking of mystical traditions, he notes:

> [The mystical tradition being examined always has] its origins in a sacred source that is transcendent to the limits of the phenomenal world. All the expressions and extensions of this tradition will then bear the imprint of the sacred, manifested in terms appropriate to the time, place, and condition of humankind. The tradition provides the means, essentially through sacred rites, for contact with and, ultimately, a return to the transcendent Principle, Origin, or by whatever name this is called. True and integrated progress on such an inner journey demands the means for accomplishing the progressive and

accumulative integration of the following elements or spiritual dimensions: (1) purification, understood in a total sense, that is, of body, soul, and spirit; (2) spiritual expansion, by which an individual realizes his or her totality and relationship with all that is, and thus integration with, and realization of, the realm of the virtues; (3) identity, or final realization of unity, a state of oneness with the ultimate Principle of all that is. Spiritual expansion is impossible without the prerequisite purification, and ultimate identity is impossible outside the realm of virtue, wholeness, or spiritual expansion. These themes of purification, expansion, and identity are inherent in all the spiritual ways of the orthodox traditions of the world.[2]

Basically the journey on the mystical path begins when any human being, who, coming into contact with the sacred, becomes aware of an ultimate transcendent reality and then feels compelled to completely change all aspects of the self—physical, emotional, and spiritual—in order to achieve unity with that transcendent reality. All who have undertaken the journey and left a record of it have noted the great difficulty they experienced in remaking the self. The process is marked by extreme swings (closer to and then away from the sacred), by encounters with the basic foundations of the self and reality, and by the painful stripping away and remolding of the personality.

Underhill's description of the process is basically the same as Brown's: Awakening of the Self (called Contact with the Sacred by Brown and assumed by him to be a necessary prerequisite to the mystical journey), Purification of the Self, Illumination (called Expansion by Brown), and Union with the Divine (called Identity by Brown). The stage Underhill called Dark Night of the Soul is in reality the most excruciating period of the purification of the Self. In fact, the mystical journey can be simplified to three elements: that first touch of the sacred, which marks the beginning; the final union with the divine, which marks its end; and the process of purification that is in between and is marked by alternating periods of destructuring and balance—some lasting many years. Underhill calls the period of greatest balance Illumination; she calls the period of greatest destructuring of the self the Dark Night of the Soul.

The tendency to mark exactly one's passage through each stage of the journey is bound to cause confusion, as in the story of a Buddhist hermit who lived alone far from any monastery. He was so far away, in fact, that his teacher could only visit twice a year, spring and fall. The student did not mind, for he enjoyed the life of a solitary hermit and he also had the companionship of his books. He was liberally supplied with many of the major writings of Buddhism, for he had been quite wealthy before taking his vows and renouncing the world, and he had brought these few works of his old life with him. He read these earnestly and daily practiced the devotions his teacher had given him; in between he took long walks in the mountains. One fall his teacher noted the student had moved to a new level of spiritual awareness and, thinking the student was well aware of it, began to talk of it.

"Revered Teacher," the student said in surprise, "you must surely be mistaken."

The teacher, surprised in turn, asked how the student came to that conclusion.

"I have read of the stage of awareness that you are speaking of. Here," the student said, retrieving a book from his library and opening it to a certain page and pointing at it. "See. The stage of which you speak has these elements, and they differ from mine in many ways." And the student went into detail about the differences, concluding with: "So you must surely be mistaken."

The teacher looked at him for a moment, then laughed. "Surely, revered student," he said, "you have confused life with a book."

awakening of the self

All religious traditions assume that there is a sacred center to all things. The name differs from religious form to religious form, but it is clear that there is an inherent tendency for human beings to encounter this sacred center, to name it, and to incorporate the human experience with it into culture. Its prevalence is quite widespread in Native American religious forms as well as among the more traditional world religions. For instance, among the Oglala peoples of

North America it is called Wakan Tanka, among the Iroquois Orenda, among the Shoshone Pokunt, among the Algonquian Manitu, among the Kwakiutl Nauala, among the Tlingit Yek, among the Haida Sgana, among the Melanesian Mana,[3] among the Omaha Wakanda, among the Mandan Ho'pinis, among the Ojibway Manido,[4] among Christians God, among Hindus Atman-Brahmin, the Tao among Taoists, Yahweh in Judaism. Within mystical traditions people begin a contemplative life when that sacred center experientially touches them in a manner that forcibly makes them aware of its existence. Christian mystics have referred to this unasked-for touching as the violence of God's love or the grace of the divine touch. The New Age movement has referred to the various manifestations of this event as peak experiences. Whatever they are called, they are experienced in much the same manner by all human beings. The experience seemingly comes out of nowhere, "abrupt and well-marked, accompanied by intense feelings of joy and exaltation."[5]

Mystics the world over note the power and penetrating depths of this experience and the irrevocable changes it causes in a person. Underhill notes that "it is a disturbance of the equilibrium of the self, which results in the shifting of the field of consciousness from lower to higher levels, with a consequent removal of the centre of interest from the subject to an object brought now into view; the necessary beginning of any process of transcendence."[6]

A primary aspect of visionary experience is that it is always uninterruptible. Once it begins it goes through to its end. Lee Irwin, in *Dream Seekers*, notes that "obtrusive, unrelated events never break into or distract the visionary from the continuity of the experience."[7] Although Irwin was looking primarily at visionary experiences among the Plains cultures of the United States, mystical writings of other traditions and cultures also point to the unbreakable continuity of mystical vision.

The experience itself is anything but analytical. Its primary, overwhelming component is the deep effect it has on the spirit of the person. One example from Christian mysticism is that of Suso in which he describes his original mystical experience. (He refers to himself in the third person and as the Servitor, or Friar.) He was at prayer alone when

of a sudden his soul was rapt in his body, or out of his body. Then did he see and hear that which no tongue can express.

That which the Servitor saw had no form neither any manner of being; yet he had of it a joy such as he might have known in the seeing of the shapes and substances of all joyful things. His heart was hungry, yet satisfied, his soul full of contentment and joy; his prayers and hopes were all fulfilled. And the Friar could do naught but contemplate this Shining Brightness; and he altogether forgot himself and all other things. Was it day or night? He knew not. It was, as it were, a manifestation of the sweetness of Eternal Life, in the sensations of silence and of rest. Then he said, "If that which I see and feel be not the kingdom of heaven, I know not what it can be: for it is very sure that the endurance of all possible pains were but a poor price to pay for the eternal possession of so great a joy."

. . . This ecstasy lasted from half an hour to an hour, and whether his soul were in the body or out of the body he could not tell. But when he came to his senses it seemed to him that he returned from another world. And so greatly did his body suffer in this short rapture that it seemed to him that none, even in dying, could suffer so greatly in so short a time. The Servitor came to himself moaning, and he fell down upon the ground like a man who swoons. And he cried inwardly, heaving great sighs from the depths of his soul and saying, "Oh, my God, where was I and where am I? [and again] Oh, my heart's joy, never shall my soul forget this hour." . . . None knew from his demeanor that which was taking place within. But his soul and spirit were full of marvels; heavenly lightnings passed and repassed in the deeps of his being, and it seemed to him that he walked on air. And all the powers of his soul were full of these heavenly delights. He was like a vase from which one has taken a precious ointment, but in which the perfume long remains.[8]

Compare Suso's account with the poem of the great Indian mystic poet Kabir:

Between the conscious and unconscious, the mind has put up a swing:
all earth creatures, even the supernovas, sway between these two trees,
and it never winds down.

Angels, animals, humans, insects by the million, also the wheeling sun and moon;
ages go by, and it goes on.

Everything is swinging: heaven, earth, water, fire,
and the secret one slowly growing a body.
Kabir saw that for fifteen seconds, and it made him a servant for life.[9]

Compare both quotes with what the great Oglala holy man Black Elk says about his experience. In his vision, when he was nine years old, Black Elk was taken into sacred realms and shown the work before him and introduced to the powers of the world who gave him things with which to help in the work he had been shown. He spent twelve days in a coma and he was thought near death while he was experiencing his remarkably detailed visions. In the book *Black Elk Speaks,* he describes the impact the visions had on him and what it was like when he came back from that touch of the Sacred:

Everybody was glad that I was living; but as I lay there thinking about the wonderful place where I had been and all that I had seen, I was very sad; for it seemed to me that everybody ought to know about it, but I was afraid to tell, because I knew that nobody would believe me, little as I was, for I was only nine years old. Also as I lay there, thinking of my vision, I could see it all again and feel the meaning with a part of me like a strange power glowing in my body; but when the part of me that talks would try and make words for the meaning, it would be like fog and get away from me.

I am sure now that I was then too young to understand it all, and that I only felt it. It was the pictures I remembered and the words that went with them; for nothing I have ever seen with my eyes was so clear and bright as what my vision showed me; and no words that I have ever heard with my ears were like the words I heard. I did not have to remember these things; they

have remembered themselves all these years. It was as I grew older that the meanings came clearer and clearer out of the pictures and the words; and even now I know that more was shown to me than I can tell.[10]

This overwhelming sense of the sweetness and ultimate reality of what is being seen and the consequent impossibility of conveying it in words are a hallmark of such experiences. As Underhill says:

Commonly, however, if we may judge from these first-hand accounts which we possess, mystic conversion is a single and abrupt experience, sharply marked off from the long, dim struggles which precede and succeed it. It usually involves a sudden and acute realization of a splendor and adorable reality in the world—or sometimes of its obverse, the divine sorrow at the heart of things—never before perceived. In so far as I am acquainted with the resources of language, there are no words in which this realization can be described. It is of so actual a nature that in comparison the normal world of past perception seems but twilit at the best. Consciousness has suddenly changed its rhythm and a new aspect of the universe rushes in. The teasing mists are swept away, and reveal, if only for an instant, the sharp outline of the Everlasting Hills.[11]

This first, deep impact of the sacred is disruptive, stripping away as it does many layers of the secular psyche. The person experiencing it has been shown, has experienced, the touch of a reality far deeper and more real than that experienced in normal reality. After the original experience has passed, the person strives to encode it in language and memory. As I noted in my book *Sacred Plant Medicine:*

To explain the experience and to retain memory of it, human beings automatically structure the direct experience of the sacred into internalized symbolic constructs. Thus the sacred comes to be expressed in visions, wondrous feelings, thoughts, and sometimes smells and tastes. This is due to the nature of human memory patterning.

Human memory patterns are constructed of aspects of the five senses; that is, memories are encoded bits of sights, sounds, smells, tastes, feelings. Thus the experience of the sacred is translated into visions, sounds, smells, tastes, and feelings even though the sacred is both all and none of these things. Examinations of the written and oral records of those encountering the sacred show that their experiences were very rich and generally included all of the five senses.

Strong visionary experience is often accompanied by imperatives for human conduct. Conveyed during contact with the sacred, these imperatives often require the person to whom they are given to act in a certain manner, engage in a specific life work, or make changes in lifestyle or behavior. Because these imperatives are usually interpreted as language when experienced, they most often take on a pattern of language that is already encoded in the person receiving them. To make the imperatives, sensible people also interpret them through previously learned cultural experiences and values. Thus, if one is raised in a primarily Christian environment, any direct experience of the divine will often tend to take on Christian forms or symbols.

All these things—sensory memory bits, linguistic and cultural structures—that give the experience of the sacred memory form, become symbols that contain in themselves the capacity to reinvoke the original sacred experience. Though these elements are used, the sacred does not become only those things. Inherent in the experience of the sacred is the memory of its transcendent nature and the human, according to his or her capacity, is forced to generate more powerful constructs out of their own existing structures to encompass the immense morphology of the sacred. In this process it is not possible for the human to retain the full experience of the sacred. It is too large a territory. Even so the human has been changed, is no longer only secular, and the symbols they retain point the way to something other and more REAL than the human.[12]

Although this touch of the sacred is the true beginning of the mystical path, those who are so touched, when viewed from the vantage point of later

life, can be seen to have been possessed of a certain restlessness of character in the years leading up to the experience of the sacred. They were searching for something, although often they did not know it. This restlessness is often viewed as the deep stirrings of the inner spirit driving them onward to that time when the sacred reveals itself. In a number of indigenous cultures this state of restlessness was recognized, and the holy people of a tribe or culture would observe the young and seek to discern those in whom the sacred was beginning to work. When detected, those children of the tribe were marked for special training and preparation for the eventual sacred experience. Interestingly, many of the deep experiences of the sacred shared through the writings of the mystics reveal that a common age for this experience is around eighteen. (Black Elk did indeed experience a tremendous resurgence of his visions at eighteen— along with a drive to begin actualizing them in the world.)

Once the person has experienced this deep awakening of the self, he is usually called to begin lengthy and unremitting personal work that serves to incorporate the power of the experience into normal daily life. In contrast to New Age movements, established mystical traditions have a huge body of writing and tradition that backs up the initial mystical experience and the realization that such "peak experiences" are in themselves nothing without the work, the yoga, or discipline that follows. Practitioners in New Age movements have begun to realize that without a dedicated and unremitting practice of daily spiritual devotion such peak experiences tend to fade, leaving the person hardly better off than before.

This dedicated practice is designed to transmute all those elements of the self that are not in harmony with the deep reality that has been experienced, to make the self more reflective of the sacred center of things than of the secular, which has been the truth of the past. Underhill calls this stage of the mystic's growth Purgation, or Purification, of the Self; this stage ultimately allows complete unification with the divine principle at the center of all things.

purification of the self

Beyond the first personality-shattering contact with the sacred lie the years of spiritual practice to incorporate the initial mystical experience into everyday life. Purification of the Self is a process during which the person follows the dictates given in the initial mystical experience and the information shared by people who have previously taken this journey; the goal is to purify or make sacred the numerous parts of the self. Many established religious traditions have charted this journey in great detail and supply deeply useful information about the terrain the traveler encounters. The works of those who have gone before us indicate clearly that this is not a "one-size-fits-all" process.

Each person faces unique problems and challenges during the purification of the self because each possesses a unique psychological and physical makeup. A person who is afraid of heights may be prodded to overcome this limitation. A willful individual who is unwilling to hold back anger might focus many years of devotional practice on this personal trait. But the process is not one merely of working to surmount psychological limitations; the point is to actively purify the self so that personal limitations do not keep one from being in harmony with the sacred.

Throughout the process further mystical experiences help refine and deepen the journey, which is often quite difficult and painful. But the exchange of love between the contemplative person and the sacred center of all things keeps one on the path. As Underhill explains:

> Here, then, stands the newly awakened self: aware, for the first time, of reality, responding to that reality by deep movements of love and awe. She sees herself, however, not merely to be thrust into a new world, but set at the beginning of a new road. Activity is now to be her watchword, pilgrimage the business of her life. "That a quest there is, and an end, is the single secret spoken." Under one symbol or another, the need of that long slow process of transcendence, of character building whereby she is to attain freedom, become capable of living upon high levels of reality, is present in her consciousness.

Those in whom this growth is not set going are no mystics, in the exact sense in which that word is here used; however great their illumination may have been.[13]

Immediately after the initial mystic experience the illumined insight of the awakened soul is turned upon itself; deep consternation greets the contrast between the land from which it has returned and its normal state. The overwhelming desire of the soul is to unite once again with the divine but it cannot. Unification can only be maintained when the muscles of the spiritual self have developed sufficiently. Each step toward the Real necessitates an expenditure of spiritual strength, which the newly awakened self has in short supply. There is a necessary and inevitable falling away from the sacred during the period in which the new spiritual muscles are developing. The process of strengthening these muscles, of transforming the self from a secular to a sacred state, may take years and is not for the faint-hearted. St. Catherine of Genoa calls this process the immersing of the self into the "divine furnace of purifying love." The love spoken of by the mystics is not the pale, insipid, sentimental love spoken of so highly in common society or the New Age movement. It is a fierce and passionate love that may, only sometimes, have the quality of gentleness. Its purpose is not to coddle the frightened soul but rather to pierce it deeply and leave no part of it untouched by the sacred fire. Thus purification of the secular self usually entails many years spent working with aspects of the self that seemingly stand in opposition to union with the sacred. As St. Augustine noted: "I was swept up to Thee by Thy Beauty, and torn away from Thee by my own weight." Every aspect of the self that tears it away from the sacred must be revealed, explored, transformed.

Despite the conscious mind's awareness of the Real and its desire to return, the unconscious realms of the self must slowly be transformed. These unconscious realms have their own particular reasons for existence and each must be dealt with and understood. The mystic, of necessity, must become adept at understanding the human psychological structure and must come to terms with his or her own internal ego family. Through years of work, the unconscious realms must be brought into alignment and agree to move

together toward the divine center of all things. The attainment of this coherence is a daily, diligent, and difficult task.

The body, as holder of many psychological patterns and possessor of its unique structural impacts on the soul, must also be transformed. Both the body and the psychological self must be transformed, not only because their secular nature stands in the way of union with the sacred but because they must be able to hold all the power of the holy at times of deep experiences of the sacred. The mystic must come to know her own body deeply. The tendencies of the body toward disease, the movement patterns of the body, the manner in which muscle patterns contain emotional reality all must be dealt with and worked with. These understandings deepen over time, and more and more subtle elements of psychology and physical manifestation are explored and understood.

The tendencies of the Christian and Hindu mystics to asceticism and denial of the body have been misconstrued by some as indicating that the mystics hated the world and material things, including their own physical form. Some of them did. But this erroneous view has more to do with the lack of understanding of secular social cultures, which are based on contractual relationships, than with the reality of mystical calling, which is based on a covenantal relationship with sacred reality. The basic agreement upon which all Western society is based is abandoned as immaterial to the journey to the divine. Thus, many in Western society and some casual readers often respond with fear and misunderstanding.

The mystic, struggling to transcend her secular self and return to the heart of the divine fire, may often feel great loathing or hatefulness for the secular self, standing, as it seems to, in the way of return. Personal weaknesses of character and of body may be viewed with anger and with a wish to just be rid of them. The long years of developing the capacity to travel in sacred domains, to return to the sacred fire, involve the development of personal compassion and loving understanding of the self's limitations. This patience of character and the emotional expression of deep sacred compassion are an inherent aspect of the purification of the self. The suffering of the self must be understood personally—experientially at its fullest depth. The darkness must be fully entered

so that the mystic traveler knows the suffering of all life and knows fully, as Mary Baker Eddy noted, that "there is no place so dark that sweet Spirit has not been there before thee and prepared thy place." The self is purified, yes, but there are other elements of this stage of the mystical journey that are as important. Here the self learns nonattachment. Here the self learns sacred compassion. Here the self learns of the inevitability of suffering. Here the self develops sacred strength and muscle development. Here the self learns the absolute unbreakable truth that she will never be abandoned by God.

The suffering of the self during purification teaches the prime, transreligious principle of nonattachment. The capacity for nonattachment (the concept so perverted in its New Age popularization) comes as an inevitable development *in its own time.* When the soul has exhausted its strength in trying to save the world from its suffering, to save itself from its own suffering, and accepts that suffering is, has been, and always will be and releases itself to the divine will, the first and most important lesson of nonattachment is learned. In time this truth is developed and expanded; the self's understanding and use of it are broadened. The universality of the lesson of this element of the stage of purification is evident in the writings of the world's mystics. Christian mystic St. John of the Cross speaks of how attachment to the secular world keeps one from the sacred:

> That thou mayest have pleasure in everything, seek pleasure in nothing. That thou mayest know everything, seek to know nothing. That thou mayest possess all things, seek to possess nothing. . . . In detachment the spirit finds quiet and repose, for coveting nothing, nothing wearies it by elation, and nothing oppresses it by dejection, because it stands in the centre of its own humility. For as soon as it covets anything, it is immediately fatigued thereby.[14]

And the need to give up attachment is absolute.

> It makes little difference whether a bird be held by a slender thread or by a rope; the bird is bound, and cannot fly until the cord that holds it is broken; still notwithstanding, if it is not broken the bird cannot fly. This is the state

of a soul with particular attachments; it never can attain to the liberty of the divine union, the soul as the remora is said to affect a ship; that is but a little fish, yet when it clings to the vessel it effectually hinders its progress.[15]

Kabir speaks to this idea as well:

> Friend, please tell me what I can do about this world
> I hold to, and keep spinning out
>
> I gave up sewn clothes, and wore a robe,
> but I noticed one day the cloth was well woven.
>
> So I bought some burlap, but I still
> throw it elegantly over my left shoulder.
>
> I pulled back my sexual longings,
> and now I discover I am angry a lot.
>
> I gave up rage, and now I notice
> that I am greedy all day.
>
> I worked hard at dissolving the greed,
> and now I am proud of myself.
>
> When the mind wants to break its link with the world
> it still holds onto one thing.
>
> Kabir says: Listen my friend,
> there are very few that find the path.[16]

Black Elk discusses the idea with Joseph Epes Brown (recounted in *The Sacred Pipe*):

Any man who is attached to the senses and to the things of this world, is one who lives in ignorance and is being consumed by the snakes which represent his own passions.[17] . . . I think I should explain to you here, that the flesh represents ignorance, and, thus, as we dance [while being pierced through the flesh in the Sun Dance] and break the thong loose, it is as if we were being freed from the bonds of the flesh. It is much the same as when you break a young colt; at first a halter is necessary, but later when he has become broken, the rope is no longer necessary. We too are young colts when we start to dance, but soon we become broken and submit to the Great Spirit.[18] . . . As I have said before, of all the created things or beings of the universe, it is the two-legged men alone who, if they purify and humiliate themselves, may become one with—or may know—Wakan Tanka.[19]

The learning of nonattachment comes, as I mentioned, not from any sense of "you have to or you're bad," but from the mature recognition of its necessity at a certain point in the soul's journey. It is grasped and developed at a particular time of great suffering of the self. And for that time and particular struggle in the stage of purification it is the only resolution possible. There is an elegance in this resolution: it is the only solution that will work and the only solution that allows the mystic to move into the next stage of the journey. Immature souls who try to mimic nonattachment because they feel it to be spiritually superior to attachment do themselves a disservice. They should concentrate on being *authentic* and real to themselves for who and what they are now. Only then can the true lessons of each step of the journey be learned. The result otherwise is a terrible caricature of spirituality and humanity.

The development of nonattachment leads, for the first time, to the first real integration of humility. Humility and nonattachment are part and parcel of the same thing, two sides of the same coin, differing aspects of the same gestalt. As Brooke Medicine Eagle notes, "*Humble* comes from the same root word as *humus* and means 'of the earth, or close to the earth.' "[20] This capacity for humility begins in an integral aspect of the original mystical vision: from the touch of the sacred a person becomes aware of just how small and ineffectual he or

she really is, and that the capacity to do comes from the sacred. As Black Elk says about his ability to cure: "Of course it was not I who cured. It was the power from the outer world, and the visions and ceremonies had only made me like a hole through which the power could come to the two-leggeds. If I thought I was doing it myself, the hole would close up and no power could come through. Then everything I could do would be foolish."[21] Although Christian religious adherents are particularly noted for taking this concept to unhealthy degrees or transforming it into aberrant behavior patterns, its primary nature is a simple acceptance of human limitations. In early life it is difficult to incorporate this idea into personal perspective. Later, after much life experience, it becomes more obvious. But a sense of humility in the face of direct experience of the sacred *is* an integral aspect of any visionary touching.

An Oglala, Lone Man, notes:

> After my return to camp I wanted to do something to show that I realized my unworthiness of the honor given me by the thunderbirds. No one told me that I ought to do this, and yet all who dream of the thunderbirds in any of their manifestations have a deep sense of their own unworthiness. I knew that I was only an ordinary mortal and had often done wrong, yet the riders in the air had disregarded this. By appearing to me they had given me a chance to redeem myself. I wanted to make a public humiliation to show how deeply I realized my unworthiness.[22]

The internal sense of humility, first encountered at the touch of the sacred, is finally integrated when the lesson of nonattachment is learned. From this time, the sacred keeps working on the soul, refining the understanding of nonattachment, moving the soul out of flight-or-fight responses (the law of the jungle) into the acceptance of and nonattachment to suffering (the law of the heart). At the same time the soul recognizes that nothing that she does will ever relieve the suffering of humankind (and in spite of this recognition, she must still respond to it). The result is an integrated and deep humility of self.

balance in the sacred—
illumination of the self

He who is called by the sacred center of all things turns all he is or can be to the task set before him. In time, when he is changed through the deep inner work necessary for transformation, when "he has arranged his life in accordance with [his vision],"[23] when the divine inner child that was called into being by the direct touch of the sacred upon it learns to walk, and the "tottering is over, the muscles have learnt their lesson, [the child is] standing upright and secure. That is the moment which marks the boundary between the purgative and illumina-tive states."[24] In another sense, when the initial, major work of purification is completed, the soul is granted a time of rest, a time in which she can dance with the sacred in exquisite balance.

Illumination, unlike popular conceptions, is not the stage in which one becomes one with God, commonly referred to as enlightenment; it is simply the time when one is balanced in the sacred, a time when the secular self has been so altered that one exudes and lives a deep and harmonious sacredness. A basic duality, I and Thou, still exists in personal experience and in the world. But the self has changed its secular nature; it is now congruent, in harmony, with the sacredness of the vision that touched it so many years before.

> He has now got through preliminaries; detached himself from his chief entan-glements; re-oriented his instinctive life. The result is a new and solid certi-tude about God, and his own soul's relation to God: an "enlightenment" in which he is adjusted to new standards of conduct and thought. In the tradi-tional language of asceticism he is "proficient" but not yet perfect. He achieves a real vision and knowledge, a conscious harmony with the divine World of Becoming: not yet self-loss in the Principle of Life, but rather a will-ing and harmonious revolution about Him, that "in dancing he may know what is done."[25]

The soul has come to know itself. It has learned its secret unconscious manners of keeping separate from the sacred, its secret ways of holding onto things, and has transformed them. It has given up feelings of superiority. It has experienced the underlying suffering of life and come to terms with it. It has surrendered to the will of the divine. It no longer holds itself back, no longer can maintain that it is in any way in control but acknowledges in the deepest parts of the personality that there is something beyond itself from which it has come that is the primary moving force of its world. There is a peace in this surrender, a clarity about many things that were not apparent before. One has entered into a house that one never completely leaves again. This is not to say that there are not times of difficulty or of doubt, "renewals of the temperamental conflicts experienced in purgation,"[26] or new challenges and upheavals in the deep self. But the struggle between the clinging self and the soul has been won insofar as the soul now knows without exception and with a certain amount of peace that it is immersed in the reality of the divine.

St. Catherine of Genoa writes of God's description of it to her: "With the souls who have arrived at perfection I play no more the Game of love, which consists in leaving and returning again to the soul; though thou must understand that it is not, properly speaking, I, the immovable GOD, Who thus elude them, but rather the sentiment that my charity gives them of Me."[27] To Underhill, the last sentence means: "In other terms, it is the imperfectly developed spiritual perception which becomes tired and fails, throwing the self back into the darkness and aridity whence it has emerged."[28] Or as St. Theresa notes: "I clearly seem to experience what St. John says, *That He will dwell in the soul,* and this not only by grace, but that He will make her [the soul] perceive this presence."[29]

In a similar vein Kabir notes:

Inside this clay jug there are canyons and pine mountains, and the maker of canyons and pine mountains!
All seven oceans are inside, and hundreds of millions of stars.
The acid that tests gold is there, and the one who judges jewels.

And the music from the strings no one touches, and the source of all water.
If you want the truth, I will tell you the truth:
Friend, listen: the God whom I love is inside me.[30]

Black Elk says:

> We should understand well that all things are the works of the Great Spirit. We
> should know that He is within all things: the trees, the grasses, the rivers, the
> mountains, all the four-legged animals, and the winged peoples; and even more
> important we should understand that He is also above all these things and peo-
> ples. When we do understand this deeply in our hearts, then we will fear, and
> love, and know the Great Spirit, and then we will live and act as he intends.[31]

Black Elk elaborates on the peace that comes from the deep experiential understanding of this stage:

> I wish to mention here, that through these rites [Hunkapi: the making of rel-
> atives] a three-fold peace [is] established. The first peace, which is the most
> important, is that which comes within the souls of men when they realize
> their relationship, their oneness, with the universe and all its Powers, and
> when they realize that at the center of the universe dwells *Wakan-Tanka*, and
> that this center is really everywhere, it is within each of us. This is the real
> Peace, and the others are but reflections of this. The second peace is that which
> is made between two individuals, and the third is that which is made between
> two nations. But above all you should understand that there can never be
> peace until there is first known that true peace which, as I have often said, is
> within the souls of men.[32]

dark night of the soul
and union with the divine

At the point of maximum balance in the process of purification, during the stage of illumination, the soul still perceives the universe as a duality. There is itself and the absolute reality from which it came, still an I and Thou. The soul, if determined or if it is in its nature to do so, eventually leaves this plateau of illumination and strives to finish its purification, ultimately achieving identity with the transcendent principle: union with the divine. In this process all the final elements of the ego are stripped away. The ego experiences this event as a complete and final death. It no longer is in service to the sacred center of things but is subsumed into it, and there is no longer a distinction between the self and Creator.

During this time the self experiences a destructuring of all basic reality perception, and all forms that one has held onto begin to fall apart. The early Christian mystical text *The Cloud of Unknowing* refers to this time as one during which one can perceive nothing with the inner eye or the spiritual heart. At this point the internal structures that a person uses to define both the self and the external world begin to break down, and a complete and total restructuring of the basic nature of the self occurs. During the process all the basic mechanisms the self uses to process information from the world and about the world quit working. As the process proceeds, more and more of the basic psychological structures of the self cease to function. In the end there is nothing left and the person feels immersed in a void that has no meaning and in which nothing can be perceived. The parts of the self that attribute meaning to things no longer function. Even the experience of the sacred, so integral a part of the mystic since the call that pulled the soul to this path, cannot be found anywhere. The person is alone in a nothingness—a void of meaning.

All the texts describe this stage of the mystic way similarly and all agree that the person is brought through the stage by personal love, longing, or devotion for the sacred. The love and the faith from many years of intimate contact with the sacred are all that is left them.

Any deep growth process that breaks down basic structures of the personality so that a new formulation of the self can occur has much in common with this ultimate dark night of the soul. For in all such processes where the most basic foundations of the self are in flux, the mechanisms for determining meaning are being broken down and their very nature changed. This process is universal, but for the mystic, the reason for the destructuring is critical—his movement toward complete immersion in the sacred, becoming seated in the place where there is no more I and Thou. And in the case of the mystic it has occurred several times before this final dark night of the soul. Prior to illumination the mystic experiences three such states: one during the restructuring of the psychological body, one during the restructuring of the physical body, and one during the restructuring of the psychic body. These initial dark nights of the soul, in part, allow the mystic to intimately understand its nature.

Fewer writings exist on this portion of the mystic way than on the journey to illumination from the awakening of the self. Underhill believes there are fewer because so few make the journey. The stage of illumination, she notes, is "the largest and most densely populated province of the mystic kingdom."[33] Those who realize that illumination is not the end goal are few. "Only the greatest souls learn this lesson, and tread the whole of that 'Kings Highway' which leads man back to his Source."[34]

But written accounts of this great purgation of the self do exist. Two of the great souls who encountered and surmounted this purgation are Buddha and Christ. Christ's temptation in the desert, his encounter with the void, with despair, and the temptations of his dying ego to hold onto the world are well known. Buddha's sitting beneath the Bodhi tree and the final acts wherein his ego struggles with the illusions of the world and its temptations are also well known. Disciples in both these traditions have spoken of the final stages they themselves struggled with, all so similar to the enlightened one whom they followed. St. John of the Cross notes:

This is one of the most bitter sufferings of this purgation. The soul is conscious of a profound emptiness in itself, a cruel destitution of the three kinds of

goods, natural, temporal, and spiritual, which are ordained for its comfort. It sees itself in the midst of opposite evils, miserable imperfections, dryness and emptiness of the understanding, and abandonment of the spirit in darkness.[35]

Within Buddhism, this experience is embodied in the image of the crossing by ferry or boat of "life's river—a journey from the common-sense bank of ignorance, grasping, and death, to the further shore of wisdom and enlightenment."[36] Huston Smith, in his book *The Illustrated World's Religions,* describes it:

> As the ferry pushes off and moves across the water, the bank we are leaving loses its substance. Its shops and streets and antlike figures are blending together and releasing their hold on us. As yet, though, the other side is not in focus either. At this interval the only tangible realities are the water with its treacherous currents and the boat that is stoutly but precariously contending with them. This is the moment for Buddhism's Three Vows: I take refuge in the *Buddha*—there was an explorer who made this trip and proved that it can succeed. I take refuge in the *dharma,* this ship to which we have committed our lives in the conviction that it is seaworthy. I take refuge in the *sangha,* the order; our crew that is navigating the ship in whom we have confidence.[37]

At the point where no shore can be seen, one can feel the currents that are affecting forward progress, currents that can take one in the wrong direction. Yet one cannot see either shore and having never left the original shore before, the traveler does not know from experience that he can make it to the other side. And at this point the extreme and soul-shattering despair of the spiritual traveler (afloat in a gray void of no-meaning) is experienced. Like the Buddhist, the Christian mystic has few things to rely on: the knowledge that Christ made this journey and said that others could, the years of devotional practice that preceded this moment in time (the seaworthiness of the craft), and personal direction of the will toward the divine (the order). It is at this point that the truth of Huston Smith's insight, that "reason is too short a ladder to reach truth's full height," comes into full experience. The traveler in both traditions

loses all landmarks that the reasoning mind can hold to. A leap of spirit must be made; in the process unessentials are left behind, and one crosses the void and comes to rest in the divine.

The writings of mystics in many traditions speak of the beginning of this final journey, which many times is accompanied by the loss of all that the mystic highly values: wife, children, reputation, holy relics from a teacher, an experiential sense of the divine, or God's love. Everything to which a mystic clings for self-definition is stripped away. It is not an act of a vindictive God against a sinful and bad person, as it might be interpreted in the Western Christian tradition, but it is simply part of the nature of this journey at this time. Final attachments are stripped away.

the journey to the divine in the earth-centered tradition

Earth-centered traditions also have their memories of great souls who have made this journey and have served as guides to their disciples. They have been, of course, remembered in oral traditions, not written. As a result they are somewhat different in form; the essence, however, remains the same.

Two of these great souls are Dawn Star and Degawanidah. Some of Dawn Star's remarkable story is told in Brooke Medicine Eagle's book, *Buffalo Woman Comes Singing*. The story of Degawanidah can be found in many places; the best-known version is in Paul Wallace's book, *White Roots of Peace: The Iroquois Book of Life*.

Degawanidah came among the Indian tribes of the Northeast and showed them the Great Law of Peace, which founded the League of the Iroquois and eventually was the model for the structure of the U.S. government and Constitution. The story of his first disciple, whom he renamed Ayawentha (sometimes called Aionwatha—popularly mistranslated as Hiawatha and confused with the

character in Longfellow's poem), is that of a man who made the crossing from one shore to the other. It is revealing that the man's original, secular name is not remembered—Ayawentha is his sacred name. It is a very long story, only a portion of which I will paraphrase and relate.

It is said that Degawanidah's birth was foretold to his grandmother by a messenger from Creator. In her sleep the messenger came to her and said that a boy would be born to her virgin daughter.

"It is the will of the Master of Life, the Holder of the Heavens, that thy daughter, a virgin, shall bear a child. He shall be called Degawanidah, the Master of Things, for he brings with him the Good News of Peace and Power. Care for him well, thou and thy daughter, for he has a great office to perform in the world."[38]

The messenger explained that Degawanidah's work in the world was to bring peace to people on Earth, to spread, what he called, the New, or Good, Mind. And she was instructed to help her grandson in any way she could, never hindering him in his work.

The grandmother related to her daughter all that had happened and in time it became clear that she was indeed pregnant. The house was made sacred and all things were done in a sacred manner and eventually the boy was born. In his coming into the world they could feel the sacredness of him and in all ways they taught him as the messenger had told them. Eventually, when he had grown to manhood, he went to them and told them it was time for him to build his canoe and go into the world to do his work.

When the canoe was finished he said goodbye to his mother and grandmother and crossed the great lake (Ontario) until he came to the land of the five nations of the Iroquois, although, of course, then it was not yet the five nations. At this time a great evil was on all the people there and they fought constantly: there was an Evil Mind, which affected them all and caused them to behave in cruel ways. The "good message of how to live had been cast aside and naked power ruled, fueled by vengeance and blood lust."[39]

Eventually in his travels, Degawanidah came to the lodge of a man who was strongly filled with the evil that affected all the people. The man was a

great warrior. It is said that just as Degawanidah arrived, the man was cutting up the body of a man he had killed and was preparing to eat it. Degawanidah climbed onto the roof of the house and looked down the chimney. The man had put the kettle on the fire and was bending over it, dropping in the chopped-up meat. The man, looking in the pot, saw Degawanidah's reflection in the water and thought it was his own. He was shocked. He was used to seeing the reflection of a man filled with the great evil that suffused all the land. In that moment of relaxed consciousness, when he least expected it, he saw the reflection of a man filled with the power of the sacred, a noble and kind man, filled with such wisdom and strength that he was wholly taken over by it. He was shocked out of his old world and saw all the power and beauty of the sacred reflected back to him.

He stepped away from the pot, marveling, then returned and again looked within it. Again he saw the reflected power of the sacred. Then, still standing there, feeling all the power of the sacred within him from this reflection, he looked deeper and saw the pot filled with the meat from a man he had killed.

"This is not the face of a man who eats humans," he said, again looking at Degawanidah's reflection. "I see, now, that it is not like me to do that."[40]

And so saying, he took the pot, carried it outside, and emptied it at the roots of a great, upturned tree. Having done this he felt better but he could not stop comparing himself to the sacred reflection that he had seen and the evil man that he had been. This caused a great sorrow inside him and he lamented what he had done, wishing to make amends for it.

"To pour out the kettle is one thing, but to change all the ways of my life and mind is harder. I am that sacred reflection which I saw in the kettle, but I do not know how to become that and leave who I was behind. I do not know how to make amends for the evil I have done. I wish there was someone here who could help me." And so saying, he returned to his house to find Degawanidah awaiting him.

There was something about Degawanidah that caused the man to tell him what had happened. Degawanidah was pleased. "This is a good thing that has happened to you," he said. "You have felt the power of the Good Mind

(New Mind) and have changed the very patterns of your life. And you are miserable because the New Mind does not live at ease with old memories."[41]

The man asked Degawanidah what he could do. And Degawanidah told him that he must act in the world for justice and peace, especially in the areas in which he had previously caused pain. He must walk among the pain he had created, balanced and at peace with himself, speaking for the New Mind, the Good Mind.

As he felt this truth go into him he said to Degawanidah, "This is a good thing, I take hold of it, I grasp it."[42] And then Degawanidah cautioned him to never go against the forces of nature but to find the flowing pattern in all things and find the way to move with it.

During the next weeks, Degawanidah explained the Great Law of Peace he had been given to bring to the people, and the man was taken by it. He wished to carry it also, to help. Knowing this, Degawanidah spoke to him:

> There is one who has taken into himself the most evil of any in this land, Tadodaho, the most powerful chief of the Onondagas. He is a great wizard and so cruel that he kills and devours any who approach him uninvited and so strong that birds flying over his lodge fall dead at his feet if he waves his hand. His body and mind are twisted by the evil he has become and his hair is a mass of tangled snakes. His voice carries terror within it for it is the mocking cry of the doubter who kills men by destroying their faith. To see him is to become afraid, no one can stand before him, but you are the one who will comb the snakes out of his hair. And so I rename you Ayawentha—He Who Combs.[43]

It was now time, Degawanidah said, for Ayawentha to go to Tadodaho and to tell him that the New Mind had come—the time of peace was at hand. "He will drive you away, but do not despair, for you shall succeed in the end." And so saying, Degawanidah left Ayawentha and continued on, taking his message of the New Mind among all except the Onondaga.

Ayawentha went to the Onondagas and they liked what he brought them. But when Ayawentha tried to go with them to take the truth of this new sacred

thing to the powerful chief, Tadodaho, they were all driven away by Tadodaho's power. Many were killed; others fell to fighting among themselves. Again and again Ayawentha tried to go to Tadodaho but was driven back. His repeated failure to get to his destination and the repeated obstructions placed in his path began to wound his mind and he was troubled.

He was trying to rest one day, trying to once again find the peace he had known with Degawanidah, when he heard Tadodaho calling his name, "Ayawentha-a-a-a-a!" The sound of his name was drawn out into a howl at the end and all the power of Tadodaho's voice filled it. Ayawentha knew some evil was about to come upon him and he was troubled and afraid. Soon his three daughters were taken ill and each died. The weight of his grief threatened to bow him down. "I cannot go on," he thought. "I cannot do the work of the Good Mind because of this pain and loss I feel."

The Onondagas, hearing his lament, came to him to help cheer him up. But soon after they arrived a mysterious bird dropped from the heavens and the crowd, trying to catch the bird, trampled Ayawentha's wife to death. At this Ayawentha's despair overcame him and he left the people and went up among the lakes and mountains of the north. He became a lonely wanderer, feeling the despair of his loss, his emptiness, but although his heart was filled with nothing but this emptiness, each day he prayed. He had picked up shells from the lake bottom and he threaded them on three strings of jointed rushes as a mark of his grief. And each night, when he built his fire, he held the three strings in his hands and said: "This would I do if I found anyone burdened with grief, even as I am. I would take these shell strings in my hand and console them. The strings would become words and lift away the darkness with which they are covered. Holding these in my hand, my words would be true."[44]

For a long time Ayawentha was alone in his emptiness, neither retreating from it nor going beyond it. He would move his camp, sometimes here, sometimes there, and each night he would take the wampum beads in his hand and say the same prayer. Then one night Degawanidah heard his prayer and came to him, and taking the wampum beads Degawanidah held them in his hand and spoke: "I wipe away the tears from thy face using the white fawn-skin of

pity. . . . I make it daylight for thee. . . . I beautify the sky. Now shalt thou do thy thinking in peace when thy eyes rest on the sky, which the Perfecter of our Faculties, the Master of All Things, intended should be a source of happiness to man."[45] And so hearing, Ayawentha's mind was cleared and he could see and think again.

Degawanidah said then: "Reason has returned, thy judgement is firm again. Thou art ready to advance the New Mind. Let us together make the laws of the Great Peace, which will abolish war."[46]

And when the Great Law was made they made wampum belts to help them remember it more easily and they took it to all the nations. The nations received them but the voice of Tadodaho was raised whenever they approached too near him, bringing despair to them all, so they left him till the last. Eventually, all the tribes had accepted the New Mind and even all the chiefs of the Onondaga except Tadodaho, and they knew it was time to return to him.

Degawanidah and Ayawentha took their canoe and together they went to Tadodaho. He used his powers but he could not put them aside. They told him that they had brought to him the New Mind. They told him of the Great Law of Peace. And he replied, "Asonke-ne-e-e-e-eh! It is not yet."[47] At this Degawanidah and Ayawentha returned across the water and gathered the representatives of the five nations and together embarked in their canoes to return. When they reached the middle of the crossing, Tadodaho raised his voice and powers against them. Despair and great winds broke against their canoes but they held their course, returning to Tadodaho.

"We have returned, united, and your power cannot stand against us." And so saying, Degawanidah and Ayawentha approached Tadodaho and made straight his body; their words made straight his mind. Then, at last, Ayawentha combed out the snakes of his hair and made it straight, thus fulfilling that which Degawanidah had foretold of him. Tadodaho was made whole and in honor of the transformation he became the first chief of the five nations of the Iroquois, the holder of the Great Law of Peace.

Ayawentha's journey from the secular world began with his experience of the sacred reflected back to him. He suffered when he then knew himself in

comparison to the sacred; he saw how he had caused pain and suffering in the world and lamented it. The sacred, through Degawanidah, taught him the actions and behaviors he should engage in to develop morally and in accordance with the sacred so that he would not be out of balance. He had been touched by the sacred; he knew it. It represented another way of thinking and feeling—the New Mind. The sacred (Degawanidah) and Ayawentha were yet two: Ayawentha was to take his understanding of the sacred out into the world, and Degawanidah would be about his own business—I and Thou.

But as Ayawentha tried to take the teachings out in the world, he encountered the voice of the crooked man whose hair is snakes. Recall Black Elk's words: "Any man who is attached to the senses and to the things of this world, is one who lives in ignorance and is being consumed by the snakes which represent his own passions." Tadodaho represented this concept at its extreme. In approaching him, Ayawentha was confronting the elemental aspect of human existence that is attached to the world, to form, to desire, to unhealthy emotions, and cannot let go. He made little headway at first in attempting to even get close to the place where Tadodaho lived, to his core location. He was driven off again and again and dissension and conflict were the outcome each time. Eventually Ayawentha began to despair and at this moment everything that Ayawentha valued began to be stripped away. Alone and in grief and despair, Ayawentha turned away from the world and in emptiness, with nothing, he walked. Each night he made his prayer to the sacred by an act of his will. He moved from place to place, but made no progress, going neither forward nor back. But in time, the sacred, again in the person of Degawanidah, heard him and came to him. Its touch cleared his mind, brought him into a state of grace, and allowed him to look upon the sacred with clear eyes, never to be confused again.

Then, together, as one, they traveled to the home of Tadodaho and told him it was time to become a part of the New Mind. Tadodaho tried to put them off but in unity he was made straight, his mind cleared, the snakes were combed out. As Underhill notes: "[The mystic] has learned the lesson of 'the school of true resignation': has moved to a new stage of reality: a complete

self-naughting, an utter acquiescence in the large and hidden purposes of the Divine Will."[48] The journey of Ayawentha, encoded in an Earth-centered oral tradition, is the same journey that all mystics have made from the beginning. It is regrettable that the oral traditions have been so little available to the world's peoples. There are many mystics who have journeyed to the sacred in those traditions. The truths they learned in their travels, such as the New Mind of Degawanidah and Ayawentha, have much to offer the world. And as in all mystical traditions, in the end Ayawentha became one with the sacred. I and Thou dissolved.

On all mystical paths, when the final aspects of the self become transmuted in the Dark Night of the Soul, the mystic has become that which he beholds. He has moved from a state of movement to a state of being. At the root of all mystic experience is the knowledge, which comes from the first touch of the sacred upon a person, that there is but one source for all things. This final act of surrender of the self, the willingness to allow the personality to die fully while the body still lives, is the sacrifice that the great mystics make—the point when all the snakes are finally combed out. Such mystics live in, and provide an example for all humankind of, the eternal now.

chapter three
the sacred earth

In Christian mysticism one specializes in the Christ Mind and the spiritual journey of the Christian saints. In Buddhism, one specializes in the vast body of knowledge that Buddhist travelers have amassed, and one seeks the attainment of non-dual reality. Nature mysticism focuses on the sacred teachings of Creator as they are expressed through the Earth. Like all forms of mysticism, it has its own body of knowledge, its own signposts, its own terrain. Those who are called to Nature mysticism learn a unique body of knowledge—their bible is the stones, the plants, the animals, the sacred breath of God as it moves within the wind and the lungs of human beings. The sacred, at the core of all physical things, also expresses itself in patterns of the Web of Life of the Earth. These patterns, too, are a part of that living bible of the Earth.

The essential elements in that living bible are similar in all indigenous cultures: At the center of all is a sacred thing that is alive and aware. It is the source of all things. It resides within each physical element of the

Earth, all physical things are made of its substance, and human beings are only one of a multitude of such physical forms on the Earth, all of which have awareness and intelligence.

We have a duty to revere the physical forms of the Earth because of the source from which they come; not to do so implies we revile ourselves and the source from which we come. All things—time, the seasons, the life of people—everything moves in cycles; nothing is linear. Because all things on this Earth are from one source, interspecies communication is not only inherent within us, it is necessary for understanding our own humanity and our own sacred nature. There are millions of interlocking and interdependent communication patterns among all the physical forms of the Earth, and with training, human beings can perceive and understand those patterns of communication. It is part of our species' purpose to do so. And human beings can travel, through the sacredness of Earth, to the center of all things.

An Oglala Sioux, Chased-by-Bears, describes this idea:

When a *man* does a piece of work which is admired by all we say that it is wonderful; but when we see the changes of day and night, the sun, moon, and stars in the sky, and the changing seasons upon the earth, with their ripening fruits, anyone must realize that it is the work of some one more powerful than man. Greatest of all these is the sun, without which we could not live. The birds and the beasts, the trees and the rocks, are the work of some great power. Sometimes men say that they can understand the meaning of the songs of birds. I can believe this is true. They say they can understand the call and cry of the animals, and I can believe this also is true, for these creatures and man are alike the work of a great power.[1]

Luther Standing Bear, also Sioux, speaks of these ideas too:

From Wakan Tanka, the Great Spirit, there came a great unifying force that flowed in and through all things—the flowers of the plains, blowing wind, rocks, trees, birds, animals—and was the same force that had been breathed into the first man. Thus all things were kindred, and were brought together by the same Great Mystery.

Kinship with all creatures of the earth, sky, and water was a real and active principle. In the animal and bird world there existed a brotherly feeling that kept the Lakota safe among them. And so close did some of the Lakotas come to their feathered and furred friends that in true brotherhood they spoke a common tongue.

The animals had rights—the right of man's protection, the right to live, the right to multiply, the right to freedom, and the right to man's indebtedness—and in recognition of these rights the Lakota never enslaved an animal, and spared all life that was not needed for food and clothing.

This concept of life and its relations was humanizing, and gave to the Lakota an abiding love. It filled his being with the joy and mystery of living; it gave him reverence for all life; it made a place for all things in the scheme of existence with equal importance to all.

The Lakota could despise no creature, for all were of one blood, made by the same hand, and filled with the essence of the Great Mystery. In spirit, the Lakota were humble and meek. "Blessed are the meek, for they shall inherit the earth"—this was true for the Lakota, and from the earth they inherited secrets long since forgotten. Their religion was sane, natural, and human.[2]

These understandings engender a natural attentiveness of mind for, as Joseph Epes Brown remarks,

The sacred powers may manifest themselves through any form or being of the natural world, which may appear visually, or which may wish to communicate through some audible message. The presence and word of the Great Mystery is within every being, every thing, every event. Even the smallest being, a little ant for example, may appear, and communicate something of the power of the Great Mystery which is behind all forms of creation. The powers and beings of the world wish to communicate with man; they wish to establish a relationship, but may only do so where the recipient is in a state of humility, and is attentive with all his being."[3]

My own particular experience of the sacred, involving as it did such a profound sense of the living spirit at the core of all physical reality, was a direct expression of these truths: a deep experience of Nature, or Earth, mysticism. That which came to me was the sacred center of all things. It had no name. It did not need one. I felt called by this sacred power to be in deep relationship with the sacredness of the Earth itself. I was introduced, so to speak, to the sacred and living Earth as the spiritual path I was to follow.

deepening the experience of the sacredness of the earth

I found my access point to the deeper elements of the sacredness of the Earth through the internal and external feelings of my body. The body is a part of this world and it responds to patterns and knowledge thousands of generations old. Our minds may be, temporarily, out of kilter, but our bodies remember. We remember in our feelings. (One of the simplest events that can stir up these ancient feelings is the sight of a young puppy or kitten. Something in us innately surges into life and reaches out to touch and be touched in return. And in spontaneous recognition of the event, our body smiles, we breathe deeply, and relaxation and calmness flood our being. We feel connected.)

This memory can often be stimulated when we are in the presence of the great trees. Standing near an ancient tree, you can feel the life force that it contains, reaching out and tugging on our basic self. In that instant there is again a relaxation, a settling into a remembrance that is fundamental to our humanness. When that feeling is allowed to grow through the body, to swell and fill us, we gather with luminous eyes once again a part of the world. And an immanent part of us reaches out and touches the tree that is touching us.

Once you have had an experience like this one and have felt its power and its beauty, tasted the rightness of it in the body, you are faced with a difficulty. You are now in possession of an experience for which, however right it seems, you will find little support in Western society—although support is growing.

Those who wish to return to the sacred Earth begin to break an unspoken, unconscious agreement with Western society: that the analytical mind is superior to all other things and that the universe is simply one great machine of inanimate matter, which the mind alone can figure out. In the experience of the sacred, one learns firsthand (in contradiction to Western thought) that the mind is quite limited and that the universe is not just one great machine of inanimate matter. It becomes clear that anything built entirely upon the foundations of the mind (and assumptions of inanimateness) is also quite limited, which brings one invariably face to face with the limits of science (a useful tool but a terrible master). And then you're done, you see—for who in the West (in their right mind) can publicly say science is missing the point?[4]

And so in the beginning, the newly touched person shuttles between the deep experience of the sacredness of the Earth and the outside world, from which he fails to gain recognition and support for that experience. Eventually, all in the West who desire to journey to the sacred Earth must give themselves permission to break that agreement with a society that tells them they must not.

In the early stages of the return to a sacred Earth one struggles between paradigms, feeling that something deeper and more meaningful than a materialistic reality exists—even if one just barely touches it from time to time. A search for the authentic begins, the nose begins to be sensitive to its scent, a winnowing process commences. In spite of strong cultural injunctions the search for the authentic begins, taking ever more precedence over time, and one begins to weed out the unauthentic so that the deeper reality is more fully present in daily experience.

John Seed, the Australian rainforest activist, tells this remarkable story of two sisters named Bradley and their "weeding."

> [They] came up with an exciting technique by which we may slowly invite back the original biotic community from denuded and scarred landscapes.
>
> Their method is essentially simple, unheroic. Nothing needs to be planted. All we have to do is to learn to distinguish the exotic from the native species right from when the tiny seedlings first emerge. Then we remove the exotics without treading on the natives.

This must be done painstakingly and methodically. And we must start from the strongest expression of native vigour in our management area. That is, let's say there's an erosion gully breaking our hearts, we want to start the repairs there at once but any attempt to heal it is doomed. What we must first do is discover and begin from some least-damaged spot. For example, in a park of introduced grasses, we find a corner that the mower couldn't reach where a few annual weeds flourish. We begin from this corner and move out. Or perhaps among all the annuals, we spot a few pioneers and begin carefully clearing the exotics from around them.

Slowly at first, the pioneer natives emerge creating shade, soil, micro-climate, then the next stage in the succession, till finally, years into the process, the conditions are ripe for the re-emergence of the climax species. We will never know whether the seeds were introduced by a bird flying by or perhaps lay dormant beneath the soil waiting for conditions that allow their germination. But years into the Bradley method of an area, to our amazement, climax native trees begin to emerge, perhaps unseen for generations and unremembered.

With each succeeding season the process becomes more vigorous and robust. By the time the spreading cover of burgeoning native vegetation reaches the erosion gully, it takes it in its stride.

The Bradley Method is more than a handy tool that teaches us how to repair the simplification that we have wrought. It also provides us with an extremely useful metaphor for the reclaiming of our own native wisdom. Buried under millennia of conditioning, suppressed by inquisitions, ridicule and doubt lie unimagined potentialities to reinhabit our interbeing with the world, to fully participate in the world once again.[5]

After the first great struggle is won, the self has permission to go whole-heartedly into that other reality and to see what a world it is. It is so complex, and the possible learnings are so numerous that a human being cannot, in one lifetime, hope to do more than scratch its surface. It is truly a world in and of itself, which is why many indigenous peoples consider the Earth the living equivalent of the Christian Bible. Genesis is contained in the Earth—not in the

words of Genesis; the act itself is engraved in the structure of the Earth. And because we are capable of interspecies communication, it is not necessary to read the Bible to hear of Genesis; the rocks will tell us the tale. Herbalist Carol McGrath recounts a native woman's view of this idea. "If you take the Christian bible and put it out in the wind and the rain, soon the paper on which the words are printed will disintegrate and the words will be gone. Our bible IS the wind and the rain."[6]

After you have given yourself permission to enter the spell of the sensuous, as David Abram calls it in his remarkable book of the same name, the second great struggle begins: validation of knowledge received from this new source.

Imagine yourself walking along a mountain path, not thinking much, just enjoying the feel of the sun upon your body, the stretch of your muscles as your legs move you along, the smells and sounds of the mountainside. You pass near a small plant to the side of the path and catch a glimpse of it out of the corner of your eye. "Hello," you hear. "If you pick me, make me into tea, and give me to your wife it will help those menstrual cramps she's been having."

Now what do you do? The mind immediately gets involved.

"Plants can't talk," you say to yourself. Or, "I'm just imagining this conversation. Some part of me is projecting the voice onto the plant." Or, "What if the plant is poison? What if I do as it says and my wife gets sick?"

You can feel the livingness of the Earth, sense the plant's life force, touch the sacred within it with your own spirit, hear its gentle humming as it lives happily rooted in the Earth. And you know it all to be good and true. But now you've come to the next struggle. You have given yourself permission to enter the sacred world but what do you do with what you find there? How do you tell if the information you find is useful or valid? What do you do with it? How do you share it with others? How do you tell people what you do for a living? Just who are you anyway and what are you doing? Perhaps there is something organically wrong with you? Would your mother mind if you just moved back home again?

So you struggle with it. You go in and out of the sacred world, in and out of the rational mind.

Then one day you begin to see and feel the interlocking patterns of communication of the Earth—how the plants think, the stones, the animals. You begin to understand their language, the words they use. You begin to make a

deep and personal relationship with residents of the Earth who live in your neighborhood. And you begin spending longer and longer times in that reality. You begin to amass interesting and surprisingly effective and useful information. And you feel good. Really, really good.

At this point on the path, if you go on, if you can move beyond learned fears, you firmly enter the indigenous world, the world of the sacred Earth. At this point you have left the confines of Western civilization and have entered an immeasurably older world. You no longer linger within the doorway, taking a look around the foyer. You have come into the house and you start to poke around the rooms and find out just what they keep in those closets. You have restored the indigenous mind within yourself.

Indigenous peoples opened many closets in this house a long time ago. One of the most beautiful examples of the interlocking patterns of communication and interdependence of the Earth encoded in indigenous wisdom is in the old Navajo saying: "If you kill off the prairie dogs, there will be no one to cry for rain." Bill Mollison, the father of Permaculture, comments:

> Amused scientists, knowing that there was no conceivable relationship between prairie dogs and rain, recommended the extermination of all burrowing animals in some desert areas planted to rangelands in the 1950's. . . . in order to protect the roots of the sparse desert grasses. Today the area (not far from Chilchinbito, Arizona) has become a virtual wasteland.[7]

Prairie dogs and all the burrowing creatures open breathing tubes in the Earth. As the moon circles the Earth, it pulls on the underground aquifers, just as it pulls on the oceans to cause the tides. This pull on the underground aquifers, causing them to rise and fall, is akin to the breathing process in human bodies. As the underground waters rise and fall, the Earth literally breathes through the fissures created by the burrowing creatures. The Earth breathes out moisture-laden air, which helps to create rain.

How did the Navajos know about this relationship? By any standards of Western thought they could not have known it. The tie between the prairie dogs and rain doesn't make sense to Western sensibilities. But when one enters the

indigenous world, becomes enfolded in the spell of the sensuous, the patterns of the Earth are readily apparent. The mind "sees" them—and yes, the Earth, the prairie dogs, the rocks, the plants tell the human being about them. This concept of rocks, animals, and plants being able to talk to human beings is found in all indigenous cultures. The elders, holy people, and the medicine people of the tribes told the Europeans who questioned them that plants, for instance, told them many things. Thus among the Mitlenos in Mexico: "The herbs and flowers also talk to her and she to them, a rapport with the natural world which is not visibly part of the lifeways of other Mitlenos."[8] And the Zuni: "The Zuni live with their plants—the latter are part of themselves. The initiated can talk with their plants, and the plants can talk with them."[9] And the Papago: "It was customary to 'talk to the plant or tree' when gathering a medicinal substance and also when administering it."[10] Amused Europeans, knowing that it was impossible for a plant to talk, labeled the idea superstition.

Kenneth Pelletier touches on the reason people can communicate with plants in nonindustrial cultures and why science has misunderstood this ability. In his book *Toward a Science of Consciousness*, he observes that the mind is capable of much finer discrimination than scientific instruments. He notes that understanding deep truths about the interactions of the universe has always been possible for human beings because all human beings, irrespective of culture and era, have had access to "the finest probe ever conceived—the trained and focused attention of consciousness itself."[11] Many non-Western cultures and religions have used their understanding of this capacity to develop fairly subtle and refined expressions of what can be called sacred science. Western scientists, in relying on external (and fairly gross) probes, have only been able to perceive rather gross truths and elements of the Earth system (see Appendix 1).

As one becomes comfortable with interspecies communication and learns how to separate projection from what the plants or stones are really saying, one begins to be drawn in a particular direction. One is called to a particular aspect of the sacred Earth; one specializes. The focus may be specific, such as sacred patterns of plant relationships, or it may expand into understanding multiple sacred patterns, such as the interrelationships of mountains, water, air, plants, human beings, and human societies.

The area of focus is not decided upon by the mind. Rather, the area that begins consuming more and more attention is determined by one's internal

nature and the calling of the sacred. Each human being contains the potential for congruent, sacred work—the doing of which fulfills the destiny of the soul. The conscious mind is rarely aware of the calling. In some manner the sacred calls the person to that work through the impact of visionary experience, through certain signs or omens, or through specific, out-of-the-ordinary events.

Sometimes a person will be walking by a plant that will begin talking to him. Or a dream may come to him when he is awake that teaches him the use of certain plants for healing. He begins, then, to learn about these plants and becomes a medicine person who learns of his place and work in ever-deepening relationship through plants. Or an animal may become a teacher. In *Teton Sioux Music*, Frances Densmore relates a story told to her by Two Shields.

> Many years ago a war party were in their camp when they heard what they believed to be the song of a young man approaching them. They could hear the words of the song and supposed the singer was one of their own party, but as he came nearer they saw that he was an old wolf, so old that he had no teeth, and there was no brush on his tail. He could scarcely move, and he lay down beside their fire. They cut up their best buffalo meat and fed him. Afterward they learned his song, which was the beginning of the wolf songs (war songs). After this, too, the warrior began the custom of carrying a wolf-skin medicine bag.[12]

This spontaneous touching of the human being by the sacred world through a particular animal or plant allows the human being access to more than human power, to a source of nonhuman knowledge. And when that source is activated in the future, as by singing the song learned from a sacred source, it can touch and change human life and experience. This body of knowledge makes up a portion of the body of sacred science that is particular to Earth mysticism.

Sometimes a person may feel that it is time to deepen his knowledge of his path. He may be restless and may realize that he needs to actively seek help from the sacred. He may go to an uninhabited place, returning to the Earth and calling on the sacred for help. The seeker opens himself to the sacred and asks for the blessing of being touched by its knowledge and caring in this manner.

As a Lakota Sioux, Siya'ka, says:

All classes of people know that when human power fails they must look to a higher power for the fulfillment of their desires. There are many ways in which the request for help from this higher power can be made. This depends on the person. Some like to be quiet, and others want to do everything in public. Some like to go alone, away from the crowds, to meditate upon many things. In order to secure a fulfillment of his desire a man must qualify himself to make his request. Lack of preparation would mean failure to secure a response to his petition. Therefore when a man makes up his mind to ask a favor of Wakan'tanka he makes due preparation. It is not fitting that a man should suddenly go out and make a request of Wakan'tanka. When a man shuts his eyes, he sees a great deal. He then enters his own mind, and things become clear to him, but objects passing before his eyes would distract him. For that reason a dreamer makes known his request through what he sees when his eyes are closed. It has long been his intention to make his request of Wakan'-tanka, and he resolves to seek seclusion on the top of a butte or other high place. When at last he goes there he closes his eyes, and his mind is upon Wakan'tanka and his work. The man who does this usually has in mind some animal which he would like for protection and help. No man can succeed in life alone, and he cannot get the help he wants from men; therefore he seeks help through some bird or animal which Wakan'tanka sends for his assistance. Many animals have ways from which a man can learn a great deal, even from the fact that horses are restless before a storm.[13]

When Siya'ka was a young man, he felt he needed such a vision. He turned to a medicine man for help. He was instructed how to proceed, a place for the quest was selected and prepared, and Siya'ka remained there alone.

As I still faced the west, after the sun had set and when it was almost dark, I heard a sound like the flying of a bird around my head, and I heard a voice saying, "Young man, you are recognized by Wakan'tanka." This was all the voice said.

All night I stood with my eyes closed. Just before daybreak I saw a bright light coming toward me from the east. It was a man. His head was tied up, and he held a tomahawk in his hand. He said, "Follow me," and in an instant he changed into a crow. In my dream I followed the crow to a village. He entered the largest tent. When he entered the tent he changed to a man again. Opposite the entrance sat a young man, painted red, who welcomed me. When I was thus received I felt highly honored, for as this was the largest tent I knew it must be the tent of the chief. The young man said he was pleased to see me there. He said, further, that all the animals and birds were his friends and that he wished me to follow the way he had used to secure their friendship. He told me to lift my head. I did this and saw dragonflies, butterflies, and all kinds of small insects, while above them flew all kinds of birds. As soon as I cast down my eyes again and looked at the young man and at the man who had brought me thither, I saw that the young man had become transformed into an owl, and that my escort had changed again into a crow.

The owl said, "Always look toward the west when you make a petition, and you will have a long life." After this the owl commanded me to look at him. As soon as I did he was changed to an elk, and at his feet were the elk medicine and a hoop. As soon as I saw him changing, I began to wonder what marvel would be next. Then I heard a song.

The hilltop where I had my dream was quite a distance from the camp. My friends knew I had gone there, and in the early morning they sent a man with my horse. I came home, and the first thing I did was to take a sweat bath. In the lodge with the medicine-man I told him my dream.

I was a young man at that time and eager to go on the warpath and make a name for myself. After this dream, my stronghold was in the east, but the west was also a source from which I could get help. All the birds and insects which I had seen in my dream were things on which I knew I should keep my mind and learn their ways. When the season returns, the birds and insects return with the same colorings as the previous year. They are not all on the earth, but *above* it. My mind must be the same. The elk is brave, always helping the women, and in that way the elk has saved a large proportion of

the tribe. In this I should follow the elk, remembering that the elk, the birds, and insects are my helpers.[14]

In my own travels in sacred space, I found that the plants began to call to me to work with them. I had been ill with an intense abdominal cramping (something between kidney stones and appendicitis). Physicians had been unable to help me (they didn't know what caused my pain but were willing to do exploratory surgery). Coincidental with the advent of my abdominal cramping, a friend, an herbalist, had shown me a plant growing near my home. The plant, osha, was specific, in part, for abdominal cramping. So in desperation, I turned to the plants growing around my house for help.

The result was remarkable. The cramping lessened immediately and eventually disappeared. For the first time I had a direct experience of the Earth healing me but more than that I could feel the spirit of the plant as a living presence in my body. I could feel its spirit healing me while its body helped my body to feel healthier.

I was galvanized. I could feel the spirit of the plants calling on me to learn about them. I began spending time with the plants in the fields and valleys around my home, getting to know them all. As I spent greater and greater amounts of time with them I found myself

entering a kind of waking-dreaming state where the plants began to come and speak with me concerning their uses as medicine. One of the most profound experiences occurred with a plant called usnea, a widespread lichen that grows on trees throughout North America. Usnea is strongly antibiotic, to some extent rivaling penicillin. As I was sitting with the plant, focusing on its feeling tone, I entered a state of mind similar to just waking or just drifting off to sleep. My vision was softened, colors seemed more enhanced. The feeling tone of usnea, usually subtle, increased in intensity of its own accord until I found myself lost in it, my normal sense of personal boundaries dissolving. At that moment the plant appeared to me in the guise of a youngish man, hair curled and growing like the plant itself. He smiled and told me that usnea's primary function in the Earth ecosystem is to heal the trees; that it acts as an antibiotic

for the lung system of the planet, and that its effects in humans are only a byproduct of its intended effects for the trees. He went on to tell me that usnea is specific for infections in any lung system. He left and I gradually became aware of my surroundings again, waking from the state I had entered.[15]

This experience with usnea gave me an understanding of "If you kill off the prairie dogs there will be no one to cry for rain." I began to understand the deeper patterns of interdependent connections between all things in the Earth. I could *feel* the connections flowing like rivers throughout the world. My sensibilities, altered by contact with the sacred, were perceiving in the very manner that human beings had perceived the world for most of our history on Earth. I was becoming aware of a basic tenet of Earth spirituality: Any element of Earth, because of its origin in spirit, can evoke all the power of the sacred, can become more than just plant, tree, or stone. It can transform itself and become PLANT, TREE, or STONE because each form of matter contains within it a divine *logos*. And when human beings come into contact with an object that expresses all the power of the holy, they can learn a great deal about their own sacred nature and the sacred world of the Earth; and they can obtain knowledge that can help them and others to cope with the human condition.

Each portion of the Earth ecosystem possesses its own essence, its own archetype. These archetypes have been explored by indigenous cultures for thousands of years: What is their nature? How do they interact with human beings? How can human beings communicate with them? What are the responsibilities of human beings to these particular archetypes? What will or can the archetypes do for human beings who contact them? How do these archetypes represent essential aspects of the sacred? The sacred elements of the Earth become teachers, illuminators of aspects of Spirit, instructors about the parts of the human self that are undergoing purification. They provide a kind of soul care—much as mystical mentors do—and aid the young soul in its work of transcendence, in its journey to the divine. These many sacred elements of the Earth and their complex relationships make up the pages of the indigenous bible. It is a living bible. The human being walks among its pages and uses the capacity of her soul for discrete and incredibly refined perception and distinctions to understand and respond to communication from the sacred center of all things.

This perception, which is built upon a rich heritage and tradition, is an incredibly effective and sophisticated way of learning about the world. The rational mind, a much grosser instrument than the soul, is less able to grasp the subtleties in the experience of a sacred Earth. When we rely exclusively on the rational mind, we begin to lose something intrinsically human in ourselves. Frequent contact with the sacredness of the Earth allows us to recontact our fundamental humanness, for in that deeper world, we developed as a species; our modern perspectives are new additions. To understand that world, to enter it wholeheartedly, to develop the necessary muscles and balance to walk there, is to become indigenous again and to relearn how the Earth *really* is.

Upon this essential experience of the sacred, all indigenous spirituality and ceremony have been developed. Without a personal experience of this ground of being, it is impossible to understand tribal peoples when they describe their worldview. However, regardless of one's birth—within or outside of an indigenous culture—everyone who has such an experience, who makes this journey, becomes indigenous and embarks upon the way of Earth. It is a part of our heritage as human beings to be able to do this. And more important, it is *essential* that we do.

the necessity of restoring earth spirituality and the indigenous mind

It is unlikely that there is anyone who does not know that our earthly home is suffering from the effects of industrialization: rainforest depletion; species extinction; the resurgence of antibiotic-resistant strains of bacteria long thought to be "conquered" by medical science; sinking water tables; pollution of air, water, soil; wars over scarce planetary resources; and the negative effects of overpopulation; (such as increases in violent crime; rapidly escalating costs of land, housing, and food; the collapse of government infrastructure). All these are in the news daily, and we can feel the impact of industrialization in our lives. Who could have thought, except in the wildest science fiction story, that

a major city (Tokyo) would offer street-corner access to several seconds of pure oxygen for a few coins inserted in a slot? It would have been inconceivable when I was a boy. The most striking thing about this phenomenon is that it goes unremarked. What more fertile ground could the sacredness of the Earth find? And if you look you will find that experiences of the sacred Earth are exploding out of the human psyche. Bookstores are filled with writings about them and workshops are proliferating. The concept of Gaia, the living and self-regulating Earth, has touched off a firestorm in the human community. As Vaclav Havel says:

> [The Gaia hypothesis reminds us] in modern language, of what we have long suspected, of what we have long projected into our forgotten myths and what perhaps has always lain dormant within us as archetypes. That is, the aware-ness of our being anchored in the Earth and the Universe, the awareness that we are not here alone nor for ourselves alone, but that we are an integral part of higher, mysterious entities against whom it is not advisable to blaspheme. This forgotten awareness is encoded in all religions. All cultures anticipate it in various forms. It is one of the things that form the basis of man's understand-ing of himself, of his place in the world, and ultimately of the world as such.[16]

However, in spite of the Gaia hypothesis and the emerging awareness of the sacredness of the Earth, never has so ferocious an assault on the Earth occurred as in our time. This almost feral attack on the Earth is most evident near places of particularly potent sacredness. As soon as a place has been des-ignated as a national park or a wilderness area, the surrounding terrain begins to look as if it had been chewed by a pack of voracious dogs.

the roots of heaven

My awareness of this assault on sacred places was heightened in 1982 when I visited Mount Olympus in the state of Washington. Although the West

has its own traditions of the sacredness of mountains (for instance, Moses' journey up the mountain on which he received the tablets), the most common Western approach to mountains is "mine them or climb them." The feeling for mountains in the East, in traditional Asian cultures, is altogether different. They are viewed as sacred and as places of Kratophany—places where power manifests. Jan Whitner, in her beautiful book *Stonescaping*, remarks:

> The early Chinese believed that they were surrounded by sacred mountain ranges . . . [which] were considered "centers of cosmic energy, the conductors of that magic electricity which . . . flashed around their peaks, while the thunder roared and grumbled in the crags." The mountains were said to generate the clouds draping their peaks and so were seen as the source of rain and the empire's fertility. They have continued to inspire spiritual awe and regeneration in the poets, wise men, and ordinary pilgrims who wandered in them throughout China's history.[17]

Western religious philosopher Rudolph Otto notes that mountains evoke a religious response in humans because of their "mightiness, fearfulness, sublimity, and overwhelming power."[18] A historian of religions, Mircea Eliade, took this idea further, saying that mountains automatically evoke an experience of the sacred in human beings "because their natural form corresponds to a transcultural archetype of 'the center of the world' where vertical passage between earth and heaven occurs."[19] Edward Canda (a specialist in cross-cultural religious experience) writes:

> According to the *I Ching*, earth is associated with the trigram *k'un*, "the receptive"; it is completely *yin* in character. Heaven is associated with the trigram *ch'ien*, "the creative"; it is completely *yang* in character. Mountain is associated with the trigram *ken*, "keeping still"; it consists of two *yin* lines topped with a *yang* line. The Chinese commentary *Shuo Kua* identifies the meaning of the mountain trigram as the junction of beginnings and ends where all things reach fruition in stillness. Another image associated with this trigram is the gate, derived from its shape: ☶ Accordingly, one may envision

the mountain as an embodiment of *yin* opening up toward *yang*. The mountain is a gateway between heaven and earth.[20]

Mountains are the places where Heaven is rooted in Earth and where Earth reaches up to touch Heaven. They are places where human beings feel the most dynamic interchange between the sacred powers of Earth and Sky. This idea is also found among North American indigenous cultures. In one Omaha song, the singers proclaim:

> Verily, one alone of all these was the greatest,
> Inspiring to all minds,
> The Great White Rock,
> Standing and reaching as high as the heavens,
> Enwrapped in mist,
> Verily as high as the heavens.[21]

Stone, the substance of which mountains are made, is considered sacred in many cultures. Particularly sacred to the Sioux were certain perfectly round stones that would sometimes help men. Brave Buffalo says:

> When I was 10 years of age I looked at the land and rivers, the sky above, and the animals around me and I could not fail to realize that they were made by some great power. I was so anxious to understand this power that I questioned the trees and the bushes. It seemed as though the flowers were staring at me, and I wanted to ask them, "Who made you?" I looked at the moss-covered stones; some of them seemed to have the features of a man, but they could not answer me. Then I had a dream, and in my dream one of these small round stones appeared to me and told me that the maker of all was Wakan'-tanka, and that in order to honor him I must honor his works in nature. The stone said that by my search I had shown myself worthy of supernatural help. It said that if I were curing a sick person I might ask its assistance, and that all the forces of nature would help me work a cure.[22]

Lone Man also speaks of the sacred stones: "The medicine-man also told me that the sacred stone may appear in the form of a person who talks and sings many wonderful songs."[23]

Canda explains the deep connection traditional Korean people have to the sacredness of mountains:

> San sin (or san sin lyong), translated here as mountain spirit, should be understood as an entity which is tangible, specific, and personal. San sin are evident to human senses through the vitality, power, and mystery of physical mountains. They also make themselves directly known through visions and dreams. San sin are localized in space, usually associated with specific mountains. They are subject to causal and magical conditioning. San sin are endowed with personalities, each having unique emotive qualities and typical patterns of behavior.[24]

According to Canda, when San sin makes contact with human beings, he may appear in the form of a benevolent old man with a long white beard. "San sin," he continues, "is supernatural not in the sense of being above and detached from nature, but rather in the sense that he is supremely natural. The mountain spirit personifies earth at its highest point of development (both literally and metaphorically) at which earth meets heaven and receives its most direct blessings and sacred communications."[25]

These descriptions touch on a pan-human understanding: Stones and mountains have the capacity to express the sacred through a particular archetype. Cultures and individuals who remain sensitive to the living fabric of the sacred world can experience the mountain archetype, communicate with it, achieve harmony with it. Our forefathers, in the myriad cultures and tribes in which they lived and experienced, touched the fabric of this underlying truth and kept the memory of it in their daily work and oral traditions.

Which brings us to Mount Olympus. Mount Olympus in the state of Washington is named after the famed mountain in Greek legend, the home of the gods. It is easy to see why Washington's Mount Olympus was so named. It is indeed a place where God is strongly present. The trees are immense in that rainforest; the understory is lush. One feels upon entering the forest that one has walked into a world that has always been known. It was there just out of

reach, almost remembered, like a familiar room once well known but not thought of for many years. One enters it again and the memories come back. They flood in and take hold, carrying one away in a wash of ancient knowledge. When I first entered the forest, I began to remember an ancient world in which I had always lived and I felt tremendous reverence for the beauty and sacredness of that place.

However, all around the boundaries of the park, around the mountain, is the most rabid assault on the surface of the Earth I have ever seen. The trees are clear-cut without any sense of reverence; all life is ground down under machinery. It looks like pictures of the battlefields of both world wars. A few splinters that were once trees stick up here and there, huge clods of Earth are thrown about, and the rocks are ground down: Nothing is allowed to live. What causes us to attack the Earth so ferociously in our harvesting of resources? What, in spite of our scientific and aesthetic knowledge of the foolishness of our actions, drives us? This question, in my opinion, is the seminal question of our time.

Rationally we know why trees are clear-cut in such fashion—the expanding need for houses and paper for an exploding population. But our feelings tell us there is something more involved. We know it so deep down that, for many of us, our minds cannot make that knowledge go away. We know that the path we are taking as a species is not sustainable; know, as Robert Heinlein once remarked, that "population problems have a horrible way of solving themselves." So the question remains, What is the underlying motivation that drives us to such ferocious assaults on the Earth? It is, in part, the purpose of this book to explain.

Encoded in the "spell of the sensuous," in our deeply buried memories of that other manner of living, is the knowledge we need to successfully inhabit the Earth. There is a basic relation between the health of the Earth and the experience of the sacredness of Earth. As connection with the sacred grows more tenuous, fewer and fewer areas of the Earth will remain alive and wild and sacred. It seems that the Earth and the sacred are both reaching out and stirring up the human population of the Earth; there is a movement toward a general understanding of the sacredness of the Earth. The Earth is calling us to remember. And it seems apparent that without remembering our very humanness may be at stake. David Abram comments: "Our eyes, after all, have evolved

in interaction with other, non-human eyes; and our ears are attuned, by their very structure, to the howling of wolves and the honking of geese. We simply cannot survive in a purely human world, a world made up only of ourselves and our own creations. Not without destroying ourselves. . . . We are human only in contact, and conviviality, with what is not human."[26]

* * *

A story appeared in a Seoul newspaper in the summer of 1979. As Edward Canda recounts it: In a remote mountain village, the mother of a two-and-a-half-year-old boy went into her house for a few minutes, leaving her son outdoors; when she came out again, she found him gone. She called, looked frantically, but was unable to find him. The next morning the police, family, and villagers searched but still they were unable to find the boy. That evening the parents fell asleep exhausted, and they dreamed. The mountain spirit appeared to them and scolded them for having, a few months earlier, without reverence, cut the branches of a three-hundred-year-old tree. When the couple awoke they were sure that a tiger (a messenger of the mountain spirit) had taken their child. Another search was begun and tiger tracks were discovered behind the parents' house, some two hundred yards into the forest. The boy was found four days later, hungry and bramble-scratched but unhurt. When asked, the boy told his rescuers that he had been playing with a tiger.

The tiger that has come to seek us out, to remind us of the sacredness of the land, is a big one. We would do well to listen to its message.

part two

objections to the return

prologue

I must admit I have always suffered from a certain naiveté. My experiences of the sacredness of the Earth were so profound and moving, I thought that the wondrousness of Earth sacredness would be widely welcomed. Well, it is . . . sort of. Many people are enthused and are joining the movement to remember the sacred Earth. But others are extremely uncomfortable with a general resurgence of Earth mysticism. As I was to learn, the opponents fall into three groups: Native American activists, militant Christians, and Western scholars and scientists. And they are beginning to organize in active opposition to a general return to Earth spirituality by people on the North American continent.

My first encounter was with Native American activists. Because they still feel the pain of their own struggle and their people's oppression, in general many of them feel that non-Indians should not worship at the sacred places on the North American continent, should

not worship with the sacred pipe, and should not return to wilderness to seek closer contact with Creator. (It became apparent that the main thrust of their arguments was that non-Indians should return to Europe.) My awareness of their strong feelings was heightened after the *New York Times,* in pursuing an article on the conflict, interviewed my wife and me and featured us on the front page of the paper. As the result of that interview and for writing articles that resemble the first three chapters of this book, we were placed on a list that was widely circulated by Native activists. It was recommended that all dissemination of our work and writings be stopped.

I was then faced with an emotional dilemma that hinged on competing values—the right to worship in the way I was called versus the pain felt by many Native Americans at the historical treatment of their people. I had to try to find in myself some path to resolution. I began studying the Native activists' objections in order to find a path to common understanding. One thing was certain, however: I was now experiencing the same kind of religious repression that Natives in the nineteenth and early twentieth centuries had experienced when they attempted to retain their ceremonies. If I did not voluntarily cease engaging in activities Creator had called me to do, I would be stopped. There was a certain irony in the fact that Indians were now the initiators of religious repression against those who carried the pipe.

As I began working on this book in early 1994, I started to keep a file of opposing articles that I would use when I began writing in earnest. In 1996, after a publisher had expressed interest in the book and I was ready to begin writing, I received some odd mail. The first was an unsolicited publication by militant Christians, articulating in detail why no one (white *or* Indian) should follow Earth mysticism or Earth-centered spirituality; and (also unsolicited) I received a great deal of material by Western scholars, attacking the sacred Earth movement; foremost among the scholars and the one who addresses the problems of a return to Earth spirituality in greatest detail was the Western philosopher Ken Wilber. Oddly, many of the objections made by these two groups and the Native Americans were similar. The coincidence of the arrival of this material just as I was beginning to write this book, their similarity of perspectives,

and their common desired outcome—the cessation of a general return to Earth spirituality—indicated there was more here than I at first supposed. Why, I wondered, was everybody so nervous?

It became obvious as I developed this book that due to space limitations it would be impossible to respond in detail to the objections of the Western scholars and those of the Christian religious groups. So I touch on those objections and their ramifications where I feel it is crucial to the text, and I have included some material in the appendices. Several people have responded to those two groups in some detail. In *Religion and the Order of Nature*, Seyyed Hossein Nasr responds quite eloquently to Ken Wilber and other Western scholars who object to the current trends in Earth spirituality. Philip Sherrard (in *Human Image—World Image*) and Father William McNamara (in a number of his works) respond in detail to fundamentalist and militant Christian objections to the concept of a sacred Earth. No one has, to this time, however, responded to the virulent objections some Native activists are raising against non-Indian participation in sacred ceremonies in North America. Because the opposition against a general return to Earth spirituality is becoming so widespread, so emotional, so strong, and so violent, I felt compelled to address the question. For without a return to a general Earth spirituality, the wounds in us and in the Earth will only grow deeper. The assault on the land as I've witnessed around Mount Olympus, where the sacred is manifested, is echoed by an assault on the manifestation of the sacred in human beings. In both instances the assault comes from human beings.

In this process I encountered most strongly the Body of Suffering in our world. You cannot find the sacred places of America without also finding her wounds. You cannot touch those wounds without also finding them in yourself, in other people, and between all of us. The spiritual crisis that has brought us to this place exists in *all* of us. The Earth-centered path, Earth mysticism, is intimately bound up in a solution to this crisis. Those who have searched for the sacred places of America have found her sacred wounds. Those wounds have been held to our eyes and ears and hearts by Native activists, militant Christians, skeptical academics, our own sacred knowledge of the darkness in

ourselves, and by the Earth itself. They lie between many of us now; we each see the other as the cause of the wounds and thus increase them. Since the wounds are spiritual in nature, they cannot be healed through merely environmental ethics, legal expression, negotiation between peoples, or racial and cultural sensitivity training—although all these methods have some value. As Degawanidah taught us, the solution must come from the sacred, from our becoming the Good Mind. Out of the pain can come a good thing. If we are to heal our world, we must be unafraid to touch its pain.

chapter four
gifts of the great spirit?

Our religions are ours.
Period. We have very strong reasons for keeping certain
things private, whether you understand them or not.
And we have every human right to deny them to you,
whether you like it or not.[1] . . . [So] if you do [respect our
proprietary rights to our ceremonies], you're an ally and
we're ready and willing to join hands with you on other
issues. If you do not, you are at best a thief. More
importantly, you are a thief of the sort who is willing
to risk undermining our sense of the integrity of our cul-
tures for your own perceived self-interest. That means you
are complicit in a process of cultural genocide, or at least
attempted cultural genocide, aimed at American Indian
people. That makes you an enemy, to say the least.
And believe me when I say we're prepared to deal
with you as such.

— R U S S E L L   M E A N S[2]

White people in this country are so alienated from their own lives and so hungry for some sort of real life that they'll grasp at any straw to save themselves. But high tech society has given them a taste for the "quick-fix." They want their spirituality prepackaged in such a way as to provide instant insight, the more sensational and preposterous the better. They'll pay big bucks to anybody dishonest enough to offer them spiritual salvation after reading the right book or sitting still for the right fifteen minute session. And, of course, this opens them up to every kind of mercenary hustler imaginable. It's all very pathetic, really.

— V I N E   D E L O R I A ,   J R .[3]

If whites are searching for the mystical, [George Tinker] suggest[s] that they research their own religions, noting for example, such fifteenth-century Roman Catholic mystics as Theresa of Avila and John of the Cross.[4]

In its simplest definition, religion is considered to be the area of human activity through which the search for meaning—and the articulation of what is found during that search—occurs. In that endeavor, human beings are *bound back* (the literal meaning of religion) to a center of meaning, a point of ultimate reference in the universe.[5] Profane, secular life exists without reference to any ultimate sense of reality, no *mysterium tremendum,* no touch with that sacred center of all things before which all other things pale. It is regulated by "little" meanings (birthdays, love of one's hometown, national ideals) but not one overriding sense of the REAL. Historians of religion examine the varieties of expression of human contact with fundamental reality, how people shape their lives after contact with the sacred, and how they shape their search for meaning.

To any historian of religion, to any theologian who understands the main thrust of the religious impulse, to anyone who has felt the touch of the sacred, the person living a secular, profane existence is by definition living a pathetic existence. (The word *pathetic* comes from the Greek *pathetos,* meaning "suffering.") How much worse would suffering be if it were also devoid of the touch of the sacred fire from which we have come? Even in a desacralized world—the

modern industrialized world—the religious impulse is not dead. It strives to make itself heard amid the clutter of internal dialogue, commercial harangues, and desensitized emotional and psychic life. In America, which has no incorporated mystical tradition, no vibrant living religious life, the religious impulse has been reduced to a degraded and furtive experience. In reaction, the children of America seek, search, reach out for meaning. A searching coming from *pathetos* in its true sense, not the sarcastic, demeaning, put-down, dehumanizing meaning to which "pathetic" is usually put.

The depth of human suffering, the experience of *pathetos*, and the importance the sacred plays in relieving it are embodied most deeply for me in a story I have thought about for many years. It is said that most of the Protestant hymns sung in America were written by one man. The account I heard holds that the man was the captain of a slave ship—a cruel and unforgiving man who had been at his trade a long time. One year, he was making the trip from Africa to America and the hold of the ship was filled with a cargo of suffering humanity. Packed top to bottom, the slaves were spooned into the shelves that lined the hold. A few inches above their faces was the next row of bunks; the slaves were chained in place. If weather permitted, they were allowed a few minutes on deck each day because the ship captains realized that fewer slaves died if they were allowed the touch of the sun and some fresh air once a day. One day, the captain, more than halfway across the sea, suddenly found himself in the presence of God. In that moment of limitless time, he saw his life examined, sorted, and reviewed, and he quailed at the darkness of his soul. Then God turned to him, reached out and touched him, and said, "You are forgiven, go and sin no more." The captain turned his ship around and took the slaves back to Africa; then he went home and sold his ship. They say (so the story goes) that the first song he wrote was "Amazing Grace."

I have always thought that the captain must have understood the deepest meaning of *pathetos*. How must it have felt to be so changed and different and to live all the rest of his life carrying the burden of the pain he had caused? I have often thought of him, for what man or woman has not caused pain to others? What person has not eventually understood the pain he or she has

caused and had to bear its burden? Many people, like the sea captain, have been touched by the power of the sacred and, in spite of the rigid form of their old life, followed its lead to a new way of being. Is this not, in part, what the sacred is for? And do we not all experience it from where we begin, our secular mundane self? To some, unfortunately, having this experience seems to be a crime for which one is castigated.

Vine Deloria, Jr., in his introduction to *The Dream Seekers: Native American Visionary Traditions of the Great Plains,* by Lee Irwin, notes:

> This book is for the serious reader and must be read with the utmost care and seriousness. It is not a manual for fools or something for New Age exploitation. It is considerably more comprehensive than the scholarly treatments that have preceded it. The most valuable thing about it is that it does not have a doctrinal point of view, a cherished anthropological "truth" or interpretation that labels and moves on without understanding what it was that happened— or happens. Thus, when Irwin describes the motives for enduring the excruciating experiences of the vision quest and mentions seeking "power," he is NOT talking about a New Age circle-jerk where a dozen affluent people spend all of two hours being informed that the world is round and that they all can have a "power panther" at their beck and call.[6]

Earlier in the introduction, he remarks:

> Bookshelves today are filled with pap—written many times by Indians—who have kicked over the traces and no longer feel they are responsible to any living or historic community, but more often by wholly sincere and utterly ignorant non-Indians who fancy themselves masters of the vision quest and sweat lodge. Lying beneath this mass of sentimental slop is the unchallenged assumption that personal sincerity is the equivalent of insight and that cosmic secrets can be not only shared by non-Indians but given out in weekend workshops as easily as diet plans.[7]

Anyone who has seriously read Deloria's work cannot help but be affected by his sincerity and depth of insight. Except for a regrettable tendency to label people by their skin color (*Red Earth White Lies*) and to assume (in the heat of passion on a topic he cares deeply about) that all non-Indians are fools and poltroons when it comes to deep experience of and commitment to Earth-centered religion, his work is remarkable. Of exceptional importance is his most recent work, *Red Earth White Lies*, in which, for the most part, he refrains from race baiting and bashing. In it, as I did in my own book, *Sacred Plant Medicine*, he makes a strong argument for the inaccuracy of current scientific models of the indigenous world. There are other ways to gain understanding about and information on the inner workings of the universe in which we live than a left-brain, rational scientific approach. Deloria makes the good (and essential) point that the conflict between Native American indigenous cultures and the European culture is a conflict between these paradigms. But he just cannot quite restrain himself: In the first paragraph in the book, he speaks sarcastically of the "multitudes of young whites roam[ing] the West convinced they are Oglala Sioux Pipe Carriers . . . on a holy mission to protect 'Mother Earth.' "

The inherent unkindness and dehumanizing tone of such words can be seen in a comment by Indian novelist Sherman Alexie.

> Last year on the local television news, I watched a short feature on a meeting of the Confused White Men chapter in Spokane, Wash. They were all wearing war bonnets and beating drums, more or less. A few of the drums looked as if they might have come from K-Mart, and one or two of the men just beat their chests. "It's not just the drum," the leader of the group said, "it's the idea of the drum." I was amazed at the lack of rhythm and laughed, even though I knew I supported a stereotype. But it's true: white men can't drum.[8]

Now, let's change the quote just a little.

> Last year on the local television news, I watched a short feature on a meeting of the Confused Red Men chapter in Washington, D.C. They were all wearing

white men's clothes and carrying briefcases and making legal arguments, more or less. Some of the clothes and a few of the briefcases looked as if they might have come from K-Mart, and one or two of the men just waved imaginary copies of the Constitution. "It's not just the Constitution," the leader of the group said. "It's the idea of the Constitution." I was amazed at their naivete and lack of legal sophistication and laughed, even though I knew I supported a stereotype. But it's true: Indians are just like simple children.

Unfortunately, when directed at whites, such racial dehumanization is often not recognized. Especially troublesome about Deloria's and Alexie's articulations is the casual reduction of a whole group of people to the dehumanizing term "white." I do not mean here that "white" is in itself a pejorative, although many Indians—and others—use it as such, but that the individual humanity of the members of a group is collapsed into a term with no differentiation. Such an act is racist, no matter the reason for doing it.[9] Indian activists seek to deny (or through denigration cause the abandonment of) a religious practice to one group of people solely on the basis of skin color.

Deloria, Tinker, and Means cannot have met or known every white person whose religious practice has been affected by Native religious forms. In their writings (whatever other opinions they may hold), they do not acknowledge that any white person feels the underlying sacredness of the pipe (for instance), knows the commitment necessary to carry a working pipe (or even knows the distinction between a working pipe, ceremonial pipe, healing pipe, and an individual pipe), knows how many years are necessary to develop the muscles and capacities necessary to walk in sacred terrains, or realizes the necessity for unrelaxed integrity in these pursuits. Could there not be one? Is there not one white person who is a "real" convert to this path and not simply an "utterly ignorant" "circle jerk"? Is there not one white man who can drum? The Native activists would have us believe that the answer to all these questions is no.

Many people, non-Indian and Indian alike, approach life and religion superficially. Mystics—those who seek deeper connection with the sacred—in all ages realize that some people seek deeper into the meanings of things than others.

Some "white" people are admittedly superficial and some of those are, no doubt, involved in Native forms of religious expression.[10]

Deloria, Tinker, and Means make sweeping generalizations: All white people are superficial; all Indians are not. All white people who participate in Native religious forms are outsiders to a religion they cannot really understand; all Indians who participate in Native religious forms automatically have an affinity with those forms because they are Indian.[11] Genetic, race-based religion is a legitimate option.[12] White people's genetic religious form is Christian mysticism or pre-Christian European paganism to which "whites" should return (and they must not engage in drumming!); Indian religion is for Indians and they should, presumably, stick with their religion.

I have met stupid Indians and smart Indians, handsome Indians and ugly Indians, racist Indians and humanity-embracing Indians, religious Indians and secular Indians, greedy Indians and generous Indians, rhythmic Indians and Indians who can't drum. In short, Indians seem to possess characteristics across the human spectrum. Native writers like Tinker and Deloria seem to be saying that Indians are superior to whites in their capacity to experience the underlying reality of Native religious forms. Or they are saying Indians are genetically predisposed to that underlying reality, as Edna Seidner (of the Bear River and Weott tribes) states: "I have always believed what my elders taught me, that when one is born to a natural birth mother, their lives are forever connected to that birth mother, no matter what race it is and their roots should be formed from that time. Why five hundred years later are [whites] trying to transplant their roots to become another nationality and form imitation tribes and doing fantasy quests into a world they can never be a part of?"[13] At the same time activists make these assertions, many—Tinker and Deloria among them—have condemned "white New-Agers" for saying that Indians seem to have access to a deeper or humanly necessary kind of religiosity. They decry the *Dances with Wolves* romanticization of Indian culture while proclaiming that Indian culture is, basically, Dances with Wolves (e.g., all red men can drum).[14]

Tinker advises whites who insist they have found something in Indian ceremonial forms to return to traditional Christian mysticism and abandon any

contact with North American indigenous religious traditions. Deloria, Means, and Seidner seem to agree with Tinker—as does Myrna Leader Charge Trimble, director of tourism on the Rosebud Indian reservation. She flatly states: "We don't want people coming here looking for answers to their spirituality that they can't find in their own religions or countries."[*][15]

This attitude can be found among members of other cultures. Nirad C. Chaudhuri, who was born in India, says in his book *Hinduism*: "[This book] is not meant for those who go to Hinduism from some personal emotional pressure, or to put it more bluntly, for those who seek in Hinduism what they feel they do not find in the religion in which they were born, or simply as an anodyne for psychological malaise. I have had to say some hard words about Hinduizing Occidentals."[16] Chaudhuri admits "he lost faith in the tenets of Hinduism and indeed in all established religions long ago"[17] and feels, apparently, that any religious impulse comes from some kind of limitation. Nevertheless, he gets upset about Occidentals (whites) converting to Hinduism and is even harsher about Hindu teachers who teach Occidentals.

> In the present enfeebled state of Western life and culture, the so-called Hindu spirituality has become a mirage to lure those Europeans who have become so de-vitalized that they feel the Western heritage of religion, ethics, and intellection as an unbearable burden (Aldous Huxley furnishes a pitiful example of this). . . . There was also, of course, throughout the West in the nineteenth century the attraction of Hindu charlantry and mumbo-jumbo for the superstitious, who thought they could get from Hinduism what was not to be had from Christianity. . . . This kind of attraction also continues, and has become more insidiously dangerous because it operates on all that is weak, unsettled, and morally debased in the West. After losing the mental stability and

---

* In spite of this statement, the *Wall Street Journal* reports that tourists from Europe are flocking to the reservations. Tour packages (promoted by tribal representatives), which include living in tipis, sweat lodges, and experiencing traditional Indian lifestyles, can cost as much as $3,200. Tribal representatives rent booths at the huge annual tourism fair in Berlin in order to promote a heavier tourist influx.

spiritual confidence which came from Christianity, many people in the West are coming around to think they can find a substitute in certain things in Hinduism, e.g. Yoga. . . . Some Hindu writers are actually writing to meet such expectations, each choosing which he would satisfy. Thus one ladles out Vedanta to the intellectually debilitated, another Yoga to the physically degenerate, and a third Tantra to the eroto-maniac who has not the courage of his lechery. So there is a good deal of misrepresentation of Hinduism.[18]

He believes that the misrepresentation by Hindus allows opportunists to line their pockets by preying on the weakness of the Western mind. He asserts that the many books written by Westerners who thought they understood Hinduism have contributed to the problem by perpetuating a filtered and changed occidentalized form of Hinduism, which has more to do with Western projections than real Hinduism. He ends by stating it is nearly impossible for a serious writer to describe Hinduism accurately because Western readers, full of romantic notions about Hindu spirituality, would not believe the description. Chaudhuri's comments are remarkably similar to comments by Native activists, particularly those of Oren Lyons: "Non-Indians have become so used to all this hype on the part of impostors that when a real Indian spiritual leader tries to offer them useful advice, he is rejected. He isn't 'Indian' enough for all these non-Indian experts on Indian religion."[19]

From Chaudhuri's comments I assume that a number of Westerners (such as Ram Dass) who have immersed themselves in Hinduism have had to deal, from time to time, with similar types of prejudice as non-Indians in this country. I have read or heard of similar comments by Buddhists and Confucianists and I have been told by Occidentals who wish to practice those religions that they also experienced racial prejudice and stereotyping. The charges and beliefs of racial separatists are similar in each case: Westerners are trying to get something their own religion does not provide, Westerners are weak and debilitated, Westerners are unable to really understand a foreign religion, Westerners should go back where they came from. Native activists, using similar words and phrases, advance the same message.

However, there are many members of other cultures, Koreans, Japanese, American Indians, who are converting to Christianity. Native activist declarations to the contrary, most of the converts would bitterly dispute any allegation that their conversion was not genuine—that they were forced to convert or that their conversion is a result of religious imperialism or that it is genetically impossible for them to experience the essential teachings of their new religion. Many Indian Christians genuinely believe in Christianity and strongly disagree with traditional Indian religious practices. One Indian minister, Eugene Rowland, notes: "The American Indian Movement is telling people that Christianity is a white man's religion and that the Indian people should go back to their Indian religion. Sometimes when I preach people mock me and make fun of me. Some Indian people still believe in yuwipi meetings and talking to the spirits, which is wrong and Christ doesn't want it."[20]

Garfield Good Plume, another Indian minister, gives similar details about Rich Ashley, the son of a well-known yuwipi man. "Rich fasted in the Black Hills and saw a vision that the destruction of Jerusalem meant the destruction of yuwipi as a sign of Christ's coming. At this conversion he turned his back on the old ways and gave himself to Christ. His father, Fred Ashley, asked Rich to take over his yuwipi practice. But Rich believed it was the work of the devil."[21]

These Indians, like many non-Indians, have come to accept a different religious form from the one in which they were raised.[22] It works for them; they find a deeper connection with the sacred center of meaning through their participation in it. People *do* explore many religious traditions and religion itself in their search for meaning and deeper contact with the sacred. Racial separatists in many cultures want, have always advocated, a restriction on this human exploration.

But Native activists, by advocating religious separation along racial lines, are ignoring a central element of humankind's relationship with the sacred: The sacred manifests itself in the manner *it* chooses and to whom it chooses. Neither human beings nor a particular human culture own or control how the sacred chooses to manifest itself.

these ceremonies do not belong to the indian alone

Members of a culture who assert that they understand the intention and drive of the sacred in its manifestations better than the sacred itself are, at best, guilty of hubris and, at the worst, of fanaticism. As Frank Fools Crow, the ceremonial chief of the Teton Sioux, widely respected Sioux elder and traditionalist, and nephew of Black Elk, said: "I do not always ask, in my prayers and discussions, for only those things I would like to see happen, because no man can claim to know what is best for mankind. *Wakan-Tanka* and Grandfather alone know what is best, and this is why, even though I am worried, my attitude is not overcome with fear of the future. I submit always to *Wakan-Tanka's* will. This is not easy, and most people find it impossible."[23] Many Native activists, however, assert that they *know*, without question or doubt, what Creator wants each people to have, how they are to worship, and what ceremonies they are to use. They are certain that such issues are to be delineated along racial or tribal lines.

But many Indians, past and present, have not agreed with this perspective. Charles Eastman, the Sioux whose Native Lakota name was Ohiyesa, asserts the universality of human beings and their capacity to equally worship the Creator, regardless of their skin color. "We of the twentieth century . . . know that all religious aspiration, all sincere worship, can have but one source and goal. We know that the God of the educated and the God of the child, the God of the civilized and the God of the primitive, is after all the same God; and that this God does not measure our differences, but embraces all who live rightly and humbly on the earth."[24] His statements are remarkably similar to those of Frank Fools Crow who, like many Natives, does not believe that these ceremonies cannot be shared. He feels that all who come should be able to receive help; none should be discriminated against on the basis of their skin color. He remarks:

This is not a thing only I can do. Anyone who is sincere with the pipe can do it, and gain the insight he wishes. If this person takes his pipe and goes out by himself, if he takes plenty of time, as long as is needed to get the message, he will learn what he wants to know. And these ceremonies do not belong to the Indian alone. They can be done by all who have the right attitude, and who are honest and sincere about their belief in Grandfather and in following his rules. This is why *Wakan-Tanka* has taught me to make proper use of the spiritual colors.

Whenever it is possible, when I am doing my ceremonies I put my black flag here (west), and that is a man; I put my red flag here (north), and that is a man; I put my yellow flag over here (east), and that is a man; and I put my white flag over here (south), and that is a man. These are the spiritual representatives of all races, and they remind me that Grandfather's spirits serve others as well as the Indian. We are the keepers of certain areas of knowledge, which we are to share for the good of mankind. And the blacks and the Orientals and the whites are each keepers of knowledge that can and should be used to benefit us.[25]

Many Native elders, it is said, foresaw a time when the children of all races would celebrate the ceremonies and sacredness of the Earth together; among them was Crazy Horse, the great Sioux leader.

He saw his people being driven into spiritual darkness and poverty while the white people prospered in a material way all around them, but even in the darkest times he saw that the eyes of a few of his people kept the light of dawn, and the wisdom of the earth, which they passed on to some of their grandchildren. He saw the coming of automobiles and airplanes and twice he saw the great darkness and heard the screams and explosions when millions died in two great world wars.

But after the second great war passed, he saw a time come when his people began to awaken, not all at once, but a few here and there and then more

and more, and he saw that they were dancing in the beautiful light of the Spirit World under the Sacred Tree even while on earth. Then he was amazed to see that dancing under that tree were representatives of all races who had become brothers, and he realized that the world would be made new again and in peace and harmony not just by his people, but by members of all the races of mankind.[26]

Many tribes have stories like the one shared by the Muskogee-Creek journalist Brian Wilkes. "I grew up with the saying that once eight generations of your ancestors are buried here, you are of this land. Nothing was said about complexion. I grew up with the prophecy that one of the elders being removed west of the Mississippi told the whites—that their descendants would gradually become Indians."[27]

Ed McGaa, who trained with Fools Crow and who is one of the Native teachers of non-Indians who has been attacked by Native activists, notes: "In all the speeches of the old Indian chiefs that I have read, every one of our leaders wanted the conquerors to change their ways, and many warned of serious consequences if this did not happen. We will have to face those leaders in the spirit world, and they will ask, what did we do to change and educate the dominant culture from this road of Earth destruction?"[28]

Harry Kindness, an Oneida Indian, recently ran across the continental United States to let people know that "this is not just an Indian issue. We all have to come together and make people aware that we need to be concerned about Mother Earth."[29] Manitonquat, an elder and a storyteller, is the spiritual leader of the Assonet Band of the Wampanoag Nation. He echoes McGaa and others: "Part of my work as a medicine man . . . is to illuminate your own [individual] vision by the light of the spiritual heritage of the ancient ones of this continent. This heritage contains all of the healing that is needed if life is to survive on this planet that is our home."[30]

Fools Crow believed that it was crucial to share the sacred pipe with all people. He (like Sun Bear, the Ojibway teacher) "believe[d] that [the pipe] is the key to the world's survival today."[31] And in some versions of the coming of

White Buffalo Calf Woman it is remembered that she told the people, "I bring you this pipe for *all* the common people." Some activists maintain that the common people are "Indian" people alone. But others do not. Lucy Looks Twice, the daughter of Black Elk, says, "We accepted that pipe from the Great Spirit through a sacred lady who brought it to all the human beings."[32]

According to Black Elk, when a person smokes the pipe it is an act joining all creation, healing all separation between people, between things and people. He related that Buffalo Calf Woman said: "All these peoples, and all things of the universe, are joined to you who smoke the pipe—all send their voices to *Wakan-Tanka*, the Great Spirit. When you pray with this pipe you pray for and with everything. . . . You must always remember that the two-leggeds and all the other peoples who stand upon this earth are sacred and should be treated as such. From this time on, the holy pipe will stand upon this red earth, and the two-leggeds will take the pipe and send their voices to *Wakan-Tanka*."[33]

Brooke Medicine Eagle, also one of the Native teachers condemned by Native activists, has said time and time again that White Buffalo Calf Woman brought the sacred pipe to the Lakota people for all people—that it was truly brought "for *all* the common people." She notes that "many who proudly exhibited the sacred pipe that White Buffalo Woman urged us to carry and use in our pursuit of oneness nevertheless practiced aggression and violence against others of the family of two-leggeds whom they judged to be outside their particular circle. Thus while they carried Buffalo Woman's form in their hands, they did not carry her song in their hearts."[34]

In a letter dated April 2, 1996, Arvol Looking Horse, the current keeper of the original sacred pipe of the Oglala people, called on all people of all faiths to actively pray together to support a healthy Earth: "The prophesies tell it is time to begin mending the SACRED HOOP and begin GLOBAL healing by working towards PEACE & HARMONY. The birth of the WHITE BUFFALO CALF lets us know We are at a crossroads either to return back to sacred places and pray for WORLD PEACE—if we do NOT do this our children will suffer."[35] Looking Horse and other involved elders apparently do not feel the same conflicts about people of all skin colors worshipping with the sacred pipe as do

Russell Means and other activists. Father Paul Steinmetz, a Jesuit priest who lived and worked among the Oglala Lakota (Sioux) on the Pine Ridge Reservation from 1961 to 1981, reveals:

> In October of 1976, I requested to pray in the presence of the Calf Pipe. [Arvol] Looking Horse conducted a sweat lodge ceremony for me and late at night opened the small house where the Calf Pipe is kept. He told me that this was the first time a priest or minister had made this request and he was pleased. During the summer of 1977 on the first day of the Sun Dance, the bundle was brought outside for a public ceremony. Sidney Keith, a prominent member of the tribe, defended my presence there against the complaint of a Lakota woman. He said that the Calf Pipe is open to anybody regardless of race and that is the way they do it there.[36]

Steinmetz eventually was given a pipe to use in his Catholic ceremonies. Iron Rope, a respected medicine man at Slim Butte, said: "I am glad this Father is interested in the Pipe. He can use this Pipe at mass. . . . I would like to have Father use the Pipe when he prays at Mass." Steinmetz says that Pete Catches echoed this feeling when he "defended my praying with the Pipe on the grounds that as a priest I was the equivalent of a 'holy man' in the traditional Lakota sense. When he put me on the hill for a two-day Pipe fast in 1974, he told me that some would criticize him for this but that this was one of the great honors of his life."[37]

Many medicine people have not limited their work with non-Indians to the pipe. In his book *Fools Crow*, Frank Fools Crow notes that he would work with anyone who came to him. "Three white people, an older man, a younger man, and a young girl—came to my home to see me, and wanted me to take them on a vision quest," which he did. His attitude seems somewhat at odds with Russell Means's position: "Our religions are ours. Period. We have very strong reasons for keeping certain things private, whether you understand them or not. And we have every human right to deny them to you, whether you like it or not."

Fools Crow's attitude is not uncommon; many Indian people believed that Native practices should be shared among all people, that the color of a person's skin had little to do with what was inside the heart, that a person's relationship with Creator was a private matter between that person and Creator. As Ohiyesa said:

We believe that God is nearer to us in solitude, and there are no priests authorized to come between us and our Maker. None can exhort or confess or in any way meddle with the religious experience of another. All of us are created children of God, and all stand erect, conscious of our divinity. Our faith cannot be formulated in creeds, nor forced upon any who are unwilling to receive it; hence there is no preaching, proselytizing, nor persecution, neither are their any scoffers or atheists. Our religion is an attitude of mind, not a dogma.[38]

Or as White Shield, the Arikara chief, said: "The color of the skin makes no difference. What is good and just for one is good and just for the other, and the Great Spirit made all men brothers. I have a red skin, but my grandfather was a white man. What does it matter? It is not the color of the skin that makes me good or bad."[39]

The Winnebago people believed the pipe should be used to bring reconciliation between peoples and to mend the pain between men and between nations; in other words, it should be used, as Creator said, for bringing about the oneness of all things:

Try to do something for your people—something difficult. Have pity on your people and love them. If a man is poor, help him. Give him and his family food, give them whatever they ask for. If there is discord among your people, intercede.

Take your sacred pipe and walk into their midst. Die if necessary in your attempt to bring about reconciliation. Then, when order has been restored and they see you lying dead on the ground, still holding in your hand the

sacred pipe, the symbol of peace and reconciliation, then assuredly they will know that you have been a real chief.[40]

But as Brooke Medicine Eagle notes, many Native activists, although carrying Buffalo Calf Woman's form in their hands, do not subscribe to this Winnebago belief; they carry dissension in their hearts. Paul Steinmetz, in *Pipe, Bible, and Peyote Among the Oglala Lakota,* remarks on Pete Catches's feelings about whites participating in other Indian ceremonies besides the pipe and militant activists trying to prevent their participation. He writes about the Sun Dance:

> The day before Pete Catches' Sun Dance in 1978, a few young mixed-blood militants demanded that no white people be present. Although he had invited Allen, a friend visiting from Hawaii, and me to be there, he gave in to the pressure but wrote a note to me: "Please, Father, don't come to the Sun Dance at all as friction here is strong against any form of white man coming here. Even Allen is not allowed to be present to look on. And I am personally very hurt by this. And I told the opposing party that if we cannot approach the Sun Dance with an open mind, then this will be the last Sun Dance here at our place. Yours sincerely and respectively, Pete Catches, Sr." This short letter perhaps best dramatizes the confrontation developing between the militants entering Lakota religion and most of the established medicine men. In 1979, the next year, Catches' Sun Dance was open to everyone to attend with the exception of any militant.[41]

But Russell Means and other American Indian Movement (AIM) activists disagree. They think that Indian ways should not be shared, that they belong only to Indians. As Means says: "Since when is the sweat not an Indian ceremony? It's not 'based on' an Indian ceremony, it *is* an Indian ceremony. So is [the] visionquest, the pipe, . . . sage, and all the rest of it."[42]

are these ceremonies uniquely indian?

Except for the sacred pipe, the ceremonies mentioned by Russell Means are, in spite of his assertion, common to many people and cultures throughout the world. And as for the sacred pipe, as I noted earlier, many Indian leaders and ceremonial leaders have felt it should be shared, that part of its purpose is to unite all people just as it unites human and nonhuman life. The sacred pipe *is* unique to North America. Many people who are not racial separatists and have seen the beauty of the pipe feel it was brought to all mankind by Creator through White Buffalo Calf Woman. Many medicine people believe that it should be shared among all people, that part of its purpose is to unite all people just as it unites all human and nonhuman life. But the sweat lodge, the use of sage, and the vision quest are not unique to North America; they are practiced on all continents and are common to all peoples.

the sweat lodge

The most comprehensive book on sweat bath customs around the world is by Mikkel Aaland and, appropriately enough, is entitled *Sweat.* Aaland found sweat baths or lodges in nearly every country on Earth. Sweat baths come in all shapes and forms: round, square, big, small, fancy, and simple. The use of a sweat bath is, in fact, an ancient and universal human custom.

The sweat house, by housing and controlling the awesome power of flame, became a sacred shrine. Early sauna bathers in Finland believed fire was heaven sent and if fueled with choice firewood and tended to with appropriate ritual, diseases and spiritual evils could be driven off. . . .

Many sweat bath cultures discovered that rocks could absorb the power of fire, and thereby acquired spiritual significance. . . . When water was splashed over them, the vapor produced became another medium for the transfer of heat

and another object of worship. The Finns named this vapor *loyly,* spirit of life. The Fox, another American Indian tribe, believed that *Manitou,* a friendly spirit, dwelled inside the rocks and was released through the vapor to penetrate the skins of the bathers and drive out sickness. . . .

A bather absorbing the heat of a sweat bath was seen as reenacting Creation, merging body and fire. Hindu mythology has several stories regarding the human absorption of heat. Pajapati created the world by heating himself to an extreme temperature through asceticism. Consequently, Hindu ascetics meditate near fire to achieve inner heat. Those who reach a communion with the Spirit are said to "burn." Those who perform miracles are called *sahib-jocks,* which means to "boil" from inner heat.

> The visible product of heat, or "waters born from the heated man," is sweat. When looked on in this spiritual light, sweat's importance . . . becomes clear. . . .
>
> Sweat, because of its indirect association with fire, was sometimes connected with the creation of humankind. Sweat from bathing gods is of special importance. In Russian and Indian folklore are tales of "God" in a sweat bath and creating "Adam and Eve" through drops of falling sweat. . . .
>
> Finnish women usually gave birth inside saunas in order to be in the presence of benevolent spirits. These spirits were thought to reduce the pains of childbirth and increase the chance of survival for both the mother and child. . . .
>
> Islamic women went to the hamman, the middle eastern sweat bath, three times during many days of wedding ceremonies, attending the final rinsing bath on the eve of the marriage.
>
> Russian mourners would heat their sweat bath in order to warm their souls and . . . the souls of the deceased.[43]

Aaland also writes of the use of the sweat bath in Japan: "While Turkish baths and Finnish-style saunas enjoy great popularity in Tokyo, their native sweat bathing culture co-exists and further confirmed what my research had already revealed—that almost every people, at some time in their history, had

devised, in one form or another, hot air or steam bathing."[44] Japan has many types of baths: "*mushi-buro* (steam bath), *kama-buro* (kiln bath) resembling a kiln, *ishi-buro* (rock bath) a cave drilled into the side of a rock formation, *kara-buro* (empty bath) empty of water and filled with hot air or steam, *todan-buro* (shelf bath), and the *Zakuroguchih*, known as the Pomegranate Entrance bath."[45] "[The] *Makuranososhi*, a book written around the 9th century, observed: 'Stones are placed inside small cottages and huts. After the stones are heated, water is poured on them to produce steam. Bamboo mats are placed around the stones so people may sit near the steam.' "[46]

Yosai Aotani, a Japanese classical scholar and poet who lived from 1868 to 1910, wrote a poem about the *kama-buro*, the kiln bath:

> *When one crawls into the* kama-buro
> *It is just like night,*
> *Then one sees the white daylight as the softening steam reaches the*
> *lungs and stomach.*
> *Sweat is released in streams*
> *And the power of this kiln bath equals hundreds of medicines.*[47]

Such a description could have been written by a medicine person from any North American tribe in any time. It is clear that the underlying power and spiritual significance of the sweat lodge transcend culture and have for hundreds, if not thousands, of years.

About the sweat lodge Manitonquat says:

My elders many years ago . . . instruct[ed] me to explain our ways to any non-Indian people who were interested to want to know about them. As I have spoken of this way in many places around the world since then, I have found that using steam for healing is very common and very ancient on this planet. At one time, all the uses for steam healing were spiritual, but these ways were lost to people as they were converted to other religions. Because of this I believe the sweat is for all people, not just my people.[48]

the use of sage

The use of sage is also a widespread human practice. In her book *Sacred Land, Sacred Sex, Rapture of the Deep*, Delores La Chappelle quotes Herbert Wright on the prevalence of the use of sagebrush throughout human history. Wright notes that North Africa, Spain, Italy, Greece, Iran, and Syria were once dominated primarily by an *Artemisia* species: sagebrush. La Chapelle remarks:

> In Southwestern Asia, as well, there was a dominance of sagebrush steppe in this same Pleistocene period. . . . [A]s the human race began during Pleistocene times in Africa, the odor of sage was everywhere present. The persistent odor of sage accompanied humans as slowly, over generations, they moved further north and into the Paleolithic cave areas of Spain and France. Then, as the climate changed, the persistent odor of the sage steppe moved further north into the areas where humans later learned to grow cereal grains. Throughout all this period of human development, sage was always present.
>
> No wonder that Artemis, one of the most important Greek goddesses has the same name as this plant. . . . *[Artemisia]* grew abundantly on Mt. Taygetus, the favorite haunt of Artemis. . . . Artemis means bear. . . . Here again we have a herb which bear first showed to humans.[49]

Various species of *Artemisia* are used regularly in Nepal and India. Trilock Chandra Majupuria and D. P. Joshi remark in their book *Religious and Useful Plants of Nepal and India* that *Artemisia* has traditionally been used for many ceremonies. "The leaves of this plant are offered to Shiva after chanting various *mantras*. In the month of *shravana* (July to August) the flowers of this plant are offered to Vishnu and Surya. After funeral ceremonies Hindus also use either flowers or leaves of this plant. The fragrance of this plant has also been said to be used by several religious people to avoid lethariness and yawning."[50]

Sagebrush (an *Artemisia* species) and white sage are both used in Native American ceremonies. Although sagebrush is used interchangeably with true sages *(Salvia* species, among which is white sage) in ceremony, it differs

botanically from them. Even so, the *Salvias* also grew throughout the Mediterranean area and in Asia, and people believed they also had strong spiritual properties that were identified long before European contact with the indigenous tribes of the Americas.

In *A Modern Herbal*, M. Grieve notes that the name of the genus *Salvia* comes

from the Latin *salvere*, to be saved, in reference to the curative properties of the plant. . . . Among the ancients and throughout the Middle Ages it was in high repute: *Cur moriatur homo cui Salvia crescit in horto?* (Why should a man die whilst sage grows in his garden?) . . . The herb is sometimes spoken of as *Salvia salvatrix* (Sage the Savior). . . . In the Jura district of France, in Franche-Comte, the herb is supposed to mitigate grief, mental and bodily. . . . The following is a translation of an old French saying: "Sage helps the nerves and by its powerful might palsy is cured and fever put to flight."[51]

An examination of the traditional European uses of sage and sagebrush shows that the plant was used to dispell unhealthy influences and to bring in good, fresh, clean influences—uses similar to those in Native American traditions.[52]

the vision quest

The recognition that human beings can contact the deep sacred powers of the Earth and Creator by spending periods of time in isolation on the Earth (in a vision quest) is common throughout the world. In fact, the knowledge that mankind must periodically return to the wilderness or the desert for renewal is implicit or explicit in many of the world's religious traditions. It is common, as Russell Means asserts, among indigenous cultures. Traces of the wilderness initiatory rite can be found in Africa, Australia, and the Americas.[53] Black Elk notes there were many reasons to go into the wilderness to seek a vision, or "lament" as he called it. "But," he says, "perhaps the most important reason for 'lamenting' is that it helps us to realize our oneness with all things,

to know that all things are our relatives; and then in behalf of all things we pray to *Wakan-Tanka* that he may give us knowledge of Him who is the source of all things, yet greater than all things."[54]

Steven Foster and Meredith Little write, in *The Book of the Vision Quest,* that one basic reason for returning to wilderness was to contact the Earth Mother aspect of the sacred. In the Essene Gospel of John, Jesus says:

> I tell you in very truth, Man is the Son of the Earthly Mother, and from her did the Son of Man receive his whole body, even as the body of the newborn babe is born of the womb of his mother. I tell you truly, you are one with the Earthly Mother; she is in you, and you in her. Of her you were born, and to her you shall return again. . . . For your breath is her breath; your blood her blood; your bone her bone; your flesh her flesh; your bowels her bowels; your eyes and ears, her eyes and ears.

Foster and Little remind us that "the gift of love for our Great Mother is given to us at birth. But we often forget to remember. That is why it is sometimes necessary to go to her, to fast, and be alone with her, so that we can fully remember the kin relationship between our bone and her stone, our blood and her rivers, our flesh and the body of nature."[55]

This understanding is also reflected in Taoist practice. Huston Smith notes the Tao

> is the *way of the universe;* the norm, the rhythm, and the driving power in all nature. . . . [A]nother feature of Taoism [is] its profound naturalism. Nature should not be exploited and abused, any more than people should be. It should be befriended not conquered.

> *"Those who would take over the earth*
> *And shape it to their will*
> *Never, I notice, succeed.*
> *The earth is like a vessel so sacred*

That at the mere approach of the profane it is marred.
They reach out their fingers and it is gone."

... Before reaching for their brushes, [Taoist] painters would go to nature and lose themselves in it, to become, say, the bamboo that they would paint. They would sit for half a day or fourteen years before making a stroke.[56]

In addition to seeking a direct experience of the sacred in its manifestation in Earth, seekers in many religious traditions (including Native American) return to wilderness to make contact with specific powers of the sacred that reside in the Earth. Many Korean religious seekers undertake periods of pilgrimage and isolation in Korea's mountains. Edward Canda explains: "The mountain spirit may act in more positive ways as an instructor for spiritual advancement. He can shed great inspiration upon sincere persons who meet him. He can be sought through quests for vision or he can manifest himself to the unexpectant worthy."[57]

Throughout history, many people in Asia, tiring of the cluttered life of the cities, would join monasteries or religious orders. Others would go alone to wilderness areas as did the Korean Buddhist monk Yi Kap-lyong. According to Canda he "began a secluded life in a cave, subsisting at times on pine needles. In the course of many dreams, visions, and illuminations the hermit established an extraordinary communication with *san sin* [the mountain spirit]."[58] Canda goes on: "[Korean] shamans [regularly] journey to mountains in order to strengthen themselves spiritually and obtain visions."[59]

This pattern of retreat to the natural world is common among Jews, Hindus, Buddhists, Sufis, Taoists, and Christians. Buddha, in leaving his kingdom, shaved his head, left all earthly things behind, and went into the forest for six years. In his later life, after his enlightenment, he spent nine months a year teaching, three in retreat in a simple, natural setting. Like Christianity, Buddhism has developed schools, or denominations, that follow different aspects of their founders' teachings. Some Buddhist schools advocate being alone in nature as a method to find the REAL; monks who went into the wilderness, like Yi Kap-lyong, are not uncommon. Some Christian orders (notably the

Carmelites) also advocate retreats. Father William McNamara writes: "The original members of my own monastic order, the Carmelites, were hermits, simple laymen, living as solitaries in a loosely connected group, in caves and huts on the side of Mount Carmel."[60] He goes on to say that without periodic return to the desert, to wilderness, people can never know God. Time alone in wilderness allows human beings to stand back from their attachments to the things of the world, to get down to basic elements of self and Earth, eventually finding the REAL, which is at the heart of all things.

> It [is] man who need[s] the utter simplicity, the silence, and solitude, the emptiness of the desert. In the desert the difference between the essentials and nonessentials is reasserted; the distinction between the vital and moribund is rediscovered. The desert is a destruction of mediocrity which is compromise worked into a system. Mediocrity becomes impossible in the desert where everything is reduced to the rigid alternatives of life and death. Man then rises up out of a sluggish culture, regains a classical human stature as he responds to reality with authenticity and sensitivity according to a hierarchy of values in accord with the Supreme Value of ultimate reality. . . . Without the desert experience, man cannot achieve his destiny or fulfill his vocation.[61]

McNamara's comments echo Siya'ka's comments on the necessity and purpose of the vision quest (quoted in Chapter 3; see note 13). In brief, he said:

> All classes of people know that when human power fails they must look to a higher power for the fulfillment of their desires. . . . Some like to be quiet, and others want to do everything in public. Some like to go alone, away from the crowds, to meditate upon many things. . . . [One who decides to vision quest knows] It has long been his intention to make his request of Wakan'-tanka [for he has thought on it a long time], and he resolves to seek seclusion on the top of a butte or other high place. When at last he goes there he closes his eyes, and his mind is upon Wakan'tanka and his work. The man who does this usually has in mind some animal which he would like for protection and help. No man can succeed in life alone, and he cannot get the help he wants

from men; therefore he seeks help through some bird or animal which Wakan'tanka sends for his assistance. Many animals have ways from which a man can learn a great deal, even from the fact that horses are restless before a storm. . . . [During my first vision quest I saw] dragonflies, butterflies, and all kinds of small insects, while above them flew all kinds of birds. . . . [And then I saw] an elk, and at his feet were the elk medicine and a hoop. . . . All the birds and insects which I had seen in my dream were things on which I knew I should keep my mind and learn their ways. When the season returns, the birds and insects return with the same colorings as the previous year. They are not all on the earth, but *above* it. My mind must be the same. The elk is brave, always helping the women, and in that way the elk has saved a large proportion of the tribe. In this I should follow the elk.

Father McNamara, like Black Elk, says that what is found in wilderness and desert places is God, the sacred center of all things. Man has always gone there to find Him. "[T]he desert, the mountaintop, and other solitary places are used synonymously in Scripture to refer to the basic wilderness experience. . . . No one can live a full life without some experience of the wilderness. . . . We need far wilder things and more wilderness places to ready us for the absolutely unmitigated wildness of God.[62] . . . [For] the desert is, above all, the place where we encounter God, the place where God visits his people. This is why the tradition of desert spirituality has persisted in the Church.[63] . . . The [Desert] Fathers went into the desert to pray, to feed on God."[64]

The Bible, he tells us, is full of examples where the Christian Fathers (Hosea and Elijah among them) and Jesus, himself, sought renewal and closer contact with God in wilderness and desert places. But more than renewal was found there—the "vision" for life's work and vocation was forged, sharpened, refined there (as many Native Americans have also noted about the vision quest).

But if Christ needed to withdraw periodically into silence and solitude, it seems an egregious presumption to assume that we can go on forever on our own steam with no direct and intimate contact with the infinite Source of our

being. . . . After St. Paul's dramatic conversion on the road to Damascus, he immediately went straight to the Arabian desert and spent a long time there. Obviously, the full meaning of his vocation could not be penetrated unless he returned to the traditional source of spiritual strength, the place where man meets God. Only after he had steeled himself by prolonged retreat in the desert did Paul plunge into his exhausting apostolic [work].[65]

McNamara notes that when Christians return to the wilderness and restore direct connection with the divine, as in Buddhist and Native American traditions, they then come out, back to the world, to help alleviate the suffering of mankind—to help their people. In addition, "the desert is a place where an egoistic and complacent humanism will not do. It will undo us. Each man must come to terms actively with the evil forces within himself."[66] The desert and the wilderness exist in part to help men with this coming to terms, to find the face of God, to restore the capacity to walk in a sacred manner, to generate the capacity to help humankind. McNamara quotes Father McKenzie: "If men will not return to the desert to find God, He will make their cities a desert where no sound drowns out His voice."[67]

Black Elk observes that a journey into the wilderness to quest, to experience "oneness with all things," may need to be taken many times.

This young man who has cried for a vision for the first time, may, perhaps become *wakan;* if he walks with his mind and heart attentive to *Wakan-Tanka* and His Powers, as he has been instructed, he will certainly travel upon the red path which leads to goodness and holiness. But he must cry for a vision a second time, and this time bad spirits may tempt him; but if he really is a chosen one, he will stand firmly and will conquer all distracting thoughts and will become purified from all that is not good. Then he may receive some great vision that will bring strength to the nation. But should the young man still be in doubt after his second "lamenting," he may try a third or even a fourth time; and if he is always sincere, and truly humiliates himself before all things, he shall certainly be aided, for *Wakan-Tanka* always helps those who cry to him with a pure heart.[68]

The need to return to the place where God dwells, to touch the basic fabric of Creation, to strip away the superficialities of daily life, to call on the sacred to help us in our suffering, to "lament," is universal. As Black Elk said of the vision quester: "All this time he is crying most piteously. . . . As he walks he cries continually, 'Oh, Great Spirit, be merciful to me that my people may live.'" And the Great Spirit does help for *"Wakan-Tanka* always helps those who cry to him with a pure heart." Father McNamara echoes this truth in the Christian tradition: "The experience begins with the free, deliberate decision to suffer. It ends with the uproariously happy surprise of being in harmony with the universe."[69] And this experience is not only for Indians, not only for blacks, not only for whites, not only for Asians, but for all people. For (as noted earlier) the desert, the wilderness, "is, above all, the place where we encounter God, the place where God visits his people." Questing in the wilderness to find God and sacred vision is not an "Indian" thing; God is *not* red or any other color. As the nineteenth-century saint and sage Ramakrishna commented:

A man entered the woods and saw a chameleon on a tree. He reported to his friends, "I have seen a red lizard." He was firmly convinced it was nothing but red. Another person after visiting the tree said, "I have seen a green lizard." He was firmly convinced it was nothing but green. But the man who lived under the tree said, "What both of you has seen is true. But the fact is that the creature is sometimes red, sometimes green, sometimes yellow, and sometimes has no color at all."[70]

but are these ceremonies dangerous?

[T]hese practices have been and continue to be conducted by Indians and non-Indians alike, constituting not only insult and disrespect for the wisdom of the ancients, but also exposing ignorant non-Indians to potential harm and even death through the misuse of these ceremonies.

— AIM RESOLUTION, 1984 [71]

[Sun Bear and the people who are following him are] playing with some very powerful things, like the pipe. That's not only stupid and malicious, it's dangerous.

— RICK WILLIAMS [72]

Many activists assert that they are only trying to protect innocent white people by prohibiting them access to these ceremonies. They insist that those who are teaching whites are exposing them to potential harm because the ceremonies are so dangerous. These assertions are somewhat duplicitous and disingenuous; they do not exist in a vacuum. In other words, the assertions are made in a context of racial separatism and accusations of illegitimacy toward those who are conducting the ceremonies for non-Indians. But separating the assertions from their context, it makes sense to look at them, to (as Robert Heinlein might say) drag them out from under the rug and let the cat sniff at them.

When I was writing my book *Sacred Plant Medicine,* a Cherokee man, an herbalist, heard of my writing and insisted to a mutual friend that I "should be careful" as I was "playing with powers I didn't really understand." I was amused rather than concerned by this remark. The man neither knew me well enough to be concerned nor knew what I was really doing or how or why. My lack of concern did not come from ignorance. I did know that there were prices to pay for the kind of relationships I had with the plants and the pipe (and the sweat lodge). I knew what could happen should I "misuse" my knowledge. The plants, the pipe, and the sweat lodge had told me all these things; we had talked them over together. I decided, in full awareness of what I was doing, to bear the

responsibility for these things. But my responsibility is to the plants, the sacred pipe (and the Spirit that called me to it in the first place), the powers of the sweat lodge (which after twelve years of work I am just beginning to know), the Earth Mother, and Creator. These beings have called me to do this work—*not* an Indian or an Indian tribe. The beings will exact the price that must be paid if I falter in my task, if I fail to keep sacred balance, if I do not act with a pure heart and cause desecration to them.

When I work with apprentices (either Indian or white) in the use of sacred plants as medicine, I am responsible for their behavior. I introduce them to a sacred world and to sacred beings, who allow the meeting to take place because I have asked it of them and they know I will keep my word to them. But apprentices do not know the importance of keeping their word. They are too caught up in the outside world. (They do argue so for the right to break their word!) The spirits of the plants come to me, and I must make it right. Indian apprentices as well as non-Indian apprentices have broken their word. Usually, the transgression is unintentional; it is a part of the learning. The young have to learn why not lying is important. But sometimes it is not unintentional: The apprentice cannot learn to subsume his or her own ego needs to the sacred agreements with the plants and other beings of the Earth and Spirit world.

Irresponsibility is not limited to breaking agreements with the plants. I have known some who carry working pipes and who have been asked to smoke for someone in need but have not done so, who have refused. The refusal to use the pipe for someone who asks is akin to refusing communion or last rites in the Catholic tradition. Such a refusal is the antithesis of the reason for the existence of these ceremonies. I agree with all true pipe carriers about this issue. A refusal to smoke for someone in need is the worst thing someone can do with the pipe other than to use it for consciously evil ends. And some people— Indian and non-Indian—are guilty of such acts. Some men who lead sweat lodges seduce women who are sweating with them—even in the lodge itself. (An Indian who seduced women regularly in Denver caused a lot of problems there. He didn't charge money for sweat lodges, however, because he thought to do so was wrong.)[73]

Misuse of power is not limited to Indians; foolishness is not limited to white people. The remedy resides in proper role models and education. Problems arise because the ceremonies are not discussed. Hatred, fear, and the misuse of power grow in a closed and darkened room. Thus, the elders of the Wampanoag Nation decided "to instruct [Medicine Story] to explain [their] ways to any non-Indian people who were interested to want to know about them."[74] It was the possibility of harm coming to the uninformed that moved the elders to instruct Medicine Story to teach non-Indians about the sweat lodge.

> You may even build an Indian sweat lodge, but unless you build it with a spiritual awareness, totally conscious of the gathering of the wood and rocks, of the building of the fire, as well as of the lodge, and unless you perform the ceremony in a sacred manner, you will not achieve the purification we now seek of body, mind, heart, and spirit. If you are careless and inconsiderate, you can do yourself much harm, for the power of this way is great.[75]

But rather than attack non-Indian participation, they decided to speak openly to all.

In contrast, Vine Deloria, Jr. (as noted earlier) simply denigrates non-Indian participation in native ceremonial forms because non-Indians are superficial, uninformed, or (he feels) interested in them for the wrong reasons. But Deloria fails to consider the possibility that people grow in insight and understanding.

Human beings do not come to this Earth with a high level of understanding. We all start from scratch. The depth of insight we attain in our lives depends on many factors, two of which are our inner drive and personal capacity. Deloria's insight (which in many instances is inspirational) is not the same now as it was twenty years ago. He acknowledges it is not. In the introduction to *Red Earth White Lies*, he writes: "I became an avid reader of popular scientific books, wanting to know as much as I could about the world in which I lived. Gradually I began to see a pattern of nonsense in much scientific writing. . . . As my faith in science decreased geometrically over the years, like many former acolytes, I was embarrassed by my former allegiance."[76]

When I teach, I often ask my students if, after they have lit a large wooden kitchen match, they hold the match straight down toward the ground. I pause then as they remember their experience with wooden kitchen matches. At first they look a little puzzled as they make the image in their minds of a box of kitchen matches. Then they see their hands opening the box and taking out a match; they see their hand holding it, they feel the square stem of wood with their fingers, hear the sound it makes as it scratches against the box. It flares into brilliance. Now they see their hand tip down, holding the flame toward the ground. They see the flame rise up the match's wood handle, then they *feel* their fingers burn. At this point they grimace and sometimes, absently, rub their hand or fingers; then they look up at me like I am an idiot for thinking anyone would do such a thing.

The lesson, I point out, is that we only learn the proper use of fire by misusing it. There is no other way we *can* learn. (In spite of all our teaching, my son still set the toilet paper on fire in the bathroom and then frantically grabbed handfuls of water from the toilet to put it out. His explanations when we got home were, to say the least, colorful.) Once we have burned ourselves with a kitchen match, we rarely do so again.

In the process of learning, it is imperative that there not be secretiveness about the proper use of fire or the proper practice of ceremonies. If the desire is to truly prevent harm, then all the information necessary to prevent harm should be accessible. "Just say no" is too simple a solution for drug use, for improper sexual activity, and for religious exploration. It is time for the elders to speak with the spirit of the sacred pipe and ask *it* if more harm than good has been accomplished from non-Indian use of the Pipe. It is time for the elders to ask the spirit of the sweat lodge if more harm than good has come from non-Indians using the sweat lodge. It is time for the elders to ask the Earth and Creator if more harm than good arises from non-Indians practicing Earth-based spirituality. It is time for us all to attend to the work before us.

The proper conduct of these ceremonies must be made clear to minimize harm. After that it is up to the pipe, the sweat lodge, the medicine wheel, the Earth, Creator, and the powers of the Earth. The young will learn, eventually.

The pipe and the others will take care of how they learn. We, as older and more knowledgeable human beings, can help. As Gandhi observes:

> what may appear as truth to one person will often appear as untruth to another person. But that need not worry the seeker. Where there is honest effort, it will be realized that what appear to be different truths are like the countless and apparently different leaves of the same tree. . . . Truth is the right designation of God. Hence there is nothing wrong in every man following Truth according to his lights. Indeed it his duty to do so. Then if there is a mistake on the part of anyone so following Truth, it will be automatically set right. For the quest of Truth involves tapas—self-suffering, sometimes even unto death. There can be no place for even a trace of self-interest. In such selfless search for truth nobody can lose his bearings for long.[77]

chapter five
selling indian spirituality

*Traditional Native healers do not charge for their healing
and doctoring. This is not the Indian Way. There are no
"ifs," "ands," or "buts" about it.*

— MEDICINE BEAR GRIZZLY LAKE [1]

*First they came to take our land and water, then our
fish and game. Then they wanted our mineral resources,
and to get them they tried to take our governments. Now
they want our religions as well. All of a sudden, we have
a lot of unscrupulous idiots running around saying they're
medicine people. And they'll sell you a sweat lodge for
fifty bucks. It's not only wrong, it's obscene. Indians don't
sell their spirituality to anyone for any price.*

— JANET McCLOUD [2]

Nothing has caused more protests from Native activists
than the practice of charging money for "Indian" ceremonies. As Janet McCloud says, "It's not only wrong,

it's obscene." And there are few, if any, teachers of Indian ceremonial forms who have not been accused of charging "fat fees" and getting rich off Indian spirituality.

Most activists, like Medicine Bear Grizzly Lake, are absolute in their pronouncements that historically, Indians have never charged fees for services. And although it might be true that some pre–European contact tribes and their members did believe that charging for services was improper, the historical evidence indicates that the norm was quite the opposite.

the historical record

For example, Eagle Shield, a Lakota Sioux holy man, who trained in the old ways before the coming of the white people to his part of this country, was a noted and powerful healer—a Lakota bear doctor. He routinely charged for services. He once treated a man whose arm was paralyzed as the result of a wound in the shoulder. Through Eagle Shield's use of yarrow, songs, and ritual, the man regained full use of his arm. "As compensation Eagle Shield received $100, a new white tent, a revolver, and a steer."[3]

Eagle Shield's fees, when placed in the context of early twentieth-century monetary values, are high. His fee, if charged today and reduced to cash equivalents, could easily be $1,000. But such high fees are not unusual. Navajo ceremonies, such as the Mountainway, can cost much more.

Historically, among the Navajo, it was believed that seeing a bear in the wild could cause great illness. "One could be cured only through an elaborate and expensive nine-day ceremony called the Mountainway."[4] Tony Hillerman, considered by many to be a knowledgeable writer and friend of the Navajo, writes of the high costs of this and other Navajo ceremonies. The cost of ceremonies can range from $400 to $1,200; additionally, the person asking for a ceremony has to prepare the site and supply food for the participants, who

sometimes number twenty or more. Thus the total fee can be very high, especially considering the average income on the Navajo Reservation.

These kinds of high charges are present in other cultures as well. Shamans in Korea are known to charge as much as $2,000 for elaborate rituals of healing and ceremony.[5] A member of the Clayquot tribe noted in 1938 that "a doctor got his wealth by treating the sick. Sometimes he got a slave, or blankets when the person got well, and sometimes they let him have whatever he asked for."[6] Ales Hrdlicka observes in his studies of the Pueblo tribes of the southwestern United States in 1908 that the medicine man "may have to be paid in advance, and not seldom exacts a large compensation."[7] Among the Valley Maidu in California, Alfred Kroeber notes that when a medicine person was summoned to heal, "[v]ery high payment was demanded for this treatment."[8] He quotes a Yuki shaman: "[A]ll his property was stacked up before him to pay me. Whenever a man is bitten by a snake he has no belongings left."[9]

Black Elk, perhaps the most widely known North American Indian holy man, relates in his book *Black Elk Speaks* that before his first curing he asked the father of the sick boy to bring him a pipe: "So I sent him back and told him that if he wanted me to go there and do a little curing that he should bring me a pipe with an eagle feather on it."[10] In the three years of his practice he usually charged and received a horse for his curings. "It's too bad they did not give me money! They gave me only horses."[11] He explained that the usual payment was horses "because the horse was about the only property we had."[12] Thus, although money itself was not present in many indigenous cultures, there were items that were deemed valuable—some more than others. The horse was often the most valuable possession and the giving of one for services was a standard of exchange, just as in the modern era money is used for a standard of exchange.

As money came to supplant other forms of exchange, it came into more common use as a means of payment for services. In 1920, among the Northern Ute, one medicine man reported: "He sings five times in one evening, cures the patient, and receives 'about five or six dollars' as compensation."[13] And in the early 1930s one member of the Karuk tribe noted that "[a]fter the Whites came they have started to fee [the medicine man] $10."[14]

Many medicine people considered it necessary for the supplicant to recognize that nothing is free in order for the healing to occur. Further, it was not the medicine person who determined the necessity of a fee. Often the "power" one had for healing required the payment. Thus, among the Paviotso tribe: "The invitation extended to the shaman by a member of the patient's family and the determination of his fee themselves have a ritual character. If the shaman asks too high a price, or if he asks nothing, he falls ill. In any case it is not he but his 'power' that determines the fee for the cure. Only members of his own family are entitled to gratuitous treatment."[15] When Frances Densmore was recording songs among the Nootka and Quileute tribes of the Pacific Northwest, a similar comment was made to her: "Mrs. Guy, a member of the Clayquot tribe, said they believed that their remedies would lose their power if used too freely, so the doctors seldom gave herb remedies unless highly paid."[16]

Fees also often depended on the wealth of the family needing help. Thus, there was a kind of "sliding scale" in many tribes. "The fees for doctoring (as a halaait [shaman]) might be 10 blankets, prepaid, for each patient, or it might be as little as one blanket. . . . The fees depended upon the wealth of the family calling for services."[17]

In some instances the fees were refunded if the cure was not successful. But, even so, the fees were as high as the market would bear. "When a patient called upon a doctor for treatment, a fee was established or the giving of a gift was implied. In most groups, if the doctor was unsuccessful in the cure, he would return all, or at least, a portion, of the fee. . . . Fees depended on the type of disease, the length and danger to the doctor of the cure, and the rank and economic status of the patient. Usually a shaman attempted to fit his fee to what the market would bear."[18] Some cultures recognized that the healer could become infatuated with the wealth to be gained from their work. Thus in Africa, "medicine men are expected to be trustworthy, upright morally, friendly, willing and ready to serve, able to discern people's needs and not be exorbitant in their charges."[19]

In many situations, the payment of a fee was expected in the form of a "gift." The nature of the gift was left up to the person giving it; however, a poor

gift was often considered inappropriate. Sometimes, if gifts were given for ceremonial healing, the medicine person might sell them for money. In certain circumstances, the healer would also charge money to cover expenses if he had to travel very far. "Whether or not any improvement is effected, the doctor must be paid. . . . The payments may take many forms. [Cloth, animals, clothing, deer hides, liquor, or] sometimes a pocket-knife is given, or some salable goods such as the beaded bracelets made for the tourist trade. . . . [The doctor is not paid with money except sometimes when he] practices his profession in Oklahoma; however, he will accept money to help cover expenses. . . . The normal price in Oklahoma is $4.00–$5.00 [in 1955], although occasionally one will pay $20."[20]

The expectation of a gift as a fee was the same for healing or for training apprentices and students. "The doctor receives from his students at intervals afterwards various gifts, such as untanned deer hides, tobacco, pipes, and knives. These he may use or sell."[21] Among the Taikomol, Kroeber reports, when children were to be initiated into the sacred ceremonies by the medicine man of the tribe, the parents would "put rope, knives, net bags, snares, furs, and other property in a pile to pay the old man who was to teach their children."[22]

According to my reading, the Iroquois seem more likely to expect a gift than money. However, in a footnote in her book *Ethnography of the Huron Indians, 1615–1649*, Elizabeth Tooker notes: "Fees are still given to fortune tellers and to herbalists. The line between 'fee' and 'gift' is a thin one in Iroquois as well as other Indian cultures."[23] But the failure to give a gift was often disastrous. Tooker quotes a medicine man: "[The woman] had not been cured because he did not get all he had demanded; particularly a pipe of red stone and a pouch for his tobacco."[24]

Training by a medicine man to cure the sick, to become a holy person, and to learn the ceremonies used by medicine people generally commanded a fee. Such payments were expected and usually demanded before training would begin. In 1920, Frances Densmore commented about fees among the Northern Ute, "Doctors, on the other hand, were accustomed to buy and sell songs, the older doctors frequently transferring songs to younger men. A good

remedy was worth a horse, this price including the herb, the history of its medicinal use, and the song without which it would not be effective."[25]

In order for the sacred traditions to continue as a benefit for the community and its individuals and to be passed to the next generation, it was understood that the holy people deserved compensation for their services in some form, whether gift or fee. The fees should depend on three things: the dictates of the holy person's power, the understanding that for all things there is a price, and the needs of the community and the individual (thus, the fees should not be exorbitant). There was within indigenous communities the understanding that problems could arise if the holy person became too involved in the accumulation of wealth and power. Members of the community recognized that the healer's or ceremonialist's ability to help the community was affected by dwelling on becoming rich. Thus among the Seminole, it was said: "Just like white doctors, some [healers] are chiefly interested in their payment while others sincerely try to cure."[26] In a similar vein, Black Hawk, the Sauk leader, said: "We have men among us, like the whites, who pretend to know the right path, but will not consent to show it without pay! I have no faith in their paths, but believe that every man must make his own path!"[27]

breaking the power of the medicine man

There is good reason to believe that the development of the idea that Natives do not charge for services came not so much from their own traditions but from Christian missionaries and Bureau of Indian Affairs agents in the nineteenth and twentieth centuries in an effort to destroy the religious culture of the Native peoples. Numerous works, printed in the early twentieth century, note the importance of breaking the hold of the medicine men on the Indian cultures; for the Indian tribes to accept subjection by the White culture, they

advise, the medicine men must be disempowered. What better way to achieve this goal than to prohibit the use of tribal languages, traditional religions, and the holy people from conducting ceremonies or making enough money (or other items of necessity such as deer meat, knives, and clothes) in their chosen line of work to support themselves. The view of medicine men as a primary obstacle to the civilization of the Indian is seen in Walter James Hoffman's comment: "The jugglers [a specific type of medicine man] were early mentioned by the Jesuits as being their greatest opponents to Christianizing the Indian; and as early as 1632 the Nipising Indians of Canada had been designated as the nation of sorcerers. The Spaniards met with similar opposition when attempting to Christianize the Mexicans."[28]

Many of the early ethnological texts that describe the cultural and religious practices of Native tribes are replete with comments to the effect that Native medicine people are charlatans and quacks, that they are agents of the devil, and that they defraud their communities and impoverish individual Indians by charging high fees for services that are basically useless. Christian missionaries were horrified by the practices of the medicine men and described their feelings in no uncertain terms, as this account by Father José de Acosta shows: "There were an infinite number of these witches, divines, enchanters, and other false prophets. There remains yet at this day of this infection, although they be secret, not daring publikely to exercise their sacrileges, divelish ceremonies, and superstitions, but in their abuses and wickedness are discovered more at large and particularly in the confessions of the Prelates of Peru."[29] Hennepin, in his *Travels Through the Interior of North America in the Years 1766, 1767, and 1768*, says of the medicine men:

> These Impostors cause themselves to be reverenced as Prophets which foretell Futurity. They will needs be look'd upon to have an unlimited Power. They boast of being able to make it Wet or Dry; to cause a Calm or a Storm; to render land Fruitful or Barren; and, in a Word, to make Hunters Fortunate or Unfortunate. They also pretend to Physick, and to apply Medicines, but which are such, for the most part, as having little Virtue at all in 'em, especially to cure that Distemper which they pretend to.

It is impossible to imagine, the horrible Howlings and strange Contortions that these Jugglers make of their Bodies, when they are disposing themselves to Conjure, or raise their Enchantments.[30]

In the *Collection of the Historical Society of Wisconsin* for 1854, Hiram Calkins notes that the medicine man "pretends that the Great Spirit converses in a heavy voice to the lesser spirit, unintelligibly to the conjurer, and the lesser spirit interprets it to him, and he communicates the intelligence to his brethren without. The ceremony lasts about three hours, when he comes out in a high state of perspiration, supposed by the superstitious Indians to be produced by mental excitement." This "fake" ceremony, to "help" in times of sickness, Calkins remarks, would not be performed until he was "paid by the Indians with such articles as they have, which generally consist of tobacco, steel-taps, kettles, broadcloth, calico, and a variety of other commodities."[31]

John G. Bourke, author of *The Medicine Men of the Apache*, states: "Notwithstanding the acceptance by the native tribes of many of the improvements in living introduced by civilization, the savage has remained a savage, and is still under the control of an influence antagonistic to the rapid absorption of new ideas and the adoption of new customs. . . . This influence is the medicine-man."[32]

U.S. Secretary of the Interior Henry Teller called attention to the problems of medicine men and the traditional religion of the tribes in 1882. "A great hindrance to the civilization of the Indians [is] the continuance of the old heathenish dances, such as the sun-dance, scalp-dance, etc." The medicine men, he continues, kept the young from attending white schools and promoted heathenish customs. "It will be extremely difficult to accomplish much towards the civilization of the Indians while these adverse influences are allowed to exist."[33]

Teller's solution was the creation of the Courts of Indian Offenses. The judges, appointed by the agents of the Bureau of Indian Affairs, had the power to hear any case brought before them. After the creation of the Courts of Indian Offenses, any medicine man conducting ceremonies or attempting to carry on the old healing practices was subject to arrest. Indian Commissioner Hiram

Price asserted, "There is no good reason why an Indian should be permitted to indulge in practices which are alike repugnant to common decency and morality; and the preservation of good order on the reservations demands that some active measure should be taken to discourage and, if possible, put a stop to the demoralizing influence of heathenish rites."[34] Violations of the prohibition on conducting ceremonies or healing were punishable by fines and imprisonment.

Individual states supported the assault on medicine men; Oklahoma, for instance, passed legislation in 1899 that prohibited "medicine men from practicing their incantations." Violators were subject to fines of up to $200 and imprisonment up to six months.[35] Christianized Indians were encouraged by the missionaries to inform the authorities about medicine men who practiced the old rites. Western medical doctors who felt that the older healing practices were dangerous superstition also informed authorities when they found Indians practicing old ways of healing. Christian missionaries hated the tradition of charging for services, which they felt to be "heathenish superstitions" carried out on an ignorant culture by devil worshippers and quacks. This account by the Reverend S. J. Digmann is typical:

A pagan Indian . . . called for a priest to baptize his dying child. I went with him on horseback to his camp, about three miles from the Mission. One of our school girls, already baptized, had dressed the one-year-old boy nicely and put a small crucifix on his breast. He was asleep. After we had said the Our Father, The Apostle's Creed, I baptized the child "Inigo." For a couple of days he had taken no nourishment, as the mother had no milk.

A boy went with me to the Mission to get milk and medicine. Mother Kostka, who was a good nurse and had knowledge of medicines, wished first to see and examine the sick child. We went on foot under the parching heat of the sun to the Indian camp, the white veil of the Sister was soaked with perspiration. A short distance before the log cottage, Grace Anayela met us saying: "The medicine man is conjuring the sick child, I do not want to be present." Arriving at the door, we heard their singing, beating the drum. . . . What a spectacle! In a corner of the room, the father was sitting

with the naked child in his arms. Along the wall four conjurors were crouching, with their faces painted red and yellow. One of them had returned from an Eastern school, understood English fairly well and spoke it tolerably. Him I addressed first: "George, you here?" He had asked me already before to baptize him. Then I continued in Sioux the best I could at the time. "Give up your devil's work. The child is baptized and belongs to the Great Spirit." George said: "Do you want that one of us shall die?" "You will not die, get out of here." They, however, continued their powwow, singing and ringing pumpkin shells. On my repeated begging they finally kept quiet. Mother Kostka examined the little patient and wanted to make hot poultices.

The conjurors had spread out on the dirt floor of the log house their medicine bags. There were also bowls with water, and a pan with burning coals. To gain room, I removed . . . the deerskin bags, gave the water to the Sister, and put the coals in the stove to start a fire. Horrified they looked at me, thinking perhaps that the Evil One would hurt me. George flung the satchel of the Sister out of the open door. The scared mother took the sick baby outside, the Sister followed. George, angry, grasped my arm to put me out, but I stood the ground. In the presence of them I told the father of the child, not to allow them to continue their conjuration, and not to let their leader take the child to his house. They promised. The firmness seemed to make an impression. George became cool. He said he did not believe himself in this powwow but there was money in it. They make parents pay in ponies, blankets, or other valuables, while at the Mission and at the Agency they would get medicine gratis.[36]

As a result of this united pressure, the medicine men were pushed into the background of tribal culture. The impact of these attitudes and laws was to impoverish the medicine people, force them underground, divert the younger generation from training with the old medicine people, and Christianize the tribes. The repositories of wisdom and information of the traditional religious forms were destroyed just as the missionaries, intellectuals, and government bureaucrats had envisioned. The belief that one does not charge for these kinds

of services began to become the norm—not because it had ever been the norm but because of pressure from "white" law and religion.

It is important, however, to underscore that *all* religious traditions consider the use of sacred capacities for secular gain unwise. This belief does not mean that an exchange of value does not or cannot occur. It means that if the sacred work is reduced to merely secular realms through the acquisition of money *as an end in itself,* the outcome is often unpleasant. It is a misuse of sacred gifts. However, the exchange of value *in the context of the sacred*—and not as an end in itself—is a part of all religious traditions. Many Native activists seem to be concerned with articulating the second point without making the distinction clear.

In the final analysis it cannot be routinely decided that the sincerity of the healer or ceremonialist is determined by the requirement or use of fees. The practice varies from person to person and is often dependent on cultural variables or the requirements of one's power and spiritual imperatives. There may in fact be people who use healing and ceremonialism only to earn money; it is doubtful that all Indians of all tribes have always been perfectly pure in their motives for healing and doctoring (as the injunction not to be exorbitant shows), just as all white people have not always been pure in their motives in the use of Christianity. All religions would be destroyed if we prohibited access to worship because some people of the same skin color were not pure in their motives. The question should be: Is one following the dictates of Spirit as best as one can in the fulfillment of the spiritual imperatives given for one's work? Native activists, in asserting that Indians have never charged for services, are, in fact, only arguing for Christian and Bureau of Indian Affairs policies that date from the late nineteenth and early twentieth centuries. They argue that Indians (or non-Indians) who are teaching whites for a fee are "enriching" themselves through the theft and subsequent sale of Native traditions. Many, unfortunately, believe this charge without having any personal knowledge of such practices. For example, some have referred to Sun Bear's teaching as a "lucrative cottage industry."[37] No one who has seen Sun Bear's house would call it "lucrative" or wealthy. It was built from found materials and donated labor.

Sun Bear lived in this house for nearly twenty years. A new house, paid for by donations, was being built for him when he died. And although he lived in part of the new house while he was dying, it was never completed.

When Sun Bear's debts were paid after his death, there was nothing left—no huge estate, no piles of cash. He had spent all he had carrying out the work that he believed Creator had given him to do. The vast majority of Indians and whites who are accused of "stealing" Indian ceremonies and selling them for profit live extremely simply and without money or riches. Most live hand to mouth, spreading a spiritual belief that they feel is crucial to the survival of the Earth. There are easier ways to make a living. With few exceptions no one is doing it for the money.[38]

all those illegitimate teachers

In his chapter "Spiritual Hucksterism: The Rise of the Plastic Medicine Men," Ward Churchill asserts that many people, Indian and non-Indian alike, have begun teaching Indian ceremonial forms solely because of the rising interest in Indian spirituality. He never explores the possibility that the movement to teach non-Indians traditional Native ceremonies might be coming out of sincere beliefs. Quite the contrary. Through personal commentary and the use of material from Native writers he charges that ceremonial teachers are "phony." He quotes Vine Deloria, Jr., who is one of many who feels that "the realities of Indian belief and existence have become so misunderstood and distorted at this point that when a real Indian stands up and speaks the truth at any given moment, he or she is not only unlikely to be believed, but will probably be contradicted and 'corrected' by the citation of some non-Indian and totally inaccurate 'expert.'"[39] Virgil Vogel, author of *American Indian Medicine*, echoes this observation: "There is sufficient interest in the practical and mystical aspects of Indian medicine to induce impostors, both red and white, to proclaim themselves the possessors of ancient secrets and to charge fat fees for performance of sweat baths, purification rites, and so forth. Such practitioners have been condemned by legitimate Indian groups."[40] Churchill agrees: "This situation has been long and bitterly attacked by legitimate Indian scholars, from Vine Deloria, Jr. to Bea Medicine."[41]

Are the teachers liars and impostors? Are they fake Indians? Those who can prove they are enrolled members of federally recognized tribes are certainly not "fake" Indians. But they are generally written off as Indian "traitors" cashing in on the lucrative market of selling Indian spirituality to non-Indians. Rick Williams says:

> Sun Bear isn't recognized as any sort of leader, spiritual or otherwise, among his own Chippewa people. He's not qualified. It takes a lifetime of apprenticeship to become the sort of spiritual leader Sun Bear claims to be, and he

never went through any of that. He's just a guy who hasn't been home to the White Earth Reservation in 25 years, pretending to be something he's not, feeding his own ego and making a living misleading a lot of sincere, but very silly people. In a lot of ways he reminds you of a low grade Jimmy Swaggert or Pat Robertson–type individual.[42]

Williams is right in one respect. By comparing Sun Bear to Swaggert and Robertson he recognizes that the Native teachers are in fact proselytizing a particular (and new) kind of spirituality to non-Indians, and thus he classifies the phenomenon as a primarily *religious* one. However, he not only attempts to deny Sun Bear legitimate status as an Indian but also attacks his creation of the Bear Tribe, an interracial society of Earth-centered religious practitioners. "Sun Bear hasn't started a new tribe. *Nobody* can just up and start a new tribe. What he has done is start a cult."[43] (It should be noted that *nobody* can revive an old tribe without a great deal of patience and money. In the Native newspaper *News from Indian Country,* an article reports that the Samish tribe was finally recognized as legitimate by the U.S. Department of the Interior "despite requests from two other tribes that the matter be reconsidered."[44] Attempts by some tribes to thwart other ancient tribal groups from gaining federal recognition is fairly common, and a number of tribes have not been recognized.)

Arguments similar to those directed toward Sun Bear's legitimacy have been made about Brooke Medicine Eagle, Ed McGaa, Wallace Black Elk, and others. But their training and tribal membership can be validated by their work: Medicine Eagle's *Buffalo Woman Comes Singing,* McGaa's *Mother Earth Spirituality,* Sun Bear's *Path of Power,* Wallace Black Elk's *Black Elk.* They have not been condemned by their teachers (many of whom were or are notable in their tribes). They are being attacked, primarily, because they are teaching non-Indians (and because of the unfounded assumption that they are getting rich being professional Indians).

Brooke Medicine Eagle and the other Native teachers who have been willing to offer Native spirituality and ceremonies to people of other ethnic groups and skin colors have come under tremendous pressure. Their position

is reminiscent of ministers in South Africa and the American South who dared offer Christian sacraments to blacks. As Joseph Leonard notes: "If Southern white churchmen follow their conviction and work for integration, they are damned at home; if they compromise their conviction and condone segregation, they are damned in the nation and the world. Many clergymen have made the difficult choice and placed themselves in the forefront of groups acting to end the 'peculiar institution' of the twentieth-century America."[45] This situation, as Leonard remarks, resulted in two separate groups of priests and ministers in America—those who ministered to whites and those who ministered to "colored." The Catholic Church "provide[d] 'a separate set of white priests— who seldom mingle[d] with the other priests—for the Negroes.' "[46] Leonard continues: "The full story remains to be told of the heroic struggles and hardships of these early priests, secular as well as members of communities, who, working against unbelievable odds and under great handicaps, were entirely devoted to the care of the Negro Catholics and the conversion of others. The fact that they were engaged in this work made them sharers and partakers of the scorn and contempt shown to the Negroes themselves."[47] The similarity between the situation of white ministers and priests who ministered to coloreds, and the price they paid for it, and the circumstances of Native teachers can be clearly seen from comments of Native activists. By teaching white people these ways, Russell Means notes, "[t]hese people have insisted on making themselves pariahs within their own communities, and they will have to bear the consequences of that."[48] Janet McCloud comments that Indians who teach whites are "thieves and sell-outs."[49] And Barbara Owl states: "Non-Indians who [share our ways with others] are thieves, and the Indians who do it are sellouts and traitors."[50]

Many white Christians, like Native activists, did not like members of their community and race offering their spirituality to people of a different ethnic and racial group. When informed of the fact that white ministers and priests were offering religious ceremonies to non-whites, they reacted strongly, sometimes turning to violence. Joseph Leonard recalls, "At the Church of Our Lady of Lourdes in Erath, Louisiana, on November 27, 1955, Bishop Jules Jeanmard of Lafayette, in a decree read at every mass, excommunicated several white

women of the parish who had set upon and beat a white catechism teacher who had been instructing white and Negro children at the parish catechism school" because they believed religion should not be taught between the races. Similar events have occurred when Native teachers offered "whites" religious ceremonies: Sun Bear and others have been physically assaulted and beaten for their work.[51] Leonard notes other instances of physical coercion being used to stop interracial religious instruction. "On October 2, 1955, a Negro priest was sent as a 'supply priest' to say Sunday Mass for a mixed congregation at St. Cecilia's Mission in Jesuit Bend. On arriving, he found a police car parked in the driveway and two men, armed and in uniform, in front of the church. Three of the parishioners told him that a Negro priest could not say mass in a white church."[52] In spite of the support given African-Americans by the church, numerous white Catholic priests refused to allow African-Americans to attend their church services. Leonard, exploring the right to worship in his book *Theology and Race Relations*, comments: "The refusal of a priest to permit a Negro Catholic to attend Mass or receive the sacraments, insisting that he must go to the colored parish for these is a source of scandal not only to the one who is rejected, but also to the white parishioners, who seeing this, are convinced that the territorial parish is closed to Negroes; and become insistent in drawing the color line in other facilities."[53] Many Indian activists, some of them theologians and ministers, hold positions similar to those of the Catholic priests who drew a color line. They refuse to permit whites to receive the sacrament of the sacred pipe, a rite brought by White Buffalo Calf Woman for *all* human beings, a rite intended to make all life interconnected and whole. And they interfere with whites being able to receive this sacrament from Indians who believe it should be available to all human beings. The Native activists' position thus violates the essential meaning and purpose of the pipe. Furthermore, their actions cause others, Indian and non-Indian, to support the denial of the sacrament of the pipe to whites. Jamie Sams, who has been attacked, insists that the word *all* as in "all our relations" means *all*. "ALL does not mean unless they are white, or New Agers, or wounded spiritually."[54]

The legitimacy of the religious work of Sun Bear, Wallace Black Elk, and others (like that of the white priests) is not being examined; opponents are only interested in *whom* they are teaching. But the underlying truth of their work should be the only criterion: Are their teachings valid? Will their work help all life on Earth move into harmony? Are the spiritual values, ceremonies, and teachings they convey true? I would assert that they are. People, white people included, are not complete fools. If there is value in a belief system, they come back to it again and again. And there is something in this teaching for both Indians *and* whites.

Many Indian teachers have been instrumental in bringing about recognition of the dignity, worth, and necessity of Indian spiritual forms. Sun Bear, for example, was one of the earliest Indian people to publicly assert that traditional Indian religious forms should be practiced by both Indian and non-Indian peoples. He gave a talk in 1965 entitled "Did the Indians know something about the Earth that white people don't?" Looking at Indian religious forms and traditional ways of honoring the Earth, he concluded they did and actively exhorted people of all colors to return to honoring the Earth through sacred ceremony. He was also one of the first Indians who insisted on accuracy in the portrayal of Indians in films. Many of his activities preceded AIM activities in the same areas.[55] Sun Bear was quite active in the restoration of Indian rights and spirituality. Although Sun Bear was often accused of abandoning his people for his lucrative cottage industry teaching whites, we can marvel at his accomplishments of forty years.

1954 Developed self-help program at the Reno Sparks Indian Colony in Nevada

1955 Worked as Indian extra in Hollywood and technical director on many films to ensure accuracy of Indian portrayals

1956 Early activist for the Los Angeles Indian Center, primarily generating food donations and giving lectures

1958 Lobbyist in Washington, D.C., for reservation housing

1960 Worked with the Los Angeles Federated Indian Tribes

1961 Began publishing *Many Smokes* magazine, the first national intertribal Indian magazine in the United States

1963 Began halfway house for Indians in California

1966 Worked for the Nevada Intertribal Council for the Reno Sparks Indian Colony—cleaning up; raising funds for house repair, groceries, park development; started Indian jobs training program; built two Indian centers

1967 In charge of developing self-help programs at twenty-three reservations

1967 Indian lobbyist: successfully lobbied in Nevada for tax-exempt status for reservation industries and businesses; successfully lobbied for $350,000 in matching funds for Indian work-incentive program; represented the Nevada Intertribal Council as lobbyist against restrictions on peyote use

1968 Economic Development specialist for the Nevada Intertribal Council: wrote grants, helped develop ideas for Indian industries and employment programs

1968 Helped Paiutes develop working ranch to raise tribal and individual incomes; supported the filming of a documentary about the Moapa Project to show how Native Americans could succeed

1969 Helped develop a Native American studies program at University of California, Davis

1970 Ran U.S. Coast Guard blockade to Alcatraz Island; covered the occupation for *Many Smokes* magazine

1970 Wrote *Buffalo Hearts,* a book about great American Indian leaders

1972–1975 Traveled the powwow circuit throughout United States

1973 Helped film a documentary at the Wounded Knee takeover; covered the occupation for *Many Smokes* magazine

1974 Worked to raise money for and publicize the Klamath Indian land rights fight

1977 Began actively speaking about the importance of Native American religious beliefs for world survival

1980 Began working more and more with non-Indians on their spiritual connection to the Earth, insisting that without their understanding the Earth would be damaged beyond healing; began holding yearly medicine wheel

gatherings where elders and medicine teachers from scores of tribes participated in a celebration of Native spirituality as part of the universality of Earth religion for all people

1992 Died at the age of 63[56]

Most of the other Native teachers have engaged in similar work for similar amounts of time. AIM's main disagreement with Sun Bear (and with other Native teachers) focuses on two issues: He was teaching whites and he was (supposedly) getting rich selling Indian spirituality. Eventually (in spite of early strong connections and support from AIM), he was condemned as an illegitimate teacher. If he really wanted to help Indian people (it has been asserted), he should have gone back to the White Earth Reservation to help "his people." That assertion is interesting in light of the conviction of several White Earth leaders on corruption charges. Darrell "Chip" Wadena, who served twenty years as tribal chairman, "and two other leaders were convicted June 24 [1996] of charges including conspiracy, theft, embezzlement and money laundering. . . . Prosecutors argued that Wadena, Rawley, and Clark lived lavishly on the impoverished reservation." The defense insisted that such behavior was an "Indian Country tradition" and should not be considered illegal.[57] Chip Wadena was the active leader of the White Earth Reservation during the period when Sun Bear turned his attention to other Indian and spiritual concerns. Williams notes that Sun Bear had not returned home to the White Earth reservation in twenty-five years; the implication of his criticism is that staying on the reservation would have given him some sort of legitimacy—like Chip Wadena has.

The troublesome aspect of determining "legitimacy" is that it is not based on an examination of the spiritual depths of the teacher's work but on a hidden premise that white people should not have access to the information. Accusations of illegitimacy are often hurled at Christian sects others do not agree with (the Catholic Church condemned Martin Luther for nearly five centuries as illegitimate—not a real Christian; he was not able to offer "real" ceremonies). This process, once started, often ends up with its advocates turning on each other, much as participants in the French Revolution did.

One method of determining the legitimacy of illegitimacy claims is to see if rampant cries of illegitimacy are the norm for a movement (they are in this case) and to see if the parties turn on each other (they do). I will look at three participants in particular: Thomas Banyacya, Ward Churchill, and Black Elk.

I have admired Thomas Banyacya's work and devotion for many years and Ward Churchill's strength of character (however much I have disliked his "Indian good–white bad" polemics). Both of them have been attacked for some—if not all—of the same actions for which they have attacked others: They have been labeled "not legitimate," "wannabes," and "opportunists" and have been accused of "getting rich" on selling Indian spirituality. (Black Elk's case is unique and I will look at it last.) Here is a brief overview of what has been said about Banyacya and Churchill.

thomas banyacya and the lucrative hopi prophecies

The best known indigenous prophecies about the dangers facing the human species are those of the Hopi. The decision to make the prophecies public was taken by a number of the holy men after the dropping of the atomic bomb because, as one said, "It is our sacred duty to inform all people about things that have been kept secret from them."[58] If they did not act, it was felt, *all* nations and peoples would be in danger. But many Hopi question the legitimacy of making these prophecies public. As one Hopi said, "The teachings of the prophecy are for the Hopi, not for other people."[59]

Thomas Banyacya (one of the Indian activists who has criticized Sun Bear and other Indian teachers for condemnation) has himself been criticized as objectionable in five areas by Hopi who are uncomfortable with the sharing of the prophecies. The Indians who find him objectionable have said:

1. The prophecies should not be shared between people of different tribes or races. Anyone who shares it is violating the Hopi. Thus, Thomas Banyacya is violating the secrecy of Hopi religious truths.

2. Traditional Hopi life is one of modesty, humility, and simplicity. Because Banyacya is making a name for himself throughout the world as a teacher of Hopi religious truths, he is engaged in ego-glorification and is, consequently, acting in an anti-Hopi, anti-Indian (white) way.

3. Hopi religious truths belong to all Hopi; no one can charge for them but Banyacya receives money to travel and talk and write about the prophecies. Thus, he benefits materially from the prophecies. The Hopi people "have not benefited materially from the publication of their prophecies."[60] As a result, "the Kiva fraternities of several villages have disassociated themselves from the most active disseminator of the prophecies."[61] The most active disseminator is Thomas Banyacya.

4. Disseminators of the prophecies do so for primarily secular, not religious reasons. They are using the interest in the prophecies to make a name for themselves and the power of that name is then used for the accumulation of political strength in the tribe. This is true of Thomas Banyacya; it is improper.

5. The most active disseminators of the prophecy are not trained religious leaders or members of the Adult Hopi religious associations. "T. B. [Thomas Banyacya] the best-known disseminator is not an initiate"[62] or trained by religious leaders and hence is illegitimate.

Banyacya is referred to in *Fantasies of the Master Race* as "a spiritual elder of the Hopi." He is quoted as saying about Indians like Sun Bear, "These people have nothing to say on the matters they claim to be so expert about. To whites, they claim they're 'messengers,' but from whom? They are not messengers of the Indian people. I am a messenger, and I do not charge for my ceremonies."[63] The point of my juxtaposing the Hopi objections and Banyacya's comments is not to cast doubt on Banyacya's legitimacy but to show that in spite of publicity to the contrary, there is a great deal of conflict among tribal members in most tribes about *everything* that concerns Indian-white interface. Many respected Hopi elders, more thoroughly trained than Banyacya, were clear in their assertions that the prophecies should be shared. That does not stop many other Hopi from being uncomfortable with it and from disliking Banyacya for exactly the same actions he condemns Sun Bear and others for. I believe

all should consider the underlying spiritual imperatives at work. Is the sharing of this information going to help in the crisis facing the Earth at this time? Are the Indians in question getting rich (or extremely well-off) or are they covering expenses only to allow them to continue their work? Are they, in fact, living simply so that others may simply live?

ward churchill:
a white man posing as an indian?

Banyacya, however, is not the only one criticized by Indian activists. Ward Churchill (oddly enough, considering his writings on the subject) has also been attacked. David Bradley, a member of the "Minnesota Chippewa tribe," remarked in a November 23, 1993, *Colorado Daily* article that Ward Churchill "is a white man posing as an Indian." Bradley went on to say that "Churchill is from the white-left, a group of New Agers who want to show the Indian people the right way. They are old hippies who have gotten more heavy-handed. They want to take over the Native American struggle." He continues, "White men have taken everything they could have possibly taken from Indians. Our land, our gold, and now they want to take our identity. [Churchill] is victimizing Indian people, politically, morally, and spiritually. The concept 'Indian' is marketable, just like gold. It's our last possession. But once white people cross that line and usurp our identity, they've gone too far."[64]

Vernon Bellecourt, an Anishanabe from the White Earth Reservation in Minnesota, echoed this idea in the same article: "There are numerous 'wanna-be' Indians at large. Churchill and Glenn Morris, a professor at CU-Denver, are two white guys who came to town and now they are playing themselves off as Indian radicals." Bellecourt continued: "A few naive people in Denver and the universities continue to be fooled and actually promote these guys."[65]

Carole Standing Elk, a member of the Sisseton-Wahpeton Dakota Nation, articulated Indian concerns about Churchill in a January 13, 1994, letter to the editor in the *Colorado Daily*. She calls him a "pseudo-Indian 'wanna-be' " who is

conning the public and real Indians. "The high-stakes con job being pulled off by this white man playing the role of a Billy Jack–style 'Indian radical' and self-proclaimed 'AIM leader' is one of the most uproarious scandals to hit Indian country in a good long time. Move over, Carlos Castañeda and Lynn Andrews, here comes the biggest charlatan of them all—Ward Churchill, Chief of the Wanna-Bes!"[66] It is odd to note (in reference to Standing Elk's commentary) that Churchill has bitterly attacked Billy Jack, Castañeda, and Andrews as some of the worst of Indian rip-offs.

The discomfort expressed by Indians about Ward Churchill comes, to a great extent, from Churchill's failure to be an enrolled member of any Indian tribe (he claims one-sixteenth Creek-Cherokee blood quantum) and because he was not raised in a tribal culture. Going simply by these activists' concerns (concerns nearly identical to those Churchill expressed about others), one might agree with Pam Colorado, whom Churchill quoted in his book *Fantasies of the Master Race:*

> The process is ultimately intended to supplant Indians, even in the areas of their own customs and spirituality. In the end, non-Indians will have complete power to define what is and is not Indian, even for Indians. We are talking here about an absolute ideological/conceptual subordination of Indian people in addition to the total physical subordination they already experience. When this happens, the last vestiges of real Indian society and Indian rights will disappear. Non-Indians will then "own" our heritage and ideas as thoroughly as they now claim to own our land and resources.[67]

The point (as with Banyacya), however, is not whether Ward Churchill is or is not "legitimate." The point is that once the debate focuses on *form*—whether it be exchange of money, color of skin, level of blood quantum, personal affiliations, or credentials of one's teacher—the content of a person's character or spirit no longer matters. The overall effect of a life's work no longer matters; the striving of the personal will and heart—the "why" of their lives—no longer matters.

Is Black Elk Catholic Catechist or an Indian Holy Man?

The controversy about legitimacy or non-legitimacy of an Indian's Indianness or teachings is also beginning to be directed toward Black Elk—*the* most respected and best known of all Indians in the world. Some scholars and Indians have decided that Black Elk's teachings in *Black Elk Speaks* and *The Sacred Pipe* are not really all that Indian. Black Elk, a Catholic catechist for nearly thirty years, was an avid proponent of Christianity. A movement (which has its roots in Native activism and Western intellectual dismay about Earth mysticism) has begun to discredit his work as not "real" Lakota either because of Black Elk's exposure to Christianity or because he never really said anything attributed to him (Joseph Epes Brown and John Neihardt made it all up).

Michael Steltenkamp, in his book *Black Elk: Holy Man of the Lakota*, notes that "after only a short time, however, I learned to my astonishment that Black Elk's prestige . . . was the result of his very active involvement with priests in establishing Catholicism among his people."[68] Steltenkamp is highly reverent of Black Elk, and his book's purpose is to complete the life story of the great holy man by sharing his deep involvement in Catholicism, showing his deep reverence for it, and revealing that Black Elk experienced little conflict between the two systems of religious devotion. Indeed, for him, both were expressions of Creator's teaching and sacred path. William Powers (the remarkable scholar of Oglala religious beliefs), in his article "When Black Elk Speaks, Everybody Listens" (although also showing respect for Black Elk), points out that many contemporary Lakota do not think especially highly of Black Elk: "They have their own leaders, and their medicine men frequently disagree with Black Elk's philosophy."[69] Powers observes that the concept of a medicine man taking on universal attributes for all humanity is a non-Lakota perspective. In fact, it is antithetical to Lakota belief. Black Elk was primarily thought of not as a medicine man and carrier of Lakota tradition but as a Catholic catechist.[70] Powers further insists that there is no way to know if *anything* that is contained in *Black Elk Speaks* is what Black Elk really said; only his son, who acted as interpreter,

and the other old Lakota who were there could know for sure. (Steltenkamp gives some support for the translation not being an accurate reflection of what Black Elk really said by noting that Lucy Looks Twice [Black Elk's daughter] thought Ben Black Elk [Black Elk's son] might have altered Black Elk's message during translation. Of additional significance, however, to Looks Twice's remarks was the dispute between Lucy Looks Twice and Ben Black Elk about which religion was more legitimate: Christianity or traditional Lakota spirituality.) Powers reprints the 1934 letter from Black Elk in which he repudiates his Indian religious forms and declares that the only religious form he believes in is Christianity. Powers argues that what the book *Black Elk Speaks* reveals is only what a white man allowed. The "Indian truth" came through a white man and, as George Tinker said about this process, it was perverted, changed, and altered into something not Indian in the process. Tinker notes:

And now it's time to take the last remaining thing that we have that makes us Indian, to take our spirituality, to transform it, mutate it into something that is usable in white, individualistic culture and then to reintroduce that mutation like a virus back into the Indian world so that the final assimilation of the Indian people, the final act of cultural genocide [can take place].[71]

Thus, when Indians read *Black Elk Speaks* they accept back into themselves something perverted and non-Indian; the white man has defined what Indian spirituality is through a devious control of Black Elk's (now spurious) message. Steltenkamp notes that other scholars, such as Holler, are making this same claim.[72]

Powers's insistence on the general lack of Lakota respect for Black Elk (except as a catechist and older person) does not seem to mesh with Frank Fools Crow's and Ed McGaa's perspectives. Steltenkamp says (and Fools Crow in his book echoes this idea) that Fools Crow, who originally decided against a book about his life, relented when being informed Black Elk had done one. "The fact that Black Elk had chosen this course demanded that Fools Crow reconsider his own position. After all, even for Fools Crow, Black Elk was a beacon. His stature,

Fools Crow knew, dwarfed that of all modern religious practitioners, including Fools Crow himself (from whom many others were taking their cue)."[73]

This nibbling at the edges of Black Elk's communications to Neihardt and Joseph Epes Brown is the beginning of a general repudiation of Black Elk; its momentum has been growing. There is every reason to believe that eventually other Indians (such as Vine Deloria, Jr.), who have embraced Black Elk's communications, will be caught up in it and also repudiated for believing white man's propaganda. Such a repudiation is already in its beginning stages. Steltenkamp notes that Deloria "suggested that the book [Black Elk Speaks] captured what was authentically Indian. Now, however, . . . some may find this later period [of Black Elk's life] tainted through 'guilt by association' with Western ways."[74] (It is relevant to note that almost every book that has been written by an Indian—or an Indian life story "as told to" a white writer—that echoes universal themes or the sacredness of the Earth is attacked for being perverted by white influences.[75] This attack on universalist Indian writings is prevalent among Indian activists, Christians opposed to Earth spirituality, and many white academics.)

Steltenkamp observes that to some Indian activists, white scholars, and fervent Black Elk Speaks literalists, "Black Elk's participation in Christianity, and that of others from his generation, is thus [being] evaluated as sincere but misguided"[76] or even the only response left to them by religious and military imperialism. One ninety-year-old relative of Black Elk disagreed and "angrily indicted her people by saying: "Younger ones now don't tell the truth. They never believed. People heard him but did not listen."[77] Steltenkamp comments that this venerated elder "did not wish to be identified in this text for fear of reprisal arising from her comments."[78] Raymond DeMallie notes that discussion of this topic usually dissolves from objective assessment to political rhetoric.[79] In particular DeMallie is referring to the issue of whether Black Elk "was, at heart, either an old-time medicine man or one who forsook the tradition in favor of something entirely new."[80] In spite of desires to place him in a neat niche, Black Elk resists such classification. He was, however, clear about his Christianity. He viewed his work as a Catholic catechist as a further extension

of his original visions and work that Wakan Tanka had given him. He was joining two worlds—white and Indian, inside himself—as Wakan Tanka wished.

As for Black Elk's communications, Powers denigrates them by placing
them in quotation marks in his text as "teachings." Indian or white attempts
to emulate or use Black Elk's communications make them, in Powers's words,
"disciples." Both white and Indian "disciples" of Black Elk are therefore deluded
in the process of finding universal truth in his words. (According to Powers, the
words are not Black Elk's but Neihardt's.) Few great religious teachers have left
writings of their own. Neither Buddha nor Christ left original texts, for instance.
They are known through the writings of their disciples. The point (from the
perspective of the human journey) is that the teachers themselves touched on
some universal principle and people are being moved to emulate them and to
try to touch on that principle themselves. Black Elk's teachings have clearly
moved people. People seem to find in his words some deep truth that is relevant for our time. Black Elk's work, as Steltenkamp notes, can be seen as a focus
on one essential: "Namely, searching for and reliance upon Wakan Tanka in
the everyday course of events."[81] Black Elk believed that it was essential for
humankind to make the attempt to lead a sacred life—to touch and be touched
by Creator. Steltenkamp comments:

> Black Elk's reprimand in later life of the Manderson Catholic community reveals the
> kind of discouragement he endured as an elder. Far from being an acknowledgement
> of his erroneous Catholic practice, *The Sacred Pipe* was simply another attempt to
> rally his people's religious fervor by whatever means were at his disposal. Earlier in
> life he respected [Thin Elk's] decision to resume traditional [Indian] participation
> and to discontinue Christian practice—not because he felt their choice was theo-
> logically more sound or because he was indifferent to their concerns or because he
> was vacillating in his own commitment. Important to Black Elk was the quest itself.
> Whereas his destiny was that of a Catholic catechist, others might pursue alternate
> paths. The Thin Elk decision, because it was apparently rooted in sincerity, was a jour-
> ney upon which he could bestow his blessing. By contrast, the elder Black Elk seems
> to have been discouraged by so many people abandoning a trek in *any* direction.[82]

The capacity of Black Elk or any human being to serve as a universal beacon calling people to journey to the Creator is not unknown in human history; Black Elk, I think, would have been glad that so many felt so strongly the call of the sacred life through his words. One of the marks of the power of his life, like those of Jesus and Buddha, is that so many people can see so much in it. His life truly has become, as Powers remarks in denigration, all things to all people. Steltenkamp seems to comment on this attribute: "One wonders if the disclosure of his story from start to finish just might be a phenomenon not guided solely by human design. It is indeed intriguing that a man's vision still unfolds these long years after his death, revealed to countless persons far removed from his place and time."[83]

Critics, seeing human limitations in people like Black Elk and Sun Bear, gleefully point and say, "See, you were supposed to be a holy man, but look at all the imperfections in your work, look at how many ways you failed to carry the sacred in your actions." What the critics have missed, however, is not that, touched by the power of the Sacred, Black Elk and Sun Bear did so little, but that suffering from the same limitations as all human beings, they did so much. As Barry Lopez has remarked, those we respect as our great teachers, "from a certain distance, were faithful. They did not break faith with their beliefs, they remained dedicated to something outside the self. As far as we know, they never became the enemies of their souls or their memories."[84]

The result of judging a person by form *is* a kind of oppression. Whether Black Elk was Catholic, Sun Bear charged money to teach, Brooke Medicine Eagle had the proper teachers, Ward Churchill obtains tribal membership,[85] or Thomas Banyacya has become too well-known is irrelevant. What matters is the "why" of their lives. Overreliance on form leads to conflict. Sun Bear spoke of this problem in a piece he wrote about 1978, just after he had purchased twenty acres for the Bear Tribe at Vision Mountain:

> Happy times. We are thankful to the Great Spirit in that we now have our 20 acre "Home Base." A temporary house is up and foundation work is going on for the permanent house. We have chickens again and gardens are planted. How smooth things go when people have learned to walk together as brothers and sisters. We are thankful for all the outside help that has come to the Bear Tribe

from business men and other friends from the Spokane area and elsewhere across the country. We are thankful that we have found Indian and non-Indian people capable of putting aside the sick racism that continues to destroy so many people, that they could come together as real people and work and help each other. We are thankful that our friends from Klamath Falls believe in us enough to sell their property there and come north to join us in our work. We are thankful that our message has reached across the country to where other Indian people are returning to land and restoring their Way.

Yes, I am glad that my Indian heritage has given me knowledge of real value. And I am glad that the Great Spirit has given me a heart that lets me feel and a brain that makes me understand. So that I can embrace an Indian of another tribe and call him Brother or a non-Indian that comes with a true heart and call them Brother. I remember back in Los Angeles when I first started publishing Many Smokes. Some wanted me to use Many Smokes in petty tribal bickering to put down other Indians and I refused. I have had support from Indian and non-Indian. And I have been stolen from by both. So I will continue to accept each person as a human being. And when the Great Spirit has brought all changes upon the land I will stand on my medicine.[86]

chapter six
genocide, race, and spirituality

*These non-Indian hucksters and charlatans are a disgrace.
They are the promoters of "spiritual genocide" against
Indian people; and while some of them may be guilty
"merely" of complicity in "genocide with good intentions,"
others have become aggressive in insisting on their
right to profiteer by exploiting and prostituting American
Indian sacred traditions. . . . It is appropriate and indeed
imperative that all supporters of American Indian
religious freedom recognize this onslaught of "New Age"
exploitation and hucksterism for what it is—a major
component in the "final phase of genocide" to which
American Indian people currently are exposed. . . .
We ask all those who care about Indian people in our
struggle for justice and peace to help us put an end to this
spiritual genocide.*

— CENTER FOR THE SPIRIT [1]

genocide

No Native indictment in this conflict carries more emotional power than the assertion that whites who participate in Native ceremonies are engaged in an act of genocide. The word "genocide" creates specific images in our minds: Auschwitz, ovens, Nazis; the term, in fact, came into common usage to describe the attempted extermination of the Jews in World War II. Images of the murder of the Jews evoke the horror of genocide and emotionally move listeners in two important ways: First, the images become emotionally and visually linked to whites, and second, the instinctive human response to protect the victims of genocide is engaged. The continual repetition of the charge of genocide tends to make the association automatic in listeners' minds. In fact, such repetition is necessary. John O'Sullivan, the editor of the *National Review,* observes about such charges: "When a worldview is false, it can only be sustained by constant reinforcement."[2] Constant repetition leads to acceptance without any question of accuracy. (And the belief that contemporary Whites are guilty of genocide against Indians is becoming widespread. I have seen it in major American newspapers, in scholarly works, even a social work journal.) As the belief becomes accepted as true at an unconscious level, the legitimacy of strong action to prevent the genocide also becomes more acceptable. Violence slowly becomes a legitimate expression of the desire to protect the victims of genocide. Thus, the charge of genocide is a dangerous one, which should be closely examined. Does it, in fact, possess merit? To do so, let us look at the dictionary meaning of genocide and how the Native activists use the term.

are earth-centered whites engaged in a process of genocide?

Genocide is defined in most dictionaries as "the systematic extermination or destruction of an entire people or national group." The word comes from

the Greek *genos*, meaning "race," and the Latin *-cida*, which means "killer", or the Latin *caedere*, meaning "to kill." Thus, the exact linguistic definition is to murder or kill a race of people. According to this definition, it is clear the answer is no; whites are not engaged in genocide toward the Indian people. There is no evidence that any white person involved in Native ceremonies has killed *any* Indians. And there is no evidence of a systematic effort by a large group of people practicing Indian religious forms to murder an entire people or national group.

Like many others, however, Ward Churchill (quoted by Annette Jaimes in her introduction to *Fantasies of the Master Race*)[3] has expanded the definition of genocide that we find in the dictionary. Specifically, he says that the genocide of a people occurs in three stages—all of which are genocide. In the first stage the destroying culture engages in direct acts of violence. During this period the destroying culture substantiates the violence by creating literature "to provoke and sanctify systematic warfare."[4] When violence has achieved its intended goal of domination, the destroying culture begins to engage in activities to accomplish the "civilizing" of the savage, such as prohibiting indigenous language, religion, and education. In this second stage, the dominant culture's literature begins to enhance "public zeal in 'civilizing' the savage."[5] Finally, the dominant group absorbs the dominated group to the extent that it "owns" the oppressed group's "truth and knowledge."[6] At that point, the dominated group has been absorbed into the dominating group so that its cultural values, aspects, elements, and expressions are a part of the dominant group. Specifically, in the case of Indian-European dynamics, at this third stage we are all Americans—no longer Indians and white colonizing oppressors, but one people. The final act of assimilation has occurred.

Churchill's argument is compelling. An examination of the historical relationship between Indian tribes and the U.S. government bears out many of his assertions. (Other groups—blacks, Asians, women, Catholics, Jews, Mormons, Quakers, Communists, and many others—have also suffered through similar patterns of violent domination and assimilation.) The early treatment of the Indian people by the U.S. government shows clear evidence of genocide

according to both the dictionary definition and Churchill's first stage analysis. From broken treaties, to abuse of the police powers of the state, to the intentional introduction of disease, the treatment of the Indian was clearly intended to destroy their culture in order to secure control from sea to shining sea.

There is much evidence of our country's dishonor. George Bird Grinnell describes the government's treatment of the Indian in *Blackfoot Lodge Tales:*

> Protests against the governmental swindling of these savages have been made again and again, but such remonstrances attract no general attention. Almost everyone is ready to acknowledge that in the past the Indians have been shamefully robbed, but it appears to be believed that this no longer takes place. This is a great mistake. We treat them now much as we have always treated them. Within two years, I have been present on a reservation where government commissioners, by means of threats, by bribes given to chiefs, and by casting fraudulently the votes of absentees, succeeded after months of effort in securing votes enough to warrant them in asserting that a tribe of Indians, entirely wild and totally ignorant of farming, had consented to sell their lands, and to settle down each upon 160 acres of the most utterly arid and barren land to be found on the North American continent. The fraud perpetrated upon this tribe was as gross as could be practiced by one set of men upon another.[7]

There is little argument (as Churchill himself notes) against this record. The first stage of genocide as Churchill has described it is clear. It is also clear that the second stage of genocide that Churchill describes occurred even though many in the eighteenth and nineteenth centuries were horrified at the government's actions and fought long and bitterly to stop them.

The literature of the time portrayed Indians as ignorant and un-Christian savages, as heathens who often worshipped the devil, as lacking any element of civilization or human decency. Religious groups, government employees, and Western scholars and scientists actively called for the civilizing of the Indian.

The need for this civilizing was heightened by continued descriptions of the Indians' lack of civilized manner, behavior, religion, and morality. For example, "a Protestant Episcopal clergyman and a member of the Misasauga tribe of the Ojibway nation of Canada" remarks: "I have been sometimes inclined to think that, if witchcraft still exists in the world, it is to be found among the aborigines of America. They seem to possess a power which, it would appear, may be fairly imputed to the agency of an evil spirit."[8] In addition, the news media, for more than a century, was filled with accounts of the atrocities committed by the "savages" in the killing of white settlers.[9] Indian cultures and lifestyles were alien—not understandable. Indians themselves were dangerous, to be feared. In attempting to counteract these beliefs and fears, many advocates for the Indians moved quite naturally into the second stage described by Jaimes and Churchill; specifically, the destroying culture, having achieved domination through violence, begins to actually "civilize" the savages.[10] George Bird Grinnell writes:

> The Indian has the mind and feelings of a child with the stature of a man; and if this is clearly understood, and considered, it will readily account for much of the bad we hear about him, and for many of the evil traits which are commonly attributed to him. Civilized and educated, the Indian of the better class is not less intelligent than the average white man, and he has every capacity for becoming a good citizen.[11]

Grinnell possessed a deep love of the Indian people, which, in fact, was shared by many who knew them well. The drive of people like Grinnell (it can be convincingly argued) came not out of a desire to assimilate the Indian but out of a desire to save their lives and cultures. If these defenders could change people's beliefs, perhaps people would leave the Indian alone and allow their culture to survive. Thus, their arguments had to directly address the fears and common beliefs of the citizenry and would be couched in decidedly nineteenth-century terms. And although there were many writers like Grinnell, they were decidedly *not* in the majority. With equal obviousness, however, *all* writers

of the time did not come from an assimilationist point of view. Churchill ascribes the universal base motives of assimilation to an entire group of people but it is clear that some people had other motivations. This assertion of the universality of evil intent (even if it is unconscious intent) by an entire people is exactly what the white did to the Indian. It is crucial to remember that it did not represent reality when it was done to the Indian. It does not represent reality when done to the non-Indian.

In spite of this, Churchill does make a brilliant point. The literature of the time clearly indicates that most people did not write from a love of the Indian. They were writing, as Churchill asserts, to foster assimilation *only*. It is clear, too, that he defines genocide not simply as the killing of a race of people but also their absorption into another, more dominant culture, in the process of which the minority culture's sense of identity begins to disappear. And, in fact, in the drive for assimilation and the civilizing of the savage Indian, much of their culture was actively attacked, prohibited, or altered. Many Indians, prohibited from speaking their own language, from teaching their children, and from practicing their religion, came to view their own culture as savage and barbaric and their religious forms as heathen and uncivilized. As a result they often rejected any identification with their own cultures. Annette Jaimes comments on this when she notes that "white domination is so complete that even Indian children want to be cowboys [in the game of cowboys and Indians].[12] Churchill's description of the forcible conversion of a culture's identity into that of another is accurate. Forcible conversion is, in fact, a form of genocide.

The third stage in this process, "absorbing the indigenous culture into the culture of the dominant group," is accomplished, Churchill asserts, through expropriation and ownership of the "truth and knowledge" of the dominated culture.[13] The writings of Carlos Castañeda,[14] Lynn Andrews, and others, Churchill maintains, are a reflection of this final stage of genocide. It is genocide, he insists, because it removes "the prime cultural symbol" of a culture. He quotes two Canadian researchers: "If people suddenly lose their 'prime symbol,' the basis of their culture, their lives lose meaning. They become

disoriented, with no hope. A social disorganization often follows such a loss, they are often unable to insure their own survival."[15] Churchill quotes Russell Means: "Spirituality is the basis of our culture; if it is stolen, our culture will be dissolved. If our culture is dissolved, Indian people *as such* will cease to exist. By definition, the causing of any culture to cease to exist is an act of genocide."[16]

Means appears to be making a sensible statement, a logical argument (if A then B, if B then C, if C then D), but is he? In reality, both his and the Canadian researchers' arguments are flawed. Means's argument goes something like this: If you use our ceremonies, it is stealing our spirituality; if our spirituality is stolen, our "prime symbol" is gone (there is just a big hole where the Pipe ceremony and Sun Dance used to be); if our "prime symbol" is gone, our culture dissolves; if our culture dissolves, we are gone and it's plain that this is genocide. Churchill concurs. He associates the "taking" of the "prime symbol" with white participation in Indian spirituality. He confirms his agreement by using Means's quote and by focusing the chapter (at least partly) on the "exploitation and appropriation of Native American spiritual traditions."[17] This *is*, he insists, genocide.

We can, I believe, agree that the first two stages are clearly genocidal. But the third stage is more tenuous, and it is more difficult to equate it with genocide, especially because of the implication that absorption into the dominant group leaves no trace of the indigenous culture. When non-Indians perform Indian ceremonies, nothing is being denied to or physically removed from the Indian. It is simply not correct to assert that Indians will have nothing left, not even their spirituality. There is, in fact, *not* a big hole where the Pipe ceremony and Sun Dance used to be; Means's reasoning is not really sensible at all. And many Indians do not agree with it. As the Wampanoag elder Medicine Story said:

From my side, I can say that no one can steal my religion. You may come and copy my ways, you may copy my songs and stories, but you have stolen nothing, because I still have my religion. You might even steal my sacred assistants,

such as tobacco, sweet grass, or my pipe, but my religion does not depend on those things. What you may make of my ways might be your religion—it certainly is not mine—and I am still, by the instructions of our old ones, willing to respect your religion, however you acquired it, if it is real for you.[18]

Jamie Sams voices a similar perspective:

The truth is that we hold our spirituality inside ourselves and no one can steal it. The truth is that nobody can come to our sacred dances and ceremonies on the Reservations and learn anything that would weaken our connections to the Earth Mother or the Creator. Our strength is internal. It rests in our hearts and our spirits. That has been proven through history and cannot be changed.[19]

The truth of these statements is self-evident. If I smoke the pipe, it does not mean that there is one less Indian who can smoke the pipe as if there are only a certain number who can do so. There is not a long line of people in which the presence of another white person forces the ejection of an Indian who immediately suffers the lack of a "prime symbol" to sustain him. Fostering such images, such untruths, is dangerous. Activists perpetuate untruths if they insist that when a white person worships through the use of the pipe, the essence of Native spirituality is killed and the prime symbol removed. And when they assert that all "real" Indians believe these untruths, race hatred and violence are generated. White motives are purported to be conscious, and the destruction of the Indian is the goal. Indians, in an equal (though covert) distortion, are presumed to be so weak and debilitated that if a white smokes the pipe, by some magical, unexplained process their spirituality, their prime symbol, is sucked out of them, never to return.

Many Natives take this process one step further. They assert that the involvement of non-Indians in Indian spirituality is specifically *intended* to supplant the Indian by "stealing" his spirituality. George Tinker states:

And now it's time to take the last remaining thing that we have that makes us Indian, to take our spirituality, to transform it, to mutate it into something that is usable in white, individualistic culture and then to reintroduce that mutation like a virus back into the Indian world so that the final assimilation of the Indian people, the final act of cultural genocide, [can take place. And that] is the individualizing of Indian communitarian structures and ceremonies.[20]

Pam Colorado's words are worth repeating in this context:

The process is ultimately intended to supplant Indians, even in the areas of their own customs and spirituality. In the end, non-Indians will have complete power to define what is and is not Indian, even for Indians. We are talking here about an absolute ideological/conceptual subordination of Indian people in addition to the total physical subordination they already experience. When this happens, the last vestiges of real Indian society and Indian rights will disappear. Non-Indians will then "own" our heritage and ideas as thoroughly as they now claim to own our land and resources.[21]

"Supplant," as it is used here, is in itself an expression of genocide: The real Indians are eliminated, fake Indians take their place, and, presumably, no one notices the difference. Although it is true that many people of many colors and nationalities are being influenced by Indian values, it is not possible to find *any* evidence of such widespread *intention* to supplant the Indian; in other words, there is no movement by "New Agers" to completely remove the Indian people—physically exterminate them—and take their place. Many non-Indians insist that they cherish and revere Indian values, that they see Indians as role models for personal and cultural conduct. Some insist they wish to become more like Indians solely because of this appreciation. And the pervasiveness of this modeling, it can be argued, means that Indian values are in the process of supplanting European values, not vice versa. The result of this (which many people assert is crucial for our Earth) is a joint holding of common values and perspectives. But the Indian is not being supplanted. Far from it.

At the dawn of the twenty-first century, the Indian nations are emerging as potent political forces in the United States; their populations are rising, they are beginning to generate large revenues and to expand. They are emerging as sovereign nations, powerfully able to shape their own destinies. Long thought by most government officials to be on their way into extinction, American Indians have done exactly the opposite.

Douglas Endreson, a nationally prominent Indian lawyer, ringingly proclaimed in 1992 to a conference of tribal leaders in Washington, D.C.:

> From the time that the Europeans arrived, tribes were forced to defend themselves, their rights, and their people. At stake was their sovereign right to govern themselves and to make their own choices. Tribal powers are now well established in federal law. The battle for recognition of sovereignty has been won. The new battles will center on the exercise of sovereignty as tribes struggle to achieve economic, political, social and religious objectives. The Indian future now depends not on the federal government, but on the choices that tribes make in the exercise of their sovereignty. Tribes are no longer on the defensive—they are on the offensive.[22]

Although the tribes still face many challenges (such as poverty, lack of education, and alcoholism), there is little evidence (or danger) of them being supplanted in *any* area. Should the trends established in the past thirty years continue, the United States could very well see a de facto country composed of fifty states and two hundred and fifty or so sovereign (tribal) nation-states, all of which have to get along with each other.[23]

But the crux of the activists' point lies in Colorado's final sentence: "Non-Indians will then 'own' our heritage and ideas as thoroughly as they now claim to own our land and resources." The message is that whites (non-minority non-Indians) are colonizers in someone else's country. They are guilty—because of their genetic connection to those who perpetuated crimes against the Indian people in the past—of those same crimes. They enjoy the benefits of their ancestors' crimes and, as children of the oppressors, partake of the same worldview as their ancestors. As such they can never be "native" here. They are alien

and always will be. No matter how many generations are born here they will never be children of this soil. The underlying supposition is that we—Indians and whites—are still at war and the war will never end until the oppressors are driven from these shores. Any act of accommodation or of peaceful coexistence between oppressor and oppressed is treason or burglary. This view can be seen in the rhetoric: If Indians teach non-Indians their spirituality, they are traitors; if whites use Indian spirituality, they are thieves. Any ideological position that does not recognize that whites are oppressors, that does not recognize that Indians are oppressed, that does not recognize that when a white has a pipe it is stealing, *is* by definition an act of oppression.[24] Those who believe we are still in a state of war assume that conditions have remained static; they do not acknowledge the unique process that has occurred: the emergence of a new people who together make one people. But to affirm this interblending is treason; to advocate it is to argue for assimilation. We are still (and we must remain), activists insist, of different cultures, different races, different tribes: one bad— the other good. No children of the oppressors are good, no children of the oppressed who fraternize are good. *No* interblending can be tolerated.

Thus, the primary concerns of the activists about non-Indians using Indian ceremonies do not really seem to be based on lack of respect for indigenous traditions, treason, theft, genocide, or any other concept that is being articulated. The "for" and "against" positions are split along one line only. On one side are those who believe in an underlying unity of all humankind and are responding from that universalism, and on the other are those who consider themselves members of an oppressed culture still at war with the oppressors. Those who support Thomas Banyacya's sharing of the Hopi prophecies are clearly universalist; those who do not support it are clearly oriented toward the ethnic, tribal, oppressor-oppressed perspective. Janet McCloud clearly reflects the latter position; Sun Bear, for example, reflects the former.

The concept of "heritage" ownership is itself troubling and is viewed quite differently from a universal perspective than from an ethnic, tribal one. Pam Colorado's assertion that non-Indians will own her heritage brings up a picture of the logical conclusion of such thinking: Each of the world's ethnic

groups crouched over their "heritage," shotgun aimed and ready. White Americans will eke out some blue jeans, penicillin, and surgical techniques from time to time. Indians will in return offer some corn and beans, a little tobacco, some insight on how the Earth ecosystem is a whole living entity. The Chinese will share some of the *I-Ching,* perhaps let someone look through the writings of Lao Tsu, insist on the return of gunpowder and the printing press. The Japanese will take back all their Zen gardens and restrict the practice of Zen Buddhism to ethnic Japanese of sufficient blood purity. The Islamic cultures will insist on the return of the number "0" and only allow its use on payment of a fee. The Greeks will take back the inclined plane, the lever, and all the writings of Plato, Aristotle, and the like. France will take the decimal system, England Shakespeare, Italy the works of Michelangelo (plus all rights to any reproduction in any form) and viaducts. Strict lines will be erected around all identifiable ethnic groups with immediate consequences for anyone transgressing boundaries.

many indians disagree

There is a tendency on the part of non-Indians who hear a definitive statement by an Indian to think that belief is held by all Indians. In reality, Indians are as diverse and rich in their opinions as any other group of people;[25] many Indians do not agree with Native activists' desire for racial separatism. Philip Martin, chief of the Mississippi Band of the Choctaws, is one.

> I don't like what this country did to the Indians: it was all ignorance based on more ignorance based on greed. . . . But I don't believe that you have to do what others did to you. Ignorance is what kept us apart. But we'd never have accomplished what we did [in recent years] if we'd taken the same attitude. We only have a short time to live on this earth. Everybody has got to get along somehow. We live here surrounded by non-Indians. We have to live with our neighbors and with our community. I don't condemn anyone by race. What kept us down was our own lack of education, economy, health care—we had no way of making a living. At first I never thought that Choctaws could fit into

the larger society and remain Choctaw. But, in fact, we don't have to give up our language, our culture, or our traditions. I believe that if we're going to fit in this country, we'd better do it on our own terms. If we can help local non-Indian communities in the process, we do it. And when we do it, we build up a lot of political and social support. We all have a common cause here: the lack of jobs and opportunities has kept everyone poor and ignorant. The future is going to bring a lot of change for everyone. It's going to be very difficult for a tribe to isolate itself and develop its own economy. We all depend on one another, whether we realize it or not.[26]

Rayna Green, a Cherokee who is director of the Native American Program at the Museum of American History, is another.

We live in a world where everything is mutable and fragile. But we are here, and we are not going to go away. Indians look around at the malls and stores of America and say, "None of this is ever going to be ours." But none of it is going to go away either. Somehow we must face the consequences of history and live with it. We don't need only to remember the tragedy, but to also remember the gift, to live in this place, to know it gave us birth, to feel the responsibility we have for it. We have to sit down and figure out how to not hurt each other any more.[27]

The need for this level of personal responsibility, of facing consequences and learning how to deal with what *is*, is also articulated by a Sioux social worker: "People still sit around crying about how it's all the white man's fault for bringing us firewater. Well, five generations later, we better start taking some responsibility ourselves—because we are committing self-genocide, breeding a new generation of idiots. If it keeps up at this rate, 50 years from now there won't be a Sioux on the reservation who can think straight even if he is sober."[28]

Spokespeople such as these are actively seeking a partnership between non-Indian and Indian and the development of a common ground that will allow the growth of a future based on friendship and cooperation. In that future

the members of *both* cultures will have to come to terms with our collective pasts. Use of polemical rhetoric, especially the word "genocide," does not foster solutions that include partnership or common ground. By its essential meaning the word "genocide" casts all dialogue in terms of race—it creates barriers between people. It cannot be used without referring to a distinct class of people—the group that can be identified as distinct and separate from all other groups—the group that is being exterminated. *Both* groups involved in genocide—oppressor and oppressed—are invariably identified through concepts of race and genetics. Historically, when the identification of a people by their racial or genetic characteristics becomes common in a culture, violence and spiritual repression will follow. Because so many activists insist on using a term that is race-dependent, it is essential to examine the concept of race itself and the historical consequences of using it as a means to redress social justice issues.

race

Each people has their own ways. You cannot mix these ways together, because each people's ways are balanced. Destroying balance is a disrespect and very dangerous. This is why it's forbidden.

— M A T T H E W   K I N G [29]

White people don't have any real feeling for these ceremonies, they are just mimicking them.

— G E O R G E   T I N K E R [30]

Suppose I took George Tinker's statement and revised it slightly so that it read: "Black people don't have any real feeling for Christian ceremonies, they are just mimicking them." I would be branded a racist, and rightly so, from coast to coast. Half the country would be up in arms if a white Christian denied black people admittance to a Christian church and said (as Russell Means did):

"Our religions are ours. Period. We have very strong reasons for keeping certain things private, whether you understand them or not. And we have every human right to deny them to you, whether you like it or not." Oddly enough, most people who hear Tinker's and Means's comments do not apply them universally. For some reason the statements seem to make sense to them when structured around Indian concerns but not if applied to other ethnic groups such as African-Americans. But the historical record is clear: When the primary criterion for anything is the color of a person's skin or ethnic origin, violence is not far away. Ethnic labeling and emphasis on skin color seem to breed violence in and of themselves.[31]

For the past thirty years it seemed that, as a culture and as a species we were finally moving away from race as a standard of humanity. We had come a long way and seemed to be on the verge of embodying Martin Luther King, Jr.'s electrifying oratory: "I have a dream that my four little children will one day live in a nation where they will not be judged by the color of their skin but the content of their character."[32] Unfortunately, recent social trends seem to indicate the pendulum is swinging the other way; even international experts have felt the need to address the issue. Lionel Tiger, Darwin Professor of Anthropology at Rutgers University, reported about an international meeting on the concept of race held in June 1996 in Schlaining, Austria, that was attended by experts in genetics, endocrinology, anthropology, psychology, animal behavior, and psychology.

> The fact is that all of contemporary population genetics and molecular biology underscores that the nineteenth century notion of races as discrete and different entities is false. There is only gradual genetic diversity between groups. We all merge smoothly into each other. Nearly all the physically observable differences reflect very limited local adaptations to climate and other specific environmental conditions. The group concluded: "Categorization of humans by distribution of genetically determined factors is artificial and encourages the production of unending lists of arbitrary and misleading social perceptions and images."[33]

He continues:

> Decent public life in the U.S. and elsewhere has been traumatized by the socioeconomic fact of racism. Now it is being violated by the idea of race as a crucial category in public policy, as much positively as negatively. Using "race" in public discourse is like being a flat-earther in NASA. The world looks flat, but it isn't. Race seems real, but it isn't.[34]

blood purity and sovereignty

Unfortunately, race is inextricably intertwined with the whole concept of "Indian" in the United States. Indian tribes are held to be sovereign nations, and to identify membership in those nations (with whom the United States has treaties), race has traditionally been used. Membership is based on minimum levels of blood purity, different for each tribe. Race and racial purity have, as a result, become entrenched in both U.S. law and culture.

Being defined as an Indian means that a person has a unique status with respect to the rest of the people in the United States. To be set aside as racially distinct, as Indian, means one partakes of that status. Indians are American citizens but also citizens of a foreign nation. Some U.S. laws apply to them, others do not. For example, reservations are exempt from separation of church and state restrictions in their government formation but the people living on the reservation are (theoretically) guaranteed freedom of religious worship. In practice, however, like many instances where people are defined as in along racial lines, the application of racially based sovereignty can be grim, and not all people find it beneficial. Fergus Bordewich, in his book *Killing the White Man's Indian*, comments on its dangers.

> On a deeper plane, the ideology of sovereignty seems to presume that racial separateness is a positive good, as if Indian bloodlines, economies, and histories were not already inextricably enmeshed with those of white, Hispanic, black, Asian Americans; it seems to presuppose that cultural integrity ought

to, or even can, be preserved. With little debate outside the parochial circles of Indian affairs, a generation of policy making has jettisoned the long-standing American ideal of racial unity as a positive good and replaced it with a doctrine that, seen from a more critical angle, seems disturbingly like an idealized form of segregation, a fact apparently invisible in an era that has made a secular religion of passionate ethnicity. . . . [This] leads inexorably toward a moral acceptance of political entities defined on the basis of racial exclusion. Although the concept of tribal sovereignty has parallels in other ideologies of racial and ethnic separatism, it is potentially far more subversive. . . . It should, moreover, be obvious to anyone that legitimizing segregation for Indians will set a precedent for its potential imposition upon black, Asian, and Hispanic Americans.[35]

And Ramon Roubideaux, a Rosebud Sioux and attorney, notes:

"Sovereignty" is often just a mask for individuals who rob people of their rights as U.S. citizens. Tribes are able to deny fundamental rights in tribal court and then hide behind the principle of sovereignty. They have the power to do anything they want to do. Many tribal court decisions have nothing to do with fairness. Without the separation of executive, legislative, and judicial powers that exists everywhere else in the United States, we have no way to enforce justice on the reservation if the tribal council says no, irrespective of the lip service that may be paid to tribal and appellate courts. Otherwise, you will see a worsening of every aspect of life on the reservation, because there is no place we can go to get an appeal on a decision. We've got to live within the legal framework of the U.S. whether we like it or not. We've got to develop along those lines because at least it has the goal of honesty and fair dealing.[36]

But the racial purity laws that have been passed by the U.S. Congress are difficult to do away with.* Ostensibly these laws were passed to help determine

---

*It is a twisted irony that the three major industrialized nations to pass laws of racial purity in the twentieth century are Nazi Germany, South Africa, and the United States.

who is or is not Indian so that the government can carry out its obligations to the sovereign nations with whom it signed treaties in the nineteenth century. The tribes receive a certain amount of government assistance based on the number of members of the tribe, and the membership in the tribe is based on blood quantum or level of blood purity. (This situation explains why many tribes attempt to restrict the recognition of new tribal entities: The more tribes there are, the less federal money to go around.) Members of federally recognized tribes also have some degree of interest in the sale of tribal assets such as mineral deposits and timber. Attendance at Indian colleges such as Haskell Indian Nations University in Lawrence, Kansas, is dependent not only on membership in a federally recognized tribe but also on a minimum of verifiable Indian blood levels. Further, in order to protect the term "Indian," the Congress of the United States passed legislation restricting the term when applied to art objects to those created by people who possessed enough blood purity to be a member of a federally recognized tribe.[37]

blood purity:
meaningful distinction or hidden racism?

The creation of standards of blood purity has led to conflict within some Indian tribes. For example, the Eastern Band of the Cherokees, located on a North Carolina reservation, is embroiled in a deep conflict that is typical of the sort that blood purity creates. The tribal members make distinctions between full bloods (or fuller bloods), mixed bloods, and white Indians. Full, or fuller, bloods are traditionally considered to be the most conservative Cherokees, have a higher blood quantum, define themselves as Cherokee, and use Cherokee as their primary language. Mixed bloods generally have a lower blood quantum, have intermixed many white values with their own Cherokee traditions, speak English more often than Cherokee (and generally consider the Cherokee language as not very useful in the modern world), and are more interested in the concept of progress. White Indians are from families in which there has been

a great deal of intermarriage with whites (particularly males), generally follow a white orientation toward life, seldom speak Cherokee, and their children often marry outside the tribe.[38] In other words, fuller bloods are generally living as much like their Cherokee forebears as possible, mixed bloods blend both worlds, and white Indians have been assimilated into the white world. This is a simplification of the situation, however; there are some Cherokees with a minimal Cherokee blood quantum who speak Cherokee fluently, are very conservative culturally, and are, generally, considered "real" Cherokees. Others are nearly full-blood Cherokees who are completely assimilated into white culture and speak little or no Cherokee and are thought of as "white Indians." This mixture of orientations is a constant source of sometimes bitter debate about who should have membership in the tribe. John Finger, in his excellent book *Cherokee Americans*, notes that this factionalism between the racially purer and the less pure in tribal politics "can be nasty, brutish, and frequently entertaining."[39] He goes on to say that although such factionalism is common in American politics, on the Cherokee Reservation it often becomes "particularly virulent."[40]

The Eastern Band of the Cherokee separated from the Cherokee Nation in 1819 and remained in North Carolina when the rest of the tribe was forced over the Trail of Tears to Oklahoma in 1838. The first tribal roll of members was begun in 1907. Once the roll was completed, each person listed could expect to receive a yearly cash payment from the sale of tribal timber—thus there was an incentive to be listed on the roll. The general consensus was that $1/16$ Cherokee blood was sufficient to be a member of the tribe. But in 1919, by a 15 to 0 vote of the tribal council, the Eastern Band decided to accept allotment by which the communal lands of the tribe were to be broken up and a portion given to each member in fee-simple title. Suddenly everyone was claiming to be Cherokee, and political pressure was brought to bear on elected officials. Congress subsequently rejected a clause in the tribal charter requiring $1/16$ Cherokee blood quantum for membership in the tribe, noting: "Congress determine[s] qualifications for tribal membership, not any state, or even the tribe in question."[41] As a result, some Oklahoma Cherokees who had as little as $1/256$ Cherokee blood were enrolled. The final decision of Congress was that anyone

with a verifiable trace of Cherokee blood who lived in the historical boundaries of the tribe was a member. This decision, which swelled the number of potential members of the tribe, was objected to by many tribal members because the money and land were to be shared evenly; the more members, the less received by each. Approximately one-half the final members were less than 25 percent Cherokee and one-half were more than 75 percent Cherokee. Because of the bitter conflict, allotment was never enacted for the Eastern Cherokees, and by 1930 the whole concept of allotment for the Indian people was abandoned. Congress finally certified the original, or Baker, roll but agreed to the Eastern Cherokee request that new members be restricted to $^{1}/_{16}$ Cherokee blood quantum or more. Generally, the $^{1}/_{16}$ requirement has remained in effect since then.

But racial purity standards for membership in a culture or tribe, even with as low a blood purity as $^{1}/_{16}$, have continued to be problematic. The Eastern Cherokee community has been concerned in recent years about children who have one Indian parent with $^{1}/_{16}$ blood quantum and one white parent, thus giving the children, at birth, $^{1}/_{32}$ blood quantum—insufficient to be a member of the tribe.* The children are raised in the tribe, immersed in its customs, speak its language exclusively, and yet are ineligible for membership. Culturally they may be more "Indian" than someone possessing a 50 percent blood quantum, but because of their insufficient blood quantum they lose possessory rights to their parents' holdings. At their parents' death, they have to leave the reservation. Concerned parental members forced a compromise in 1987 whereby children with less than $^{1}/_{16}$ blood quantum, although unenrolled, would still enjoy the benefits of their parents' estate. This right would, however, not be passed on to their children.

---

*This problem is not unique to the Eastern Band of the Cherokee. The children of Robert Hoag, a former president of the Seneca Nation, are ineligible for tribal membership in spite of being raised in the tribe, speaking its language, and possessing a high blood quantum. Membership in the tribe is matrilineal and Hoag's children's mother is white. Thus, although they are considered Indians by whites, Indians consider them white. Culturally they are Indian.[42]

Blood quantum standards continue to affect all areas of Eastern Cherokee tribal life. In the mid-1980s a Bureau of Indian Affairs proposal to limit educational benefits to tribal members with ¼ blood quantum or more created a "storm of opposition." Finger reports: "Frederick Bradley, a teacher and former school board member, complained to the BIA that such a change would destroy the local school system and expose Indians with even a low blood quantum to racism in the public schools. In closing he wrote, 'FUND THE SCHOOLS AT CHEROKEE FOR CHILDREN AND NOT DEGREE OF BLOOD.' "[43] Schooling is not the only factor affected by the controversy; many lesser-blood Indians find that they are often excluded from tribal lifeways (such as ceremonial events) solely because their blood quantum level is low.

Some tribes take blood purity to even greater extremes. The Tonawanda Band of Seneca has removed members of the tribe who are critical of tribal government policies from tribal rolls, in effect making them (and their children) "white." The offenders are no longer considered Indian by either the United States, tribal government, or other Indians and, as such, they no longer can influence tribal politics.[44] Legal appeals to correct this inequity have been denied. With few exceptions (the U.S. government still sets blood purity levels for some tribes), the tribal council of each tribe now has exclusive and total control over who is or is not a member of the tribe. Because of the many financial and ownership benefits that accrue to membership in a tribe, the capacity to determine who is or is not a member brings with it tremendous political power. Thus, controlling access to things Indian by actively verifying blood quantum is becoming the norm. Inevitably this includes religious ceremonies. As Charla Hermann noted in 1993: "Because of so many games and foul play, we now have to justify our belief of our honor to carry Cannunpa [the sacred pipe], to Vision Quest or even Sun Dance. More and more places we found this year wanted all participants to provide Indian roll numbers to prove our worthiness to participate in the rigors of these ways."[45]

spirituality

Connecting religious participation with blood purity bears many similarities to South African race-based religious repression. "An article in *Time* on 'Apartheid,' spoke of the lack of charity manifested by the South African Dutch Reformed churches, most of whom refused to admit any native to their services. The article reported the story of a South African policeman who discovered a native in a white church on his knees. Being informed that the Kaffir was scrubbing the floor, the officer replied, 'Alright, but God help you if I catch you praying.'"[46]

Many Indians, feeling that the ceremonies were handed down by their forefathers or were given directly to them by Creator, strongly believe that a roll card and sufficient blood purity are legitimate determinants of religious participation in Indian religious services.[47] Joseph Leonard observes: "Essential to the defense of [this kind of racism] is the claim that it was not instituted by modern-day members of society, but rather came to them as a sacred and ancient tradition from their forefathers; an inherited way of life. [Because of this the] individuals or groups [involved] proclaim their impotence to alter the situation or to defy the tradition."[48] When the actions involve Indians, few will call it racism—which is what I deem it to be—because of rampant guilt feelings about white domination of the Indian peoples. As Leonard succinctly observes about this hesitancy: "[The] term 'racist' has acquired a pejorative meaning, and men shy away from the application of 'racist' or 'racism' to their pattern of thinking. However, abandonment of the term does not mean abandonment of the theory. Actually, a euphemism has been substituted. This is the term 'blood,' which has a certain mystical connotation."[49]

The arguments of Native activists directly connect the concept of "blood" and the mystical essence it contains with allowing "white" participation in Native ceremonies. "Whites," identified by blood, do not have the proper blood essence to participate in or carry on Native ceremonials. But the activists' arguments are not new. They have been applied to black slaves in the American

South, blacks in South Africa, the Jews in fifteenth-century Spain and again in Nazi Germany, and the Serbs, Croats, and Muslims in the former Yugoslavia. Because these arguments are so similar and take such a familiar historical path, it is important to explore them to see just how closely Native activists' arguments parallel them.

the american negro and the ariel controversy

Published in 1867 and titled *The Negro: What Is His Ethnological Status?*, this tract became more popularly known as "The Ariel Controversy" because of the pseudonym (Ariel) of its anonymous author. Ariel was, in fact, the Nashville publisher and clergyman Buckner H. Payne. His writing attempted to show, using the Bible and science as authorities, that the Negro was of a separate species from the Caucasian and therefore should be treated differently in both religious and social affairs.

By an elaborate use of the Bible, Payne argued that Negroes were not human beings but were created before Adam and Eve and were, therefore, beasts, for the use of human beings. Using the genealogical history of the Bible, he "proved" that Negroes were not descendants of Adam and Eve (who, as everyone knew, were white-skinned, had high foreheads and long straight hair). And if they were not descendants of Adam and Eve, they were not then descended from Noah and his children. Since all creatures now living came out of the ark, then the Negro must have existed before Adam and Eve and be a part of the beasts that Noah gathered to save in the ark. "[I]t follows indubitably," he then asserted, "that the negro is not a *human* being."[50]

This is an essential act of racism—the denial of membership in the human family to the person or group in question. Through the application of complex theories, the group to which a person belongs is shown to be lacking in human characteristics. Payne eventually applied it specifically to the question of whether the Negro could legitimately participate in, or even feel the depth of, Caucasian (Christian) religious ceremonies. Like Native activists who claim "whites" cannot participate in Indian rituals, he asserted that "blacks,"

the Negro, could not really engage in any Christian religious ceremonies. That Negroes appeared to do so was only out of their capacity for clever mimicry. They had, surreptitiously, watched the sons of Adam and, without the permission of either God or the sons of Adam, began to copy Christian ceremonies. This imitation, he charged, profaned the ceremonies:

> They can see the exact time (A.M. 235), when men—the negro—erected the first altar on earth; they had seen Adam, Cain, Abel, and Seth, erect such altars and call on the name of the Lord. They, too, could imitate them; they did then imitate; they then built their altars; they then called on the name of the Lord; they are yet imitating; they are yet profaning the name of the Lord, by calling on his name.[51]

George Tinker's comment about whites and mimicry is eerily similar. As he noted in the *Good Morning America* interview: "White people don't have any real feeling for these ceremonies; they are just mimicking them." Payne's belief that real religious participation by the Negro in Christianity was impossible on genetic grounds is echoed by John Boles in *Masters and Slaves in the House of the Lord:* "Some thought the Christian gospel too precious or refined an inheritance to be simplified sufficiently for the blacks' capabilities without perverting the message."[52] Again, this idea bears eerily similar parallels to Native activists' claims that participation by "whites" in Indian religious forms is impossible because they can neither understand their underlying reality or that such participation "mutates" or perverts the ceremonies themselves.

Payne continues his arguments by making the distinction that the Negro was a man—not a Man. For God said he wanted to create a Man in his image. The Negro, a man, was created first but not in God's image. He was an animal able to mimic Adam but still only an animal. Thus, any acceptance of equivalency between the Caucasian and the Negro was an error. Moreover, acceptance was blasphemy against God's laws. In fact, God flooded the world, he asserts, because the sons of Adam and Eve had been interbreeding with the Negro and thus weakening the race. Moreover, they were, as beings with souls, engaging

in intercourse with beasts possessing no souls. Thus, God punished them. Any future interblending would again result in divine anger.

> You can not elevate a beast to the level of a son of God—a son of Adam and Eve—but you may depress the sons of Adam and Eve, with their impress of the Almighty, down to the level of a beast. God has made one for immortality, and the other to perish with the animals of the earth. . . . The states or people that favor this equality and amalgamation of the white and black race, God will exterminate.[53]

The paths allotted for each race were distinctly different. Payne asserted: The Negroes had no soul and would die when their bodies died; Caucasians were possessed of immortal souls and would live again in Christ. These two ways could not be combined; it would be against the order of God's universe. Anyone who tried to violate that order—to combine ways and peoples who are by nature separate and distinct—would face divine retribution. Or as Matthew King, the Oglala Lakota elder, said: "Each people has their own ways. You cannot mix these ways together, because each people's ways are balanced. Destroying balance is a disrespect and very dangerous. This is why it's forbidden."[54]

The argument that each race possesses distinctly different "ways" that should not and cannot be combined is a hallmark of racist belief. Parallel assertions can be found in German racism, South African apartheid, and Black Nationalism. For instance, Alan Davies comments on common German theological beliefs just prior to World War II:

> Not only did the pietists rebel against the Enlightenment understanding of religion as merely another aspect of universal humanity, regarding it as an "abomination," but they emphasized the particularity of each historic form of the Christian faith. No longer was a universal natural religion detected underneath every particular religion and defined as the real religion of humanity. Instead, Christianity was individualized in much the same way as Germany: religion was a fundamental facet of each separate cultural and national entity,

a part of the living organism of the nation itself. . . . God, moreover, has imparted to each nation its own distinctive ethos, marking out "bounds and limits for the habitations of the different races of men on the face of the earth." . . . Nations, once they have developed to a "certain height," are degraded if they receive foreign elements into their corporate life; to do so is to act in an unnatural fashion. . . . [and they] will become imbued with an alien instead of a native spirit.[55]

South African theories of apartheid echo this idea:

Apartheid is sometimes described as a separate development, a term which suggests that under apartheid different races are given the opportunity of pursuing their respective and distinctive social and cultural evolutions. It is argued that only in this manner will these races be doing the will of God.[56]

And further:

[Specifically, it is suggested that] The races are like trees. Hence they must grow apart: each tree has its distinctive roots in the deep soil of its own proper spirituality, and each must grow as its own organic nature dictates. What is suitable for whites is not suitable for blacks, and vice versa.[57]

And it appears again in the writings of Black Nationalist writer W.E.B. Du Bois (compiled by Alan Davies):

"For it is certain that all human striving must recognize the hard limits of natural law, and that any striving, no matter how intense and earnest, which is against the constitution of the world, is vain." Natural law and the constitution of the world . . . [leave] us only to recognize the "subtle, delicate, and elusive" differences between the races . . . that constitute the "central thought in all history" Physical differences are real . . . but the deeper differences of mind and spirit—which, however, are related to the physical differences—are the truly important ones. Each race, consequently, is creative in its own way."[58]

the jews in spain in the fifteenth century

There are also close parallels to many of the propositions of Native activists and to many of their actions in a number of writings and events of fifteenth-century Spain. B. Netanyahu, in his seminal work *The Origins of the Inquisition in Fifteenth-Century Spain,* discusses at length the role racism played in the Inquisition and "the concept and advocacy of 'purity of blood' that so influenced Spanish society from the middle of the fifteenth century on."[59]

A great many Jews had been forced to convert to Christianity in the late fourteenth century. From the early to the middle of the fifteenth century these *conversos,* or New Christians, were an economically and socially influential group in the country. Some Old Christians felt disadvantaged in various sectors of the society, notably in employment in government, ascension to the nobility, and private enterprise. The Old Christians, thus, began a campaign to discredit the New Christians so as to be able to enact laws that would disenfranchise the *conversos* from their perceived strongholds in society. The Old Christians found their lever when they began to argue that race "endows man, among other things, with his basic moral qualities and dispositions, which in turn affect his religion."[60] Thus, despite their conversion to Christianity, the *conversos* were racially—genetically—still Jews and could never become "real" Christians. They would continue to be motivated by behaviors that were inherently—genetically—Jewish, behaviors that, by their essential nature, would corrupt Christianity and Spanish culture. Older, economic accusations with which the *conversos* had been labeled were restated and attached to this new (and ultimately more effective) assertion.

> Nor did the racists abandon the charges leveled at the conversos in the socio-economic field. Rather did they affirm, emphasize and broaden them by a multitude of new and even harsher charges, so that all the conversos' social-economic deeds appeared as one long sequence of offenses. Never did they suggest that any of these offenses stemmed from such circumstances as distress, or fear, or moral confusion, or provocation, or the like, which so often

lead man to crime. All the [conversos'] misdeeds, they stressed, had only one source: the converso's race, his mental constitution, his urge to do evil to all men of goodwill, and the ruthless egotism that unscrupulously commands him to use his victims' assets for his own profit. Thus we see how the racists grafted the social-economic crimes ascribed to the conversos onto the trunk of their racial theory.[61]

Discrimination against Jews on the basis of their race was not new, it had been common ever since the death of Christ. As early as the fourth century Christian writers had portrayed the Jew as "a creature whose mission in life was to serve the Devil and do his heinous work." Behaviors attributed to Jews were "such ghastly atrocities as the murder of Christian children for religious rites, the torture of Hosts by piercing or boiling them, and the use of sorcery to inflict cruel death upon multitudes of Christians."[62] (Those who have studied Indian history in the United States will recognize these behaviors as also being attributed to Indians and used as part of the justification to destroy indigenous cultures.) Netanyahu continues:

> What is most ominous about these charges is that all of them, save one or two, were attributed to all conversos. Accordingly, a whole people, or at least a whole tribe, numbering hundreds of thousands of individuals, consisted of criminals and base, vile men. Not one of them was presumed to be decent. All of them, regardless of their class or profession, were vicious, ruthless, and villainous. Their officials were traitors, their doctors killers, their druggists poisoners, their priests blackmailers, and all of them hardened habitual criminals devoid of any moral sense. Could there be such a society of men? Were the [conversos] such a society? Did none of them do a decent day's work, earn a living by honest toil, conscientiously fulfill the duties of office, or devote himself to higher ideals than robbery? The authors of this literature wanted people to believe the answer to all these questions was no.[63]

It is not hard to see where this thinking led: to the wholesale killing of converted Jews. There is an inexorable movement from this kind of thinking to violence. Historically, American Indians suffered from the same process.

Now, Indian activists call the other residents of the North American continent "whites," reducing a whole population to one term, and these "whites" are described in terms identical to those used to describe the *conversos*. "Whites" don't have any essential capacity to feel Indian ceremonies; they are naturally noncommunitarian and materialistic; they are seeking to turn all Indian spirituality into money-making ventures (indeed, they are concerned only with money); they do not care about Indian cultures or peoples; they commit genocide against Indians; they are intentionally trying to supplant Indians. In short there is nothing good or honest or honorable or wise about them. The best of them (as Deloria, Churchill, and others have commented) are "wholly sincere and utterly ignorant" people (still complicit in genocide nevertheless). The majority of them possess traits, because of their genetic makeup—their race alone—that make them dangerous to all Indians, however well-meaning they might seem. Mervyn Wright, director of the tribal water program for the Piute tribe, expresses this attitude in Bordewich's *Killing the White Man's Indian*. He argues that for the Indians to work together with whites to ensure enough water for all, white and Indian, is to engage in "white man's thinking." He comments that "to compromise is to risk corruption, to risk becoming like whites."[64]

Like the Old Christians in fifteenth-century Spain, the Native activists cannot acknowledge that someone of a different ethnic group can experience sincere conversion, that "white" people can experience the underlying spiritual reality of "Indian" ceremonies. They believe, as the Old Christians argued, that race "endows man, among other things, with his basic moral qualities and dispositions, which in turn affect his religion." And because the traits with which "whites" are endowed cause them to engage in behaviors that are dangerous to the survival of Indian peoples, violence is an inevitable, acceptable, and necessary response.

The Use of Violence in Restricting
Access to Religious Practice

Walter Echo-Hawk, a member of the Pawnee Nation and an attorney for the Native American Rights Fund (NARF), stated in a *Good Morning America* interview (March 6, 1994): "Native People are becoming increasingly concerned about the exploitation of Native religion by non-Indians in the United States. Just recently the National Congress of American Indians essentially declared war on this particular issue." His comment is of particular concern for several reasons. Echo-Hawk's work in the field of religious freedoms has been of great benefit to many people, as has the work of the Native American Rights Fund. However, his comments imply (he relates the information calmly and casually without distancing himself or NARF from the National Congress position) that he and the Native American Rights Fund (for whom he is shown as working in the interview) support the National Congress of American Indians' position and also advocate "war" against non-Indians who are following the religion of their choice.

Echo-Hawk, a tireless advocate for the repatriation of the bones of Indian ancestors and religious artifacts held in museums across the country, has insisted that the First Amendment be applied *equally* to all Americans (including Native Americans). He has frequently lamented the double standard (when officials carry out the law) of discriminating against one group because their form of worship is offensive or misunderstood by some. He ends one of his articles on the subject ("Repatriation, Reburial, and Religious Rights") with a strong and unambiguous statement: "The formation of productive and positive relationships between culturally diverse people should be based upon bonds of mutual respect—not chains of religious oppression."[65] His refusal to publicly recognize that people of all skin colors may be called to a particular religious devotion and his justification of the attempt by an Indian group (because of their strong feelings) to limit a particular religious or social activity to persons of certain skin color or ethnicity or blood purity through the threat of violence (war) *is*, however, a form of religious oppression. Robert Heinlein

commented on this long ago: "When any government, or any church for that matter, undertakes to say to its subjects, 'This you may not read, this you must not see, this you are forbidden to know,' the end result is tyranny and oppression, no matter how holy the motives."[66] The position of Indian activists in condoning violence to keep "their" religion out of the hands of those they deem offensive to them is tyranny. Regrettably, it is also historically common.

The control of religious practice and insight, ceremonies, and religious objects through the use of force has been attempted before, notably by the Catholic Church in the Middle Ages. Frank Darling's three-volume history of Christian healing looks at this episode in some detail, noting that after the Vatican had consolidated its power, "it stressed the view that the church was the sole and final authority in the interpretation of the Bible and Christian doctrine."

> The church took punitive measures when this policy was challenged by the Cathars (also called Albigenses) and the Waldenses who embraced "heretical" forms of Christianity and who translated portions of the Bible. These dissidents living in southern France and northern Italy were brutally suppressed through the use of military action by French civil rulers and by Inquisition directed from Rome. In 1227 a church council forbade any layman from owning any part of the Bible.[67]

After this edict from Rome, the church began using it to persecute individual offenders.

> In 1380 John Wycliffe, an Oxford scholar, completed an English translation of the Bible that quickly spread among many clergy and the laity. Wycliffe had been assisted by Nicolas de Hereford, who was condemned for heresy and tortured by orders from the Vatican. In this controversy church officials declared that "the jewel of the clergy has become the toy of the laity." The replacement of Latin with an English translation was described as "the grunting of pigs and the roaring of lions." Wycliffe died in 1384 before he could be punished by the church, yet his bones were exhumed and burned and his ashes thrown into the Swift River by an order from clerical authorities.

Other suppressive actions were taken by the church. In 1396 every squire in England was required to take an oath not to read or possess a copy of the Bible translated by Wycliffe and his assistants. In 1401 the church ordered English Bibles to be burned. In 1415 a church restriction stated: "It is forbidden under pain of cursing that no man should have or draw any text of holy scripture into English without license of the bishop."

In the early fifteenth century a Czech scholar named John Hus was influenced by Wycliffe's translations during Bohemia's struggle for religious and national freedom. Among the writings of Hus was the "Scripture Principle" proclaiming that "the only law of the church is the Bible, above all the New Testament." He was condemned by the church and burned at the stake in 1415.

Another English scholar, William Tyndale, who lived near the end of the Middle Ages, succeeded in translating the Bible into the English language and distributing it throughout England. . . . Tyndale met much opposition from church authorities in England, and in 1524 he fled to the continent. He was captured in Belgium by Vatican officials, and in 1536 he was executed for heresy. These early advocates of the right to translate the Bible into the vernacular helped in preparing the way for Martin Luther and the Protestant Reformation. One of Luther's major issues with Rome was the right of every Christian to have direct access to the Bible.[68]

Through World War II the Catholic Church publicly denounced Martin Luther, claiming that he was an agent of the devil and that all Christians other than Catholics were deluded and guilty of creating a bastardized version of Christianity that was not the true religion. Protestantism was, in fact, a "virus," which had been injected into the body of Christ to confuse the faithful.[69] However, to many people, the spread of the use of sweat lodge and sacred pipe is akin to the emergence of Protestantism. Amanda Porterfield notes that "in certain hidden but important ways, American Indian spirituality is like a Christian reform movement within American society. . . . [Native spiritual teachers] call all Americans to a truer and purer understanding of God, to an ethic of peace and justice, and to an aesthetic of natural simplicity."[70] But, in response,

like the Catholic Church, Native activists are supporting a declaration of violence against a religious group because of their ethnicity and the temerity of their group to follow a particular kind of religious worship. Like the church in the Middle Ages, individual activists and activist groups are asserting that the Bible (or the Pipe or the Sweat Lodge or the Vision Quest) be prohibited to certain groups of people. The pipe, the "jewel of the [Indian], has become the toy of the [white]." An "outrage[d]" Ward Churchill has called on people, Indian and white, to "shut down the movement's meetings, burn its sweatlodges, impound . . . the sacred objects it desecrates, and otherwise make its functioning impossible." As for those who use Indian ceremonies in a way he finds offensive? He asserts it is an appropriate response to kill "whites" who use Indian ceremonies—although he finds the prison sentences for such acts "daunting."[71]

Bruce Lee, like Native teachers such as Sun Bear, faced similar opposition when he began teaching martial arts to non-Chinese in California in the mid-1960s. The Chinese elders in the Bay Area insisted he stop sharing "secrets" with whites. When he refused, arguing that he would teach any who came to him, his back was broken. Not expected to walk again, his hospital recuperation lasted a year.

The Native activists, like Lee's detractors, feel that they have to protect their culture and religion from the contamination of whites. They believe that it is wrong for "all the common people" to have access to the bibles of Earth-centered spirituality. And many of them would like nothing more than to have the powers of the Catholic Church of the Middle Ages to remedy the situation.

cleansing the tribe of infection

The dangers of this kind of thinking and labeling are, of course, well known. Nazi Germany epitomizes it in its most virulent form. Although best known for their attempted extermination of the Jews, the Nazis were attempting to exterminate any group of people they felt to be a danger to the strength,

spiritual integrity, and purity of the German, the Aryan, people. (Aryan, for the Germans, did not mean "white" people. The Aryans were the original indigenous tribe of Germany, and it is this tribal group that the Germans are referring to when the word "Aryan" is used. It is the equivalent of Lakota or Ojibway.) Thus, the Nazis began ethnic cleansing of gypsies, homosexuals, the handicapped, blacks, and the Slavs. Some twenty million were killed, primarily Jews (six million) and Slavs (eleven million).

According to their writings, the Nazis did not act out of hatred but as physicians. In their minds they were curing the German people of the corruption that had infected them—the virus in their blood.

> Hitler and the extreme theorists around him literally believed that the Aryan race had become ill, that it had been rendered ill by the Jewish infection. The Jews were a special problem, but other inferior races were also a problem. Therapy took the form of getting rid of the infection. That meant getting rid of the Jews. The object of therapy was not the Jews or the Gypsies or any other group; it was the Aryan race. The way of curing the Aryan race was to get rid of whatever had made it ill.[72]

This obsession with the purity of the race sprang from a resurgence and blending of occultism, spiritualism, and science in late nineteenth-century Europe. The idea of a specific "life force," which was carried in the blood of a people or tribe and from which their power as a people came, was a central component of one form of the spiritualism that flowered in Europe from 1880 to 1930. This life force could be weakened and the people as a tribe and culture also weakened if the blood was contaminated by being blended with that of other races, especially races that were inferior or carried undesirable traits in their "blood force." Hitler seized on this concept in his propaganda campaign during his rise to power. The German people embraced the belief that they would again be happy and strong if they could only purge the blood of the German people of its contamination.[73] They felt that their sorry condition, their lack of strength and power, was a result of being contaminated by other racial

thinking, culture, and blood. The horror with which the Nazis viewed con-tamination by the Slavic peoples, for instance, can be seen in this passage from the German SS main office.

> The sub-human, this apparently fully equal creation of nature, when seen from the biological viewpoint, with hands, feet, and a sort of brain, with eyes and a mouth, nevertheless is quite a different, a dreadful creature, is only an imitation of man with man-resembling features, but inferior to any animal as regards intellect and soul. In its interior, this being is a cruel chaos of wild, unrestricted passions, with a nameless will to destruction, with a most prim-itive lust, and of unmasked depravity.
> For not everything is alike that has a human face.[74]

Native activists' assertions have clearly begun to reflect strong elements of this kind of thinking. Indian alcoholism, poverty, and lack of education are caused by whites. The general debility, lack of strength, and purity of Indian culture are the fault of whites. Any Indian who freely interacts with whites has been contaminated and consequently has begun to think like whites, to focus on money and ego-glorification, and is now a danger to the culture. The focus is on some special essence that Indians possess and that has to be protected from infection by whites. As one Lakota woman noted, "The Creator gave each Lakota their own special Lakota genes."[75] And these genes, this essence, this blood, have to be protected—period.

The views of Native activists bear another similarity to German ideology. Nazi leaders such as Adolf Hitler and Anton Drexler asserted that Jewish ele-ments in German society were creating works of art that, by their very existence in society, undermined German strength and national life. They insisted on "legal action against a tendency in art and literature which undermines our national life, and the closing of cultural events violating the preceding demands."[76] Like Nazi ideologues, Native activists such as Ward Churchill and the National Indian Youth Council (NIYC) have insisted that no action is too strong if it stops the spread of Native spirituality to whites by people they deem "offensive."

The NIYC asserted: "Anything you can do to [the Bear Tribe] will not be enough"; and Churchill, in December 1990, said that people should take actions such as "denouncing," "boycotting," and "demanding that local book stores stop carrying [their books]."[77] Following a similar thought process in May 1933, the Nazis issued "the first blacklists for lending libraries and book-stores . . . including more than 150 'unacceptable' authors."[78] The Florida Indian Alliance, sixty years later, issued a list (to be regularly updated) of teachers and authors whose work, they assert, is undermining the Indian nations and their spiritual life. The list contains over 200 names, both Indian and non-Indian.[79] Some bookstores have canceled appearances or stopped carrying books by authors who are on the list.[80] It is reasonable to assume that if white activists advocated the prohibition of Indian writings and were able to convince book-stores to stop carrying their material or cancel their public talks, there would be loud charges of First Amendment violations.

The results of Nazi tactics and assertions are well known; the conse-quences were horrible. Less well known, but crucial to an understanding of this phenomenon, is that the Germans, like the American Indians, had been bit-terly conquered by a European power—the French under Napoleon. Their response to this was similar to that of Native American activists—activist Ger-man writers began advocating the restoration of the purity of the German tribe and the spiritual traditions that had been degraded by subjugation from a for-eign race. Interestingly, some of the German comments echo George Tinker's assertion that the final act of cultural genocide against Indians "is the individ-ualizing of Indian communitarian structures and ceremonies." German purists insisted that "such institutions as communal rather than private property were distinctive 'marks of the Aryan race'" and that the domination of Germany (the Aryan tribes) by the French had destroyed their communitarian structures.[81]

The German approach was not the only one of its kind in this century. In South Africa the state policy of apartheid was used to repress the blacks; and in Bosnia, ethnic cleansing and genocide have occurred. Bosnia is instructive because at one time the rhetoric of Serbian intellectuals was, like that of Ward Churchill, only rhetoric. The three cultural groups in the region occupied by

Yugoslavia (known as the Balkans)—Moslem, Croat, and Serbian—represent ethnic enclaves of three of the world's major religious and cultural civilizations. In this one small region of the world the Moslem-Arabic-Ottoman empire, the Catholic-Western European-Roman empire, and the Eastern Orthodox–Slavic–Russian empire all meet. Throughout history the major powers have periodically (militarily and diplomatically) played out their influence in world affairs in this region. The region's people go through periods of relative peace where they intermarry and form rich and culturally diverse communities. Then power interests begin capitalizing on old beliefs, fears, and prejudices to gain power in the region.

In the latter half of the twentieth century, Bosnia, and especially the town of Sarajevo, was a place where people of many cultural traditions lived in peace. The factionalism that had last torn the country during World War II seemed permanently resolved. But after the death of Tito, groups seeking to gain control of Yugoslavia begin playing on old ethnic and religious grievances. During World War II, many Croats, called the Ustashas, had worked with the Nazis and engaged in horrendous acts against the Serbs. The wounds from those atrocities, to a great degree healed under Tito, were inflamed after his death by a number of politicians.

A group of university intellectuals, headed by Dobrica Cosic, from the Serbian Academy of Sciences published a document called the Memorandum in 1986. In it they set forth the arguments for keeping the Serbian people separate and distinct and the rationales later used to justify ethnic cleansing in Yugoslavia.[82] The only way for the Serbian people to be strong again, they claimed, was to assert their identity and begin eliminating any elements that would weaken or had weakened it. This same thinking eventually took hold in Croatia and among the Moslems until all three parties were polarized. Personal identities in the region began to be described in an exclusively ethnic and religious manner. Misha Glenny, a journalist who covered the Balkan conflict from its beginning, reports in his book, *The Fall of Yugoslavia*, that "this process of differentiation [of people's ethnicity and religious orientation] was the initial step towards war in the republic."[83] The process of differentiation continued,

the rhetoric became more strident, passions were inflamed, violence began to break out. Civil war began; the war escalated until the most horrible acts of ethnic cleansing became routine.

The grim reminder in the lesson of Yugoslavia's collapse is that it was, like Germany, a modern, peaceful, cultured, twentieth-century nation. But that did not stop their collapse. Once groups begin singling out others along racial lines, justify and use violence to achieve ethnic ends, all sides end up in the same position. There is then no difference between them or their positions.[84]

Glenny says of Yugoslavia:

Croats and Serbs argued endlessly with me as to why Serbs and Croats, respectively, were congenital monsters. They would cite history, religion, education, and biology as reasons. . . . In extreme situations, nationalism appears to neutralize that part of the mind which is able to fathom complex equations. Instead, action is motivated by a single Leninist principle: "Those who are not for us, are against us." Or as George Orwell paraphrased it in *Animal Farm:* "Four legs good. Two legs bad!"[85]

Or as Russell Means puts it:

If you do [respect our proprietary rights to our ceremonies], you're an ally and we're ready and willing to join hands with you on other issues. If you do not, you are at best a thief. More importantly, you are a thief of the sort who is willing to risk undermining our sense of the integrity of our cultures for your own perceived self-interest. That means you are complicit in a process of cultural genocide, or at least attempted cultural genocide, aimed at American Indian people. That makes you an enemy, to say the least. And believe me when I say we're prepared to deal with you as such.[86]

In Bosnia, as the rhetoric and violence increased, the more polarized the positions became. Each group summed up the other in simple terms—"Croat," "Serb," "Moslem"—and those simple terms, denoting a whole people, took on all the demonizing elements that the rhetoric had attributed to the particular group in question. Any contact—marriage, shared communities, shared

countries—came to represent a danger to the purity of the group. As Glenny observes: "The doctrine of including a minority group . . . becomes less acceptable as the doctrine of 'national purity' strengthens."[87] Members of the different groups, often close friends, came to passionately believe the most horrible things about the other side. And each atrocity committed as the war progressed confirmed those beliefs. One Moslem noted: "They want to create a Moslem reservation, like the ones in North America for Indians, only with much less land. The only industry which the Moslems will then have is tourism—people will then come and pay to see the only indigenous Moslems in Europe."[88] Croats believe that the Serbs are inhuman beasts who only live to destroy Croats and Moslems; Moslems think that about both of the others; Serbs are sure that Croats and Moslems are a virus, a horrible disease infecting the region. "The Orthodox, the Catholics, or the Moslems can only claim victory when the heretics have been wiped out or expelled from their homes."[89] The only way to preserve their way of life, their unique culture and identity, is to destroy the others. One Serb policeman told Glenny: "We cannot let them [the Moslems] form an Islamic state here . . . I don't understand why you people outside don't realize we are fighting for Europe against a foreign religion."

Eventually the positions were completely polarized and as the fighting intensified, with bodies everywhere, it was not uncommon to find the dead with their faces literally sliced off—they no longer had an identity, a "face." They are the faceless, unknown, unrecognized, nonhuman enemy. The Croats, Moslems, or Serbs could not then see themselves in the other, could not see any common humanity. Glenny reveals a deep insight when he says: "It is the awful recognition that these primitive beasts on the other side of the barricade are their brothers which has led to the violence assuming such ghastly proportions in Bosnia. The only way that fighters can deal with this realization is to exterminate the opposite community. How else does one explain the tradition of facial mutilation in this region?"[90]

Those who play the race card and utter cries of genocide should go to Bosnia to see genocide in its physical expression. The viciousness of people

polarized around racial identity is beyond a matter of opinion; we have seen that option explored to terrible dimensions during this century. Unremittant dehumanizing attacks on "whites" or "Euro-Americans," to the extent that their culture and humanity are denied any substance, will polarize people in this country just as they were polarized in Bosnia. It is, however, possible to find avenues of *mutual* connection; we must find them or we have before us only the Bosnian solution.

Raoul Hilberg, a professor specializing in studies of the Jewish holocaust, makes an important point about how conflicts between people eventually become genocidal. After years of research, he concludes that it is not the common people who begin these conflicts; they begin among the most highly educated. Academics and scholarly writers formulate a theoretical position outlining the inferiority of a group or the superiority of another (usually one they belong to); eventually the body of writing becomes acceptable and is, slowly and over time, incorporated into the country's laws. The state, through its exercise of police powers, then carries out the new laws. Hilberg notes that the scholars were endlessly concerned with essential identity (Indian or white). They argued endlessly with what to do with the half-Jew; what to do with a mixed marriage. What rights would they have? What could they own? Where could they live? Legally, could their temples be closed? (Or should they be burned like "white" sweat lodges?)[91]

Hilberg's progression seems universal: Professors find a seemingly intelligent rationale for the inferiority of an identifiable group of people, lawyers draft laws based on the rationale (in order to protect the society), legislators pass the laws that begin a process of removing rights from the identified group, the police and courts carry out the laws. As this process escalates, the common people become more and more caught up in the rhetoric, and violence begins to break out. The initial stages of the process are incremental and lead predictably, logically, to genocide. If there is an ancient wound, old emotions of pain upon which to build such a process, so much the better. And so, speaking at the Conference on Evil, Hilberg asks with a slight smile, "Who did it?" And he answers with a chilling vividness. "The professionals."[92]

Native activists are participants in a process that is inexorably leading to conflict along racial lines. Whites, many of whom are sympathetic to Indian claims (and many of whom are in the New Age communities that are being attacked) are in the beginning stages of a backlash to activist polemic; they are, in turn, becoming polarized.[93] Academics and scholars, such as Ward Churchill, are developing a body of work exclusively built on the dangers and inherent inhumanity of the white race. Most or all white acts are the actions of oppressors against oppressed groups coming out of either conscious or unconscious motivations. Any disagreement with this party line, any discussion of freedom of religion or minority racism is de facto an act of racism. Churchill makes this point by quoting Kwame Turé (Stokely Carmichael): "Where the old racism ruled through physical violence, racism in its new form asserts its dominance through sheer mendacity. Racism has become covert in its expression, hiding behind a mask of calm and reason. The key to understanding racism today is that it inevitably parades itself about, cloaked in the garb of anti-racism. It is therefore far more dangerous, powerful, and difficult to combat than ever before."[94]

This kind of academic pursuit and its conclusions are coming to be accepted more and more casually. White people are beginning to have their individual faces removed. They no longer can be good friends, neighbors, people capable of love and a deep experience of the sacred, people who also fear, or people who struggle toward personal humanity. They are "white." What remains is a culture from which all individual humanity is removed. If they disagree with the Churchill-Means position on allowed spiritual activities, they are enemies and the activists are "prepared to deal with [them] as such."

Arguments presented by many Native activists match nearly word for word arguments presented by the fifteenth-century Christians about *conversos*, Nazis about Jews, South Africans and Americans in the southern states about blacks, Bosnians about each other, *and* Christians and Europeans about Indians.[95] This road will not lead to a place any of us want to go. The increasingly regular occurrences of war along ethnic and racial lines should alert all of us to be extremely cautious whenever the process begins again—however innocuous it seems. Once we become locked into a polarization of each other based on skin

color, ethnic origin, religious orientation, sex, or any other factor along these lines, we are a million miles from the sacredness of Earth, from any connection to our sacred source. There is a learning—a deep teaching—in this separation from the Earth and the sacred, but I think, I hope, I pray we have learned all of it that we need to.

part three

healing our wounds

prologue

Ahimsa teaches us to entertain the same respect for the religious faiths of others as we accord to our own, thus admitting the imperfection of the latter. This admission will be readily made by a seeker of Truth, who follows the law of Love. If we had attained the full vision of Truth, we would no longer be mere seekers, but have become one with God, for Truth is God. But being only seekers, we prosecute our quest, and are conscious of our imperfection. And if we are imperfect ourselves, religion as conceived by us must also be imperfect. We have not realized religion in its perfection, even as we have not realized God. Religion of our conception, being thus imperfect, is always subject to a process of evolution. And if all faiths outlined by men are imperfect, the question of comparative merit does not arise. All faiths constitute a revelation of Truth, but all are imperfect and liable to error. Reverence for other faiths need not blind us to their faults. We must be keenly alive to the defects of our own faith also, yet not leave

it on that account, but try to overcome those defects. Looking at all religions with an equal eye, we would not only not hesitate, but would think it our duty, to blend into our faith every acceptable feature of other faiths.

Even as a tree has a single trunk, but many branches and leaves, so there is one true and perfect Religion, but it becomes many, as it passes through the human medium. The one Religion is beyond all speech. Imperfect men put it into such language as they can command, and their words are interpreted by other men equally imperfect. Whose interpretation is to be held to be the right one? Everybody is right from his own standpoint, but it is not impossible that everybody is wrong. Hence the necessity of tolerance, which does not mean indifference to one's own faith, but a more intelligent and purer love for it. Tolerance gives us a spiritual insight, which is as far from fanaticism as the North Pole from the South. True knowledge of religion breaks down the barriers between faith and faith.[1]

chapter seven

the restoration of the indigenous mind

I am the son of white slave owners and black maids; dead Union soldiers and rich southern plantation owners; a signer of the Declaration of Independence and English aristocrats; Cherokee tribal people and implacable Indian killers; fundamentalist Chris-tian ministers and Indian, Celtic, and European pagans; powerful political physicians who outlawed alternative medicine and midwives and herbalists; Irish freedom fighters and English soldiers; poor Irish, Scottish, Dutch, English, German, Austrian, and American farmers and peasants and rich industrialists and landowners; and my body is made of the soil, rocks, trees, and air of North America. My mind has been formed by human beings out of long years of history and continents that I have never seen. My spirit has been forged by the hand of God, the sweet breath of the sacred pipe, and the upwelling sacred power of Earth.

The heady rhythms of tribal Africa, diluted by ocean miles and four hundred years, were rocked into my body through the sweet smells and gentle walking of my grandmothers' maids; the songs of Ireland, muted by distance and generations, still sing melancholy sacred wisdom in my blood; the primal pipes of Scotland call me to stand with my people; and Cherokee plant song stirs me to dawn awakening. Over and above them all thunders the sacred song of Universe and of Earth. It is a cacophony of sound or a great symphony of the song of humankind and the sacred in interblended harmony. Sometimes, simultaneously, it is both.

healing the ancestors

I am the son of this land and of these people. Their lives, in part, shape my life; their spirits live within me. How can there be harmony on this continent if these ancestors war among each other in ourselves and between ourselves? It would be easier, perhaps, to be the son of an unblemished, sacred, healed, tribally pure father and mother whose healthy purity stretches back into the dawn of time—I, their whole expression. But there are few of us that can make any such claim. We play the hand that Creator has given us.

When the first stirrings of the sacred call us to begin the journey to our own humanity and the sacred center, we begin where we are and the lessons that we learn are specific to our selves, the environment in which we live, the country in which we are born, the ancestors who throb in our history, and our particular destiny. We have in common with others elements that overlap; most basic to us all is our expression as matter out of spirit.

Malidoma Patrice Somé, the Dagara teacher from Burkina Faso in West Africa, makes the seminal point that it will be impossible for healing to occur in this country until the spirits of our ancestors are healed. The descendants of tribal peoples and the descendants of Europeans, of slaves and slave owners, of persecutors and of persecuted, feel daily the unhealed spirits within ourselves. The spirits of our ancestors cry out for healing in all of us.

In *Living by the Word*, Alice Walker has written of her struggles to accept the white slave owner who is her ancestor through rape. He comes; she does not like it, but still he comes, saying, I am in you, I am you, I am. How difficult to accept the face in the mirror. Easier to accept the one done to than the one who did. How difficult to find in ourselves, intricately interwoven into sinew, blood, and bone, those we have demonized—those whose faces we removed long ago.

For one's sacred path to mature, the ancestors—*all* the ancestors—must eventually be honored. Their spirits live in this land, in these trees and rocks, in the air, and in ourselves. Their influences can be felt in motivations, feelings, thoughts, and uncalled-for memories of other times. They sometimes come in the night and speak to us. We learn them through long years, one by one. We will never learn them all.

Like the land and its stories of Genesis, the ancestors do not need books and photographs in which to learn their bloody deeds and their pain; they speak it each day in rhythms and patterns of breath, skin, walk, gesture. Oppressed and oppressor live, breathe, eat, and sleep in all of us. As our consciousness is focused more deeply, refined to ever subtler distinctions, their lives come ever more clearly into our awareness.

As I mature, I struggle ever to accept them, love them, grant them peace. The closer they are to me in time, the more distinct they are, the clearer their influence. They hover, eager for attention, for peace, for forgiveness, for that misused word—love. When they receive it, they begin to sleep a peaceful sleep—they do not need to wander restlessly. With this healing, I—and we— begin, as Chief Joseph of the Nez Perce said, "to wash out the bloody spots from the face of the earth that were made by brothers' hands."

Healing the ancestors begins with those who come easiest to mind and heart and it progresses to those we wish never to forgive, never to love. It begins with their image in a picture or in our minds, the feelings those images engender, until we know them in ourselves, until we feel them rest comfortably in ourselves, until we understand that their face is our face.

Some of them are very bad: They committed acts of cruelty and genocide and rape. Some of them are decent and kind: They healed the sick, taught their

children to love, sacrificed themselves in war for higher ideals. But the blood of all of them flows in our veins, their teachings echo in us in family scripts and patterns—the good and the bad. Without making the journey to honoring them, they—and we—find no rest.

The rhetoric between "Indian" and "white" is polarized to that of oppressed and oppressor. There are few "pure-blood" Indians in this time and land; the blood of other nations flows within their veins as it does in mine. We are all mixed bloods to one extent or another. It is not only "all our relations" that is truth but also "all our ancestors." The lack of honor of *our* ancestors hangs between us and keeps us polarized. Indians have bitterly fought for a healing of ancestral dishonor especially through the repatriation and reburial of bones and remains. For ancestral healing, non-Indians must support this process and, in addition, I suggest, explore two other avenues.

First, they should come to terms with the ancestors who participated in crimes against the Indian peoples in the past and forgive them so that they, too, can find rest. Indian people also must come to terms with the whites that live within them, who are their ancestors. For all of us, to fail to do so is to hate the self. Non-Indians must resolve their feelings of shame and hatred for their ancestors; they must forgive them and understand them.

Second, I suggest, I affirm, that no lasting healing can occur between Indian and non-Indian peoples until the government of the United States makes a formal apology to the Indian peoples for its lack of honor in past dealings. If our country is ever to find honor again, the government must take this action. Governmental actions have made a mockery of the Bill of Rights and the Constitution and placed a rot within the body politic that will continue to undermine our peoples.

The scars, of course, cannot be completely erased. But they can be acknowledged, and forgiveness can be asked. It is not necessary for forgiveness to be given but it must be asked for if honor is to be restored. A precedent for a governmental apology has been set by the recent gesture toward Japanese-American internees of World War II. The damage to the Japanese-Americans cannot be totally repaired by a monetary payment, but the impact on long-term healing has been great.

We will, from time to time, fail to live up to the highest behaviors and ideals, but we must make the journey toward them and toward healing. The Constitution, based as it is on the sacred gift of Creator through Degawanidah, offers this possibility. As African-American legislator Barbara Jordan acknowledged on July 25, 1974 (at the impeachment hearings of Richard Nixon):

> Earlier today we heard the beginning of the preamble to the Constitution of the United States—"We the people." It's a very eloquent beginning, but when that document was completed on the 17th of September in 1787 I was not included in that "We the people." I felt somehow that George Washington and Alexander Hamilton just left me out by mistake. But through the process of amendment, interpretation, and court decision I finally have been included in "We the people." . . . My faith in the Constitution is whole, it is complete, it is total.[1]

Degawanidah's mission was successful. He did bring the Good Mind to the people and it lives still in the Constitution and the Iroquois Nation.[2] It is more than a document of secular humanism. It carries within it the sacred power of Creator and it has touched all people on this Earth. It is a good thing that Degawanidah brought this Good Mind embodied in the Great Law of Peace. For it to continue to work for the people, there is only one hope—that all people be equally treated under the rule of law; that government makes no promises it does not keep; that there is no group, identified by race, religion, or profession, that is ever allowed to dominate the freedoms of others—no matter how holy or beneficial they believe their objectives to be. The expression of the Constitution must be whole, it must be complete, it must be total. And in making things whole, as Barbara Jordan noted, "it must be reason and not passion which must guide our deliberations, guide our debate, and guide our decision."[3] The vilification of a whole race of people is not reason—it is passion and it undermines the fabric of that which was brought to us by Degawanidah. This fabric must be made whole. It cannot *be* whole unless the government of the United States is willing to make it whole—by apologizing to the Indian nations.

This proposal is, of course, idealistic. It may never happen. But if it is never proposed, it will never even be considered. But consider how wondrous it would be if, one day, representatives of the United States went to each of the sovereign Indian nations and delivered a formal apology and asked for forgiveness. How much difference it would make in our relations. But, of course, this idea is visionary. It is . . . imaginative. It may never happen.[4]

In addition, we must strive toward peace and resolution in our own hearts. It is fitting to remember Black Elk's comments.

> The first peace, which is the most important, is that which comes within the souls of men when they realize their relationship, their oneness, with the universe and all its Powers, and when they realize that at the center of the universe dwells Wakan-Tanka, and that this center is really everywhere, it is within each of us. This is the real Peace, and the others are but reflections of this. The second peace is that which is made between two individuals, and the third is that which is made between two nations. But above all you should understand that there can never be peace between nations until there is first known that true peace which, as I have often said, is within the souls of men.[5]

One of the basic preludes to finding that peace with our own hearts is to forgive and heal our ancestors. Then when we come to make peace between nations, our ancestors will not be crying and we will not be feeling shame for them. This shame, which so many feel and which so many descendants of oppressed peoples activate in dialogue, is a great wound between us. Its presence in dialogue and heart makes more wounds. There are those who have sought to understand and heal these kinds of wounds. Two of the most powerful avenues to this kind of healing can be found in Steve Karpman's drama triangle analysis and Gandhi's development of *ahimsa*.

the drama triangle and ahimsa

The drama triangle, formulated in the late 1960s by Steve Karpman, a transactional analysis psychotherapist, reflects a basic interaction pattern that is composed of three positions: persecutor, victim, rescuer.[6] Karpman chose a triangle as the symbol of this dynamic because a triangle can balance or stabilize on any of its bases. He points out that none of the positions are what they seem; they are all aspects of the same underlying emotional worldview. And that worldview can express itself in three forms—persecutor, rescuer, victim. Especially important is his observation that because of this basic identity *any person in the drama triangle can change position at any time to any other position.* Resolution of the problems being acted out in the drama triangle is not possible unless the game is abandoned. The drama triangle dynamic is its own end. Brooke Medicine Eagle remarks on this dynamic:

> Studies have shown for years that there is a dreadful cycle set up when there is victimization. It is known as the victim-persecutor cycle, and reminds us that when someone is victimized and abused, they tend, in turn, to victimize others through blame and abuse. History and personal experience make it clear that Native people all around the globe have been terribly victimized. This makes them very vulnerable to this cycle of victimizing others; and this certainly shows up many times in the current cross-cultural conflict.
>
> They are often joined by another player in this vicious cycle—the rescuer. This is someone who gets their self-worth by "saving others" . . . who wants to "be somebody" by "defending the victims." Often this turns into more abusive tactics.
>
> What we all need to do rather than play savior or find another victim to abuse is to get out of the system altogether, and find ways of cooperating for the health and well-being of all.[7]

In the drama triangle, one always begins in the victim position. An act of abuse occurs; pain and damage are the result. In attempting to come to terms

with the abusive action, the individual struggles with many of the emotions of being a victim: "It was my fault. I deserved it. God wanted it to happen. If I am good, maybe it will go away." This stage often gives way to anger as the pain of abuse is worked through. The anger is expressed as the victim draws a line in the sand and declares, "This far and no farther"; the victim becomes a kind of warrior and finds within a certain strength of purpose. Victims will often then begin an active assault on their abuser (for instance, an alcoholic or abusive father) or join groups (such as Mothers Against Drunk Driving) that attack a segment of society in which their abuser can be included. At this point, the dynamic solidifies. The rescuer "helps" victims who have suffered from a similar hurt and persecutes anyone perceived to be a victimizer or persecutor.

To people in the drama triangle every other player is defined in drama triangle dynamics. If you are not a victim or a rescuer, you are, by a process of elimination, a persecutor. (At the very least you are allied with persecutors and that makes you complicit in a process of persecution.) People who have been persecutors but who come to understand their behavior often wish to make up for their past harm and shift position on the triangle. They become victims (for example, children of adult alcoholics), or rescuers of people like those they used to victimize, or persecutors of similar victimizers. Many people, locked into one of the positions, actively invite people to play either of the other two positions, often using subtle and well-established interaction patterns to engage people in the dynamic. The only way to sustained healing, however, is to stop playing and depart the drama triangle completely. The only way to win the game is not to play.

Many Native activists, however, are stuck in the victim-persecutor cycle; through the lens with which they see the world, everyone is in one of the three positions. They cannot see the world in any other way. Because they are stuck in the dynamic, they perpetuate it through emotional and physical assault on others. The cycle of abuse continues.

Gandhi, one of the few social activists who understood that resolution can never occur in the drama triangle, was actively concerned with finding a social, spiritual, and personal resolution of this dynamic. There are close

parallels between Gandhi's understanding of the successful attainment of ahimsa and the journey through the drama triangle. Ahimsa, a Jainist and Buddhist doctrine, is based on the principle of avoiding injury to any sentient creature through act or thought. It literally means "not harming" and is often translated as nonviolence, love, or even lack of resistance. Gandhi applied it as a powerful force of dissent and political action. By using ahimsa in political action, one receives suffering without trying to keep it out of the heart; one does not respond to suffering by violence or running away; one embraces the source of the suffering. Gandhi used the principle of ahimsa to respond to the colonization of the Indian people, many of whom reacted to abuses of the British government as either victims or persecutors. In other words, they either were too afraid to do anything (just felt beat down) or they became angry and responded with revolutionary violence and rhetoric.

Within the tradition of ahimsa, Gandhi noted similar roles to those that occur in the drama triangle. He identified them as the coward, the violent man, and the social activist who has not given up attachment. When these are given up for authenticity, when one "quits the game," one achieves ahimsa in political dissent and social activism. The coward, Gandhi noted, is often mistaken for a person of nonviolence. But, he notes, "he who trembles or takes to his heels the moment he sees two people fighting is not nonviolent, but a coward. A nonviolent person will lay down his life in preventing such quarrels."[8] Eventually, the coward becomes ashamed or tired of his cowardice, of his victimization, and he transforms it into anger in order to charge himself up to enter battle. This transformation is crucial. Gandhi observes: "My creed of nonviolence is an extremely active force. It has no room for cowardice or even weakness. There is hope for a violent man to be some day nonviolent, but there is none for a coward."[9] The violent person is closer to ahimsa because he is willing to die for something he believes in. The danger in this transition, however, is that the use of anger (of persecution and the rescuer) may become permanent, which will never be effective in the long run. Gandhi says: "I object to violence because when it appears to do good, the good is only temporary; the evil it does is permanent. . . . However much I may sympathize with and admire

worthy motives, I am an uncompromising opponent of violent methods even to serve the noblest of causes. . . . Experience convinces me that permanent good can never be the outcome of untruth and violence."[10]

There is a tendency, when trying to transcend the drama triangle or break out of the coward-violent dynamic, for one to assume the role of the loving rescuer. This position greatly resembles the one exhibited by those who transcend the drama triangle altogether, but it is not. The determining factor is attachment to an outcome. Attachment to an outcome can usually be detected by the presence of one of three behaviors: The people involved will still be demonizing (using dehumanizing language about) those they are in conflict with; they will be upset if they are not thanked or appreciated for their effort; they will become upset about suffering that they experience in the process of trying to alleviate suffering. To achieve this transcendence of attachment, we must love those who hate us and actively work for their good, give up any desire for or attachment to outcome, and finally, understand the inevitability of suffering and accept it whether it is our own or the suffering of others. The foundation of the drama triangle is an underlying belief that one should not suffer or that suffering can be prevented entirely—that one has a right to live a life that has no suffering. When suffering occurs, this belief is translated into outrage. The understanding that suffering is inevitable (by suffering, I do not mean indulgent wallowing in emotional pain) allows the underlying belief systems to be circumvented. Alleviation of suffering without feeling that it should (or can) be completely prevented and the absence of a belief that those who cause it are inherently inhuman (demonizing) are then possible.

The movement from involvement in drama triangle dynamics to transcendence of it is, by nature, painful. The goal must be one of intimacy and authenticity, willingness to accept suffering without blaming as a result of understanding its inescapable presence in life, willingness to forgive, and a commitment to alleviating suffering even knowing that nothing one does will ever completely alleviate it. Gandhi notes: "Suffering is the law of human beings; war is the law of the jungle. But suffering is infinitely more powerful than the law of the jungle for converting the opponent and opening his ears, which are

otherwise shut, to the voice of reason."[11] He further comments: "Nonviolence is the law of our species as violence is the law of the brute. The spirit lies dormant in the brute and he knows no law but that of physical might. The dignity of man requires obedience to a higher law—to the strength of spirit."[12]

Chief Dan George expresses the same idea:

My friends, how desperately we need to be loved and to love. When Christ said that man does not live by bread alone, he spoke of a hunger. This hunger was not the hunger of the body. It was not the hunger for bread. He spoke of a hunger that begins deep down in the very depths of our being. He spoke of a need as vital as breath. He spoke of the hunger for love.

Love is something you and I must have. We must have it because our spirit feeds upon it. We must have it because without it we become weak and faint. Without love our self-esteem weakens. Without it our courage fails. Without love we can no longer look out confidently at the world. We turn inward and begin to feed upon our own personalities, and little by little we destroy ourselves.

With it we are creative. With it we march tirelessly. With it, and with it alone, we are able to sacrifice for others.[13]

The love that Dan George and Gandhi speak of is not the sentimental emotion that is usually called love. It is not concerned with feelings of safety or being taken care of; it is not soft and sugar-candy nurturing. It is ahimsa, whose source is the sacred center of all things. One finds it, learns to live from it, and to express it; but it does not have its beginning or end in the self. Like any art form it takes a great deal of practice to master its expression. A useful meditation to master the expression of ahimsa is to attempt to remove all influences of flight or fight from personal actions while still engaging in activities for the alleviation of injustice. In other words, all internal feelings, thoughts, and outward actions should be examined to determine if any fight nor flight feelings underlie them. Actions, thoughts, or feelings coming out of flight or fight should be reconsidered and alternatives explored. Once a limit is placed on flight or fight as an option, as with all addictions, the pattern escalates in

an attempt to reassert itself. If, in spite of all emotional escalation, flight or fight is still denied as an option, alternatives begin to make themselves known. One begins to move into ahimsa as a pattern of behavior. It becomes clear at that point that the persecutor and victim positions are expressions of either flight or fight, while the rescuer is a subtle variation of them both.

forgiving the unforgivable

Resentment underlies the development of the drama triangle dynamics that are played out among members of various religious, racial, and ethnic groups. Always present is an action by one group that harmed another. This act is fixated upon and enshrined; it is used to inflame feelings of victimization and violent reactive response. This process, which has occurred in many places (Bosnia is a recent example), is happening in this country between Native activists and non-Indian Earth spiritual practitioners. All groups that have been harmed and have eventually gained power have then victimized other groups. As R. J. Rummel, a scholar of genocide, notes, "Absolute ideology coupled with an absolute power of the state is absolutely deadly to human life."[14] Although there are few ways to interrupt this cycle, two difficult actions are essential. The descendants of the oppressors must receive the pain of the unthinkable; the descendants of the oppressed must forgive the unforgivable.

The final act of healing for those who carry within us the ancestors who engaged in unthinkable acts is to receive the pain of the unthinkable. We must allow the immense horror of our ancestors' actions to be present in our lives and our feelings, and we must grieve. It may seem that when we allow the truth to be present in our lives, the pain of it will never end. But it does end . . . eventually, as Robert Kennedy noted:*

---

*Kennedy recited this poem from memory to a crowd of African-Americans who had come to hear him speak. He, and through him, they, had just been informed that Martin Luther King, Jr., had recently been murdered. He stood before them, a "white" man, and spoke of the bitterness that comes to those whose family members have been killed by hatred. We can find the good between us, he insisted; we do not have to remain "white" and "black." Sixty-one days later he, too, was dead. (The poem, from the ancient Greek, is carved on his memorial at Arlington National Cemetery.)

Even in our sleep, pain which cannot forget
Falls drop by drop upon the heart
Until in our own despair comes wisdom
Through the awful grace of God

Allowing the full weight of the pain of the unthinkable to come upon us has no rationale other than that it must be done. It is not done because we wish to be thought better of by Indians or because we wish they would stop hating us as "whites." It is a part of the inevitable coming to terms with the suffering of the world as it is expressed through our lineage. It is part of the process of moving out of the drama triangle. Only by coming-to-terms with the horror that has happened can one find a way to forgiveness and understanding. One works through the shame of the ancestors. A resolution has to be found within our own hearts. If the shame and horror are denied, no movement occurs. One does it because one must. It is a difficult and painful process, as Maya Angelou recognizes:

> Throughout our nervous history we have constructed pyramidal towers of evil ofttimes in the name of good. Our greed, fear, and lasciviousness enabled us to murder our poets, who are ourselves, to castigate our priests, who are ourselves. The lists of our subversions of the good stretch from before recorded history to this moment. We drop our eyes at the mention of the bloody torturous inquisition. Our shoulders sag at the thoughts of African slaves lying spoon fashion in the filthy holds of slave ships and the subsequent auction blocks upon which were built great fortunes in our country. We turn our head in bitter shame at the remembrance of Dachau and the other gas ovens where millions of ourselves were murdered by millions of ourselves. As soon as we are reminded of our actions, more often than not, we spend incredible energy trying to forget what we have just been reminded of.[15]

Forgiving the unforgivable, on the part of those who have been victimized, is an equivalent action. One grieves and in so doing one grieves for all

who have suffered. The inevitability of suffering is recognized, embraced, accepted. The refusal to demonize the other does not mean condoning victimization; and one does not cease to work for a world in which victimization cannot occur. It does, however, allow us to embrace our essential humanness and find reconciliation. Barbara Jordan speaks eloquently of this process.

> I believe that I personally can move through my black experience, cut through the experience of my blackness, and find reconciliation and love. And I believe that I can do this because I think, instinctively and at base, each human being has good within the individual. . . . I believe that the good within me can overcome whatever distortions I have suffered because of my blackness and find that reconciliation and love.[16]

As a young Swiss doctor, Elisabeth Kubler-Ross, who went to help survivors of the Nazi concentration camps, came to one that had contained a great many children. Kubler-Ross was overcome by the horror. She noticed a young woman, a survivor whose siblings had been killed, at the gate. The woman seemed almost serene and peaceful. When Kubler-Ross asked how she could be so calm, the young woman explained that she had learned in the camp that she had to forgive the Nazis for what they were doing. "If I do not," she said, "I will become like them. For you see, there is a Hitler in every one of us. And if everyone of us does not learn this and come to terms with it, then these things will never stop."[17]

Without these two actions, both of which must occur within ourselves first, the drama triangle remains our home and our destination. If we respond neither from flight (avoiding the pain of the unthinkable) nor fight (refusal to forgive the unforgivable), a new world opens up—the world that Degawanidah was sent to bring. But there are many who find the resurgence of Earth spirituality—the healing of the wounds between Indian and white—threatening. And, as I noted earlier, they fall into three main groups: Indian activists, Western intellectuals, and militant Christians.

a chorus of objections

The painful relations between the descendants of our ancestors are not being addressed well. Why are these old hurts being inflamed rather than resolved? Why are we moving toward hardened positions and a dehumanization of the other? Why do so many oppose a return to Earth spirituality? Why are the criticisms of non-Indian participation in Earth spirituality similar? Why is the rhetoric becoming violent, emotional, ideologically totalitarian? Who will gain from a lack of Earth spirituality and the wedge of hatred between Indian and non-Indian?

We may be able to answer these questions if we examine some of the objections to New Age neo-paganism. Their similarity in many areas is striking. It is decidedly odd that the assault on the "New Age threat" should bring together three groups who are traditionally in opposite camps. All of them see New Age neo-paganism as a primary threat; two of them advocate violence as a legitimate response; all of them condemn it as shallow, as an illegitimate religious movement and a danger to the structural integrity of their particular group. (They are all responding somewhat in the manner of the Catholic Church's response to the rise of Protestantism.)

the objections of the indians

[W]e are issuing this bulletin to draw public attention to the scandalous commercialization and bastardization of American Indian spiritual traditions by "plastic medicine people" and other professional charlatans who peddle their counterfeit Indian spirituality at New Age gatherings. . . . We urge you to resist and actively oppose the harmful fantasies and stereotypes that these New Age pseudo-Indian workshops promote.[18]

White people in this country are so alienated from their own lives and so hungry for some sort of real life that they'll grasp at any straw to save themselves. But high tech society has given them a taste for the "quick-fix." They want their spirituality prepackaged in such a way as to provide instant insight, the more sensational and preposterous the better. They'll pay big bucks to anybody dishonest enough to offer them spiritual salvation after reading the right book or sitting still for the right fifteen minute session. And of course, this opens them up to every kind of mercenary hustler imaginable.[19]

[By taking our sacred ceremonies] these . . . non-Indians . . . think they will be better Indians than we are.[20]

White people don't have any real feeling for these ceremonies, they are only mimicking them.[21]

[This use of Indian spirituality is intended to] transform it, mutate it . . . and then to reintroduce that mutation like a virus back into the Indian world so that the final . . . act of cultural genocide [can take place].[22]

Only when white males themselves . . . rather than we begin to shut down the movement's meetings, burn its sweat lodges, impound and return its sacred objects it desecrates—will we be able to say [that they have accepted us. Only then will they] be accepted among us on our shores.[23]

[If white New Agers do not stop their use of this spirituality] that makes [them] an enemy, to say the least. And believe me when I say we're prepared to deal with [them] as such.[24]

the objections of the christians

TV evangelists increasingly warn against the New Age threat, which as one preacher heard by one of the authors proclaimed, really embodies the ancient sin of Adam: the blasphemous presumption that through secret knowledge one can become as God. Another TV evangelist affirms that the conflict between Christianity and New Age religion represents the greatest war since the prophet Elijah vindicated Jehovah on the mountain and destroyed the six hundred priests of Baal! Books warning against the spread of New Age philosophy proliferate in Christian bookstores. "New Age ideas have already begun to infiltrate and undermine the church from within!" announces a bulletin from the Evangelical Book Club.[25]

[The New Age neo-pagans will be punished because] they turned aside from worshipping the Creator and unto creation.[26]

[They are worshipping a false and shallow religion.] The only source of true, clean spiritual power comes from Jesus Christ, and a life submitted completely to him.[27]

New Age mysticism may be replacing Godless communism as the central symbolic contrast category which evokes the demonic in the exemplary dualist system of fundamentalist and charismatic Christianity.[28]

[New Age neo-paganists claim it is a real religion and that they] only want to help people, but in reality they are using the same dark powers that belong to the devil [and this is witchcraft]. . . . In fact, the old testament law of Moses specifically states that witches should be put to death, that is how strongly God feels about the sin of witchcraft.[29]

The decisive eschatological significance of New Age movements is posited by premillennial warnings; for example: "Because the New Age is the last age, it will conclude with the emergence of a powerful world teacher, the New Age false 'Messiah,' the famous Antichrist" (Evangelical Book Club Bulletin). An anti-premillennial dominion theologian sees cultural disintegration leading to a final conflict between New Age occultism and a revitalized conservative Christianity.[30]

the objections of the western intellectuals

The United States, in recent years has witnessed a resurgence of shamanistic cults among all classes and races. . . . The revival of shamanism in the United States is probably symptomatic of the weakening of orthodox religion's ability to regulate social behavior and to maintain social values. . . .[31]

We contend that a Natural State . . . idealized by movements with a tendency to look toward the past, does not exist and has probably never existed . . . insofar as humanity has always progressed by increasingly harnessing Nature to its needs and not the reverse. . . . We are however worried, at the dawn of the twenty-first century, at the emergence of an irrational ideology.[32]

[This idealized past and the drive toward the attribution of sacredness to the land] might very well establish a "religious servitude" on federal public lands.[33]

[It also] results in various forms of what has correctly been called ecofascism.[34]

[T]hese folks become incredibly belligerent and intolerant, claiming that all the strands in the web are equally important, but despising the strands which disagree with them. . . . [M]ore often than not these approaches completely sabotage and derail actual transcendence and transformation, and simply encourage the various fragments to retribalize at their own level of adaptation.[35]

[New Age neo-paganists] simply identified Nature with nature. . . . And thus, instead of moving forward in evolution to the emergence of a Nature of Spirit (or World Soul) . . . [they] simply recommend "back to nature." Not forward to Nature, but back to nature.[36]

This naive notion of one-step transformation has now been hooked up with a purely flatland [biocentric, sacred Earth] worldview, so that "cosmic consciousness" has come to mean simply that we all go from the Nasty Newtonian ego to the new-physics web-of-life one-with-Gaia self. We become one with flatland and we are enlightened and that saves the planet.[37]

It is only with scientific knowledge . . . that men and women can actually attune their actions with the biosphere. A simple or sacred respect for nature will not do. . . . [It] is modern science, and modern science alone . . . that can directly show us how our actions are corroding the biosphere.[38]

who benefits?

I find it interesting that the old wounds of the Indian peoples are being inflamed to cause them to attack their primary ally in the recognition of the legitimacy of their spirituality and the sacredness of land in general. The result is a feeling between natural allies that the other is dangerous and harmful.[39] The situation provokes a number of questions. Who will support repatriation of Indian remains? Who will support Indian rights to worship on federal land? Who will support an absolute freedom of religious practice for the Indian? The answer to all these questions is: the white New Agers—who are being attacked by the Indian. Who would be natural allies in the assignment of sacredness to land and thus to its protection from environmental abuse? Indians and New Agers. Who are becoming entrenched in opposite camps? Indians and New Agers. This state of affairs benefits neither the Indian nor New Agers. Who might benefit? Who benefits if land remains non-sacred? Who benefits if the common people fight among themselves and do not hold in common that land is sacred? Who benefits if the sacred ceremonies are not performed by thousands or millions of people? Who benefits if a conflict between Christians and pagans is stirred up? Who benefits if scientists' attachments to a reductionistic materialism are inflamed by fears that their favorite paradigm is about to come crashing down on their heads? It isn't the New Agers and it is not the Indians. An answer may be found if we explore the nature of colonization itself.

Many years ago, Canadian herbalist Carol McGrath introduced me to the concept of the Colonizing Mind. The recognition of the existence of the Colonizing Mind and the gift of a name for it have helped me in my process of restoring the Indigenous Mind. She notes:

The issues we face, living as the descendants of colonizers and colonized have more to do with the attitudes of takeover and control inherent in the colonizing process itself, what I call the Colonizing Mind, than they have to do with any physical or racial differences we may have. We need to learn to see this Colonizing Mind wherever it may be operating, whether it's a government cutting down trees, a pharmaceutical company allowing water, soil, and air in a factory town to be polluted so it can keep its profits up, or a colleague telling us we need to make all our herbal tinctures "official." We need to constantly ask: "Who benefits?", so we know what the real agenda may be.[40]

Once when Carol and I were talking, she noted in her strong Irish accent, "Ah, you know, the first thing the Colonizing Mind does is cut you off from your connection to the land; then it takes your language, so you can't describe that world of connection; and finally it stops you from performing the ceremonies and rituals that make the connection happen. And when it does all that, it's got you." At this exclamation her hand swept across in front of us, fist clenched, holding something cut off, separated from the Earth. The reason, she went on, is that people cannot be controlled, their access to life-necessary resources regulated (with resultant financial benefits to the controller), unless they are separated from the Earth and kept that way. Her points are seminal. Once people are firmly separated from the land, they begin to take on, they are infected by, the Colonizing Mind. They take on its mannerisms, its expressions, its assumptions. And when the colonized peoples then fight against the control of the Colonizing Mind, they begin using the mechanisms and viewpoints of it in their fight. They become what they hate.

The continuing growth of the Colonizing Mind can be seen in its control over agricultural processes worldwide. The mass control over seed stock, water, fertilizer, and pesticides and the manipulation that makes all people dependent on those seed stocks, fertilizers, and pesticides will result in a few being in complete control of all food production on Earth. The reality of this process is confirmed by the declining number of farmers and increasing number of agribusinesses. Buckminster Fuller called the people behind multinational

agribusinesses the Great Pirates. But by this term, as he makes clear in *Critical Path*, he means more than robber barons and corporate capitalism—he means the Colonizing Mind. To maintain control the Colonizing Mind must prevent, at all costs, the restoration of the Indigenous Mind, the sacredness of Earth, and Earth spirituality (see Appendix 1).

Although he refers to it as the Machine, Malidoma Patrice Somé also has some cogent remarks about the Colonizing Mind:

> The Machine has made itself look beautiful by making other ways of life that have existed for tens of thousands of years look silly, shameful and uncivilized. But the truth is that the Machine must eliminate every alternative to itself and focus attention on itself because it knows its purpose is not to give life, but to suck the energy out of it. . . . [T]he Machine is the specter of the Spirit, and in such a state, it does not serve because it can't serve. It needs servants.[41]

Somé makes the crucial observation that ritual is anti-Machine; by its very nature, ritual subverts the Machine. It reconnects the human to the land and to the rhythms of an authentic life. As Somé notes: "To say that ritual is needed in the industrialized world is an understatement. We have seen in my own people that it is probably impossible to live a sane life without it."[42] Native activists like Ward Churchill are doing their best to prevent the restoration of Earth ritual by non-Indians on this North American continent. And again, one must ask: Who benefits? Only the Colonizing Mind, only the Machine, only those who control the land and have reduced it to inanimate matter, devoid of living spirit. It is not the New Agers who have called on people to burn the sweat lodge temples, to impound the sacraments of the pipe and deny it to others, and to stop all meetings of sacred Earth worship. Indian activists (like Ward Churchill) have called for these actions, and they stir up others to call for them as well. When they do so, the cycle of violence goes on and, in the end, the Earth and the common people lose—as always.[43]

the transformation of the colonizing mind

The solution to the wound in our peoples and in the world lies not in drawing racial barriers between us, but in the transformation of the Colonizing Mind. I have thought (and it is a perilous thought to utter) that the Colonizing Mind cannot change without eating the heart of its enemy. Once that irrevocable step is taken and the Indigenous Mind is inside, it will begin to grow in its own way through suffering. The inevitable would then take place: Slowly the Colonizing Mind would begin to be perverted, changed, subdued. The Science Mind, focused on reason alone, would never change. It would have to be subverted to the use of heart. In a paradox, reason alone would never convince Reason to change. Like any ego state that has outlived its usefulness, it must be subverted by a greater good—by a broader, more loving, and inclusive self—to change. Attempts to destroy the disliked ego state result in it taking on great power; attempts to repress it result in its deformation. Both present great dangers. The first results in warlike aggression as the ego state takes control over behavior and action; the second results in Auschwitz. Gandhi recognized the universality of this process and applied it in India. His recognition of it led him to understand that the Western mind must be changed without the use of force. "Nonviolence," he said, "is like radium in its action. An infinitesimal quantity of it embedded in a malignant growth acts continuously, silently, and ceaselessly till it has transformed the whole mass of diseased tissue into a healthy one."[44] When the Colonizing Mind conquered the American continents, it literally ate the heart of its enemy, and in that process the Indigenous Mind entered the belly of the Colonizing Mind. Slowly each year, each decade, the Indigenous Mind has been making a greater and greater impact. It has not been without cost; there has been a tremendous price in suffering paid for it. It has been much like the black maids who took into their hearts the children of their racist employers. By injecting love into the process, by being willing to absorb

the pain into themselves—to see its human face—they turned hatred to love, the dehumanization of skin color to the experience of universal humanity. Ohiyesa evokes the deep understanding of this sacrifice and gift:

> Is there not something worthy of perpetuation in our Indian spirit of democracy, where the Earth, our mother, was free to all, and no one sought to impoverish or enslave his neighbor? Where the good things of Earth were not ours to hold against our brothers and sisters, but were ours to use and enjoy together with them, and with whom it was our privilege to share?
>
> Indeed, our contribution to our nation and the world is not to be measured in the material realm. Our greatest contribution has been spiritual and philosophical. Silently, by example only, in wordless practice, we have held stoutly to our native vision of personal faithfulness to duty and devotion to a trust. We have not advertised our faithfulness nor made capital of our honor.
>
> But again and again we have proved our worth as citizens of this country by our constancy in the face of hardship and death. Prejudice and racial injustice have been no excuse for our breaking our word. This simplicity and fairness has cost us dear. It has cost us our land and our freedom, and even the extinction of our race as a separate and unique people.
>
> But, as an ideal, we live and will live, not only in the splendor of our past, the poetry of our legends and art, not only in the interfusion of our blood with yours, and in our faithful adherence to the ideals of American citizenship, but in the living heart of the nation.[45]

The sacrifice that Ohiyesa speaks of began a process that has as its end the subversion of the Colonizing Mind; it began the moment Europeans landed and began to live on this continent. As Carol McGrath notes:

> In the early days of European–North American contact it was quickly recognized by the colonial authorities that in order to gain influence in the "new" territories, they would have to break the power of the medicine people on whom native people depended for healing and spiritual counseling.

Many attempts to do so were made and much damage was done, despite the fact that the colonists themselves needed and were often freely given medical information by these same medicine people. However, anyone as directly dependant on nature as were the colonial people, MUST become observant of the natural environment—water, wind, trees, soil—in order to survive. We begin to notice when the deer come to drink, where particular beneficial plants grow and when they do so, where certain birds lay their eggs . . . and slowly counter acculturation occurs, we start to understand WHY the indigenous people of a certain environment have many of the customs they do. We begin to realize that our true roots begin with the land itself, that the environment of a particular place shapes cultural traditions and language, and that what we bring from one place may not be suitable to another.[46]

Wallace Stegner also touches on this truth:

[W]hile we were demonstrating ourselves the most efficient and ruthless environment-busters in history, and slashing and burning and cutting our way through a wilderness continent, the wilderness was working on us. It remains in us as surely as Indian names remain on the land. If the abstract dream of human liberty and human dignity became, in America, something more than an abstract dream, mark it down at least partially to the fact that we were in subtle ways subdued by what we conquered.[47]

This heart of the Indigenous Mind, the heart of the enemy that had been eaten, has its origins in the land. The people who were conquered, displaced, and murdered lived in societies that were themselves expressions of the land on which they lived. When other peoples came to live here, the land began its work on them, too. For the spirit of the land is its own force and is the source of the Indigenous Mind.

As Vine Deloria, Jr., notes in *God Is Red:* "Each land projects a particular religious spirit, which largely determines what types of religious beliefs will arise on it." He continues: "The fact that Druidism is once again rising in parts

of Europe may indicate that those lands, in largely determining the shape and beliefs of religious experience, are Druid lands."[48] Joseph Epes Brown remarks: "One explanation for the current new willingness to understand Native Americans and their lifeways is that, being rooted in this American land for thousands of years, the Indians' otherwise very diverse cultures have all come to express rich spiritual relationships with this American land."[49] Brown goes on to note that parallel religious callings or practices between differing ethnic groups or cultures do not suggest "borrowings, but rather one may say that where the hearts and souls of men are exposed to the powers inherent in legitimate sacred traditions, there appears a common quality of spiritual realization which transcends cultural differentiations."[50]

The point, which is central to this book, is that the land on which we live shapes our experience of the sacred and that, in fact, certain religious movements, ceremonies, and artifacts are present in the land itself. If a people reside on the land for a long period of time, these impulses and forms, which are present in the land, begin to make themselves known and come to life again. As John Seed observes about the weeding practices of the Bradley sisters (Chapter 3): "Years into the Bradley method of an area, to our amazement, climax native trees begin to emerge, perhaps unseen for generations and unremembered."

Years into this process, to our amazement ceremonies, states of mind, and understandings of the land begin to emerge, perhaps unseen for generations. We do not have to have "evolved" here to understand the religion generated by the land on which we live. As Deloria notes:

> Nearly as important may be the fact that lands can apparently be consecrated by a particular religious group wishing to place its roots in the land. The persistence of some religions on originally foreign lands would appear to testify to the fact that peoples and lands can relate to each other in a very powerful manner to develop a spiritual unity. . . . Christians would be well advised to surrender many of their doctrines and come to grips with the lands now occupied. To admit that certain lands will create divergent beliefs and practices and to change to accommodate to those realities is certainly preferable to

extinction. . . . That a fundamental element of religion is an intimate relationship with the land on which the religion is practiced should be a major premise of future theological concern.[51]

The remarkable influx of so-called Indian religious forms into the popular consciousness is, in my opinion, not the last grasping reach of the Colonizing Mind in its final genocidal push, but the lands of this continent reaching out to their children, calling them home. It is the presence of the Indigenous Mind making itself known inside the Colonizing Mind's belly, subverting the scientific murder of the Earth and reinfusing its perspective with living spirit. The new Earth-centered spiritual forms in America are arising in response to profound religious encounters and experiences of the numinous, *activated by the spirit of the land itself.* Many of the negative responses to this process can be seen as the fearful objections of the Colonizing Mind, of the Machine, to this turn of events. And these objections play on, and use, the bitter pain that lies between the many cultures and races of North America. The conflict interferes with the process of the land, by which it inserts its essential spirituality into its people. The wound in the Earth, like an erosion gully breaking *our* hearts, lies deep and bleeding between us. And I wonder, when they get to the erosion gully breaking our hearts, will the sacred power of land and the Indigenous Mind, like the Native plant species John Seed spoke of, also take it in stride? I hope so. I do not know of anything else that can.

Even though certain Indians are uncomfortable with non-Indians being converted to, moved by, and adopting Native religious forms, many Earth-centered ceremonial forms are intruding themselves into the American psyche. No one has really asked why the Lakota origin story of the pipe has gained such wide acceptance in North America when there are at least five others. Why are the sweat lodge and vision quest becoming so prominent among non-Indians rather than the Keeping of the Soul or the Throwing of the Ball (two other Oglala Sioux ceremonies)? Why is the Medicine Wheel touching so many people, moving them to understand their lives and path in the world, rather than the Pawnee Hand Game or the Midéwiwin ceremonies of the Ojibway?

Why has the Iroquois Great Law of Peace made such an impact on the popular psyche (even reflected in the governmental structure of the United States) rather than other tribal government forms? Why have the Hopi prophecies—rather than others—touched so many people around the world? Why does Black Elk's story (rather than Frank Fools Crow's story, for example) continue to spread each year, touching more and more people? Why has Chief Seattle's speech touched so deep a chord, but not others as eloquent? (And why is it the most bitterly attacked of all indigenous statements? Why is it necessary to prove it false?) Why is the concept of Mother Earth welling up in people and finding expression in the concept of Gaia? There is something in these ceremonies and lives and concepts that the spirit of the North American land is extruding into the consciousness of the people that live here and, subsequently, the spirit of all humanity.

The sacred places of America (to, finally, directly answer the French couple's son) can be found in each place of its land where the sacred extrudes itself into human awareness, where each ceremonial archetype works itself into the human psyche and will not go away, where the pervasive and eternally recurrent feeling that all things of the Earth are alive and we are but a part of the multitude exists. In secret, the remnants of indigenous cultures have maintained their practices at many of the sacred places in America and across the world. But in addition to those sacred places, thousands of others are being found again by the children of colonizers. The land has taken them over, subdued them, changed their Mind (and this has not escaped notice, as the "outrage" over it shows). But it is essential. As Deloria notes: "Unless the sacred places are discovered and protected and used as religious places, there is no possibility of a nation ever coming to grips with the land itself. Without this basic relationship, national psychic stability is impossible."[52] And in spite of his distaste for "white, New Age circle-jerks," what he has discussed as necessary is coming to pass. In fits and starts, with dignity and without, Indian and non-Indian are coming into a sacred awareness of America's holy places. By all of us allowing the sacredness of this land to emerge in us, the Indigenous Mind of this continent comes alive again, comes to fruition within us. In this process, we can

either speak with hatred of our differences or speak with love of our common humanity. We can let the snakes grow in our hair or we can make the difficult journey to the place where Tadodaho lives and comb them out.

Those who walk among us and speak for all humankind, who seek a resolution of peace among all people, who carry Buffalo Pipe Woman's pipe in their hearts as well as in their hands, their names have become *They Who Comb*—and they come among us to make the body of our people straight, to comb out the snakes of our hair. By this we shall know them.

For Our People

epilogue

[Black Elk] appreciated his earlier tradition but adapted it to a historical ethos that made his religious quest a response to Wakan Tanka in the changing circumstances of the here and now. . . . [It was] the desire of Wakan Tanka that "had chosen him for this work."[1] Witness to and participant in th[e] unfolding drama [of Indian/non-Indian contact], Black Elk embodied traditional Lakota ideology as he manifested a resilient willingness to let go of what was and to experiment with what might be the disclosures of Wakan Tanka for his life.[2] [He] derived his own strength and inspiration from the Lakota/Catholic religious sphere and . . . used [it] to challenge his people unto renewal.[3]

The Great Spirit has promised one day that the tree of [Black Elk]'s vision was to root, grow, and blossom—to give out its sweet scent for everyone, and become a symbol of life.[4] At the time before he died, he had a sad tale. He said he didn't do his part in accomplishing [the flowering of the tree] and that

the tree was dying. People were not walking the right path. But he still hoped the tree would be able to give forth its branches before it was entirely dead.5 "Perhaps," he said, "in the sixth generation the tree will blossom as in my vision."[6] As [he] waited for death, he [said], "Do not worry, there is a man who comes to see me everyday at three o'clock. He is from overseas, and he comes in to pray with me—so I pray with him. He is a sacred man (Wicasa Wakan)."[7] [Black Elk] was patient with his suffering right up until the end.[8] [He] said, toward the end that "I have a feeling that when I die, some sign will be seen. maybe God will show something. He will be merciful to me and have something shown that will tell of his mercy."[9]

[And this was true for] When we came back from the wake, the sky was lit up, and you could see those flames going into midair. It was something like a light being played on a fountain which sprays up. It seemed like it was rising and moving. There would be some flames going at a great distance way up into the sky above us. And others would be rising and coming into various groups and then, all of a sudden, spurt off on this side and then another side and then off to the center again. It was almost like day when we returned.

Everything was constantly moving. . . . [I]t was all coming up from east and the south, the north and the west. And they'd all converge up to the top where they'd meet—rising up into the sky, and it was a tremendous sight. They weren't stars or meteors, but rather, well, they were beams of flashes. And there was a variation of color effect in there—the whole horizon seemed to be ablaze. . . . There were different formations in the sky that night which, to me, looked like spires, like tremendous points going up—then flashes. And it seemed like they were almost like fireworks in between. It was something like when a flare goes off in the sky—some sparkle here and there, but spread over such a vast area.[10]

What we saw that night was the sky in a way we never saw before. The northern lights were brighter than ever, and we saw those figures—the number 8 and a ring, or circle. They were separated by a short distance, but they were there—an 8 and a circle.

I always wondered what that meant.[11]

appendix one
science and the destruction of a sacred earth

Oddly enough, Native activists' objections to white participation in Earth spirituality echo a similar discomfort
to that expressed by many Western intellectuals. And
strangely, the origins of Native activists' tendencies to
separate people according to skin color, to attribute to
each different inherent capacities and behaviors, lie in
Western science and philosophy. Such distinctions are
not inherently indigenous. The influence of Western
thought is so pervasive in Indian-white relations and the
wounds in the Earth that it is important to explore it, at
least briefly. The assertion upon which racism is based
has its roots in the same perspective that has created the
unprecedented degree of environmental degradation we
are witnessing today. The assertion is that the universe is
a great functioning machine, set in motion in some past
original beginning-of-time, whose rules can be understood and used in the creation of technology. The theory

of evolution came from this concept, and together these fundamental beliefs about the nature of reality have removed *all* attribution of sacredness from matter—inanimate and animate. This divorces inherent ethical action from any contact with the Earth or human beings because universe-as-machine and evolutionary theory are, by nature, amoral. Attempts to attribute innate equivalent sacredness to all matter, and thus reinfuse morality into actions toward the Earth, are being bitterly resisted.

The assertion that there is dumb inanimate matter at the bottom, and incredibly amazing human information finders at the top, finds its own expression in the work of Western philosopher Ken Wilber. Much of the context of his two books, *Sex, Ecology, and Spirituality* and *A Brief History of Everything* is a strong, emotional defense of several of the primary foundational theories of science: the inanimate nature of matter and evolution. Although Wilber tries to salvage the Western paradigm from those who attack it by agreeing that matter should have equal extrinsic value (or depth), he denies to it equal intrinsic value or depth.

He notes that if stones (among other things) and people are given equal depth value, "it paralyzes pragmatic action and cripples intrinsic values." He insists that we must be able to "realize that it is much better to kick a rock than an ape, much better to eat a carrot than a cow, much better to subsist on grains than on mammals."[1] Wilber is correct when he notes that many (Western) people intuitively feel that sentence is true. He is also correct when he notes that people who feel it is true have an internal hierarchy of value. But he is incorrect when he states that the assignment of equal depth to all matter would paralyze pragmatic action and cripple intrinsic value. He, in fact, does not point to any instance where such a belief system has paralyzed pragmatic action. It is an assumption on his part. What if such a belief were held by the people in a society? In the West, intellectuals and scientists have an almost knee-jerk antagonism to the concept. In the East, the reaction is different.

Traditional Korean society, for instance, as the story about Korean mountain spirit indicates, has embedded within it the equal assignment of depth to stones and to people. They are different physical manifestations but each is

considered to be of (potentially) equal intrinsic depth. And those cultures do not exhibit a crippling of pragmatic action. In fact, a balancing process occurs. Sometimes the rights of stones take precedence; sometimes the rights of people. As another example, Jainism in India contains within it the attribution of equal intrinsic value to all life-forms. The most devout Jains take this idea to such an extent that they avoid any behavior that may lead even to the inadvertent killing of insects. Not only have they not experienced a paralysis of pragmatic action or crippling of intrinsic values, they exercise an influence in Indian life far out of proportion to their numbers. It is the refusal to accept the "easy" necessity of common pragmatism that has forced their behaviors into new and untried expressions of living. In fact, it was Jain behavior that influenced Gandhi to embrace ahimsa. The balancing process that occurs when equal inherent depth is extended to nonhumans is very much like the process that occurs in this country when different inherent rights must be balanced between competing demands. Wilber's objection is a variation of that voiced by private property proponents when arguing against the recognition of the sacredness of specific geographic areas in Native American worship. Private property activists (including government land managers) argue that if sacredness (in theoretical or legal principle) is conferred on land, any place of the Earth can be designated sacred at any time. This designation will remove people's ability to control inanimate matter and paralyze pragmatic action. There is no reason to suppose this position is true as U.S. court cases in similar circumstances have shown.

In the United States, when entities that according to Wilber's reasoning could be argued to have less depth than people (such as boats, corporations, states, universities, and so on, and are considered to be persons) come into conflict with people, an arbitration process occurs. The rights of each "person" in the system are articulated, the conflict examined, and the impact of the conflict is weighed until a balance is reached. The court system does sometimes make errors; it is imperfect. However, the balancing process is of long-established duration. If a corporation can bring action because its intrinsic worth is affected by the behavior of others, then there is no reason that land cannot bring action (through an intermediary such as the Sierra Club or a Native American tribe)

for a redress of wrongs to its intrinsic worth. Although this idea might seem too complex for human beings to make sense of in their day-to-day lives (all things having the same depth of intrinsic worth), nevertheless they can and do make sense of it when it has occurred in other areas (such as extension of equal depth value to women, slaves, and others).

Attorney and law professor Christopher Stone, in his law review article "Should Trees Have Standing?", remarks on the process of extending rights to wider and wider circles of beings.

> Throughout legal history, each successive extension of rights to some new entity has been, theretofore, a bit unthinkable. We are inclined to suppose the right-lessness of rightless "thing" to be a decree of Nature, not a legal convention act-ing in support of some status quo. It is thus that we defer considering the choices involved in all their moral, social, and economic dimensions. And so the United States Supreme Court could straight-facedly tell us in *Dred Scott* that Blacks had been denied the rights of citizenship "as a subordinate and inferior class of beings, who had been subjugated by the dominate race. . . ." In the nine-teenth century, the highest court in California explained that Chinese had not the right to testify against white men in criminal matters because they were "a race of people whom nature has marked as inferior, and who are incapable of progress of intellectual development beyond a certain point . . . between whom and ourselves nature has placed an impassable difference. The popular con-ception of the Jew in the 13th century contributed to a law which treated them as men *ferae naturae*, protected by a quasi-forest law. Like the roe and the deer they form an order apart. . . . The first woman in Wisconsin who thought she might have a right to practice law was told she did not, in the following terms:
>
> > The law of nature destines and qualifies the female sex for the bearing and nurture of the children of our race, and for the custody of the homes of the world. . . . [A]ll life-long callings of women, inconsistent with these radical and sacred duties of their sex, as is the profession of the law, are departures from the order of nature; and when voluntary, treason against it.

The fact is, that each time there is a movement to confer rights onto some new "entity," the proposal is bound to sound odd or frightening or laughable. This is partly because until the rightless thing receives its rights, we cannot see it as anything but a *thing* for the use of "us"—those who are holding rights at the time. In this vein, what is striking about the Wisconsin case above is that the court, for all its talk about women, so clearly was never able to see women as they are (and might become). . . . Such is the way the slave South looked upon the Black. There is something of a seamless web involved.[2]

The opinions in these court cases are not so very different from Wilber's position: Lower depth holons (basically, matter such as rocks) have less intrinsic value even though they have the same extrinsic value. If we give them equal intrinsic value, we will interfere with the natural order of things. And the natural order of things is intrinsically people on top, rocks on the bottom. Men as lawyers, women as childbearers.

Wilber reveres indigenous cultures, he says, because they are the "foundation" upon which so much rests. But, he notes, any attempt to utilize the insights of indigenous cultures in our own interaction with the Earth is evolutionarily "regressive" and against the basic order of life. His argument against attributing equal intrinsic value to "inanimate matter" is really the same argument as that used against attributing equal intrinsic value (as that possessed by white men) to nonwhite men and women. The court opinions regarding blacks, Chinese, Jews, and women are basically objections to equal depth of value between those different groups and white men. As with Wilber and rocks, it was argued that there is some ultimately *intrinsic* element that makes those groups possess less depth value from white people, and that intrinsic something comes from nature itself. ("Hey!" it was argued. "It's the great machine—I didn't make the rules. It's just the way it is. It is out of my hands.") Anyone who tries to go against that most obvious of truths is either regressing evolutionarily (in Wilber's point of view) or treasonously going against the laws of nature (the courts' opinion).

The arguments against the extension of depth or rights to the land, that it will paralyze pragmatic action, do not hold up when we look at the adjustments society has made at the successive extension of rights or depth to Blacks,

Chinese, Jews, and women. In his dissent in *Sierra Club v. Morton,* Justice Blackmun agrees. He notes that the extension of rights to land "should be no cause for alarm. . . . We need not fear that Pandora's Box will be opened or that there will be no limit to the number of those who desire to participate in environmental litigation. The courts will exercise appropriate restraints just as they have exercised them in the past."[3]

Wilber's objections to the equal extension of depth to all "strands in the web of Gaia" (basically the Western objection to attributing equal sacred livingness as that possessed by human beings to inanimate matter) and federal land managers' objections to the extension of sacred recognition to traditional Indian ceremonial sites are really just another form of objection to the extension of depth and rights to a new group. Yet Christopher Stone argues that such extension is almost certainly crucial:

> The time may be on hand when these sentiments, and the early stirrings of the law, can be coalesced into a radical new theory or myth—felt as well as intellectualized—of man's relationships to the rest of nature. I do not mean "myth" in a demeaning sense of the term, but in the sense in which, at different times in history, our social "facts" and relationships have been comprehended and integrated by reference to the "myths" that we are co-signers of a social contract, that the Pope is God's agent, and that all men are created equal. . . . I do not think it is too remote that we may come to regard the Earth, as some have suggested, as one organism, of which Mankind is a functional part—the mind perhaps: different from the rest but different as a man's brain is from his lungs.
>
> . . . Before the forces that are at work, our highest court is but a frail and feeble—distinctly human—institution. Yet, the Court may be at its best not in its work of handing down decrees, but at the very task that is called for: of summoning up from the human spirit the kindest and most generous and worthy ideas that abound there, giving them reality, shape, legitimacy. Witness the School Desegregation Cases which, more importantly than to integrate the schools (assuming they did), awakened us to moral needs which, when made visible, could not be denied. And so here, too, in the case of the environment, the Supreme Court may find itself in a position to award "rights" in a way that

will contribute to a change in popular consciousness. It would be a modest move to be sure, but one in furtherance of a large goal: the future of the planet as we know it.[4]

The insistence of Sacred Earth proponents, Gaia proponents, that intrinsic depth should be extended to the Earth and all of its parts can be viewed as the same insistence that urged all Blacks, women, Chinese, Jews, and others to be given equal intrinsic depth. The calls for equal depth assignment have not disappeared because the right has not been recognized. And based on the integration of such depth recognition in Jainist cultures and the past experience of the society and court system in expanding to include greater depth, there is no reason to believe that equal depth of sacred recognition would paralyze intrinsic worth and pragmatic action.

Seyyed Hossein Nasr makes, however, a seminal observation in his work *Religion and the Order of Nature.* He notes that the real contribution of Galileo was his formulation of the concept that the universe was a great machine imbued with no underlying intelligence, composed of inanimate matter, whose workings any could get to know and (therefore) manipulate. Wilber and other academics make the argument that indigenous tribes were horribly destructive of their environment and that our current problems are not anything new (except in degree). Nasr makes the strong argument (based on exhaustive research) that without this attribution of lifelessness to matter the current environmental problems we face could never have occurred.[5] The resurgence of a sense of a sacred Earth can be viewed not simply as a linear progression of rights attribution but as the impossible-to-repress recognition of a basic truth emerging in the human species.

In response to sacred Earth proponents' assertions that a sense of the sacred will automatically engender more cautious and sustainable behaviors toward the Earth, many Western writers argue that it will not. To emphasize this point they assert that Indians committed a great many acts of environmental degradation. Wilber notes: "Some primal tribal societies were ecologically sound, and some definitely were not. Some tribes practiced cut and slash and burn, and some were responsible for the extinction of numerous species.

[A] 'sacred' outlook toward nature did not in any way guarantee an ecologically sound culture, although there is a certain antimodern outlook that likes to imagine so."[6] Others, however, disagree with Wilber's assessment. Dinesh D'Souza and Delores La Chapelle, for instance, in separate works note that early visitors to the North American continent found a virtually pristine, ecologically sound continent—many early explorers thought they had returned to the Garden of Eden.[7]

Undoubtedly, some Indian tribes probably were not all that ecologically sound in their behavior when compared to others or even scientific perspectives. Given, however, that there were between three hundred and five hundred tribes in North America, it seems odd to make a blanket statement without conducting extensive fieldwork to determine if there was a correlation between the level of sacredness a culture afforded the Earth and the degree of environmental degradation its members caused. That so many people are claiming it is a factor (and others rather emotionally denying it) seems to indicate there is something worth investigating. Astonishingly, no one has ever attempted to assign relative degrees of Earth-sacred perception to different tribes and to then ascertain the resulting degree of environmental impact. Wilber's assertions have not been verified.

In reviewing the records of Korean treatment of the land, mountains, and forests over a 2000-year period, researcher Hong-key Yoon showed that Korean geomantic (*poong soo*) beliefs influenced both government and cultural treatment of the land at differing levels of impact based on numerous factors during the periods in question. Irrespective of short-term actions, the long-term impact of a sense of the sacredness of the Earth in Korea was to preserve ecological health. There might have been periods of one or two hundred years where environmental degradation would occur (forests would be overharvested, for instance), but eventually the cultural value put on geomantic auspiciousness would assert itself and areas of degraded land would be set aside as sanctuaries for several hundred years and allowed to regenerate.[8] This interweaving of sacred and pragmatic drive in a culture shows that each drive may, from time to time, gain ascendancy but that they can coexist in culture. Pragmatic action is not paralyzed.

Brief looks at indigenous cultures show instances in which a sacred respect for nature has protected the environment from degradation. In Kenya, the sacred groves and forests of the Mikikenda people are called *kaya*. These areas of forest surround the native villages and passage is limited to one or two pathways through the forest. The use of the groves is

> limited to gathering of medicinal herbs. Cutting of trees for timber, grazing of livestock, and clearing for farmland [are] strictly prohibited. These rules [are] strictly enforced by the kaya elders who [are] also responsible for the acre of sacred objects (*fingo*) which [are] buried in the kaya and [are] believed to be essential to the well-being of the community. The kaya forests [are] also places for prayer, not only by the elders on behalf of the community but also by individuals seeking help in problems facing their daily lives.[9]

By 1993, due to increasing development, almost the only remaining forests in the area were sacred kaya groves around villages (which were themselves being actively nibbled upon by the development at their edges). All the other land had been cleared by Western and local developers. "More than half of the known rare trees and shrubs of Kenya exist in Coast Province, many of them in the small patches of rapidly degrading kaya forest."[10] The protection of sacred groves based on purely religious motivation is not an isolated event. Worldwatch researchers note:

> South Asian and Southeast Asian farmers have traditionally honored sacred groves, believed to be the homes of powerful deities. The kuna and Embera-Choco Indians of Panama leave patches of old-growth forest as supernatural parks, refuges for both wildlife and spirits. Waterways as well as forests are protected by the Tukano Indians of Brazil, whose taboos guard as much as 62 percent of nearby streams as fish sanctuaries.[11]

Vine Deloria, Jr., offers an explanation for why the Indians are being accused of having caused wholesale extinctions in North America.

> Conservative newspaper columnists, right-wing fanatics, sportsmen's groups, and scholars in general tend to see the "overkill" hypothesis as symptomatic of a lack of moral fiber and ethical concern for the Earth among Indians.

Some people are offended by the idea that many people believe that Indians were more concerned and thoughtful ecologists than modern industrial users. Advocating the extinction theory is a good way to support continued despoliation of the environment by suggesting at *no* time were human beings careful of the lands on which they lived.[12]

In light of this comment, consider Wilber's statement again: "Some primal tribal societies were ecologically sound, and some definitely were not. Some tribes practiced cut and slash and burn, and some were responsible for the extinction of numerous species." His sentence structure is interesting. Usually in structuring such sentences, one would say, "Some tribal societies were ecologically sound, and some definitely were not. Some tribes protected large areas of forest from being degraded, and some were responsible for the extinction of numerous species." The symmetry of my version is A and B, A and B. Protected/not protected. Protected/not protected. The human mind automatically (and unconsciously) makes this association when encountering such sentence structure. In Wilber's sentences, the message subtly shifts from protected/not protected to simply not protected. Further, at the unconscious level an association is made between the first statement "some . . . were ecologically sound" and the second statement "some . . . practiced cut and slash and burn."[13] The point is that Wilber (like almost all Western thinkers) does have a bias that is present all through his writings on this subject. Rather than presenting his thesis clearly and allowing the reader to decide on the basis of his argument, he uses a number of techniques (perhaps unconscious) to shift the emotional stance of the reader where he wants it to be. As Deloria notes, the point is to convince modern readers that "at *no* time were human beings careful of the lands on which they lived." The implication, human beings were at one time careful as a matter of cultural viewpoint and we now are not, is frightening to many people.

As Malidoma Somé notes: "The truth is that the Machine must eliminate every alternative to itself and focus attention on itself because it knows its purpose is not to give life, but to suck the energy out of it."

appendix two

christianity and the subversion of the first amendment

Many militant Christians strongly echo Native activist assertions. They believe that tolerance of other religious expressions or faiths is not really a Christian virtue and those who
express it are really not Christian. This extends, actively, to
Christian faiths other than their own. As militant Christian
John Morris notes:

> Outwardly, leaders such as Vice-President Gore, who
> professes to be a "Baptist," and who mumbles a sort of
> allegiance to the Creator, also speaks repeatedly in his
> book of the "sacredness of nature," with every tree and
> rock being stamped with "the image of God." He also
> believes in a "wisdom to be distilled from all
> faiths," . . . his compassion and sincerity are not to be
> confused with a true Biblical faith.[1]

Like Native activists, militant Christians assert that only
the Christians *they* recognize as legitimate are in fact legitimate. Only those Christians who realize that they are in a

war against sin under God and Christ's banner are real Christians; the others are "religious hypocrite Christians [who] will be taken in their own net and lose out with God."[2]

The First Amendment was passed specifically to prevent adherents of such groups from denying other people the right to practice their faith. That it offers only tenuous protections against such ideologies is clear in any exploration of American history, especially in any examination of the Mormons. Their experience is particularly appropriate to American Indians.

The Mormons, to escape the religious persecution that left their founder dead, eventually settled in Utah. But the United States, in its westward expansion, reached Utah. Still disliked, the Mormons were considered a threat to the internal security of the country and to Christian values. The United States, in legal action, and through the action of its military forces, made the decision to destroy the Mormons completely and without recourse unless the Mormons changed certain of their religious practices, notably polygamy. In 1862 the Congress of the United States passed the Mormon Act. Section 1 prohibited bigamy; section 2 voided the territorial legislature's incorporation of the Church of Jesus Christ of Latter-Day Saints; section 3 provided that no religious or charitable association in the United States could acquire or hold real property worth more than $50,000 in any *territory* of the United States (Utah was then a territory). This so-called mortmain statute provided that all real estate in violation of this statute "shall be forfeited and escheat to the United States." (The statute was not repealed until 1978.) After the statute's enactment the Mormons offered up several test cases to the Supreme Court, but lost them all. In 1882, Congress passed the Edmunds Act, which outlawed cohabitation with more than one female per household in the United States (also not repealed until the 1970s, it was actively used against the hippie movement); prohibited any Mormon from holding office; and declared all voter registration and elections in Utah null and void. Bounty hunters began to descend on Utah to "crack down on Mormonism." Challenges to the federal actions went nowhere. In *Davis v. Beason* the court declared it was *constitutional* to enact a law making it a crime to be a Mormon. In 1887, Congress ordered the attorney general of the United States to begin forfeiture proceedings against the Mormon church. All property of the church excepting burial grounds and church buildings used exclusively for worship were to be seized by troops of the United States. Force was to be used against any resistance.

The Supreme Court ruling in favor of the U.S. actions upheld the position that the First Amendment was a guarantee of religious freedom *only* if a substantial number of fellow citizens do not become annoyed by a particular belief. (The court also asserted that religious *belief* was the only thing protected by the First Amendment; the founding fathers, it asserted, never intended religious *behavior* to be protected.) Should any religious belief system be found offensive to a majority of the country's citizens, the court permitted the state or federal government to:

(1) criminally prosecute anyone who practices the disavowed religion;

(2) ban any member of a sect from voting or holding public office, regardless of whether he or she practices the disfavored acts; and

(3) abolish the church as an institution and seize all of its property (including burial grounds and houses of worship if Congress so decrees).[3]

Writing for the court, Justice Joseph Bradley stated that the practices of the Mormon church were

abhorrent to the sentiments and feelings of the civilized world. . . . It is contrary to the spirit of Christianity and of the civilization which Christianity has produced in the Western world. The question therefore, is whether the promotion of such a nefarious system and practice, so repugnant to our laws and to the principles of our civilization, is to be allowed to continue by the sanction of the government itself.[4]

This decision in First Amendment law was cited by the Supreme Court when allowing the State of Oregon's (legal) assault on the Native American use of peyote in 1990. Without exception, at that time, *all* the religious governing councils in the United States saw the danger to their own religious beliefs from the "peyote case." They banded together to force the passage of the Religious Freedom Restoration Act (RFRA), itself now under attack. Justice Antonin Scalia remarked at the passage of RFRA that such liberalized thinking could once again lead to the emergence of religious practices repugnant to all civilized men (such as polygamy). The danger of the Supreme Court rulings is that they encoded in law the justification for one religious orientation to

completely subvert the beliefs and practices of another up to and including the use of genocidal violence to accomplish it—the very thing the First Amendment was passed to prevent. These legal precedents have never been overturned and, as the peyote case so vividly demonstrated, can be resurrected at any time.

It is important to recognize that *all* attempts to limit the religious freedom of others are based upon what seem to some to be legitimate and important rationales. In spite of our country's historical orientation toward religious freedom, religious freedom has often not been extended to what have been considered fringe groups. *All* religious movements, Baptists and Methodists and Christians and Buddhists and Quakers included, began from individual religious revelations. *All* of these faiths have been singled out for persecution at one time or another. When that persecution occurred, elements of the new faiths were determined to be dangerous to the stability of society or detrimental to certain groups within society. Indian tribal religions were felt to be devil worship and, as Justice Bradley noted about the Mormons, "abhorrent to the sentiments and feelings of the civilized world." Native activists, in pursuing a course of religious restriction because of perceived dangers to their group, are allying themselves with historical tendencies of militant Christianity to subvert the law to carry out social and religious missions. In orienting themselves with the thinking of groups like militant Christians, Native activists are allying themselves to a process and group that holds (and has a legal basis to do so) that Indian religions themselves are dangerous and uncivilized—a group that has and will continue to support the implementation of the Mormon statutes against Earth-based religious forms.

The history of Christian subversion of the First Amendment makes clear that the amendment itself must remain inviolate. It represents one of the greatest innovations of our time and allows the exploration and development of many forms of religious expression—a status that the founding fathers felt was essential to the unfettered development of humankind. The alternative, as they well knew, was religious repression and war. The historical maltreatment of American Indians in the practice of their own faith should be clear warning to Native activists that *any* subversion of the First Amendment, no matter how holy the motives, has as an end result only tyranny.*

---

*As the final galleys for this book were being prepared, the Supreme Court overturned the Religious Freedom Restoration Act; the standard for the regulation of religious behavior is, once again, the Mormon statutes. Justice Scalia was exuberant.

notes and references

PART ONE: **prologue**

This account was suggested by an article a friend shared with me seven or eight years ago from a book he liked. I don't remember the rest of the article, the title, or even the author, but the French couple's son's question impacted me greatly and it has stayed with me ever since. I began to ask myself the same question.

CHAPTER 2: **the mystic way**

1. William McNamara, O.C.D. *The Human Adventure* (Rockport, MA: Element, 1991), p. 94.

2. Joseph Epes Brown, *The Spiritual Legacy of the American Indian* (New York: Crossroad, 1982), p. 113.

3. William Powers, *Oglala Religion* (Lincoln: University of Nebraska Press, 1982), pp. 46–47. There is a regrettable movement among scholars to insist that the sacred center of meaning as it appears and is named in the world's religious traditions is *not* the same from religion to religion. For some discussion of this trend see Denise Carmody and John Carmody, *Mysticism: Holiness East and West* (New York: Oxford University Press, 1996), pp. 3–27. This trend is cause for concern because

if it is eventually accepted that each religion is talking about a different *essence* at the center of its practice, it will—in my opinion—reignite the worst forms of conflict over whose religious form is the most superior. Although it may be true that manifestations of the sacred center are perceived in a variety of forms specific to each religion (Christ in Christianity or Manido among the Ojibway), it is my opinion, based on numerous scholars' assertions, the words of mystics themselves, and my own experiences of the sacred, that the center from which all these terms spring and to which they all point is identical and that therefore the terms apply to the same referent.

4. Stephen Harrod Buhner, *Sacred Plant Medicine: Explorations in the Practice of Indigenous Herbalism* (Boulder: Roberts Rinehart, 1996), p. 110.

5. Evelyn Underhill, *Mysticism* (New York: E. P. Dutton, 1961), p. 169.

6. Ibid., p. 176

7. Lee Irwin, *Dream Seekers: Native American Visionary Traditions of the Great Plains* (Norman: University of Oklahoma Press, 1994), p. 121.

8. Quoted in Underhill, *Mysticism*, pp. 187–188.

9. Robert Bly, *The Kabir Book* (Boston: Beacon Press, 1977), p. 11.

10. John Neihardt, *Black Elk Speaks* (Lincoln: University of Nebraska Press, 1988), pp. 48–49.

11. Underhill, *Mysticism*, p. 178.

12. Buhner, *Sacred Plant Medicine*, pp. 7–8.

13. Underhill, *Mysticism*, p. 198.

14. Quoted in ibid., p. 206.

15. Quoted in ibid., p. 212.

16. Bly, *The Kabir Book*, p. 50.

17. Joseph Epes Brown, *The Sacred Pipe* (Norman: University of Oklahoma Press, 1953), p. 4.

18. Ibid., p. 85.

19. Ibid., p. 138.

20. Buhner, *Sacred Plant Medicine*, p. xiii.

21. Neihardt, *Black Elk Speaks*, pp. 204–205.

22. Frances Densmore, *Teton Sioux Music* (Washington, D.C.: Smithsonian Institution, Bureau of American Ethnology, Bulletin 61, 1918), p. 164.

23. Ibid., p. 157.

24. Underhill, *Mysticism*, p. 230.

25. Ibid., p. 234.

26. Ibid., p. 241.

27. Ibid., p. 228.

28. Ibid.

29. Ibid., p. 243.

30. Bly, *The Kabir Book*, p. 6.

31. Brown, *The Sacred Pipe*, p. 6.

32. Ibid., p. 115.

33. Underhill, *Mysticism*, p. 238.

34. Ibid., p. 239.

35. Ibid., p. 391.

36. Huston Smith, *The Illustrated World's Religions* (San Francisco: HarperCollins, 1994), p. 94.

37. Ibid., pp. 94–95.

38. Paul Wallace, *White Roots of Peace: The Iroquois Book of Life* (Santa Fe: Clear Light Publishers, 1994; originally published Philadelphia: University of Pennsylvania Press, 1946), p. 33.

39. Oren Lyons, "Land of the Free, Home of the Brave: Iroquois Democracy," *Earth Ethics* (Washington: Center for Respect of Life and Environment), vol. 4, no. 4 (Summer 1993), p. 7.

40. Wallace, *White Roots of Peace*, p. 43.

41. Ibid., p. 44.

42. Ibid.

43. Portions of this passage quoted in ibid., p. 45.

44. Ibid., p. 55.

45. Ibid.

46. Ibid., pp. 55–56.

47. Ibid., p. 60.

48. Underhill, *Mysticism*, p. 412.

CHAPTER 3: the sacred earth

1. Frances Densmore, *Teton Sioux Music* (Washington, D.C.: Smithsonian Institution, Bureau of American Ethnology, 1918), p. 96.

2. Kent N. Nerburn and Louise M. Mengelkoch, eds., *Native American Wisdom* (San Rafael: New World Library, 1991), pp. 43–44.

3. Joseph Epes Brown, "The Question of 'Mysticism' Within Native American Traditions," in R. Woods, ed., *Understanding Mysticism* (New York: Doubleday, 1980), p. 208.

4. See Seyyed Hossein Nasr, *Religion and the Order of Nature* (New York: Oxford University Press, 1996), esp. chaps. 3–4.

5. John Seed, "I Call on the Spirit of Herbs," in Stephen Harrod Buhner, "Plants of Power: Earthkeepers of Six Nations Speak of the Sacred Power of Plants," unpublished manuscript.

6. Carol McGrath, "The Colonizing Mind," in Buhner, "Plants of Power."

7. Bill Mollison, *Permaculture: A Practical Guide for a Sustainable Future* (Washington, D.C.: Island Press, 1990).

8. Ellen Messer, "Present and Future Prospects of Herbal Medicine in a Mexican Community," in Richard Ford, *The Nature and Status of Ethnobotany* (Ann Arbor: University of Michigan Museum of Anthropology, Anthropology Paper 67, 1978), p. 146.

9. Matilda Coxe Stevenson, *Ethnobotany of the Zuni Indians* (Washington, D.C.: Smithsonian Institution, Bureau of American Ethnology, 1915), p. 36.

10. Frances Densmore, *Papago Music* (Washington, D.C.: Smithsonian Institution, Bureau of American Ethnology, Bulletin 90, 1929), p. 90.

11. Kenneth Pelletier, *Toward a Science of Consciousness* (New York: Delta, 1978), p. 66.

12. Densmore, *Teton Sioux Music*, pp. 188–189.

13. Ibid., p. 184.

14. Ibid., pp. 185–188.

15. Stephen Harrod Buhner, *Sacred Plant Medicine* (Boulder: Roberts Rinehart, 1996), p. 19.

16. Vaclav Havel, Address of the President of the Czech Republic, His Excellency Vaclav Havel, on the Occasion of the Liberty Medal Ceremony, Philadelphia, Pennsylvania, July 4, 1994.

17. Jan Whitner, *Stonescaping* (Pownal: Storey Communications, 1992), pp. 8–9.

18. Quoted in Edward Canda, "The Korean Mountain Spirit," *Korea Journal*, vol. 20, no. 9 (September 1980), p. 12.

19. Quoted in ibid.

20. Ibid.

21. Quoted in Delores La Chappelle, *Sacred Land, Sacred Sex, Rapture of the Deep* (Silverton, CO: Finn Hill Arts, 1988), p. 189.

22. Densmore, *Teton Sioux Music*, pp. 107–108.

23. Ibid., p. 214.

24. Canda, "The Korean Mountain Spirit," p. 13.

25. Ibid.

26. Jim Cummings, "A New View of Language: A Crosswinds Conversation with David Abram," in *Crosswinds* (Santa Fe: July 1996), p. 11.

CHAPTER 4: gifts of the great spirit?

1. Ward Churchill, *Fantasies of the Master Race*, edited by M. Annette Jaimes (Monroe, Me.: Common Courage Press, 1992), p. 221.

2. Ibid., p. 193. Means's comments are similar to Barbara Owl's: "We have many particular things which we hold internal to our cultures. These things are spiritual in nature, and they are for us, not for anyone who happens to walk in off the street. They are ours and they are not for sale."

3. Ibid., p. 216. Vine Deloria, Jr., is a theologian; a graduate of Augustana Lutheran Seminary, 1963; an attorney; a graduate of University of Colorado Law School, 1970; a professor (since 1990) at the University of Colorado; and author of a number of well-selling and landmark books on Indians such as *Custer Died for Your Sins* (1969), *God Is Red* (1973), and most recently *Red Earth White Lies* (1996). He is the son of Vine Deloria, Sr., an Episcopalian priest who ministered to the Pine Ridge and Sisseton-Wahpeton Reservations (Susan Avery and Linda Skinner, *Extraordinary American Indians* [Chicago: Childrens Press, 1992]). Deloria's remarks are similar to Janet McCloud's: "These people [whites] run off reservations acting all lost and hopeless, really pathetic" (Churchill, *Fantasies of the Master Race*, p. 217).

4. David Johnston, "Spiritual Seekers Borrow Indian Ways," *New York Times*, December 27, 1993. George Tinker is a theologian at Iliff School of Theology in Denver, Colorado. Although I have not verified this information with Tinker, I have been told by a former board member of his church and a member of the Denver Indian Center that Tinker is also a minister who has his own church in Denver. His church, I have been told, offers services that are a mixture of Native religious forms and Christianity.

5. "Religion: the beliefs, attitudes, emotions, behavior, etc., constituting man's relationship with the powers and principles of the universe, especially with a deity or deities." From the Latin *religare*, meaning to "bind back" (*Reader's Digest Great Encyclopedic Dictionary* [Pleasantville, N.Y.: *Reader's Digest*, 1977], p. 1136).

6. Lee Irwin, *The Dream Seekers: Native American Visionary Traditions of the Great Plains* (Norman: University of Oklahoma Press, 1994), p. x.

7. Ibid., p. vii. Oddly enough, Deloria has, at times, explored slightly different perspectives. In his introduction to the commemorative edition of *Black Elk Speaks*, Deloria "noted how Neihardt's work had 'become a North American bible of all tribes' . . . and contended that it must be considered an essential canon of Native spirituality from which further theological reflection ought to arise. . . . Aware of authorship problems, Deloria nonetheless gave the work his blessing because of the 'transcendent truth' it spoke to *all* people" (Michael Steltenkamp, *Black Elk: Holy Man of the Oglala* [Norman: University of Oklahoma Press, 1993], p. 154; italics mine).

8. Ward Churchill, *From a Native Son* (Boston: South End Press, 1996), p. 399, quoting Sherman Alexie, "White Men Can't Drum," *New York Times Magazine,* October 4, 1992.

9. "Racism . . . is a worldview, variously defended on biological, cultural, historical, and even religious grounds, in which the idea of race is placed at the centre of human concerns as a first principle" (Alan Davies, *Infected Christianity* [Montreal: McGill-Queen's University Press, 1988], p. x).

10. In attempting to restore the Indigenous Mind in themselves, people who have been cut off from it for a long time (see Malidoma Patrice Somé's work, for example, *Of Water and the Spirit* [New York: Penguin, 1994]) are necessarily a caricature of authenticity as are all those who are manifesting *pathetos.* In time the situation corrects itself.

11. In a similar line of thought, Alan Davies observes that Aryan proponents asserted: "It was Luther's German soul, his profound German soul, that was the true source of his religious wisdom and immense creative powers." The German tribe had the capacity to touch deeper religious truths not accessible to other races because of their unique relationship to the Earth and God (Davies, *Infected Christianity,* pp. 28–29).

12. This brings up the nagging image of a member of an Indian tribe who is of 25 percent Indian and 75 percent German-Irish extraction. Does the 25 percent Indian blood have some magical essence that "overwhelms" the 75 percent German-Irish blood, which causes the Indian to experience deeper realities? Or can the Indian only experience 25 percent of that deeper reality because of the dilution of his or her blood? This kind of theological problem is not new: "Of course the pious who accepted the new theory blandly assumed that Adam and Eve were the progenitors of the Caucasian species, but even they had to face the theological implications of hybridization. Was the mulatto half-saved, half-damned? And the theological problems presented by the quinteroon and octoroon led one into higher mathematics" (Joseph Leonard, S.S.J., *Theology and Race Relations* [Milwaukee: Bruce Publishing, 1963], p. 55).

13. Mary Moore and Sudie Llaneza, "Activists in the Trenches Speak Out on Spiritual Genocide," *Sonoma County Free Press* (Occidental, Calif.) vol. 6, no. 4 (September 1992).

14. Oren Lyons, in "Land of the Free, Home of the Brave: Iroquois Democracy," an address given to the U.S. Senate Committee on Indian Affairs in 1987, noted that when the Peacemaker came to the Iroquois "a great war of attrition engulfed the lands, and women and children cowered in fear of their own men. The leaders were fierce and merciless. They were fighting in a blind rage. Nations, homes, and families were destroyed, and the people were scattered. It was a dismal world of dark disasters where there seemed

to be no hope. It was a raging proof of what inhumanity man is capable of when the laws and principles of life are thrown away." This quotation seems to clearly indicate that prior to the "white discovery" of the new world, Native tribes engaged in periods of genocide. As Lyons noted, there is a *common* inhumanity of man when laws and principles are thrown away (quoted in *Earth Ethics*, vol. 4, no. 4 [Summer 1993], p. 7).

15. Timothy Aeppel, "At One with Indians," *Wall Street Journal*, August 6, 1996, p. A6.

16. Nirad Chaudhuri, *Hinduism* (New York: Oxford University Press, 1979), p. xi.

17. Ibid.

18. Ibid., pp. 8, 9.

19. Churchill, *Fantasies of the Master Race*, p. 216.

20. Paul Steinmetz, S.J. *Pipe, Bible, and Peyote* (Knoxville: University of Tennessee, 1990), p. 154.

21. Ibid., p. 164.

22. Is an Indian who has been raised as a Christian, perhaps even third generation, connected to his or her birth religion—Christianity? Or to an Indian religion? What about a "white" person who has been raised from birth in the tradition of the pipe, sweat lodge, and vision quest, knowing no other way? Is that person's birth religion "Indian"? Or should that person be forced to return to Christianity even if he or she doesn't want to? Should Indians raised as Christian be forced to return to their ancestors' birth religion even if they don't want to?

23. T. Mails, *Fools Crow* (Lincoln: University of Nebraska Press, 1979), p. 184.

24. Charles Alexander (Ohiyesa) Eastman, *The Soul of an Indian* (San Rafael: New World Library, 1993; originally published 1911, quoted from the Classic Wisdom Collection edition), p. xix.

25. Mails, *Fools Crow*, pp. 51–52. Fools Crow, it is often noted, was a signatory to the "Resolution of the 5th Annual Meeting of the Tradition Elder's Circle," which opposed "plastic" medicine men. This action seems puzzling; Ed McGaa who was named and trained with him, Fools Crow's own words, and other biographical material by people who knew him report a completely different position on his part. However, the resolution can be interpreted as it is called—an attempt to address superficiality and lack of spiritual knowledge among *some* Earth-centered proponents. The resolution generally, however, is used to "prove" that any ceremonial sharing between Indian and non-Indian is wrong and condemned by "legitimate" Indians.

26. Vinson Brown, *Crazy Horse Hoka Hey!* (New York: Macmillan, 1971), p. 166f, quoted in Rudolf Kaiser, *The Voice of the Great Spirit: Prophecies of the Hopi Indians* (Boston: Shambhala, 1991), pp. 131–132. Although Crazy Horse is considered by many to be a

great leader of the Sioux, he, like many others, is encountering assaults on the "legitimacy" of his standing. In his article "When Black Elk Speaks, Everybody Listens," in Christopher Vecsey, *Religion in Native North America* (Moscow: University of Idaho Press, 1990), William K. Powers states that the legend and standing of Crazy Horse have been "refuted by some Indians who did not believe that Crazy Horse was a chief to be revered" (p. 147).

27. Brian Wilkes, "Who Is Indian?" *Wildfire Magazine*, vol. 7, no. 1 (Winter 1996), p. 41.

28. Ed McGaa, "Condemning the Wrong People," *Wildfire Magazine*, vol. 7, no. 1 (Winter 1996), p. 32. McGaa's position echoed that of the Catholic Church during the civil rights movement in the 1960s in the United States. Joseph Leonard notes that "attempts of Catholics to drive Negro Catholics from their church through the manifestation of contempt or hatred, either by act or word, are not only sins against justice because they are trying to deprive them of a right given by the general law of the Church to attend territorial parishes, they are also sins against charity, because of the hatred involved, and sins of scandal. Obviously those who attempt to drive them out through threats of violence, or actual use of force or fear, sin mortally through the use of unjust means or physical harm" (Joseph Leonard, S.S.J., *Theology and Race Relations* [Milwaukee: Bruce Publishing, 1963], pp. 235–236).

29. Kevin Moore, "Kindness Crosses Country Again," *News from Indian Country,* mid-July 1996, p. 12A.

30. Manitonquat, *Return to Creation* (Spokane: Bear Tribe Publishing, 1991), p. 17.

31. Mails, *Fools Crow,* p. 58.

32. Michael Steltenkamp, *Black Elk: Holy Man of the Ogalala,* (Norman: University of Oklahoma Press, 1993), p. 107.

33. Joseph Epes Brown, *The Sacred Pipe* (Norman: University of Oklahoma Press, 1953), pp. 6–7. This is similar to Catholic assertions about the Eucharist and its applicability to all people of all races. Speaking about Negroes and whites sharing religious devotion, Joseph Leonard says: "One of the effects of the Eucharist is to unite one in a mystical union with Christ and with His members through a bond of charity" (Leonard, *Theology and Race Relations,* p. 59).

34. B. Medicine Eagle, *Buffalo Woman Comes Singing* (New York: Ballantine, 1991), p. 293.

35. Arvol Looking Horse, "Nation World Peace and Prayer Day," *Urban Indian News* (Newsletter of the Native American Brotherhood Church), vol. 1, no. 5 (May 1996), p. 3.

36. Steinmetz, *Pipe, Bible, and Peyote,* p. 16.

37. Ibid., p. 190.

38. Eastman, *The Soul of an Indian,* p. 2.

39. Kent N. Nerburn and Louise M. Mengelkoch, eds., *Native American Wisdom* (San Rafael: New World Library, 1991), p. 88.

40. Ibid., from an unnamed source, p. 33.

41. Steinmetz, *Pipe, Bible, and Peyote*, pp. 34–35. The struggles between advocates of free religious sharing and racial restrictions are not limited to Indians. As Joseph Leonard notes in *Theology and Race Relations*: "Segregation in the church violates something that is basic in the nature of the church. How can a church exclude from 'the church of God' those who are children of God? How can it, as 'the body of Christ,' withhold the privilege of worship from those who have been brought into union with Christ. . . . We must confess that there are churches, and they are not all in the South, that are thoroughly committed to the continuance of segregation in society and also within the church. We believe that such an attitude, which is the epitome of racial pride, cuts the very heart out of the Christian gospel and the Christian ethic. It imperils the soul of the church itself. How tragic it would be if the churches became 'the last bulwark of racial segregation!' What a paradox if secularism and secular institutions 'out-christianize Christianity!' " (p. 218).

42. Churchill, *Fantasies of the Master Race*, p. 218. Alan Davies notes that racism begins "when religion [is] seen as an expression of race, and . . . when theology permit[s] its central ideas and symbols . . . to be recast in a racist mould" (*Infected Christianity*, p. 25).

43. Mikkel Aaland, *Sweat: The Illustrated History and Description of the Finnish Sauna, Russian Bania, Islamic Hammam, Japanese Mushi-buro, Mexican Temescal and American Indian and Eskimo Sweatlodge* (Santa Barbara: Capra Press, 1978), pp. 15–16.

44. Ibid., p. 137.

45. Ibid., p. 139.

46. Ibid.

47. Ibid., p. 140.

48. Manitonquat, *Return to Creation*, p. 25. Because of Manitonquat's willingness to follow the instructions of his elders to teach "whites," he too has been placed on a list of Indian "traitors" who are defiling Indian religious traditions.

49. Delores La Chapelle, *Sacred Land, Sacred Sex, Rapture of the Deep* (Silverton, CO: Finn Hill Arts, 1988), p. 272.

50. Trilock Chandra Majupuria and D. P. Joshi, *Religious and Useful Plants of Nepal and India* (Latipur Colony, Lashkar, India: M. Gupta, 1989), p. 239.

51. M. Grieve, *A Modern Herbal* (New York: Dover, 1971), p. 701.

52. Stephen Harrod Buhner, *Sacred Plant Medicine* (Boulder: Roberts Rinehart, 1996).

53. Mircea Eliade, *From Primitives to Zen* (New York: Harper & Row, 1967); also Wendell Beane and William Doty, eds., *Myths, Rites, and Symbols: A Mircea Eliade Reader* (New York: Harper Colophon, 1975).

54. Brown, *The Sacred Pipe*, p. 46.

55. Steven Foster and Meredith Little, *The Book of the Vision Quest* (New York: Prentice Hall, 1988), p. 24.

56. Huston Smith, *The Illustrated World's Religions* (San Francisco: HarperCollins, 1994), pp. 126, 138.

57. Edward Canda, "The Korean Mountain Spirit," *Korea Journal*, vol. 20, no. 9 (September 1980), p. 14.

58. Ibid.

59. Ibid., p. 15.

60. William McNamara, O.C.D., *Mystical Passion* (Rockport, MA: Element, 1991), p. 97.

61. Ibid., p. 84.

62. McNamara, "The Desert and the City," *Desert Call*, vol. 20, nos. 2, 3 (Summer-Fall, 1985), pp. 21–22.

63. McNamara, *Mystical Passion*, p. 88.

64. Ibid., p. 96.

65. Ibid., p. 95.

66. Ibid., p. 87.

67. Ibid., p. 102.

68. Brown, *The Sacred Pipe*, p. 66.

69. McNamara, "The Desert and the City," p. 22.

70. *The Gospel of Sri Ramakrishna*, p. 559, quoted in Joseph Campbell, *The Masks of God: Primitive Mythology* (New York: Viking Press, 1959), p. 463. This sort of conflict between religions is legion. All groups think their way is the *only* legitimate way. Even as refined a thinker as William McNamara, the Carmelite monk, falls into this trap, labeling Earth-centered religious practice "quasi-religious" and Oriental religious practice by Westerners "religious regression" (William McNamara, *The Human Adventure: The Art of Contemplative Living* [Rockport, MA: Element, 1991], p. 112). Similar remarks appear in Buddhist commentaries I have seen that describe Christianity as a lower form of religious practice, which only appeals to the spiritually inferior.

71. Churchill, *Fantasies of the Master Race*, p. 226.

72. Ibid., p. 217. Matthew King also makes similar remarks. "For someone who has not learned how our balance is maintained, to pretend to be a medicine man is very, very

dangerous. It is a big disrespect to the powers and can cause great harm to whoever is doing it, to those he claims to be teaching, to nature, to everything. It is very bad." Ibid., p. 220.

73. Board member, Denver Indian Center, personal communication, 1995.

74. Manitonquat, *Return to Creation*, p. 25.

75. Ibid., pp. 24–25.

76. Deloria, *Red Earth White Lies*, pp. 9–10.

77. Eknath Easwaran, *Gandhi the Man* (Petaluma, CA: Nilgiri Press, 1978), p. 151.

CHAPTER 5: selling indian spirituality

1. Linda Hurwicz, "Native American Protests: No Easy Answers," *NAPRA Trade Journal*, vol. 4, no. 4 (Fall 1993).

2. Ward Churchill, *Fantasies of the Master Race*, edited by M. Annette Jaimes (Monroe, ME: Common Courage Press, 1992), p. 217. This message is echoed by more activists than can be listed. Clyde Bellecourt allows that nonmonetary gifts are okay: "True medicine people accept only tobacco and food as payment," but he is clear that no money should ever change hands (Karen Lincoln Michel, "Non-Indian Use of Ritual Offends," *Dallas Morning News*, reprinted in the *Denver Post*, May 6, 1994).

3. David Rockwell, *Giving Voice to Bear* (Boulder: Roberts Rinehart, 1991), p. 81.

4. Ibid., p. 89.

5. Edward Canda, personal communication, 1994.

6. Frances Densmore, *Nootka and Quileute Music* (Washington, D.C.: Smithsonian Institution, Bureau of American Ethnology, Bulletin 124, 1939), p. 294.

7. Ales Hrdlicka, *Physiological and Medical Observations Among the Indians of Southwestern United States and Northern Mexico* (Washington, D.C.: Smithsonian Institution, Bureau of American Ethnology, Bulletin 34, 1908), p. 222.

8. Alfred Kroeber, *Handbook of the Indians of California* (Washington, D.C.: Smithsonian Institution, Bureau of American Ethnology, Bulletin 78, c. 1925), p. 423.

9. Ibid., p. 198.

10. Raymond DeMallie, *The Sixth Grandfather* (Lincoln: University of Nebraska Press, 1984), p. 236.

11. Ibid., p. 240.

12. Ibid., p. 237.

13. Frances Densmore, *Northern Ute Music* (Washington, D.C.: Smithsonian Institution, Bureau of American Ethnology, Bulletin 75, 1922), p. 129.

14. Kroeber, *Handbook of the Indians of California*, p. 231.

15. Mircea Eliade, *Shamanism* (Princeton: Princeton University Press, 1972), p. 302, quoting Willard Park, *Shamanism in Western North America: A Study in Cultural Relationships* (Evanston and Chicago: Northwestern University, 1938), pp. 46, 48ff.

16. Densmore, *Nootka and Quileute Music*, p. 311.

17. Joan Halifax, *Shamanic Voices* (New York: Dutton, 1977), p. 187.

18. Lowell John Bean, "California Indian Shamanism and Folk Curing," in Wayland Hand, ed., *American Folk Medicine* (Berkeley: University of California Press, 1976), pp. 118–119.

19. John S. Mbiti, "African Religions and Philosophy," in Hand, *American Folk Medicine*, p. 297.

20. W. C. Sturtevant, *The Mikasuki Seminole: Medical Beliefs and Practices* (Yale University Ph.D. dissertation, 1955), pp. 140–142.

21. Ibid., p. 102.

22. Kroeber, *Handbook of the Indians of California*, p. 184.

23. Elizabeth Tooker, *Ethnography of the Huron Indians, 1615–1649* (Washington, D.C.: Smithsonian Institution, Bureau of American Ethnology, Bulletin 190, 1964), p. 84.

24. Ibid., p. 118.

25. Densmore, *Northern Ute Music*, p. 127.

26. Ibid., p. 136.

27. Kent N. Nerburn and Louise M. Mengelkoch, *Native American Wisdom* (San Rafael: New World Library, 1991), pp. 41–42.

28. Walter James Hoffman, *The Menomini Indians* (Washington, D.C.: Smithsonian Institution, Bureau of American Ethnology, Annual Report 14, c. 1925), p. 138.

29. Ibid., p. 132.

30. Ibid., p. 141.

31. Ibid., p. 146.

32. John G. Bourke, *The Medicine Men of the Apache* (Washington, D.C.: Smithsonian Institution, Bureau of American Ethnology), p. 451.

33. Francis Paul Prucha, *The Great Father* (Lincoln: University of Nebraska Press, 1986), pp. 646–647.

34. Ibid., p. 647.

35. Christopher Vecsey, *Handbook of American Indian Religious Freedom* (New York: Crossroad, 1993), p. 45.

36. Steltenkamp, pp. 37–38. The need to hide traditional religious training and practice from other Indians was apparently somewhat common. A Cree elder and medicine teacher told me in spring 1997 that his first contact with a medicine man of his tribe

occurred in his twenties. He hadn't known the man was a medicine person for the man had kept his profession secret. This was because, as the Cree elder noted, many of the tribal members would inform on him and he would be arrested for practicing the old ways.

37. Avis Little Eagle, "Sisseton Elder Hurt at New Age Meeting," photocopy of article with written notation indicating it was from *Lakota Times*. Newspaper name and date clipped off. Churchill, in *Fantasies of the Master Race*, also claimed that Sun Bear "has been able to make himself rather wealthy over the past few years" (p. 190).

38. If the issue of legitimacy is reduced to amount of compensation one receives for being Indian, a comparison between Sun Bear's detractors and Sun Bear is invariably going to favor Sun Bear. Ward Churchill, George Tinker, and Vine Deloria, Jr., are all tenured and well-paid professors at prestigious institutions. Russell Means is now well remunerated for his work as an Indian actor. His roles include *Last of the Mohicans* (a remarkable, even beautiful, performance) and *Pocahontas*. If the point is taken even further to be that of receiving lucrative remuneration as a professional Indian while at the same time distorting Indian history or values, Means will fare badly for his role as the voice of Pocahontas's father. The Disney production, as was widely noted in reviews, was badly flawed. Pocahontas was only a young girl when she met John Smith, was captured and held hostage (after the John Smith episode) by Captain Samuel Argall and converted to Christianity. She then married John Rolfe and traveled to England, and died of smallpox the following year.

39. Churchill, *Fantasies of the Master Race*, p. 190. Undoubtedly, in spite of all the sources I quoted, both Indian and non-Indian, my disagreement with the historical veracity of Indian claims that they never charge for services will be cast in this light.

40. Virgil Vogel, *American Indian Medicine* (Norman: University of Oklahoma Press, 1970), p. ix.

41. Churchill, *Fantasies of the Master Race*, p. 216.

42. Ibid., pp. 219–220.

43. Ibid., p. 220. "The word 'cult,' which formerly referred to an organized system of worship, is now a term that slanders any religion that you don't know about and don't like. The term 'cult' is pejoratively applied to many different types of groups, and its use dehumanizes people, and thus sanctions violence against them, the way 'nigger' dehumanized African Americans and sanctioned violence against them. . . . Prejudice against religions that are perceived as not being mainstream is still not being questioned. . . . Prejudice against religions condones unnecessary aggressive actions against a group that results in deaths of innocent children, women, and men." Catherine Wessinger (associate professor of Religious

Studies, Loyola University, New Orleans), "Religious Intolerance—not 'Cults'—Is the Problem," *Communities Magazine*, Fall 1995, p. 33. Tim Miller, associate professor of Religious Studies at the University of Kansas, Lawrence, comments in ibid.: "When the word 'cult' enters the typical American conversation, the jury has already returned. From that point on we're discussing the sentence, not the verdict" (p. 31).

44. "Samish Officially Recognized," *News from Indian Country*, late June 1996, p. 2A.

45. Joseph Leonard, S.S.J., *Theology and Race Relations* (Milwaukee: Bruce Publishing, 1963), p. 217.

46. Ibid., p. 221.

47. Ibid., p. 227.

48. Churchill, *Fantasies of the Master Race*, p. 221.

49. Ibid., p. 218.

50. Ibid., p. 193.

51. Wabun Wind, personal communication, 1966; and David Johnston, "Spiritual Seekers Borrow Indians' Ways," *New York Times*, December 27, 1993, p. A10.

52. Leonard, *Theology and Race Relations*, p. 225.

53. Ibid., pp. 237–238.

54. Jamie Sams, portion of letter on Native American Tribal Traditions Trust letterhead, Sante Fe, N.M., no date. Many Indians who teach non-Indians, as noted, are considered sellouts or ones who are going against what nature intended. Black Nationalists made similar arguments about the teaching of Christianity to whites in biblical times. Arguing that Jesus and all the early Christian fathers were black (and that Christianity was supposed to remain a religion among black people only) they noted that "Paul, the black Hebrew 'Uncle Tom' of antiquity, turned the black religion of Christianity into a white slave religion by imposing a white theology on the followers of Jesus and thereby selling out to the Roman oppressors" (Alan Davies, *Infected Christianity* [Montreal: McGill-Queen's University Press, 1988], p. 112).

55. Paul Smith and Robert Warrior, *Like a Hurricane: The Indian Movement from Alcatraz to Wounded Knee* (New York: New Press, 1996).

56. Wabun Wind, personal communication, 1996. Also, Sun Bear, *Path of Power* (Spokane: Bear Tribe Publishing, 1983). I never knew Sun Bear although my wife apprenticed with him from 1987 until his death. Our community now owns his land at Vision Mountain. Much of our payment for the land went to pay IRS back taxes, Washington State back taxes, a bank lien, and medical bills accrued from Sun Bear's illness. I did not work with Sun Bear, and I never met him (despite my wife's affiliation). So I can say that my perspective, which will undoubtedly be disputed, is fairly unbiased. There are some

things he did that I do disagree with, including certain aspects of *how* he taught some Earth ceremonies. But none of those behaviors, I assert, justify violence or religious prohibition. He was genuine in his devotion and work.

57. Amy Kuebelbeck, "White Earth Leaders Convicted of Corruption," *News from Indian Country,* mid-July 1996, p. 5A.

58. Rudolf Kaiser, *The Voice of the Great Spirit: Prophecies of the Hopi Indians* (Boston: Shambhala, 1991), p. 136.

59. Ibid., p. 135.

60. Ibid., p. 136.

61. Ibid., p. 137.

62. Ibid., p. 138.

63. Churchill, *Fantasies of the Master Race*, p. 218.

64. Jodi Rave, "Few Who Know Churchill Are Indifferent," *Colorado Daily,* Boulder, Colo., November 23, 1993, p. 3.

65. Ibid.

66. Carol Standing Elk, "Time to Bring Ward Churchill to Account," *Colorado Daily,* Boulder, Colo., January 13, 1994, Letters to the Editor section.

67. Churchill, *Fantasies of the Master Race*, p. 191.

68. Steltenkamp, *Black Elk: Holy Man of the Oglala*, p. xvii.

69. William K. Powers, "When Black Elk Speaks, Everybody Listens," in Christopher Vecsey, *Religion in Native North America* (Moscow: University of Idaho Press, 1990), p. 148.

70. Ibid., pp. 137, 147, 148.

71. George Tinker, CNN interview, "Invisible People—Plastic Medicine Men," November 18, 1994.

72. Steltenkamp, *Black Elk: Holy Man of the Oglala*, pp. 154–155.

73. Ibid., p. xiii.

74. Ibid., p. 146.

75. See Powers, "When Black Elk Speaks, Everybody Listens," especially pp. 147–148. These attacks become particularly virulent whenever a work begins to attain universal appeal, for example, Chief Seattle's comments, the book *The Education of Little Tree,* and the especially virulent attacks on Carlos Castañeda's work. Any work that begins to be widely absorbed into the awareness of the general population is assaulted in the same manner as holy places on the North American continent (see Chapter 3). The existence and relevance of Indian spirituality and its applicability to people in general are now beginning to be challenged. It is evident that this trend will continue until Black Elk—who so far has escaped—is thoroughly discredited.

76. Steltenkamp, *Black Elk: Holy Man of the Oglala*, p. 156.

77. Ibid., p. 155.

78. Ibid., p. 191.

79. Ibid.

80. Ibid., p. 157.

81. Ibid., p. 164.

82. Ibid., pp. 164–165.

83. Ibid., p. 88.

84. Barry Lopez, comment in *Earth Island Journal*, Fall 1995, p. 34.

85. In February 1997, just as this manuscript was being completed, I learned that Ward Churchill had bowed to pressure and, in spite of prior assertions he would not submit to "identity police," became an enrolled member of the Keetoowah Band Cherokee.

86. Sun Bear, original manuscript, n.p., ca. 1978.

CHAPTER 6: genocide, race, and spirituality

1. Center for the Spirit, "Alert Concerning the Abuse and Exploitation of American Indian Sacred Traditions," Oakland: no date, 2 pages. Carole Standing Elk, a principal founder of the Center for the Spirit, has been denounced for undermining Indian values—just as she denounced others. A letter signed by George Martin (of the National Advisory Council for Leonard Peltier) and other Native activists states that Carole Standing Elk (and others) are "disgraceful impostors." Ward Churchill demanded (*Colorado Daily*, January 13 [? date obscured], 1994, p. 12) that Vernon and Clyde Bellecourt and Carole Standing Elk "should be brought before a representative tribunal of [American Indian] Movement elders to answer the charges of, among other things, subverting AIM, misappropriating resources, and collusion with federal agencies." The letter signed by George Martin also attacked Dennis Banks, one of the original founders of AIM. "It seems ironic that it was Dennis Banks who appointed FBI provocateur Douglas Durham to the National Security Director position. . . . Dennis Banks has a history of these kind of appointments. First Douglas Durham, now Carole Standing Elk and Fern Mathias."

2. John O'Sullivan, "A Yale Colloquy on Race," *Wall Street Journal*, April 17, 1997, p. A22. He continues his comments, which have special relevance: "Hence the liberal psychodramas in which racism is uncovered somewhere, those guilty made to confess (like victims of the Red Guards during China's Cultural Revolution) and sentences of political re-education ('sensitivity training' in American English) imposed. Their reward for compliance is that the offense is then lifted from their shoulders and attributed to the unconscious racism of society. In that larger social picture, someone can be guilty of racism even

when shown to be innocent. Indeed, a guilty verdict may be especially vital in such cases to allay suspicions that the general theory is false."

3. Ward Churchill, *Fantasies of the Master Race*, edited by M. Annette Jaimes (Monroe, ME: Common Courage Press, 1992). Churchill's argument was explored and developed specifically in reference to the literature a colonizing or oppressor culture produces at various stages in its relations with a colonized or oppressed culture. His observations are extremely interesting. I'm not sure anyone has explored this perspective as much as it warrants. Of the three stages he gives the shortest attention and development to the third, which theorizes that the final stage is concerned with the oppressor culture absorbing the values and truths of the oppressed culture into it. A cursory glance at the literature *seems* to support his assertion. What it really means, however, is something else again. He could offer a great deal to the understanding of oppressor-oppressed processes should he decide to examine this thesis historically and cross-culturally.

4. Ibid., p. 2.

5. Ibid.

6. Ibid.

7. George Grinnell, *Blackfoot Lodge Tales* Lincoln, NE: Bison Books, 1962), p. xi.

8. Quoted in Walter James Hoffman, *The Menomini Indians* (Washington, D.C.: Smithsonian Institution Bureau of American Ethnology, Annual Report 14), p. 143.

9. Members of my adoptive family line Harrod, through my great-grandfather, were heavily involved in such atrocities. James Harrod, one ancestor in that line, came home to find his wife killed and scalped, her finger cut off to remove her wedding ring. He spent the rest of his life hating Indians and he killed them whenever he could find them. I find this history deeply ironic considering a descendant of this man—a country doctor, my great-grandfather, Cecil Gardner Harrod—inspired my deep love of the Earth and encouraged me to strive toward deeper humanity.

10. Churchill, *Fantasies of the Master Race*, p. 35.

11. Grinnell, *Blackfoot Lodge Tales*, p. xiv.

12. Brooke Medicine Eagle, personal communication; also Churchill, *Fantasies of the Master Race*, p. 4.

13. Churchill, *Fantasies of the Master Race*, pp. 2, 3.

14. In spite of the intense assaults on Castañeda's work one fact remains—it was his work alone that sparked the beginning of acceptance of indigenous religious forms as legitimate expressions of the sacred journey. He is attacked by Churchill and others as presenting a fictionalized (and self-serving) account of tribal spirituality; nevertheless it is his work that began the process of proselytizing and converting non-Indians to Earth-centered

religious forms. The public awareness of the beauty of this kind of non-Christian spirituality from his work directly led to public support for Indian religious freedoms.

15. Ibid., pp. 194–195.

16. Ibid., p. 194.

17. Ibid., p. 187.

18. Medicine Story, "Using Native Traditions," *Talking Stick*, Spring 1996, p. 4.

19. Jamie Sams, portion of a letter on Native American Tribal Traditions Trust letterhead, Sante Fe, N.M., no date.

20. George Tinker, CNN interview, November 18, 1994.

21. Churchill, *Fantasies of the Master Race*, p. 191.

22. Fergus Bordewich, *Killing the White Man's Indian* (New York: Doubleday, 1996), p. 336.

23. Ibid.

24. Churchill (in *Fantasies of the Master Race*) reflects this tendency throughout: When Gary Snyder is quoted as remarking that spirituality cannot be owned by one culture, Churchill asserts that such a statement automatically becomes a "proprietary" act by an oppressor (p. 192). The universality of religious experience is not dealt with in the book. Many Indians assert that if whites sincerely cared about Indians and their struggles, they would not use any Native spirituality out of respect. When "whites" do not comply, Indians consider them disrespectful by definition. This behavior is then deemed essentially (and genetically) non-Native. (See Churchill, *Fantasies of the Master Race*, p. 193 or, for instance, Mary Moore and Sudie Llaneza, "Activists in the Trenches Speak Out," *Sonoma County Free Press*, vol. 6, no. 4 [September 1992].) Some of the quotes in their article reflect the common thought that "respect" (or its lack) is what the debate about white participation really concerns: "What it's all about is lack of respect for Indian people." "Respecting a different culture means that you must give it the space to be itself. [When non-Indians use Indian ceremonies] this is not respect. When Indians speak out about this issue, they are ignored or are told they are rude and selfish. This is not respect."

25. There are, at a generous estimate, perhaps twenty-five Indians who are actively decrying (in print) "white" use of their ceremonies. They present themselves as speaking for a population of 5 million people. The diversity of positions on this issue, however, is about what you would expect to see in a population that size. For instance, Tamsin Carlisle says ("Controversial Diamond Mine Is Given Green Light by Canadian Government," *Wall Street Journal*, November 4, 1996) that the diamond mine project "has driven a wedge through certain native communities in the Yellowknife region. Some local native groups and individuals are keen project supporters. . . . Others, including some tradition-minded

68. Ibid., pp. 37–38. With all this in mind it is interesting that a Singapore court recently "convicted a 72-year-old woman of owning a Bible and other banned books. . . . Yu Nguk Ding could be sentenced to serve up to two years in prison." The woman is a member of the Jehovah's Witnesses, which was banned in Singapore because the government did not like that group's religious worship (*Lawrence Journal-World*, July 2, 1996, p. 5A).

69. This particular conflict between Protestants and Catholics still exists in Ireland (among other places). The *Wall Street Journal* reported that in Harryville, Ireland: "Harassing Mass-goers, unruly Protestant crowds fling bottles, anti-Papal abuse and petrol bombs." Outside the church the Protestants "snarl 'It's not a church—It's a Fenian hole!' " The article notes that " Fenian" is a slur roughly as offensive as "nigger" (Lionel Shriver, "Northern Ireland's Fragile Peace," *Wall Street Journal*, December 31, 1996, p. 6).

70. Amanda Porterfield, "American Indian Spirituality as a Countercultural Movement," Vecsey, *Religion in Native North America*, (Moscoe, ID: University of Idaho Press, 1990), p. 162.

71. Churchill, *From a Native Son*, pp. 371-372, 396. This religious quarreling by Indians, it has been said, is contrary to traditional Indian ways. As Chief Joseph of the Nez Perce noted: "We do not want churches because they will teach us to quarrel about God, as the Catholics and Protestants do. We do not want to learn that. We may quarrel with men sometimes about things on this earth. But we never quarrel about God. We do not want to learn that" (Kent N. Nerburn and Louise M. Mengelkoch, *Native American Wisdom* [San Rafael: New World Library, 1991], p. 42). But learn it they have.

72. R. J. Rummel, *Democide: Nazi Genocide and Mass Murder* (New Brunswick, NJ: Transaction Publishers, 1992), p. 79. This underlying attitude of the Nazis is well established in the literature. See, for instance, Glenn R. Cuomo, *National Socialist Cultural Policy* (New York: St. Martin's Press, 1995), p. 7, wherein the author writes: "The Nazis' definition of what was German was based on a biomedical worldview that posited a fictitious German norm and resulted in the argument that anything deviating from this norm was to be 'removed' like a cancer from the fictitious body of a German people, or *Volk*. . . . [The German] body had to be protected from or immunized against the influence of 'degeneration.' "

73. Simon Taylor, *Prelude to Genocide* (New York: St. Martin's Press, 1985), p. 9.

74. Rummel, *Democide: Nazi Genocide and Mass Murder*, p. 80.

75. John Moore, "Native Americans, Scientists, and the HGDP," *Cultural Survival Quarterly*, vol. 20, no. 2 (Summer 1996), p. 61. Although this comment was expressed to address the regrettable surge in human gene mapping, it is relevant. I say regrettable

because despite the good uses to which this information *can* be put, it is inevitable it will be put to bad ones (note the radiation testing carried out by doctors and scientists on uninformed patients through the 1970s). The exploration of this particular arena, however, has been a subject of intense controversy. The researchers, like anthropologists in the bone repatriation controversy, are perplexed by the outcry. The Human Genome Diversity Project (HGDP) is mapping human genetic diversity, one outcome of which is mapping the genetic structure of indigenous cultures in attempts to isolate potentially useful gene structures. The ethical problems are immense. The project itself (like the theory of evolution) is enhancing ethnic distinctions, causing people to pay attention to ever subtler levels of racial and ethnic divergence. HGDP is causing more, not less, racial strife. One particular question it raises is, Who owns a people's gene structure? If two members of a tribe share gene structure and one insists that the Lakota have special genes from Creator and that they are not for sale but another Lakota sells his to researchers, can the researchers legitimately buy them? Do they now own them? The problem here for me (and I *do* make a distinction between this and the pipe, for instance) is that there is no guarantee that the scientists will use the material in a beneficial manner. They are, after all, generally for sale to the highest bidder and will do nearly anything in the pursuit of "science." Nazi medical experiments, for instance, are still a subject of controversy. Many medical researchers are trying to get the experimental records opened, "for the good of the world's peoples." They are being stopped by Jewish activists who feel (I believe rightly) that to make use of them would be ethically horrendous. The particular problem in the HGDP, as I noted, is that the HGDP itself is increasing racism by allowing ever more sophisticated levels of racial and ethnic distinction.

76. Glenn Cuomo, ed., *National Socialist Cultural Policy* (New York: St. Martin's, 1995), p. 8.

77. Churchill, *Fantasies of the Master Race*, p. 222.

78. Cuomo, *National Socialist Cultural Policy*, p. 11.

79. Plastic Medicine Man/Woman List, St. Petersburg: Florida Indian Alliance, June 1993.

80. Notes from Wabun Wind conversation with Sedona Cahill, June 27, 1993.

81. Davies, *Infected Christianity*, p. 83. One of the readers of an early draft of this book insisted that although the Native activists were making nearly identical statements to the historical groups I discuss in this section, the *reason* they are making such statements is different. Therefore, even though the behavior is the same, Indians should not be held to the same standards as these other groups. He further argued that political and social justice issues, post-traumatic reactions, and colonization factors make Indian actions

"understandable," and therefore, I should not discuss them in this light. Historically, as far as my research could determine, with the exception of slaves in the United States (and perhaps the Jews in the fifteenth century) all ethnic cleansing and racial repression began in attempts to redress social justice issues, post-traumatic stress, and colonization. When racial distinctions become an integral part of redressing social justice issues, the process is dangerous in and of itself. Joseph Leonard concurs when he asserts: "The overstressing of Justice in the field of race relations may produce the opposite of the desired effect, namely an emphasis and greater awareness of separateness of the races evidenced by the existence of separate rights and obligations" (Leonard, *Theology and Race Relations*, p. 63).

82. Misha Glenny, *The Fall of Yugoslavia: The Third Balkan War* (New York: Penguin, 1993), p. 33. I have notes, but cannot locate my copy of the article in which the *Wall Street Journal* developed the major role that this document played in the evolution of ethnic cleansing in Bosnia.

83. Glenny, *The Fall of Yugoslavia*, p. 143. Lionel Tiger also remarks on the trans-cultural truth of this process: "In his landmark book, *The Organization Man*, William Whyte notes that 'the more exquisite distinctions are, the more important they become.' Our widespread use of 'terms of tribe' has magnified and reified in public life private antipathies and inequities" (Lionel Tiger, "Trump the Race Card," *Wall Street Journal*, February 23, 1996, p. A12).

84. This seems to be a historical pattern. Even today the Nazis are considered to be nonhuman or subhuman; they have taken on in history the prime attribute that they gave to the peoples they tried to exterminate. It can also be argued that at this time, like the Nazis, white Europeans are, in commentary, beginning to take on the prime attributes that they forced on less technologically advanced peoples—inferiority, absence of civilization, nonauthentic spirituality.

85. Glenny, *The Fall of Yugoslavia*, pp. 85–86.

86. Means and other Native activists are participating in a renewal of Indian pride and culture in an attempt to counteract centuries of domination. However, the use of racial exclusion to achieve those goals is dangerous. The same approach was used, as I noted, in Nazi Germany (after Germany's long domination by Napoleon). "In the struggle for national renewal, when the church was obliged to take seriously its duty as a national church, those who could not share in Germany's destiny should, following the new principle of exclusion adopted by the state, certainly not be mixed with Germans in Christian congregations through official or pastoral roles. In effect, Althaus and Elert sacralized the Aryan laws as a legitimate means of national self-defence against assimilated Jews" (Davies, *Infected Christianity*, p. 51). It was the same earlier in France: "With the publication of

Edouard Drumont's *La France Juive* in 1886, the new generation of French antisemites received their spiritual testament, making them well-equipped to fight for the soul of the nation. . . . [The] Jew, especially the Rothschild type of Jew, was portrayed as both the religious and racial enemy of France." Ibid., p. 66. And in the Black Nationalist movement in the U.S.: "For blacks, [the] authoritative truth is the black liberation struggle and nothing else. If something assists this struggle, it is true, and being true, also moral and the will of God; if something hinders this struggle, it is false, and being false, also immoral and the will of Satan" (Davies, *Infected Christianity*, p. 111).

87. Glenny, *The Fall of Yugoslavia*, p. 187.

88. Ibid., p. 167. Like the Bosnians, many Indians will believe whatever is repeated. Many are certain Sun Bear and other Indian teachers are as horrendous as the Croats, Moslems, and Serbs think the others are without ever having met them. Some Native elders (such as Matthew King) have spoken out condemning Indian spiritual teachers (such as Sun Bear) without ever meeting them or questioning them directly about their work and training. See Churchill, *Fantasies of the Master Race.*

89. Glenny, *The Fall of Yugoslavia*, p. 172.

90. Ibid.

91. Raoul Hilberg, speaking at The Conference on Evil, recorded by Bill Moyers for the NPR program "Facing the Evil," 1988. This assertion is borne out in numerous other instances. Alan Davies notes that in the late nineteenth century "writers in many fields, but especially the social sciences, became infatuated with the new popular enthusiasm." This included the "scientific, philosophical, artistic, political, and religious thought of the modern world" and authors spoke of "bio-psychological" perspectives and the principles of "ethno-mytho-bio-psychology" and their influences on culture, nation, and race. "The fact that such a peculiar blend of science, myth, and fantasy could even have been published during this period, and have been taken seriously to boot, reveals the extent to which racism had captured the public mind" (Davies, *Infected Christianity*, pp. 24–25). The point to keep in mind, however, is that at the time few scientists thought it fanciful. It was considered to be the apex (the *summum bonum*) of the current scientific, philosophical, and religious thought (see Appendix 1). It was *scientists*, the leading thinkers of their day, who developed theories of racial inferiority as an expression of the impartial workings of the great machine of the universe. Evolutionary theory, it is often forgotten, is *only* a theory. Assumed to be true, its social implications are inevitable—they are embedded in the theory itself. This understanding is explored by many writers (such as Seyyed Hossein Nasr in his *Religion and the Order of Nature*) and fought against just as bitterly by many, notably Ken Wilber.

Wilber notes (ignoring evolution's theoretical base): "Most traditional religious thinkers don't even think evolution has occurred" (Ken Wilber, *A Brief History of Everything* [Boston: Shambhala, 1996], p. 323). He attacks, strongly, any deviation from scientific theories of evolution. We started as amoebas and we are going to a glorious future. The past is inferior, the present isn't as good as the future, only the future really matters.

In spite of Wilber's more subtle form of evolutionary certitude it isn't all that different from nineteenth-century forms of its expression. For instance, a pre-Darwin publication, *Vestiges of the Natural History of Creation*, published in England in 1844 by Robert Chambers, asserted that "apes are rude and imperfect men who only after centuries will become men. . . . In this work he denied the fixity of species and maintained that creation was accomplished by progressive evolutions. These he explained by a divinely bestowed impulse to advance through grades of perfection" (quoted in Leonard, *Theology and Race Relations*, p. 29). This perspective of "rude and imperfect men" cannot help but be projected on technologically less complex groups. The concept of a "divinely bestowed" impulse to progress is seen in Wilber's orientation as well—other cultural and technological options are "regressive" and a movement away from the journey to non-dual reality, which he asserts is the ultimate end of mankind's evolutionary journey. Wilber's assertion about his reverence of tribal cultures fits in here as well: "The primal tribes are literally our roots, our foundations, the basis of all that was to follow, the structure upon which all subsequent human evolution would be built, the crucial ground floor upon which so much history would have to rest" (Wilber, *A Brief History of Everything*, p. 47). The worth of the technologically less complex cultures and tribes is only that they are the foundation of twentieth-century culture, thought, and science. Compare Wilber's perspective to an earlier quote in history by the French philosopher and father of the Aryan myth, Count Arthur de Gobineau: "Human history is like an immense tapestry. The earth is the frame over which it is stretched. The successive centuries are the tireless weavers. As soon as they are born they immediately seize the shuttle and operate it on the frame, working at it until they die. The broad fabric thus goes on growing beneath their busy fingers. The two most inferior varieties of the human species, the black and yellow races, are the crude foundation, the cotton and wool, which the secondary families of the white group make supple by adding their silk; while the Aryan group, circling its finer threads through the noble generations, designs on its surface a dazzling masterpiece of arabesques in silver and gold" (quoted in Davies, *Infected Christianity*, pp. 23–24). There is not much difference between them.

The contrast between the "foundations" of our culture (i.e., "the primitive cultures") and the towering edifice of modern technology and science found in all evolutionary

proponents' writings leads inevitably to distinctions of better and less good. Cultural domination of technologically less advanced cultures found its basis in this "legacy of the European Renaissance" (Davies, *Infected Christianity,* p. 24). As Davies notes, "The Europeans flattered themselves, regarding their own racial lineage as the *summum bonum* of the entire historical process and the key to its meaning" (ibid.). This emphasis on contrasts *between* peoples inexorably led to racism based "in terms of civilization and barbarism, progress and backwardness, evolution and regression, knowledge and ignorance, morality and immorality, adulthood and childhood" (ibid., p. 62).

This linear progression of evolution is a nineteenth-century expression. Alan Davies asks, "Was not the advance of Anglo-Saxondom much the same thing as the advance of nature and humanity as a whole? Who, then, could reasonably oppose [such thinking] since human betterment itself was at stake?" (ibid., p. 80). "[It] only remained, therefore, to relate this scientifically revealed knowledge to the great theme of divine providence, and to seek God's purpose in so guiding the hand of the evolutionary process" (ibid., p. 81). The thrust of Wilber's work in *Sex, Ecology, and Spirituality* (and as explained in *A Brief History of Everything*) is, in fact, a divining of God's purpose in the evolutionary process. The inexorable path from scholarly affirmations of cultural superiority, even in terms of better than what was before, to racism and cultural domination is expounded in Dinesh D'Souza's book *The End of Racism* (New York: Simon and Schuster, 1995), in which he notes that the rise of scientific thought about culture and technology, scientific theories of evolution, and comparisons to the technological primitiveness or sophistication of cultures were the foundations of modern racism; racism was not primarily theologically or skin-color related until scientific thought developed it. Upon its growing acceptance in the popular mind, it then began to be reflected in theological writings, art, and skin color preference. D'Souza notes: "Racism originated as an assertion of Western cultural superiority that was eventually proclaimed to be intrinsic" (p. 65). Especially, see his chapter "Ignoble Savages," pp. 25–65.

It is crucial to understand this point. The underlying worldview originally developed by scientists has now so influenced thinking and perception that Native activists themselves are arguing for many of its basic positions.

92. Hilberg, "Facing the Evil."

93. There are calls for protecting the American gene pool, as in Chilton Williamson's book *The Immigration Mystique: America's False Conscience,* wherein he says that "the United States has a right, not to mention a duty . . . to ensure the ethnic and racial composition of the people a half-century hence" (quoted in John J. Miller, "Yearning to Breathe Free? What Nerve!" *Wall Street Journal,* July 26, 1996, p. A11).

94. Churchill, *Fantasies of the Master Race*, p. 163.

95. Similar comments were also made in instances in which one people was culturally oppressed by another: "This is clearly the form of rule that our Gauls had before they were subjected to the power of the Romans." Another comment: Membership in the French tribe was determined by "birth alone . . . producing a rigidity that forbade any crossing of class lines through intermarriage or promotion" (Davies, *Infected Christianity*, pp. 55–56). Or in the Anglo-Saxon conflicts between Charles I (Norman) and parliament (Saxon). The Saxons insisted that their original tribes were the creators of all human liberty through "the Saxon chieftains Hengist and Horsa who supposedly carried the sacred torch of freedom from Germany to England after the withdrawal of the Roman legions. . . . Saxons and Saxons alone . . . possess an innate (racial) capacity for true democracy" (ibid., pp. 73, 74). Whenever the minority "oppressed" culture obtained power, the most brutal repression of the former "oppressor" was carried out. Some cultures have learned the bitter truth of this trend. Lionel Tiger was in the parliamentary gallery in Ghana just after the country became independent in 1960: "A cabinet minister introduced a successful vote of censure of a member who referred to a parliamentarian 'in terms of tribe.' This was considered highly dangerous in post-colonial democracy. The Ghanaians understood the potential factiousness of categories based on primordial factors such as tribe" (Lionel Tiger, "Trump the Race Card," p. A12). I hope that we will be as wise.

PART THREE: **prologue**

1. M. K. Gandhi, *Sarvodaya* (Ahmedabad, India: Navajivan Publishing House, 1954), p. 25.

CHAPTER 7: **the restoration of the indigenous mind**

1. Barbara Jordan, Nixon impeachment hearings, July 25, 1974.

2. Many scholars have attacked the assertion that the Iroquois were in any way an influence in the formation of the Constitution. Responding to such an attack, Professor Bruce Johansen comments ("The Iroquois: Present at the Birth," *Wall Street Journal*, April 10, 1997, p. A15): "[Such skeptics] may wish to examine a speech by the Iroquois sachem Cannasatego, in 1744, in which he advises the colonists to form a union like that of the Iroquois. [They] also should note [Benjamin] Franklin's publication of Cannasatego's admonition on his own press, his advocacy of an Iroquois-style government in 1751, and his application of this idea in his Albany Plan of 1754. . . . Our history is not as simple as [the skeptics] seem to think, nor is the case that is being made for Iroquois influence on the evolution of democracy. We can have our Greeks, and our Iroquois, too."

3. Ibid.

4. Such an apology has already been made by representatives of ten major American church groups. The document, "A Public Declaration to the tribal councils and traditional spiritual leaders of the Indian and Eskimo peoples of the Pacific Northwest," formally apologized for the churches' involvement in degrading and attempting to exterminate traditional Indian religious forms. The church representatives further acknowledged the legitimacy of traditional Indian religious forms and pledged their support of the rights of traditional religious practitioners, access to sacred land sites, and the use of traditional religious symbols such as feathers and tobacco. The document was signed by representatives of the Lutheran Church, Baptist Church, Episcopal Church, United Church of Christ, Regional Christian Church, Roman Catholic Church, Presbyterian Church, and Methodist Church. It appeared in many major American newspapers and magazines.

5. Joseph Epes Brown, *The Sacred Pipe* (Norman: University of Oklahoma Press, 1953), p. 115.

6. Steven Karpman, "Script Drama Analysis," *Transactional Analysis Bulletin,* vol. 7, no. 26 (April 1968), pp. 39–43.

7. Brooke Medicine Eagle, "A Fully Human Path," *Wildfire,* Winter 1996, p. 28.

8. Eknath Easwaran, *Gandhi the Man* (Petaluma, CA: Nilgiri Press, 1978), p. 90.

9. Ibid., p. 87.

10. Ibid., pp. 42–43.

11. Ibid., p. 161.

12. Ibid., p. 154.

13. Kent N. Nerburn and Louise M. Mengelkoch, *Native American Wisdom* (San Rafael: New World Library, 1991), pp. 35–36.

14. R. J. Rummel, *Democide: Nazi Genocide and Mass Murder* (New Brunswick, NJ: Transaction Publishers, 1992), p. 84.

15. Maya Angelou, comments at The Conference on Evil, recorded by Bill Moyers for NPR program "Facing the Evil," 1988.

16. Barbara Jordan, Nixon impeachment hearings, July 25, 1974.

17. Elisabeth Kubler-Ross, personal communication, c. 1979.

18. *Center for the SPIRIT,* Public Alert, n.p., n.d.

19. Ward Churchill, *Fantasies of the Master Race,* edited by M. Annette Jaimes (Monroe, ME.: Common Courage Press, 1992), p. 216.

20. David Johnston, "Spiritual Seekers Borrow Indian Ways," *New York Times,* December 27, 1993; reprinted in *Boulder Daily Camera,* December 29, 1993.

21. George Tinker, *Good Morning America* interview, March 6, 1994.

22. Churchill, *Fantasies of the Master Race*, pp. 219, 220.

23. Ward Churchill, *From a Native Son* (Boston: South End Press, 1996), pp. 396–397.

24. Churchill, *Fantasies of the Master Race*, p. 221.

25. Thomas Robbins and Dick Anthony, *In Gods We Trust: New Patterns of Religious Pluralism in America* (New Brunswick, NJ: Transaction Publishers, 1991), p. 499.

26. Peter Green and Jim Green, "Native American Religion," *Battle Cry Sounding* (El Paso: Aggressive Christianity Missions Training Corps), no. 124 (May 1994), p. 5.

27. Ibid., p. 9.

28. Robbins and Anthony, *In Gods We Trust*, p. 491.

29. Green and Green, "Native American Religion," p. 9.

30. Robbins and Anthony, *In Gods We Trust*, p. 499.

31. Peter Farb, *Man's Rise to Civilization (as Shown by the Indians of North America from Primeval Times to the Coming of the Industrial State)* (New York: Dutton, 1968), p. 182.

32. Quoted in Krug, "Western Civ Has Got to Go," *Battle Cry Sounding*, No. 124. (May 1994), p. 14.

33. Steven C. Moore, "Sacred Sites and Public Lands," in Christopher Vecsey, *Handbook of American Indian Religious Freedom* (New York: Crossroad, 1993), p. 97.

34. Ken Wilber, *A Brief History of Everything* (Boston: Shambhala, 1996), p. 103.

35. Ibid., pp. 205–207.

36. Ibid., pp. 287–288.

37. Ibid., p. 151.

38. Ibid., pp. 55–56.

39. While working on this book, I met a number of non-Indians who had once been active in Indian affairs, seen Indians in a positive light, and supported their goals; they have been emotionally wounded by Indian activists. Some of these non-Indians are in positions of power and influence, in universities, on commissions for Indian rights, and in the arts. They are beginning to withdraw their support and now view Indians as a source of racial hatred. During interviews, several of them cried from the wounds that had been inflicted.

40. Carol McGrath, "Destroying Our Roots: The Colonizing Mind," in Stephen Buhner, ed., "Plants of Power: Earthkeepers of Six Nations Speak of the Sacred Power of Plants," unpublished manuscript.

41. Malidoma Patrice Somé, *Ritual: Power, Healing and Community* (Portland, OR: Swan Raven, 1993), pp. 85–86.

42. Ibid., p. 35.

43. There is much to fear from the wedge being driven between the Indian and the non-Indian people. The danger to the non-Indian is of longer duration because his servitude to the Machine will last for many generations. The danger to the Indian is more immediate. For the first time the Indian has the goodwill and support of a majority of the non-Indian inhabitants of North America, but this state of affairs is tenuous. Because of the actions of some Native activists, old wounds have been rubbed open, and people who were beginning to come together, beginning to see each other as human, and beginning to see their own face in the other are now reassessing. Many are pulling back. The American people have pressured the government to enforce the treaties and Bill of Rights. Without the power of the majority of the people, the Constitution has always proved a feeble protection in spite of those of us who would die for it.

The establishment of Indian sovereignty, however firmly established, is a threat directly to the Machine and the Colonizing Mind. It challenges the internal security of the United States as it directly limits its power within its own borders. It is also readily apparent that the states understand what is happening and do not like it. Although the courts have established protected spheres of sovereignty for the tribes, the states and tribes are still struggling over just where the boundary lines of the tribes' powers are to be drawn. It is also readily apparent to many Indian leaders that this situation exists only at the sufferance of the U.S. government. Should the tribes ever present a threat to the integrity of the country, any and all rights they have obtained will be removed, by force if necessary. The history of our country makes this plain. This struggle has little to do with "whites" or "Indians" and a great deal to do with the nature of power and government—if an Indian were president he would still order the destruction of the tribes in such a situation (as BIA politics show). Because the tribes exist at the sufferance of the most powerful government on Earth, wise leaders will focus on long-term friendly relations —recognizing what *is* not what might have been. There are about 250 million non-Indians in the United States and 5 million Indians. The wisdom of the willow is neither cowardice nor accommodation to evil. Conflict and hostility can only strengthen the belief in the minds of the powerful that the tribes are a danger to the country. The alienation of the New Age support—a not inconsiderable force for Indian rights—is only in the best interests of those who benefit from the continued weakness of Earth spirituality and strength of corporate landownership. Neo-hippies, environmental activists, white separatists, black nationalists, the Branch Davidians, the Randy Weaver family, drug dealers, Mormons (see Appendix 2), and Indians are all in the same boat: *Anyone* who is perceived a threat to the internal security of the government will face its nearly unlimited force and

the Bill of Rights will prove a very feeble shelter. Gandhi recognized this danger and he strongly warned of it. "South Africa is a representative of Western civilization while India is the centre of Oriental culture. Thinkers of the present generation hold that these two civilizations cannot go together. If nations representing these rival cultures meet even in small groups, the result will only be an explosion. The West is opposed to simplicity while Orientals consider that virtue to be of primary importance. How can these opposite views be reconciled? Western civilization may or may not be good, but Westerners wish to stick to it. They have shed rivers of blood for its sake. It is therefore too late for them now to chalk out a new path for themselves. Thus considered, the Indian question cannot be resolved into one of trade jealousy or race hatred. . . . [If] Westerners [are forced] to the wall [no good will come of it]. Westerners in South Africa are not prepared to commit suicide and their leaders will not permit them to be reduced to such straits" (Eknath Easwaran, *Gandhi the Man* [Petaluma, CA: Nilgiri Press, 1978], pp. 156–157).

The increasing dissension and alienation between us as peoples play into the hands of those who do not want the Indian nations to firmly establish sovereignty. Who will benefit if the Indian nations are eventually destroyed? Who will come to own their land and control its resources? Who will benefit if they are no longer here to perform their sacred ceremonies? Not the New Agers. The alienation of non-Indians is a most dangerous course. It is not with hatred that they will become the ally of the Indian but with friendship. Only when both sides cease to identify themselves as positions on the drama triangle will the game be stopped. Only then will the Colonized Mind lose its food and its source of power.

44. Ibid., p. 156.

45. Charles Alexander Eastman, *The Soul of an Indian* (San Rafael: New World Library, 1991), p. 59.

46. McGrath, "Destroying Our Roots: The Colonizing Mind."

47. Wallace Stegner, "Wilderness: The Geography of Hope," *Earth Island Journal* (San Francisco) vol. 10, no. 4 (Fall 1995). This theme is developed even further by Seyyed Hossein Nasr in his book *Religion and the Order of Nature* (New York: Oxford, 1996). He notes that the Greeks absorbed the Romans into them and not vice versa; the barbarians who overran Rome were in their turn subdued by that which they conquered.

48. Vine Deloria, Jr., *God Is Red* (Golden: Fulcrum Publishing, 1994), p. 288.

49. Joseph Epes Brown, "The Question of 'Mysticism' Within Native American Traditions," in Woods, ed., *Understanding Mysticism* (New York: Doubleday, 1980), p. 205.

50. Ibid., p. 207.

51. Vine Deloria, Jr., *God Is Red*, pp. 288–289.

52. Ibid., pp. 287–288.

EPILOGUE

1. Michael Steltenkamp, *Black Elk: Holy Man of the Oglala* (Norman: University of Oklahoma Press, 1993), p. 136.

2. Ibid., p. 160.

3. Ibid., p. 171.

4. Ibid., p. 110.

5. Ibid., p. 111.

6. Ibid., quoting Raymond DeMallie, *The Sixth Grandfather,* (Lincoln: University of Nebraska Press, 1984), p. 265. It is now the sixth generation.

7. Ibid., p. 129. I have heard it said that the one who came was Dawn Star.

8. Ibid.

9. Ibid., pp. 131–132.

10. Ibid., p. 133.

11. Ibid., p. 132.

APPENDIX 1

1. Ken Wilber, *A Brief History of Everything* (Boston: Shambhala, 1996), pp. 39–40.

2. Christopher Stone, *Should Trees Have Standing?* (Los Altos, CA: Kaufmann, 1974), pp. 7–9.

3. Ibid., p. 91.

4. Ibid., pp. 51–53.

5. Seyyed Nasr, *Religion and the Order of Nature* (New York: Oxford University Press, 1996).

6. Wilber, *A Brief History of Everything,* p. 47.

7. Dinesh D'Souza, *The End of Racism* (New York: Simon and Schuster, 1995), p. 59. Delores La Chappelle, *Sacred Land, Sacred Sex, Rapture of the Deep* (Silverton: Finn Hill Arts, 1988), p. 48.

8. Hong-key Yoon, *Geomantic Relationships Between Culture and Nature in Korea* (Taipei: Chinese Association for Folkore, 1976).

9. Celia Nyamweru, "Sacred Groves Threatened by Development," *Cultural Survival Quarterly,* Fall 1996, p. 19.

10. Ibid.

11. J. Ryan, *Life Support: Conserving Biological Diversity,* WorldWatch Paper 108 (April 1992), p. 17.

12. Vine Deloria, Jr., *Red Earth White Lies* (New York: Scribner, 1996), pp. 112–113. A parallel can be seen with Alan Davies's comment that racism has roots in the "thirst for

proof that the white peoples of the earth had a great and glorious destiny" (Alan Davies, *Infected Christianity* [Montreal: McGill-Queen's University, 1988], p. 25). Western culture proponents refuse to compare other cultures to Western civilization, which might show it in a bad light. The continuing assertion that Western culture is humankind's apex and that it is the only way to continue to climb upward is too close to Davies's comment to ignore.

13. One reader of my early manuscript asserted that "cut and slash and burn" *is* an ecological activity. In response I contacted two professionals whose job is the reclamation of damaged ecosystems, read them Wilber's statement and my reader's comments, and asked for their opinion. They both responded that, in their opinion, while there was some evidence that tribal cultures practiced burning, none used "cut and slash"—they hadn't the technology to do so. Further, they noted that "cut and slash and burn" is a modern technique to combat extreme cases of environmental degradation caused by inappropriate use of technology and is rarely used. Both felt that if Wilber had truly intended to communicate ecological soundness in his argument, he would have chosen another example to indicate it. People, they noted, do not hear the terms "cut and slash and burn" as ecological activity but as its obverse—an act of environmental degradation.

APPENDIX 2

1. John Morris, "Food for Thought," *Battle Cry Sounding* (El Paso: Aggressive Christianity Missions Training Corps), no. 124 (May 1994), p. 24.

2. Ibid.

3. Frank Conclin and James Vaché, "The Establishment Clause and the Free Exercise Clause of the Washington Constitution—A Proposal to the Supreme Court," *University of Puget Sound Law Review,* vol. 8, no. 411 (1985), p. 430.

4. Ibid., 136 U.S. at 48–50, quoted in Conclin and Vaché, p. 428. The Mormons eventually capitulated to the U. S. government and were admitted to the Union with an *unrepealable* section of the Utah state constitution forever outlawing polygamy.

index

Looking Horse, Arvol, 96–97

Lyons, Oren, 91

machine mind, 213

Manitonquat (Medicine Story), 95, 102, 245, *see also* Medicine Story

McCloud, Janet, 117–118, 131, 157, 241

McGaa, Ed, 95, 130, 142, 243, 244

McGrath, Carol, 61, 211–212, 215–216

McNamara, Father William, 21, 81, 107–109

Means, Russell, 83, 88, 89, 90, 97, 99, 100, 104, 131, 153, 160–161, 184, 187, 249, 255–256

Medicine Bear Grizzly Lake, 117–118

Medicine Eagle, Brooke, 47, 96, 99, 130, 144, 199

medicine men, breaking the power of, 122–127, 248–249

Medicine Story, 113, 153–154

militant Christians, objections to earth mysticism, 209, 233–236

Mollison, Bill, 62

mormons, religious oppression of, 234–236

mountains, as sacred, 71–72, 73

Muslims, 169, 182–188

mystic, the early restlessness of the, 33

mystic conversion, 31

mystic path, 21–54, stages of, 25–54

mystical traditions, origins of, 25–26

Nasr, Seyyed Hossein, 81, 229

Native American Rights Fund, 176

nature mysticism, vii, 55

    backlash against, viii, 79–82

    essential beliefs of, 55–57

ABOUT THE TYPE

This book was set in Garamond, a typeface originally designed by the Parisian type cutter Claude Garamond (c. 1500–61). This version of Garamond was modeled on a 1592 specimen sheet from the Egenolff-Berner foundry, which was produced from types assumed to have been brought to Frankfurt by the punch cutter Jacques Sabon (c. 1520–80).

Claude Garamond's distinguished romans and italics first appeared in *Opera Ciceronis* in 1543–44. The Garamond types are clear, open, and elegant.

ABOUT THE AUTHOR

RICH COHEN is the author of the *New York Times* bestsellers *Monsters: The 1985 Chicago Bears and the Wild Heart of Football*, *The Chicago Cubs: Story of a Curse*, and *Pee Wees: Confessions of a Hockey Parent*, among other books. He is a columnist for *The Wall Street Journal*, the co-creator of the HBO series *Vinyl*, and a contributing editor at *Vanity Fair* and *Rolling Stone*. He lives in Connecticut.

authorrichcohen.com